THE SELECTED WORKS OF GORDON TULLOCK

VOLUME 4

The Economics of Politics

THE SELECTED WORKS OF GORDON TULLOCK

VOLUME 1 *Virginia Political Economy*

VOLUME 2 *The Calculus of Consent: Logical Foundations of Constitutional Democracy* (with James M. Buchanan)

VOLUME 3 *The Organization of Inquiry*

VOLUME 4 *The Economics of Politics*

VOLUME 5 *The Rent-Seeking Society*

VOLUME 6 *Bureaucracy*

VOLUME 7 *The Economics and Politics of Wealth Redistribution*

VOLUME 8 *The Social Dilemma: Of Autocracy, Revolution, Coup d'Etat, and War*

VOLUME 9 *Law and Economics*

VOLUME 10 *Economics without Frontiers* (includes a cumulative index for the series)

Gordon Tullock

THE SELECTED WORKS OF GORDON TULLOCK

VOLUME 4

The Economics of Politics

GORDON TULLOCK

Edited and with an Introduction by

CHARLES K. ROWLEY

Liberty Fund
Indianapolis

This book is published by Liberty Fund, Inc., a foundation established to encourage study of the ideal of a society of free and responsible individuals.

The cuneiform inscription that serves as our logo and as the design motif for our endpapers is the earliest-known written appearance of the word "freedom" (*amagi*), or "liberty." It is taken from a clay document written about 2300 B.C. in the Sumerian city-state of Lagash.

Printed in the United States of America

Paperback cover photo courtesy of the *American Economic Review*
Frontispiece courtesy of Center for Study of Public Choice, George Mason University, Fairfax, Virginia

C 10 9 8 7 6 5 4 3 2 1
P 10 9 8 7 6 5 4 3 2

Library of Congress Cataloging-in-Publication Data
Tullock, Gordon.
The economics of politics / Gordon Tullock ; edited and with an introduction by Charles K. Rowley.
p. cm.—(The selected works of Gordon Tullock ; v. 4)
Includes bibliographical references and index.
ISBN 0-86597-523-X (alk. paper)—
ISBN 0-86597-534-5 (pbk. : alk. paper)
1. Social choice. I. Rowley, Charles Kershaw. II. Title.
HB846.8.T8 2004
320′.01—dc22 2004040867

LIBERTY FUND, INC.
8335 Allison Pointe Trail, Suite 300
Indianapolis, Indiana 46250-1684

CONTENTS

INTRODUCTION

The Economics of Politics brings together Gordon Tullock's wide range of contributions to public choice, one of the most important new fields of inquiry in the social sciences during the second half of the twentieth century. In selecting the title of this volume I deferred to Professor Tullock, who is of the opinion that "public choice" is not truly descriptive of the field, whereas "the economics of politics" surely is.[1]

Public choice is a relatively new science located at the interface between economics and politics. It was founded in 1948 by Duncan Black, who died in 1991 without ever achieving full recognition as the founding father of the discipline.[2] Scholars schooled in public choice theory seek to understand and predict the behavior of political markets by utilizing the analytical techniques of economics, most notably the rational choice approach, in modeling the behavior of political markets.[3]

Public choice, as defined above, is primarily a positive science concerned with what is or might be. As such, it is to be distinguished from its normative counterpart, social choice, which concerns itself, without reference to real-world institutions, with what should be.

This does not imply that normative analysis is impossible within the framework of public choice; rather, normative policy discussions are advanced on a realistic basis of "politics as it is." From this latter perspective, Tullock has not been averse to evaluating alternative policy solutions to alleged problems of market failure.

The Economics of Politics consists of nine parts, each depicting a separate component of public choice.

Part 1, "The Nature of Public Choice," brings together three papers that focus on the nature and origins of public choice, outlining Tullock's evolving perspective over a period of forty years.

1. Gordon Tullock, "Origins of Public Choice," in *The Makers of Modern Economics*, vol. 3, ed. Arnold Heertje (Aldershot, U.K., and Brookfield, Vt.: Edward Elgar, 1997), 125.

2. Charles K. Rowley, "Duncan Black: Pioneer and Discoverer of Public Choice," *Journal of Public Finance and Public Choice* (Summer 1991): 83–87.

3. Charles K. Rowley, "Public Choice and Constitutional Political Economy," in *The Encyclopedia of Public Choice*, vol. 1, ed. Charles K. Rowley and Friedrich Schneider (Dordrecht/Boston/London: Kluwer Academic Publishers, 2004), 3–5.

"An Economic Analysis of Political Choice," a direct precursor to chapter 6 of *The Calculus of Consent*,[4] introduces the elementary principles of the economics of politics through a concrete example concerning the appropriate governance mechanism for maintaining access roads by a small farming community. Tullock expands this example to define more generally an ideal constitution for simple, direct democracies such as New England town meetings and Asian village assemblies.

"Origins of Public Choice" is a unique personal reflection on the origins and evolution of public choice. Tullock traces the frustrated beginnings of public choice in eighteenth-century France through its reemergence during the 1940s, its evolution into a recognized field of scholarly study during the 1960s, and finally through later advances in the wake of Tullock's own insight into the nature of rent-seeking behavior.

"People Are People: The Elements of Public Choice" identifies the bonds that have developed between economics and political science during some forty years of the public choice revolution. As Tullock notes, *Homo politicus* and *Homo economicus* are the same species; each is driven largely by self-interest to pursue vigorously such personal objectives as wealth, power, prestige, and income security to the extent possible within the particular domestic and work environments they occupy. In this respect, they are driven largely by solipsism rather than by altruism. Economists and political scientists working outside the public choice research program typically assume, in contrast, that *Homo politicus* is motivated by altruism to serve the public interest, that government is omniscient and impartial, and that political markets are perfect mirrors of the majority vote. As Tullock notes, the public choice scholar knows that this is not the case.

Part 2, "What Should Government Do?" assembles seven papers that analyze the actions government should take once it is understood that solipsism governs political as well as private markets.

In "Mosquito Abatement" Tullock argues that a central element of making an efficient decision is the presence or absence of geographical contiguity. The distinction between a scale economy that can be achieved only if customers are located next door to each other and one that can be attained without such geographical contiguity is basic to both public and private choices. He then launches the discussion with a concrete example, namely the imple-

4. James M. Buchanan and Gordon Tullock, *The Calculus of Consent: Logical Foundations of Constitutional Democracy* (Ann Arbor: University of Michigan Press, 1962).

mentation of aerial spraying, through either private or public initiative, as a means of mosquito abatement.

In "Property, Contract, and the State" Tullock applies public choice principles in describing the complex relationship among property, contract, and the appropriate role of the state. Efficiency—and efficiency alone—is the normative principle that guides him through this politically sensitive maze. Tullock notes that private property rights are necessary, but not sufficient, for economic efficiency.

"Bargaining" shifts the discussion away from externalities in general to the nature of the bargaining costs that prevent adverse third-party effects from being resolved through mutually beneficial exchange. Again focusing on situations of geographical contiguity (in this case real-estate exchanges in urban renewal projects), Tullock identifies a significant problem that confronts private bargains in that holders of real estate perceive an incentive to prolong negotiations in the expectation that they may extract large payments as residual holdouts (referred to in economics as the holdout problem).

In "Externalities and All That" Tullock takes up the case of the externality that cannot be eliminated privately because of high bargaining costs. The standard public finance solution in such a situation is to impose on the output of the perpetrator of the externality a marginal tax equal to the marginal monetary harm suffered by the third party. Even if such taxes, known as Pigovian taxes, could be efficiently calculated and effectively imposed, Tullock argues, it would not replicate a market solution because the taxes would be sequestered by government. Only if those harmed by the externality are also paid a marginal subsidy equal to the marginal monetary harm that continues to be imposed on them in the post-Pigovian tax situation will economic efficiency result.

The nature of the costs associated with government is the focus of "The Costs of Government." As Tullock notes, important costs arise in the form of a loss of potential benefits to individuals because government electoral platforms are bundled into indivisible packages rather than tailored, as in the case of private markets, to match divergent individual preferences. Because individual voters perceive themselves to be unimportant in determining the outcome of an election, they have little incentive to become well informed about the precise composition of the competing policy portfolios that an election offers. Such rationally uninformed voters are unlikely to exercise good judgment in the selection of a government.

In "Remedies" Tullock reviews a range of alternative solutions to externality problems, albeit with a clear warning about the law of unintended consequences that confronts anyone who attempts to play God in the policy arena. Tullock justifies his preference for reliance on the private associations that emerge to accommodate members who share common goals and interests and that exclude individuals of a different persuasion. In the literature of economics this is referred to as the club principle. If the club principle cannot be effectively applied, his preference is for small, decentralized governments that facilitate outward and inward migration of individuals by providing competing taxation and expenditure portfolios.

In "The Social Costs of Reducing Social Cost" Tullock explains why government intervention tends to impose additional social costs rather than to eliminate those costs that trigger intervention in the first place. In part, the explanation for this lies in the nature of democratic government. Tullock closes with the suggestion that democracy may not be the most efficient form of government and that resources should be devoted to exploring potentially superior alternatives.

Part 3, "The Vote Motive: An Essay in the Economics of Politics," reproduces a widely cited monograph by Tullock on that subject. Written in 1976, when the public choice research program was still struggling to make its impact on mainstream economic thinking in the United States and was virtually unknown in Europe, this monograph illustrates, through a sequence of compelling examples, the power of using economic analysis to understand and predict the behavior of political markets. The monograph was instrumental in invigorating public choice research and discussion during the late 1970s and early 1980s in the United Kingdom and throughout Western Europe.[5]

The papers in part 4, "Rational Ignorance and Its Implications," explore the likely consequences for political markets when a significant part of the electorate chooses to be poorly informed not only about the electoral platforms of competing political parties but also about the actual policies of elected governments (a situation referred to in public choice as rational ignorance).

"Political Ignorance" adapts the model of voter abstention developed by Anthony Downs in 1957 to explain why many potential voters remain politically ignorant concerning the policy positions of competing candidates in

5. Gordon Tullock, *The Vote Motive*, Hobart Paperback Number 9 (London: Institute of Economic Affairs, 1976), 1–58.

large-scale elections.[6] Tullock demonstrates that such ignorance is rational whenever the cost of acquiring information exceeds the expected value. Politicians recognize this and therefore design policies that concentrate benefits on clearly identifiable minorities while dispersing the costs as invisibly as possible across a wide constituency.

In "The Politics of Persuasion" Tullock segments the electorate into the ignorant, the casually informed, and the well informed (the latter being a very small minority). The casually informed voter is susceptible to persuasion through the media, mass and specialized, which opens up opportunities for political advertising. Tullock explains how television newscasters, newspaper columnists, radio announcers, and others who secure a significant audience or readership through the mass media are able to use their positions to promulgate their political prejudice to a large audience at almost zero cost under the guise of information. Such job opportunities attract individuals endowed with a relatively intense desire to influence electoral outcomes.

"The Economics of Lying" refocuses the discussion to take account of lies and deception within the political marketplace. Tullock once again develops a simple, formal model that categorizes the costs and benefits of making statements that one knows to be untrue. Such actions, he claims, are more effective when dealing with the completely uninformed and the casually informed voter than when dealing with the well-informed voter. The absence of any legal penalty for lying during political campaigns increases the net benefits of lies in political as compared with economic markets.

"Some Further Thoughts on Voting" is a discussion of why rationally ignorant voters vote in elections. Tullock argues that, for most individuals, the cost of voting is very low. In such circumstances, rational individuals go to the polls in response to social pressures rather than as a response to any effort expended in a decision-making process.

Part 5, "Voting Paradoxes," brings together six papers that explore and evaluate two apparently troubling voting anomalies. The first such anomaly, initially identified by Kenneth Arrow,[7] demonstrates that when at least three voters make pairwise choices over at least three policy alternatives, the out-

6. Anthony Downs, *An Economic Theory of Democracy* (New York: Harper and Row, 1957).

7. Kenneth J. Arrow, *Social Choice and Individual Values* (New York: John Wiley and Sons, 1951).

come may be a majority vote in favor of policy A over policy B, a majority vote in favor of policy B over policy C, and a majority vote in favor of policy C over policy A. Such an intransitive outcome implies that the majority vote rule is susceptible to cycles. The second such anomaly, first identified by Anthony Downs,[8] asks why voters who have no instrumental incentive to vote, because their individual votes are clearly nondecisive in large group elections, nevertheless turn out in significant numbers at the polling stations.

"A Measure of the Importance of Cyclical Majorities" (coauthored with Colin Campbell) and "The Paradox of Voting—A Possible Method of Calculation" investigate the empirical significance of the above-mentioned Arrow vote-intransitivity paradox. Because sufficient real-world data concerning pairwise voting outcomes were unavailable, Tullock substituted computer for human resources using the Monte Carlo method, which relies on computers to generate pseudorandom numbers that mimic the random processes hypothesized to generate (in this case) pairwise voting data. The technique, relatively sophisticated at that time, is now widely used by economists and political scientists when real-world data cannot be assembled.

In "Computer Simulation of a Small Voting System" (coauthored with Colin Campbell) Tullock again uses computer simulations to demonstrate that the Arrow problem is less significant when voting occurs more or less continuously in small committees.

Tullock addresses the second voting anomaly in "The Paradox of Not Voting for Oneself" and "Avoiding the Voter's Paradox Democratically," deconstructing a wide variety of attempts by public choice scholars to explain why many voters do not abstain from voting when the expected value of their votes is markedly less than the cost of voting.

In "An Approach to Empirical Measures of Voting Paradoxes," coauthored with John L. Dobra, Tullock takes advantage of the real-world information provided by faculty voting at Virginia Polytechnic Institute to evaluate the frequency with which Arrow's voting paradox occurs and the frequency with which there is a dominant majority outcome in which one option defeats every other available option in pairwise voting.

The two papers in part 6, "The Median Voter Theorem," are Tullock's evaluations of early public choice contributions suggesting that competing candidates or parties, concerned to maximize votes, will be driven by cen-

8. Downs, *An Economic Theory of Democracy*.

tripetal pressures to support the preferences of voters located at the policy center (the median voter).

"Duncan Black: The Founding Father" is Tullock's 1991 obituary for Duncan Black, to whom Tullock refers with the Chinese toast as "the father of all of us." Tullock demonstrates that Black, not Arrow, first discovered the problem of vote intransitivity and the associated vote cycle. Having determined that vote cycling may occur, Black then identified the specific condition under which it would not occur, namely the conjunction of voters with single-peaked preferences over one identifiable issue dimension (for example, if each voter identifies one most-preferred level of defense expenditure and is less satisfied as the level of such expenditure is either less or more than that preferred level).

In "Hotelling and Downs in Two Dimensions" Tullock reviews earlier contributions by Harold Hotelling, who developed a theory that explains why competing stores locate closely together on the main street and do not space themselves to minimize the transportation costs of potential customers; and Anthony Downs, who deployed Hotelling's theory to explain why competing political parties tend to converge rather than diverge in political policy space. The theories of both Hotelling and Downs focused on competition in single-dimensional space. Tullock widens the discussion to embrace elections in which the parties compete over two separable issue dimensions, for example, defense and the economy, when logrolling is feasible across these dimensions and when more than two political parties enter into the competition.

Part 7, "Vote Trading and Logrolling as Mechanisms of Political Exchange," is a compilation of three papers evaluating the role and relevance of logrolling for spatial theories of democratic voting.

In "A Simple Algebraic Logrolling Model" Tullock emphasizes that, with logrolling, the political equilibrium changes whenever individual voters have different preference intensities over several policies and when transaction costs of vote trading are low. He distinguishes between explicit logrolling, most often observed as deals between politicians within the legislature, and implicit logrolling, which occurs when political parties or candidates bundle policy platforms for electoral purposes.

Examples of vote trading and logrolling among committees within a legislature, among the separate chambers of a bicameral legislature, and among political parties within the legislature are explored in depth in "More Complicated Log-rolling." In Tullock's view, this kind of logrolling explains the high degree of stability evident in most political systems despite the existence of the Arrow cycling problem.

In "Efficiency in Log-rolling" Tullock argues that logrolling protects minorities from significant harm from majorities and often leads to exchange efficiency.

Part 8, "More on Demand Revealing," brings together three papers that explore the strengths and limitations of a tax innovation designed by Tullock to ensure that individuals represent their true demands for a public good.

"Some Limitations of Demand-Revealing Processes" (coauthored with Nicolaus Tideman) acknowledges that the demand-revealing approach has a number of potential defects. Specifically, it may undermotivate participants to obtain all relevant information, may lead to a waste of resources when the number of participants is small, may result in the bankruptcy of some participants, and may be subject to manipulation. The authors note, however, that an overall judgment on the demand-revealing approach must be based on a comparison between it and other real-world alternatives, all of which are vulnerable to free-rider and strategic manipulation problems.

"Coalitions under Demand Revealing" (also coauthored with Nicolaus Tideman) acknowledges that coalitions may arise to manipulate collective choice outcomes even under the demand-revealing approach. The authors make a strong case, however, that such coalitions are much less likely than they are with other methods of determining the optimal outcome of public good provision.

Finally, "More Thoughts about Demand Revealing" challenges the view that the demand-revealing approach does not allow individuals to reflect altruistic preferences for a public good. As Tullock notes, individuals' demand curves reflect both selfish and altruistic preferences. Tullock argues that individuals are selfish 95 percent of the time.

Part 9, "Voting Methods and Political Market Behavior," consists of six papers that evaluate a range of voting rules and political institutions typically ignored or downplayed by public choice scholars.

"Proportional Representation" addresses the potential advantages of proportional representation over plurality-based voting methods in democratic elections. Tullock notes that political scientists in the United States misuse the term "representation." A left-leaning Democrat elected into office in Massachusetts does not represent the interests of a right-leaning Republican constituency. Under the plurality system, an elected politician may advance legislation representative of as little as 25 percent of his constituency. In contrast, with proportional representation, legislation requires a minimum coalition of 50-plus percent of the voters.

"Democracy as It Really Is" explores the weaknesses of democracy in responding to the informed preferences of special-interest groups at the expense of the general voter. Tullock argues that the federal system, although it does not completely resolve this weakness, nevertheless provides a net gain for society as a whole.

"A Bouquet of Governments" and "Thoughts about Representative Government" outline the wide diversity of democratic institutions utilized in different countries and at different levels within a country. Tullock once again manifests a strong preference for decentralization under a federalist framework.

In terms of legislative outcomes, "Voting, Different Methods and General Considerations" looks at the importance of methods actually used to determine a majority vote and focuses on problems posed by agenda control when the number of alternatives in the final vote must be reduced to two.

Problems of agenda control, as Tullock notes, are especially evident in the voting behavior of legislative bodies. The final paper in this volume, "A Bouquet of Voting Methods," outlines and briefly evaluates a wide range of voting methods used throughout the history of democracy. Tullock concludes the paper by commending the demand-revealing process as the best method ever devised, albeit a method that, as yet, is deployed only in small, private communities.

The Economics of Politics demonstrates the immense range and depth of Tullock's contributions to public choice. Equally confident in both the normative and the positive branches of the discipline, and well versed in the wide variety of institutions and practices of democracy across time and nations, Tullock expands the effective horizon of the continuing public choice revolution and makes a case for a return to the more catholic approach to political economy advanced by the great eighteenth-century scholars of the Scottish Enlightenment.

CHARLES K. ROWLEY

Duncan Black Professor of Economics, George Mason University

Senior Fellow, James M. Buchanan Center for Political Economy, George Mason University

General Director, The Locke Institute

PART I

THE NATURE OF PUBLIC CHOICE

AN ECONOMIC ANALYSIS OF POLITICAL CHOICE

It is sometimes hard to follow extremely abstract reasoning in a new field. Since the field to be discussed is new to most economists,[1] I have decided to begin by discussing a concrete example rather than presenting an abstract and fully general model. Constitutional problems of a small and rather peculiar community will be discussed in the early part of the article. The theory developed of this particular community will then be converted into a general model.

Consider, then, a community of 100 farmers owning more or less equivalent farms who live in a township cut by a number of main highways. These highways are maintained by the state government, but they are limited access roads and can be entered only from local roads. These local roads are the responsibility of the township. Four or five farmers are dependent on each of the local roads to reach the main highways. The maintenance and improvement of these roads is the only political problem of the township and, as our final restriction, the taxing power of the township government is limited to a general property tax which will mean that costs will be relatively equally shared by all the farmers.[2] The question to be discussed is: What would be the ideal voting rule for these farmers to use in determining which roads will be repaired or improved?

One possible rule, which has simplicity if nothing else to commend it, would be to let any individual order repairs or improvements on any road he

Reprinted, with permission, from *Il Politico* 16 (1961): 234–40.

This paper was presented by the author, professor of International Studies at University of South Carolina, to the third congress of Southern Economic Association (Atlanta, Georgia, November 1960).

1. The only economists to whom it will not be new will be those who have seen the mimeographed version of *The Calculus of Consent* (James Buchanan and Gordon Tullock, University of Michigan Press, forthcoming). Although this article is not directly drawn from the book, it follows the same general line of reasoning and is intended as a sort of introduction to this new field.

2. The relationship between this model and the one I introduced on page 573 of my article, "Problems of Majority Voting" (*Journal of Political Economy*, December 1959, pp. 571–79), is obviously close. The "Problems" model, in fact, is a single point on the continuum to be introduced on the next few pages.

wished. Thus, any farmer could simply call up the township government and order some road repair project and the cost would then be assessed to all the farmers. Since each farmer would be able to get his own road repaired while paying only 1% of the cost under this rule, I presume it is obvious to an audience of economists that there would be vast overinvestment in road facilities. We would have a Galbraithian world in which splendid highways connected hovels and in which the congestion problem had been solved by putting cars with tail fins beyond the purse of most farmers. The costs of this overinvestment on the farmers we will call "external costs," and we will find that there is an external cost for every voting rule short of unanimity.

A method of improving the situation would be to require that several farmers agree on each road maintenance project. This would mean, of course, that some time would be spent in negotiating the agreement, but let us for the time being ignore the problems of reaching agreement and concentrate our attention on the results that could be expected if the parties were able to reach agreements costlessly. Increasing the number of farmers required to agree to a given repair or maintenance job would make only a minor difference as long as the number was small enough so that those farmers living on a given road are sufficient to get it repaired. Let us, therefore, consider a rule requiring 10 farmers to agree to any given road repairing project, which would insure that farmers along at least two roads would have to agree.

Clearly, the farmers along one road could get agreement to its repairs from the farmers on another only by promising to agree to the repair of the other road. If this is so, then they must count the cost of repairing the other road as part of the cost of repairing their own. Thus, the real cost to them of repairing their road is something close to 10% of the total cost. (An easy way of thinking of this process is to consider how much the voter, under various rules, must pay in taxes for each $100.00 worth of road repairing. Under the one voter choice rule he would have to pay $1.00, under our present 10-voter rule $10.00 and under a unanimity rule, $100.00.)

Clearly, with our new 10-voter rule, the amount of road repairing undertaken would be much less than with the single voter rule, and, hence, the external cost imposed on each member of the community would be less. (It may appear peculiar to refer to this cost as "external" since in normal usage the term usually refers to some private activity, not to governmental action, but a little reflection will indicate that government action can impose external costs. If I am taxed to pay farmers subsidies so that they will reduce their production and thus raise my food costs, clearly I am suffering an external

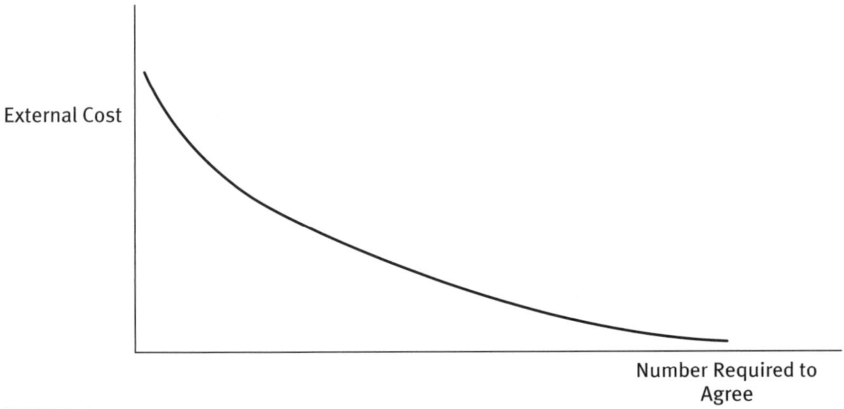

FIGURE 1

cost under the usual definitions of the term. The really peculiar phenomenon is the failure of economists in the past to use external costs in discussing political decisions, not our present usage.)[3]

Our community, of course, can require more than 10 voters to agree to any given road repair or improvement project. Each increase in the number required to agree will increase the number of necessary parties to a bargain, and hence raise the cost to each individual of a given amount of road repairing. The larger the number of farmers required to agree, the closer the cost of having the road repaired to each individual farmer will approach the real cost, hence, the less wastage of resources and the less external cost imposed on the farmers. We can represent this process by an idealized curve with the external cost of the voting rule very high at the single voter extreme and zero at the unanimity end.

Note that the curve in Figure 1 is perfectly smooth; there is no kink or irregularity at the 51-voter point. In view of the role played by simple majority voting in most of our present political ideology, this is most interesting. I would devote more attention to the simple majority case which is given so

3. Costs associated with shifting some activity from the private sector to the public are, of course, frequently discussed by economists. These costs, however, have normally been essentially the bureaucratic costs of administration, not the intrinsic costs of the decisions themselves. For a partial exception, see "Free Enterprise and Competitive Order," in Friedrich A. von Hayek, *Individualism and Economic Order*, Chicago, 1948, pp. 107–18.

much emphasis by traditional political scientists if I had not already published an article, "Problems of Majority Voting" in the *Journal of Political Economy*,[4] giving an analysis of that particular point on the curve. Perhaps it would be better to say that the present paper is consistent with "Problems of Majority Voting" rather than the other way around since it was my discovery that simple majority voting led to external costs which started me on the chain of reasoning which we are now reviewing.

Note that in Figure 1 there are external costs for every voting rule except unanimity. Only by requiring unanimous agreement for each road repair project could we make certain that the cost to the "decision makers" and the real cost coincided, and hence eliminate overinvestment. In the real world, of course, requiring unanimity would be impractical because of the problem of obtaining unanimous agreement. This brings us to the problem of the investment of resources in bargaining. Again, we are in an area which has been largely overlooked by economists. Clearly, chaffering and higgling consume resources; equally clearly, in choosing between two possible social arrangements the amount of this type of cost to be expected under each is a relevant consideration. Nevertheless, the subject has been almost completely overlooked in economic discussions, probably because these costs in economic matters are frequently insignificant in magnitude. There has been some discussion of whether bargaining problems might not be so severe in certain cases as to make reaching of agreement impossible, but that is all.[5]

Regardless of the reasons which have led to this subject being almost ignored by economists, it is highly important for our present investigation and consequently must be discussed at some length. One cost of bargaining which may sometimes be overlooked is the loss of desirable opportunities due to a failure to conclude the deal. Clearly, any decision rule will sometimes lead to desirable proposals failing and presumably the number of such proposals which would fail would be a positive function of the difficulty of reaching agreement under a series of different rules. Turning to more obvious costs, the actual process of bargaining and reaching agreement certainly consumes resources, and this again would be a positive function of the difficulty of reaching agreement.

4. December 1959, pp. 571–79. See also Dr. Anthony Downs's comment, "In Defense of Majority Voting," in the February 1961 issue (p. 192), and my "Reply to a Traditionalist" in the February 1961 issue (p. 200).

5. See "The Pure Theory of Public Expenditures," Paul A. Samuelson, *Review of Economics and Statistics*, 1954, p. 387.

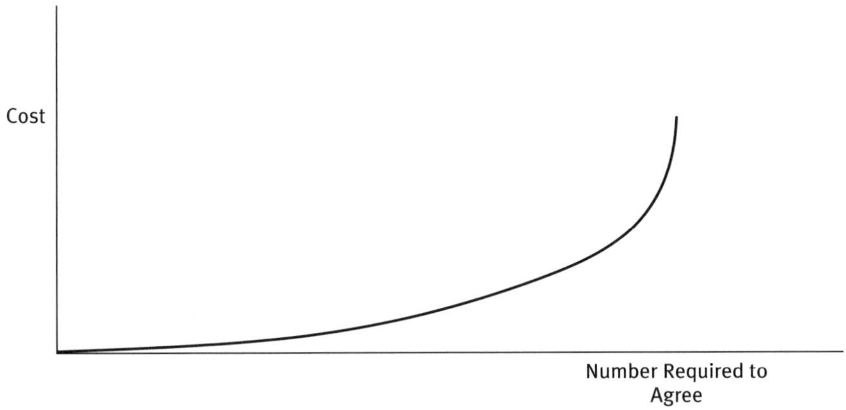

FIGURE 2

Let us now reconsider possible decision rules for our small community of farmers from the bargaining cost aspect. Our simplest rule, permitting any individual to order road repairs, would involve no bargaining costs. If agreement of two persons were required, this would surely impose some bargaining costs and these costs would increase as the number of people required to agree was raised. It should be remembered that bargaining costs have been defined to include the "cost" resulting from a failure to make bargains which, in the abstract, would be desirable. Thus, we can draw a cost of bargaining curve (Figure 2) similar to our external cost curve. It, of course, has the opposite slant from the external cost curve.

The rather odd shape of this curve, as I have drawn it, requires some explanation. The basic reason is simply that the bargaining situation at unanimity or near-unanimity is radically different from that where the number required to agree is smaller. To take the extreme case, if the agreement of only two farmers is required for a road repair project, there is apt to be little bargaining in the normal meaning of the term. Each party will be fully aware that the other can readily turn to someone else if his terms are too high. In consequence, the process of higgling in this case is likely to involve little actual bargaining, in the sense of trying to beat prices down (or up). The simple procedure if the first person you approach asks too much for his support is to go to someone else. As long as there are plenty of possible alternatives, there is no reason to waste time trying to bargain with some individual. Thus, in the lower range, the investment of resources in bargaining is likely to take the

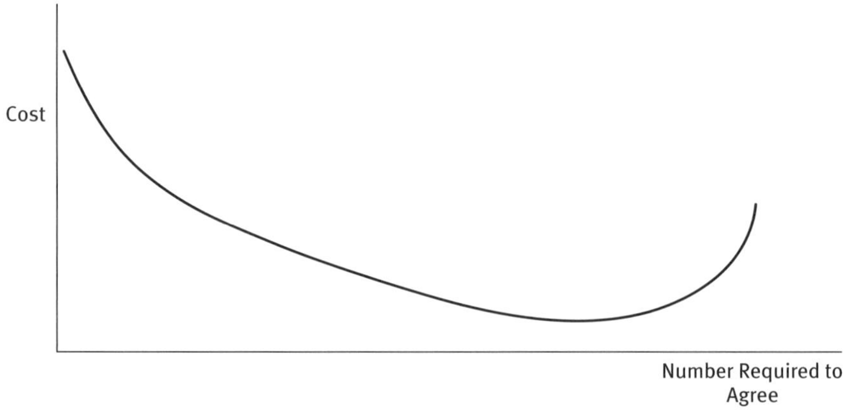

FIGURE 3

form, predominantly, of time and effort spent in trying to get the best terms by obtaining information on possible alternatives. Obviously, investment in higgling and chaffering would increase exponentially as the number required to agree increased in this range, but at a relatively moderate rate.

To turn to the other extreme, unanimity, this means that each farmer is an essential party to the agreement. Since each farmer has a monopoly of an essential resource, his consent, each farmer can aim at obtaining the entire benefit of the agreement for himself. Bargaining, in the sense of trying to maneuver people into accepting lower returns than they would desire by argument, is the only resource which the farmers can use under these circumstances, and it seems highly likely that agreement would normally be impossible. Certainly, the direct costs of making such an agreement would be extremely high and, if we count the likelihood that no agreement will be reached and hence that no roads will be repaired, the bargaining costs would probably approach infinity. This, of course, is the extreme, but somewhat similar conditions would begin to develop as the number of parties required to approve road repair projects approached 100. As a result, we have a cost line with the rather peculiar shape I have drawn (Figure 3).

With these two cost functions, we can obtain a general cost curve for any voting rule on our continuum by simple geometric addition.

The low point on this curve would indicate for each individual voter, as well as for "society in general" if that phrase has any definite meaning, the optimum rule. At that point, the costs of the political process, including the opportunity costs of lost chances for carrying out beneficial projects would be minimized.

Economists in discussing resource allocation by government have traditionally recommended the matching of marginal cost and benefit without, however, considering the political process which would lead to such a decision.[6] We have approached the problem from the other direction beginning with the political process; nevertheless, we end up with what is really an improved version of the traditional marginal criteria. Our minimum point differs from the traditional matching of marginal costs and benefits in only two respects: we specify whose value judgements are to be used in measuring cost and benefit and we include additional costs arising out of the political process of decision making. From the standpoint of any individual, decisions made under our "ideal" decision making rule will result in the marginal cost to him of road repairing equalling the marginal benefit he receives.[7] The inclusion of intrinsic political costs imposed by the decision making process itself among the total costs to be considered seems reasonable and our procedure guarantees that this "non-traditional" cost will be minimized.

Now we have completed our survey of our peculiar small community's political problems and produced a theory which would permit its citizens to select their ideal "constitution." Let us see if we cannot extend our reasoning to a more general and realistic model. In the first place, it is clear that our model is not bound solely to road repairing. Any project which uses general revenues to benefit a minority of the people would lead to the same results. Since such projects make up the overwhelming majority of modern legislation, this means that our model is of considerable practical value. Further consideration, however, leads to the conclusion that the model has an even wider application; it is not limited to fiscal measures, but also applies to all cases where minorities favor various measures and where the intensity of their desire for these measures is such that they would engage in vote trading to get them enacted. This still further widens the scope of our model.

6. See Richard A. Musgrave's *The Theory of Public Finance* for the most developed treatment of the problem in the traditional system.

7. Strictly speaking, this is true only for the whole series of decisions on road repairing. Since our model provides that each individual road repair project be voted on separately and since such a project directly helps only those living along that particular road, costs and benefits do not match for each individual on each project. It is only when we consider road repairing in general that the margins match.

Thus, the theory covers all cases where there is a minority whose desires are more intense than those of the majority. Surely, this covers the overwhelming majority of all the legislative activity of Congress, but equally surely it does not cover all. Situations in which intensity of desires are more or less equally distributed must occur, even if they are rare. They are susceptible to analysis using much the same tools we have utilized in the intense minority case. I cannot present this analysis here because of shortage of time, but I can say that the results are different from but not inconsistent with those we have been discussing. The same may be said for the extremely rare case in which the majority feels more strongly than the minority.

Thus, it would appear that we have a good theoretical system for simple direct democracy governments. Such simple governments do, of course, exist. The New England town meeting is one example and the village assemblies which are so common in Asia provide another. Nevertheless, most major democracies use representative rather than direct democracy, and the question arises whether they also can be analyzed by the same methods. The answer to the question is, fortunately, yes. Using the same principles as those used in this paper, it is possible to develop complex models which involve representative democracy, parties, two house legislatures, and federal-state division of authority. These complex models, which cannot be presented in a single article, permit analysis of existing constitutions and their comparison with other existing or proposed organizational structures.[8] The field is, to me, a highly exciting one because it seems likely that further research will lead to the discovery of methods of improving the efficiency of democratic governments. Since such improvements would be of great benefit to each of us, it seems that research in this new field should be encouraged.

8. For a comprehensive discussion of the work so far done in this field, see the forthcoming *Calculus of Consent*, cited above.

ORIGINS OF PUBLIC CHOICE

Public Choice in a way started long ago with the Marquis de Condorcet, and in modern times Kenneth Arrow, Duncan Black, and Anthony Downs have written books which are to this day read as classics. But if we talk about the development of this particular sub-discipline in sociological terms, it actually started when Jim Buchanan and I produced *The Calculus of Consent*, and I then began the journal, *Public Choice*. The Public Choice Society grew rather naturally out of these beginnings. This being so, a little biographical material is worthwhile.

I begin with an account of my own career and then go on to my collaboration with James Buchanan. The course of my development had a very unusual start; I began by studying law and got a DJ from the University of Chicago. The University of Chicago law school required all of its students to take certain non-legal courses, and one of these was one quarter of economics taught by Henry Simons. Although he was an immensely important person in the economics department, he was formally a professor of economics in the law school. I believe that I received the highest grade he ever gave to any one in the law school, although that isn't very much of a commendation since the law students tended to do very badly in the course. In any event, this is the only course in regular economics I ever took and in a real sense it changed my life.

After a short waste of time in the military, I finished law school, spent a few months in a law firm in downtown Chicago, and then went into the diplomatic service. As a result of Henry Simons's course, however, I had been "hooked" by economics, and began reading the principal economics journals more or less from cover to cover. That is something I do not do now.

In the foreign service I quickly realized that the political officers were its aristocracy. Therefore, I decided to study things that might be useful to a political officer. Since I was at the very bottom of the service, I did not aim at grand politics. I thought that I should look into the political literature on the lower ranks of the bureaucracy which is where I not only found myself, but

Reprinted, with permission, from *The Makers of Modern Economics*, vol. 3, ed. Arnold Heertje (Aldershot, U.K., and Brookfield, Vt.: Edward Elgar, 1997), 122–39.

where I could assume most of my dealings with foreign countries would lie for many years.

As I quickly realized, the material available was not very helpful. I had the good fortune, from this standpoint, that communists seized the city I was posted to and for a year we were mostly out of contact with the Department of State. We had access to the USIS (United States Information Service) Library and I was able to read in that extensively. My principal reaction was disappointment with the quality of materials on politics, particularly on low-level bureaucratic politics.

On my return to the United States, I was ordered to become a Chinese language officer, and that meant that I spent three academic years studying Chinese and related subjects at Cornell and Yale. When I was in Yale at the beginning of this period I walked into the co-op and saw a big pile of books entitled *Human Action* by a man (von Mises) whom I had never heard of. I bought one of the books, read it, and was impressed. I should deviate here and say that although I was and still am greatly impressed by von Mises, I am not an Austrian economist.

On rereading *Human Action*, I realized that his methods offered a general approach to bureaucracy; I could take his methodology, revise it, and apply it to the study of bureaucracy. I didn't do anything about this at that time, as I was moved off to Hong Kong, Korea, and then to the Department of State. It was an interesting period of my life, but from the standpoint of Public Choice it was wasted. I eventually resigned and settled down to write a book on bureaucracy, which became *The Politics of Bureaucracy*.[1]

I was not an economist at the time, and my first academic job was in the department of international relations at the University of South Carolina. At that time the University of South Carolina was at a much lower intellectual level than it is now, but the tiny department of international relations was quite distinguished. The head was one of the best China scholars in the United States, and it was my Chinese connections that led him to hire me.

In the meantime I had a number of copies of my book roughly printed and bound, and was attempting to get it published. This turned out to be extremely difficult. I sent a copy of the manuscript to Warren Nutter, my old debating partner at Chicago, who in turn showed it to other people at the University of Virginia.

1. Gordon Tullock, *The Politics of Bureaucracy* (Washington, D.C.: Public Affairs Press, 1965).

I must now talk about Jim Buchanan, then chairman at the University of Virginia. After wartime service in the navy in which he rose to the rank of commander, Jim Buchanan had enrolled in economics in Chicago and had fallen under the influence of Frank Knight. Knight was one of the great economists of this century, but was also deeply interested in philosophy. His interest was carried on by Buchanan, who entered upon a most distinguished career as an economist while I was wandering around the Far East.

When Jim Buchanan became head of the economics department at Virginia, he established the Thomas Jefferson Center for Political Economy and Social Philosophy. He had funds for various things, and I was given a postdoctoral fellowship, mainly on the strength of my manuscript (later published as *The Politics of Bureaucracy*). I was their first postdoctoral fellow.[2]

At that time my technical knowledge of economics was still pretty rough. Buchanan cured that and in general improved my technique a good deal. I reciprocated by convincing him, I think, that one could take economic methods over and apply them to political areas. He had been groping in that direction, and had written an important article criticizing Arrow's general impossibility theorem, but had been mainly concerned with economics, not possible political applications of the same methods. Needless to say, once I had been taught economics and he had accepted the possibility of economic penetration into politics, we worked out a very good partnership, and *The Calculus of Consent* was the outcome.[3]

I had gone to the University of South Carolina (we wrote the book by mail), but I came to Virginia after the book was published. While in Virginia we got the NSF (National Science Foundation) to fund a conference of the tiny little group of people who were interested, in many cases only very indirectly, in the subject. The conference was held in a small inn owned by the university.

One of the participants in this initial meeting was William Riker, a man who had an immense impact on the development of Public Choice. As head

2. Since there was another fellowship for a distinguished scholar, I invented the title "undistinguished scholar" for myself. One of my colleagues, John Moes, said that although they had many other undistinguished scholars after I left, there was never one that was as truthfully undistinguished as I was.

3. James M. Buchanan and Gordon Tullock, *The Calculus of Consent: Logical Foundations of Constitutional Democracy* (Ann Arbor: University of Michigan Press, 1962. Paperback, 1965; Spanish translation, 1980; Japanese translation, 1980; Russian translation, forthcoming).

of the political science department at Rochester, he had set up a graduate programme built around mathematical and economic applications. He did not publish a great deal, although what he did publish was very good, but the graduate students he turned out were for a long time the backbone of the political science side of Public Choice. He played an important role in the actual organization of the society as will be recounted below.

That first meeting was followed by another, not financed by anybody except those attending, held in a splendid resort hotel on top of the Blue Ridge mountains. The attendance was about the same as at the first meeting, but this time those present were more likely to be Public Choice types since by then we knew more about who was engaged in Public Choice and, of course, we had made some converts. It was at this meeting that Riker was formally elected chairman of a proto-society which as yet had no name.[4]

It is interesting that Kenneth Arrow and Anthony Downs rather dropped out of Public Choice, not because they became idle, but because they became interested in other matters. Meanwhile, we were able to arrange fellowships to bring Duncan Black to the United States. This gave him the opportunity to greatly improve his reputation in the US, where he had been practically unknown when he was living in England. It is interesting that although he wrote before we did, in essence we were his intellectual sponsors in the Public Choice area. This is an indication of how difficult communication in the field was.

From the Public Choice standpoint, the founding of the journal, *Public Choice*, was of vast importance, but it started by accident. I knew there were a number of articles floating around which could not be published because of their subject matter. Economics journals would regard them as political, and political science journals would object to their economic methodology. In conversation over morning coffee with the university printer I discovered that putting together a small volume would be easily affordable.[5]

I decided to put a bunch of these articles together and produce a small book. The title was *Papers on Non-Market Decision Making* essentially because I had written an article, "Information without Profit," on charitable activi-

4. Buchanan and I, although we never held formal office, are counted as past presidents of the society as a result of organizing the first two meetings. Riker is also so listed although his title was chairman.

5. As an indication of the tiny finance available, the first volumes were bound in whatever colour the printer had in excess supply. He gave me a discount, but the colour changes from issue to issue.

ties, and I wanted to put it in. The other articles were all on what we now call Public Choice. My original intent was to pay for it out of my own pocket, but I received a tiny research grant, through the good will of Jim Buchanan, which I could spend on anything I wanted, and I spent it on this.[6]

The publication of this book led to further articles, and I was able to produce another volume, and then realized that it would be possible to produce a journal. Arranging for a new title was sensible, and I should say that the title was changed by a vote of the members of the society, at a meeting in Chicago.

From this little journal the discipline of Public Choice developed. This may seem like an exaggerated claim, but academic life is highly competitive. Writing articles that cannot be published is not likely to get you very far, regardless of the quality of the articles. The existence of a journal on the subject made it feasible for many academics to write articles on Public Choice where they certainly would not have done so before.

The earlier articles had all been written by people who were more strongly motivated than the average academic, and in most cases were temporary deviations from their main work. The journal made it possible for people to specialize in this area, and for a group of Public Choice scholars to develop.

While dealing with this early development, the penetration of these ideas into Europe should be emphasized. Two Swiss professors, Peter Bernholz and Bruno Frey,[7] were important founders of the movement in Europe. For those who think that Public Choice is essentially a right-wing development, I should point out that Frey held a professorship as a sop to left-wing students. From lengthy conversations with him I can say that he was never remotely close to being a communist or even a socialist, but he was well to the left of the American Democratic party. In any event, Bernholz and Frey organized a European Public Choice meeting in Basle. Bernholz did most of the work, but Frey brought an enthusiastic group of young economists.

It is interesting that the actual funds for this meeting were provided by a foundation which did so at the request of one of the quasi-communist members of the academic community. Furthermore, although this person obvi-

6. Gordon Tullock, *Public Choice* (formerly *Papers on Non-Market Decision Making*; Charlottesville: Thomas Jefferson Center for Political Economy, University of Virginia, 1966). This publication started out as a book and developed into a journal which was published by the Center for Study of Public Choice, Virginia Polytechnic Institute and State University, Blacksburg, Va., until 1978, but it is since then published by Kluwer Academic Publishers, Dordrecht, The Netherlands, under the name *Public Choice*.

7. At the time Peter Bernholz was still a German, but he was working in Basle.

ously thought that, following the usual communist techniques for manipulating groups, he would be in control, he found himself dealing with people who knew even more about procedure and organization of meetings than he did. As a result, after attending a few more meetings he dropped out. This was a case of the communist being exploited instead of exploiting.

In any event, out of this has developed the European Public Choice Society, which by now is about the same size, and holds similarly interesting meetings, as the American Public Choice Society. Bernholz was president in the early years. Although Frey has always refused the presidency, he has played a major role as an almost permanent member of the board.

Membership in either society is largely a matter of subscribing to *Public Choice* and attending the meetings. Now that there are a number of competing journals it is likely that some arrangement for a permanent list of members and a secretariat will be needed. At the moment in both the United States and Europe the president of each society organizes annual meetings. Since the president changes annually in Europe and every other year in the United States there is no permanent organization which keeps a list of members. Notices are normally sent out to all people who subscribe to *Public Choice*. Those interested in the subject who don't subscribe to *Public Choice*, perhaps reading the library copy, must learn about meetings indirectly.

Professor Udagawa in Japan became interested in Public Choice, and he and a number of other Japanese, basically his former graduate students, but with others, have organized the Public Choice Study Group. Considering how close together the Japanese universities involved are, and the convenience of the bullet trains, instead of holding annual meetings they hold a series of informal meetings from time to time during the year. They are vigorous and publish a journal, but the group is still small.

At the moment there seems to be a possibility that a general Far East Public Choice Society, with members from Korea, Taiwan, Hong Kong, and the Philippines in addition to the Japanese will be organized. The only thing published in this area on a regular basis is the Japanese journal, but it may be possible for an English-language journal specializing in Asiatic problems to develop. Considering the role that English already plays in the Far East, it will probably be in English.

During the 25 years I edited *Public Choice* it gradually grew to more, more, and more articles. For a long time I was alone but I am happy to say that competition developed. There are now eight journals in the field, including the one in Japanese. Furthermore, and even more importantly, there are now many Public Choice articles in either the regular economic or the regular political science literatures. In other words, a new sub-discipline has been created.

When I say Public Choice is the use of economic methods in political science, I frequently find that people assume that we are Marxists. This is not the only case where this confusion with Marxism has caused difficulty. The obvious correct name for "Public Choice" is "Political Economy." We could not use that, in part because it was the old name for economics, but even more importantly because the Marxists had taken over that title for their work. They still use it for their "economic analysis." Public Choice is a perfectly suitable name, but not what we would have liked.

Having said what Public Choice is not, I should turn to what it is. The first thing to be said is that we regard people as being much the same both in politics and the market. Indeed, Kalman attacked me with great vigour for having said "the man in the voting booth, and the man in the supermarket are the same man."[8]

The traditional view about politics has been that it is essentially a moral matter. This originated with the Greeks and continued, with the only single deviation being Machiavelli, until very recently. Strauss held that politics was "the science of right action." Most political scientists were not members of his particular school, but moral principles were important in their work.

Thus the simple assumption that people were mainly trying to maximize the well-being of themselves or their families in politics was rather shocking. I was a little surprised that it was shocking. I had noticed in the Department of State that almost everybody considered their future career prospects when making policy decisions. Further, if one looks back through the regular literature you will find this attitude commented on from time to time, but always as something which is unfortunate, rather than a fundamental principle.

This can also be said about voting and politicians. The previous political scientists were not fools, and they knew that people were likely to object to competition if they could avoid it and that politicians were interested in winning elections. All of this was regarded as something that was unfortunate and would be criticized. We switched over and gave it the full treatment.

If I may quote a statement I've made in many papers:

> The traditional political scientist, or ordinary citizen, in his public presentation talks about politics as essentially an effort to get the proper policies

8. Interestingly enough, although I was the one who put this in print, it was actually Buchanan who first said it. Since he said it orally, and I plagiarized him, I get either the credit or the blame.

> in the terms of the public interest. Privately, over a beer they might say that politicians are all crooks, and that the voters vote in terms of narrow selfish interest. They would be shocked if you would say so publicly.

What we did was to take the bar-room approach to politics, and bring it out in the open.

At the time we were doing this, the economics profession was divided very sharply into the Keynesians and the anti-Keynesians, with the Chicago anti-Keynesians being a very small minority. Both Buchanan and I were members of the latter school. Those who feel that Public Choice started on the far right should bear in mind that Kenneth Arrow regarded himself as a socialist, that Duncan Black voted for Labour, and that both Anthony Downs and Mancur Olson are members of the left half of the Democratic party.[9]

Nevertheless, the view that Public Choice was on the right has a certain element of truth in it. Public Choice scholars are rarely enthusiastic about having the government do anything. They may believe that in certain areas it works better than the market, but they believe that there are other areas where it works worse, and in those areas where it works better than the market they don't think it comes near perfection. They don't think that the market is perfect, but neither is the government.

Public Choice had some influence in the long war between the Keynesians and the Chicago School. The Chicago School in the long run won, albeit the current general view is not by any means identical to what the Chicago School thought originally. I don't think that Public Choice had any vital impact on the demise of Keynesian economics, but it made it possible for people to talk about things like protective tariffs in a different language than before.

It should be said here that the problem of protective tariffs had a tendency to drive people from pure economics into different disciplines from the beginning. Both Sumner and Pareto had moved from economics into sociology in an effort to explain protective tariffs. Frank Knight had gone into philosophy partially for the same reason.

Almost all of the political scientists were on the left, although this does not mean they were communists or socialists. They tended to be rather left-wing supporters of the Democratic party. There were a few exceptions to this rule, but most of them fell into that category.

9. I have not mentioned Mancur Olson thus far, as he came a little later than the other people, but the impact of his book, particularly in political science, was large enough so that he certainly can be listed as one of the founding fathers.

A friend of mine who was working for a conservative foundation trying to develop the conservative view in early 1960s academe, said that, of the few allies that he found, a good many were conservative because they had not read anything for some time. There was also a small group of people, essentially interested in political philosophy, who also regarded themselves as conservative. They were Aristotelians, or something of that sort. It should be emphasized that among the people engaged in what was then called "political theory," and what I would call "history of political thought," most were moderate leftists, like the rest of the profession.

The other problem was that, leaving aside a number of Ph.D. candidates who were being generated by William Riker at the University of Rochester, the bulk of the political scientists were poor in mathematics. In many cases it seemed as if they had become political scientists in order to avoid having to do more in the way of mathematics. Being poor in mathematics was a serious problem for many of them because the bulk of them tended to handle statistics very badly and, since the 1920s, the principal drive in political science had been the use of statistical tools. The tests were normally used to confirm some basically moral proposition and distinguished statistical work was carried out using very simple tools.

From my standpoint, the change in this work is one of the great steps forward in political science. If you read *American Political Science Review* today, the articles, in mathematical elegance and statistical sophistication, are as good as those in the best economics journals. This was not the case when *Public Choice* first began.[10]

As a result of all this, Public Choice was in danger of becoming almost entirely economics. Fortunately, from the very beginning Riker and a number of his bright students were always present, but they tended to be outnumbered. Today a Public Choice scholar is as likely to be a formal economist as a formal political scientist. This is distinct progress.

Further, it is not only economists and political scientists who are engaged in Public Choice. James Coleman, a very prominent sociologist, has been president of the American Public Choice Society, and Melvin Hinich, the last president, is almost impossible to classify because of the number of different

10. To give one example, I recall reading an article (citation forgotten), in which a hypothesis was tested with seven independent variables, and six observations. Today, the computer would not permit you to do that, but this was in the early days of the computer. A set of numbers was generated and solemnly published.

disciplines in which he has published. I think he considers himself an electrical engineer. But he could be called an economist, political scientist, statistician, or even an expert on acoustics.

As can be seen from this description of regular economics and political science back when Public Choice began, both disciplines have changed a great deal. I think the fact that they were undergoing major internal revolutions is one of the reasons that Public Choice was able to break into both of them. If a firm orthodoxy had been there, they would have been more resistant.

As a matter of fact, fairly early in economics, and not too late in political science, one began finding people who were not in Public Choice mentioning Public Choice ideas in their articles, and most students were becoming fairly familiar with them. The change in these two professions, which has been radical over this period, was helpful for Public Choice.

As I mentioned, the actual foundation of the society and its original work were in essence set off by *The Calculus of Consent.* What we might refer to as the general philosophical aspect of *The Calculus of Consent* has remained important in the profession since that time. The idea that government exists primarily to deal with externalities; that it is not perfectly efficient; and that the voters exercise control which is really strong, even if not well informed, are all orthodox today. Nevertheless, the specific technical aspect of *The Calculus of Consent*, the study of log-rolling, has never been a major feature in Public Choice. As the inventor of the log-rolling model, I regret this. I think the lack of attention it has received is a mistake, and I hope we can revive it; and in fact, I am working on the subject at the present time.

At the time Public Choice was invented, there was an orthodox opinion about government and the economy. This opinion is perhaps demonstrated by the title of an important book, *Private Wants and Public Needs.*[11] The prevailing view was simply that for various reasons the market did not work perfectly. This is true. But it was further deduced that the government should enter for purposes of filling in the gaps, and correcting the errors of the market. In retrospect, it is hard to see how anybody could have thought this was sensible. It implies a hidden assumption that the government is perfect, and I don't think that anybody has ever thought that is so.

Amusingly, there is a mirror image of this in what I call the American anarchists. They demonstrate, normally quite easily, that the government is do-

11. Edmund S. Phelps, ed. *Private Wants and Public Needs: Issues Surrounding the Size and Scope of Government Expenditure* (New York: W. W. Norton, 1962).

ing badly in some particular area, and then assume if you switch into the market it will function perfectly. This is as erroneous as the majority error I have just mentioned.

Both the government and the market are highly imperfect instrumentalities. Fortunately, the imperfections do not occur exactly in the same area. One can choose whether government or the market is the best instrumentality in dealing with the given problem without assuming that it will solve the problem perfectly. We assume a good deal of error and friction, but still can decide which of them, for any particular problem, would have had the least error and friction. Indeed much research has gone into this particular problem.

Another problem which was of great importance in the early days of Public Choice, but has rather vanished, was the existence of very severe paradoxes in all known voting methods. The basic problem was discovered by the Marquis de Condorcet shortly before he died in the French Revolution. It was brought to public notice by Black after World War II, and then formalized by Kenneth Arrow.

Arrow showed that apparently no voting method can avoid severe paradoxes. In the early days efforts to find ways around this were important aspects of Public Choice. None was found, and the eventual outcome was a simple ignoring of the problem. It ceased to be a major problem, but it remains in the back of the minds of most Public Choice specialists.

My feeling in this particular area from the very beginning was that Arrow's theorem was perfectly correct, but it dealt with a model of voting which was not what we actually observed. In other words, there was no determinant point outcome to voting, but voting could get us into a small region. I have published a number of articles in this area, but the mathematicians working on the theorem have generally disapproved of my work, perhaps because I had said they were wasting their time. I think as a matter of fact I won the debate. In other words, the Arrow theorem is true, but unimportant.

To repeat, Public Choice became a significant area of study. At the time of writing, I have just returned from the European Public Choice meeting. There was a large and active group, and in some way they were too active. It was in Valencia, and I had hoped to spend some time looking around that very pretty old town, but found that most of my time was spent in meeting rooms listening to papers. The same thing would have occurred in the United States, except that since the American meeting was held in Austin, Texas, no one would want to look around town.

Thus we have the combination of two and a half Public Choice societies, which are active and vigorous, and a very substantial penetration of Public Choice ideas and personnel into both regular political science and regular economic channels.

The passage of time has not only meant partially forgetting about logrolling and the Arrow theorem, it has seen positive developments. The bulk of these positive developments are re-examinations of various institutions of the sort that are normally examined by political scientists with the use of the special tools developed by Public Choice scholars, essentially rooted in economics. This has yielded a large number of specific results and a general change in attitude. One of the achievements of Public Choice has been to bring some of the imperfections of government out in the open.

As I said earlier, if one talked to a traditional political scientist he would have found that in public, teaching his class, giving lectures, he talked a great deal about the public interest and desirability of following ethical courses of action. (This was particularly true of the followers of Strauss.) As I mentioned before, if you met him afterwards in a bar, and had a few drinks, you would find him talking about specific cases in which governments or politicians behaved in a highly unethical way. In this they were like the general public.

The students and, for that matter, the average citizen, followed much the same pattern. On ceremonial occasions they would talk about public interest and virtuous government, and in private would remark that politicians were all a bunch of crooks, and the bureaucrats were incompetent. In Public Choice we melded these two points of view. We would talk in the open about bureaucrats trying to maximize their own well-being, and politicians trying to get elected. The voters also would vote in terms of their interests for themselves and their families. This openness shocked a great many people such as Kalman.

I think that we have made the point. Conventional social scientists now publish articles in which they demonstrate that congressmen vote primarily in the interest of their constituencies, voters vote primarily in their own interest, and both are generally badly informed.

There are few students these days who think that the civil service is unremittingly in pursuit of the public good. All of this in a quiet way is a revolution, and a revolution that is comparatively inconspicuous if you read the current literature. It is only by comparing what is now said in the average empirical study of voter behaviour, with what was said in the standard textbooks

40 years ago, that you realize how large the change has been. In other words we now have a much more accurate view of what government does, and what government does to the rest of the economy.

This new way of looking at the government in itself would be a step forward, but there have been many other improvements. One of the more important of these is the discovery of rent-seeking. This term is a misnomer. I made the original discovery, but I am not responsible for the name, so I do not apologize to the readers, and don't feel particularly guilty.

The basic discovery of rent-seeking was that the issuance of special privileges, as in government, or private monopoly, is more costly than had been previously thought. The previous theory, which today it is a little hard to believe anyone actually held, was that if monopoly was created either privately or by government, the basic cost was simply the small triangle showing the deadweight loss of consumer surplus.

In this traditional theory the profits of the monopolist were part of the total of society's income and equalled the bulk of the cost to consumers. Since the monopolist was part of society, the two amounts cancelled each other out and there was no social loss here. If the government raises the price of butter by 5 cents per pound, the butter producers get 5 cents more and the consumers pay 5 cents more, but that is a transfer from one to the other. Hence it is not, in this view, a true social cost. True social cost would only be the lost consumer surplus from the fact that not as much butter was purchased.

Note that this assumes (and I must confess I have made this assumption for much of my life) that the government rule in this case is obtained with no resource investment, possibly a gift of God or some politicians who think it is just a good idea. This is an absurd assumption. You have to work for these things. Further, there is no reason to believe that the return on capital invested in getting special privileges out of the government is any higher than that obtained by investment on other things. The area that appears to be a transfer in the traditional view is actually a cost run by the people who receive the transfer.

This isn't simple because there is a very high element of risk in these cases. Many people maintain lobbies in Washington, but only a few of them achieve major monopolies. In a way, setting up a lobby in Washington is like buying a lottery ticket. If you win, the return will be very high, but most of the people who buy do not win. The same is true with monopolies and government lobbying. The number of people who make large gains by pushing the government into giving them some special privilege is small, and for those people it is very profitable. Unfortunately, their profits are matched by the expenditures of other people who don't get the privilege.

One of the problems of this new approach is the difficulty of measuring the rent-seeking costs. Those who have empirically attempted to do so have got figures anywhere from 3 per cent to 30 per cent of GNP. A summary of the general debate with my solution is presented in my *The Economics of Special Privilege and Rent Seeking*.[12]

It must be that discounting for risk, etc., a company deciding to build a factory, rather than going to Washington and getting some special privilege which will produce as much profit as the factory, would never build the factory unless these two activities discounted for risk were about equally profitable, or the profitability of investing the money in lobbying was, again discounting for risk, less than that of the factory.

Thus, the new approach implies that monopolies, special privilege in the government, etc. cost society not only the small deadweight loss once they are in existence, but the cost of the resources needed to obtain them. This is a larger amount, but, to repeat, it has turned out to be difficult to measure. Even if it is as low as 3 per cent of GNP, the lowest empirical measure derived, it is obviously a major cost. If we assume that it is in the middle of the range of empirical measurements, somewhere around 15 per cent, then it may be one of the largest net wastes in our society.

Rent-seeking is currently the most exciting single topic in Public Choice, but the really impressive characteristic of Public Choice over the last 30 years is its growth. Earlier I mentioned I had just returned from the meeting of the European Public Choice Society. It attracted 170 scholars. The American meeting running at the same time had somewhat more participants, and as I have said there is also a proto Far Eastern Society. Using these as measures, Public Choice has grown from 15 to 20 scholars at the time the first meeting was held to something in excess of 500.

It has to be admitted that the recent work in Public Choice, although sound, has not been revolutionary. We are progressing in learning about government by many small steps instead of by a few giant ones. Rent-seeking, discussed in the last few paragraphs, is the only major single step in recent work. Nevertheless, it is probably true that the steady progress made in other areas, both in the seven journals now specializing in Public Choice and in the papers read at the meetings, is very considerable and significant. Further, as

12. Gordon Tullock, *The Economics of Special Privilege and Rent Seeking* (Boston and Dordrecht: Kluwer Academic Publishers, 1989).

I mentioned, Public Choice papers are regularly published in both the standard economic literature and the normal political science literature.

This is a large growth, but the potential for further growth is even greater. First, one of the characteristics of the Public Choice Society's meetings is that the average age of the participant is much lower than the average age of the participants in the American Economic Association meetings. This is because it is a new field attracting new practitioners. Many people who are studying Public Choice for Ph.D.s are engaged in formal economics, but many of them are also engaged in formal political science.

Not only is Public Choice growing, it is beginning to have an influence on policy. In a way the principal reason for studying in the social sciences is to improve our societies. Economics, from its very beginning, has been in essence a crusading science which attempts to improve government economic policy. Perhaps the oldest chestnut in economics is the desirability of free trade, and economists have on the whole made very considerable progress, although not as much progress as most of them would have liked.

It is interesting that the role of protective tariffs in leading to the initial development of Public Choice is significant. First, the work on log-rolling in essence explained why democracy would tend to adopt protective tariffs together with any other measures that would give special privileges to small groups.

I believe it has been the traditional view in democracy that normally a policy not approved by the majority of the citizens would not be adopted. An important advance made very early in Public Choice is the realization that, through log-rolling, measures benefiting minorities at the expense of the majority are not only adopted, but actually dominate the political process.

The realization that this is the case could lead to the reform of political process so that these net harmful projects would not be implemented. So far, these efforts at reform, although frequently ingenuous, have not in general been directly adopted. I am in favour of something called "demand revealing" which would greatly improve democracy in this area. I remarked on one occasion to Milton Friedman that the prospects of it being adopted in the near future were very small. Friedman replied: "You are exaggerating its chances."

Other proposals for a change of a less radical nature have only entered into the discussion process, but have not shown any signs of being adopted. Still, the fact that such things are being discussed in the academic literature, even if at the moment only a small sub-set of the academic literature, is a favourable augury. Ideas have to start somewhere, and have to develop support in minorities at the beginning. We hope that they will eventually become acceptable to the majority. The fact that there are a very considerable number of members of the various Public Choice Societies, or students studying under them who are in favour of fairly drastic reforms, or, at least, discussing them, is a favourable sign.

One should not simply adopt such reforms on the basis of the little work that has been done so far. Further study and the continuous drumfire of new research and particularly the continuance of empirical testing of various theoretical propositions indicates that we are not likely to go off on a tangent. When Public Choice begins to have influence, it will be certain to be an accurate influence.

As an example, new propositions in Public Choice are almost immediately tested empirically and sometimes experimentally. If the first test is favourable, this does not normally lead to the widespread adoption of the proposition. Instead, a favourable first test result will lead a number of other scholars to seek out other information so that the suggestion can be further tested. After seven or eight independent tests there is a high likelihood that the theory is correct.

The movement from a tiny part of the learned community to, say, a core of 500 serious students and a periphery of something like 2,000 scholars who are at least interested in Public Choice is a big step. Many of the 2,000, of course, are primarily engaged in other fields of study, but their concern for Public Choice is still helpful. Further, it is notable that active politicians and other people involved in making policy now frequently show at least some familiarity with Public Choice, and use terminology and ideas drawn from Public Choice to some minor extent in their policy.

In Reagan's second term, the director of Office of Management and Budget was a student of Jim Buchanan and myself. I was living in the outskirts of Washington and was occasionally invited to have lunch or breakfast in the White House mess. There is no doubt that Jim Miller was fully aware of Public Choice procedures and favours the Public Choice approach. He is also a practical politician, and knew that he couldn't do too much in the way of applying what is now an idea held only by a certain number of professional scholars.

It is notable that during Miller's tenure as director of Office of Management and Budget[13] he was able, for the first time in a long period, to actually

13. For the benefit of non-Americans this is a cabinet position; in fact, one of the more important cabinet positions.

get down the percentage of GNP absorbed by the federal government. It was done in general by using his Public Choice knowledge to eliminate wasteful projects. As far as I know he did not do anything in the way of reducing the actual useful part of the government. Still, there is plenty of waste left and much more could be done. Unfortunately, Darman, who took over the directorship in the Bush administration, reversed almost all of his reforms.

Going further, the majority leader of the House of Representatives is a Public Choice enthusiast, and there are a number of Public Choice scholars in the high ranks both of the American bureaucracy and of those international organizations like the World Bank who have headquarters in Washington.

All of this does not mean that Public Choice is likely to be adopted tomorrow as the official theory of American or, for that matter, foreign governments. We are making progress. The whole thing started only about 30 years ago, and we are obviously doing very well.

I am, as the reader may have noticed, an enthusiast for Public Choice and the reader may discount my views accordingly. It seems likely to me that we are now part of the academic community and the policy advising community that cannot be ignored. We are likely to continue expanding our influence.

There are three areas where we should obviously push. One of these is simply learning more about government. If we are to attempt to reform the structure of government in order to make it work better, we obviously have to know more than we do now. I am very much impressed by how much we have learned in the last 30 years. In essence, we have a new science which is well established and has a large body of well-tested theory. Still, there is an opportunity for much further work and I hope that this will be done. I go farther and say I am convinced that it will.

The large number of young and enthusiastic, bright and well-trained scholars now entering the profession is a guarantee that the necessary work will be carried out. Thus, at the end of the next 30 years we certainly will know a great deal more about government and have even better ideas of how it can be reformed than we do now.

We can continue to spread our ideas and our influence in the scholarly community, adding on to our achievements to date. Surely this will continue. It is promising to note that there are now no less than five elementary textbooks designed for teaching undergraduate courses in Public Choice. In two of these cases, there is now a new and revised second edition. This indicates that the publishers think this is a market, i.e., there is going to be more teaching of Public Choice.

There has been for some time a very good book designed for graduate students or professors who want to get a start in Public Choice. This is Dennis Mueller's *Public Choice II*. This book, as its title implies, is the second edition. Basically, it is a critical bibliography of most of the existing literature, together with a careful introduction to most of the principal points in the literature. It is on the whole too hard for use with beginning students, but graduate students or members of the faculty will find it very straightforward. It does cover the entire field.[14]

Teaching is important because it produces more research and, secondly, a collection of people who understand the subject, hence are apt to pass it on, either formally or informally. If Public Choice is to have an effect, it must get into government circles, and as I have said before, it already has. I should point out that the so-called think tanks, in particular the Institute of Economic Affairs in London, and the American Enterprise Institute in the United States, have begun showing strong signs of recognizing the importance of Public Choice.

As mentioned above, politically active people are beginning to show signs of taking Public Choice on board. In a democracy we must wait until the ideas are spread among the public, but the general attitude the average citizen has towards government is such that this should be fairly easy once we get over the initial barriers.

Although I wish we had made more progress in the first 30 years than we have, we still have made progress. I hope that the next 30 years will be even more prosperous.

Additional References

WORKS BY GORDON TULLOCK

"Problems of Majority Voting," *Journal of Political Economy* 67 (December 1959), 571–79. Reprinted in Kenneth Arrow and Tibor Scitovsky (eds.), *Readings in Welfare Economics*, Homewood, Ill.: Richard D. Irwin, 1969, pp. 169–78. Translated "Problemi del voto a maggioranza," in Francesco Forte and Gianfranco Mossetto (eds.), *Economia del Benessere e Democrazia*, Milan: Franco Angeli Editore, 1973, pp. 459–71. Reprinted in Thomas Schwartz (ed.), *Freedom and Authority: An Introduction to Political Philosophy*, Encino, Calif.: Dickenson Publishing Co.

14. Dennis C. Mueller, *Public Choice*, 2d ed. (Cambridge: Cambridge University Press, 1989).

A Practical Guide for the Ambitious Politician, Columbia: University of South Carolina Press, 1961.

"An Economic Analysis of Political Choice," *Il Politico*, 16 (1961), 234–40.

Entrepreneurial Politics, research monograph no. 5, Thomas Jefferson Center for Political Economy, University of Virginia, February, 1962.

"Entry Barriers in Politics," *American Economic Review*, 55 (May, 1965), 458–66.

The Organization of Inquiry, Durham, N.C.: Duke University Press, 1966. University Press of America, 1987.

Toward a Mathematics of Politics, Ann Arbor: University of Michigan Press, 1967. Paperback, 1972.

"The General Irrelevance of the General Impossibility Theorem," *Quarterly Journal of Economics*, 81 (May, 1967), 256–70. Translated "L'irrelevanza generale del theorema della impossibilita generale," Francesco Forte and Gianfranco Mossetto (eds.), *Economia del Benessere e Democrazia*, Milan: Franco Angeli Editore, 1973, pp. 261–76.

"The Welfare Costs of Tariffs, Monopolies, and Theft," *Western Economic Journal*, 5 (June, 1967), 224–32.

"Federalism: Problems of Scale," *Public Choice*, 6 (Spring, 1969), 19–29. Reprinted in Ryan C. Amacher, Robert D. Tollison and Thomas D. Willett (eds.), *The Economic Approach to Public Policy*, Ithaca, N.Y.: Cornell University Press, 1976, pp. 511–19; reprinted in Bhajan S. Grewl, Geoffrey Brennan and Russell L. Mathews (eds.), *Economics of Federalism*, Canberra: Australian National University Press, 1980, pp. 39–49.

Private Wants, Public Means: An Economic Analysis of the Desirable Scope of Government, New York: Basic Books, 1970. Spanish translation, 1979; Japanese translation, 1984; University Press of America, 1988.

The Logic of the Law, New York: Basic Books, 1971. University Press of America, 1988.

The Social Dilemma: The Economics of War and Revolution, Blacksburg, Va.: Center for Study of Public Choice, 1974. Japanese translation, 1979.

Explorations in the Theory of Anarchy, Blacksburg, Va.: Center for Study of Public Choice, 1974.

Further Explorations in the Theory of Anarchy, Blacksburg, Va.: Center for Study of Public Choice, 1974.

Tullock, Gordon, with Richard B. McKenzie, *The New World of Economics: Explorations into the Human Experience*, Homewood, Ill.: Richard D. Irwin, 1975; 2nd edition, 1978; 3rd edition, 1980; 4th edition, 1984 (see ch. 4, "Competing Monies." pp. 52–65); 5th edition, 1988, revised 1994, McGraw-Hill; 6th edition, retitled *The Best of the New World of Economics . . . and Then Some*, 1988. Spanish translation, 1980; Japanese translation, 1981; German translation, 1984.

The Vote Motive, with a British commentary by Morris Perlman, London: Institute of Economic Affairs, Hobart Paperback No. 9, 1976. Spanish translation by

Maria Jesus Blanco, Madrid: Espasa Calpe, 1980; French translation, *Le Marche Politique*, 1978, Paris, France: Association Pour L'Economie Des Institutions; revised and expanded English edition, forthcoming; Swedish translation, *Den Politiska Marknaden*, by Eric Jannersten, Avesta, Sweden: Timbro, 1983, new, revised and expanded edition, Timbro, 1994; Italian translation, *Scelte Pubbliche*, 1984, Florence, Italy: Le Monnier; Korean translation, 1994.

Trials on Trial: The Pure Theory of Legal Procedure, New York: Columbia University Press, 1980.

Tullock, Gordon, with James M. Buchanan and Robert D. Tollison (co-editors), *Toward a Theory of the Rent-Seeking Society*, College Station: Texas A&M University Press, Series 4, 1980.

"Efficient Rent Seeking," in Buchanan, Tollison and Tullock, *Toward a Theory*, pp. 153–79.

Toward a Science of Politics: Papers in Honor of Duncan Black, Blacksburg, Va.: Center for Study of Public Choice, 1981.

Economics of Income Redistribution, Hingham, Mass.: Kluwer-Nijhoff Publishing, 1983. Second printing, 1984.

The Economics of Wealth and Poverty, London: Wheatsheaf Press, 1986.

Autocracy, Dordrecht: Martinus Nijhoff, 1987.

Wealth, Poverty, and Politics, Oxford: Basil Blackwell, 1988.

Tullock, Gordon, with Charles K. Rowley and Robert D. Tollison (co-editors), *The Political Economy of Rent-Seeking*, Amsterdam: Kluwer Academic Publishers, 1988.

Economic Hierarchies, Organization and the Structure of Production. Studies in Public Choice, Norwell, Mass./Dordrecht: Kluwer Academic Publishers, 1992.

The New Federalist, Vancouver: Frazer Institute, 1994. Serbo-Croatian translation by Ljubomir Madzar, Belgrade: The Institute of Economics and "Ekonomika," 1992; Russian translation, Centre of Children's and Adults' International Initiatives for Peace and Cooperation, Moscow, 1994; Korean translation, 1994.

On the Trail of Homo economicus: *Essays by Gordon Tullock (In Search of the Economic Man)*, edited by Gordon Brady and Robert Tollison, Fairfax, Va.: George Mason University Press, 1994. This is a collection of essays (papers) by Gordon Tullock, together with some critical bibliographical notes.

The Economics of Non-human Societies, Tucson, Ariz.: Pallas Press, 1994.

Tullock, Gordon, with Gordon Brady (co-editors), *Intellectual Biography of Duncan Black*, Dordrecht: Kluwer Academic Press, forthcoming.

Tullock, Gordon, with Gordon Brady and Arthur Seldon (co-editors), *Primer on Public Choice*, Dordrecht: Kluwer Academic Press, forthcoming.

OTHER SOURCES

Arrow, Kenneth J., *Social Choice and Individual Values*, New York: John Wiley, 1951.

Black, Duncan, *The Theory of Committees and Elections*, Cambridge: Cambridge University Press, 1958.

Breton, Albert, *The Demand and Supply of Public Goods*, Chicago: Rand McNally, 1968.

——, *The Economic Theory of Representative Government*, Chicago: Aldine, 1974.

Kau, James B., and Paul H. Rubin, *Congressmen, Constituents and Contributors*, Boston: Martinus Nijhoff, 1981.

Mueller, Dennis C., *Public Choice*, 2nd edition, Cambridge: Cambridge University Press, 1989.

Olson, Mancur, *The Logic of Collective Action*, Cambridge, Mass.: Harvard University Press, 1965.

Ostrom, Vincent, Elinor Ostrom and Robert Bish, *Local Government in the United States*, San Francisco: ICS Press, 1988.

Phelps, Edmund S. (ed.), *Private Wants and Public Needs*, New York: W. W. Norton & Company, 1962.

Riker, William H., *The Theory of Political Coalitions*, New Haven: Yale University Press, 1962.

——, *The Art of Political Manipulation*, New Haven: Yale University Press, 1986.

PEOPLE ARE PEOPLE

THE ELEMENTS OF PUBLIC CHOICE

"*Homo politicus* and *Homo economicus* are the same. The critical implication of this assumption of universal self-interest is that the observed differences between public choices and private choices emerge not because individuals adopt different behavioral objectives in the two settings, but rather because the constraints on behavior are different. Different outcomes emerge not because public choices are guided by motives different from those guiding private choices, but rather because in private markets self-interested voters and politicians make choices that mainly affect themselves, while in political markets self-interested voters and politicians make choices that mainly affect others."[1]

Political Actors and the "Public Interest"

Public choice is a scientific analysis of government behaviour and, in particular, the behaviour of individuals with respect to government. Strictly speaking, it has no policy implications except that in some cases it might be demonstrated that a particular policy is impossible or extremely unlikely to achieve its stated policy goals. For example, students of public choice would not be particularly impressed with a policy of "maximising the public interest" and would recognise the inherent difficulties of obtaining free trade or achieving a balanced budget in seven years. They would regard these policy objectives as rather like telling the pilot of a Boeing 747 to get to London faster than the Concorde.

Until the days of Adam Smith (1723–1790),[2] most social discussion was essentially moral. Individuals—whether they were businessmen, civil servants, politicians, or hereditary monarchs—were told what was the morally

Reprinted, with permission, from *Government: Whose Obedient Servant? A Primer in Public Choice*, ed. Gordon Tullock, Arthur Seldon, and Gordon L. Brady (London: Institute of Economic Affairs, 2000), 3–18.

1. F. S. McChesney and W. F. Shughart II, *The Causes and Consequences of Antitrust: The Public Choice Perspective*, Chicago: The University of Chicago Press, 1995, pp. 9–10.

2. See Adam Smith's *The Nature and Causes of the Wealth of Nations* (1776). There are many editions.

correct thing to do and urged to do it. It was implicitly assumed that all these people should be, and perhaps were, engaged in maximising the public interest. Machiavelli (1469–1527)[3] and Hobbes (1588–1679)[4] were major exceptions to this rule; nevertheless, in both cases their influence was much less than their readership might suggest. They were taken by most of their readers as wickedly arguing against morality, rather than producing a scientific system which was essentially amoral.

David Hume (1711–1776)[5] was the first to make significant cracks in this monolithic approach. He took the rather obvious view that most people pursued their own interest in their behaviour rather than a broadly based public interest, and in several essays applied this line of reasoning to economics. Forerunners to his work can be found in European and, indeed, non-European thought. But, until the time of Hume and his friend, Adam Smith, the prevailing view of human nature and government was that the moral or public interest approach was dominant. Adam Smith developed modern economics by assuming that individuals were very largely self-interested and working out the consequences of that assumption in the realm of economics. In *The Nature and Causes of the Wealth of Nations*, Smith devoted three chapters to government, while retaining the moralistic or public-interest model.

From the time of Plato (428–347 BC)[6] and Aristotle (384–322),[7] political science was viewed simply as a matter of producing morally correct policies. The claim by Leo Strauss (1899–1973)[8] that political science was "the science of right action" was extreme, but not untypical. There was no formal theory of how government works outside such moral and ethical foundations.

Throughout the 19th and well into the 20th century, economists assumed that individuals are primarily concerned with their own interest and worked out the consequences of that assumption. On the other hand, during this same period political science largely assumed that political actors are mainly concerned with the public interest. Thus, an individual who enters a super-

3. Niccolò Machiavelli, *The Prince* (1532) (many editions).
4. Thomas Hobbes, *Leviathan* (1650) (many editions).
5. David Hume, *Essays Moral and Political* (1741–42) (many editions).
6. Plato, *The Republic* (many editions).
7. Aristotle, *Politics* (many editions).
8. Leo Strauss; almost any one of his books.

market and purchases items of his choice is assumed, when he enters the voting booth, to vote *not* for the politicians and laws which will benefit him, but for politicians and laws which will benefit the nation as a whole. The person in the supermarket mainly buys the food and other goods that are, granted their price, found to benefit him and his family.[9] However, once he becomes a politician, a transformation is assumed to occur so that a broader perspective guides him to make morally correct decisions rather than follow the course of behaviour which pleases the interest groups which supported him or the policies which may lead to re-election.

The Bifurcated View of Human Behaviour

Economists changed this bifurcated view of human behaviour by developing the theory of public choice which amounts, in essence, to transplanting the general analytical framework of economics into political science. The statement that the voter in the voting booth is the same person as the customer in the supermarket does not seem radical, but is nevertheless a very dramatic change from the political science literature. Indeed, the author of this Part I has often been denounced with great vigour at professional meetings by conventional political scientists for expounding this view.

This bifurcation of the individual psyche is particularly impressive when it is remembered that the economic system based upon self-interest assumptions can be demonstrated to produce a result not totally out of accord with the classical ideas of the public interest. On the other hand, until very recently, there was no proof that the government would generate an output in accord with the classical ideas of public interest. Indeed, the first demonstration that the government might tend to produce an outcome which, in any sense, was optimal came from people who adopted economic assumptions about political behaviour.

Since the *same* people engage in market activities and in politics, it seems simpler to assume that their behaviour has the same motivation in both of these areas. Indeed, it is rather difficult to understand how the bifurcated view of individual behaviour has been maintained. Nevertheless, it has been and remains the dominant view. Of course, empirical confirmation of any theo-

9. He may, and most people do, make charitable contributions from time to time. These are usually a fairly small part (5 per cent or so) of his total income.

retical proposition is more important than analytical elegance. Most people realise that when considering the behaviour of any individual politician, he behaves in a self-interested way, and similarly, when considering the factors that affect votes, most people assume that personal gain is certainly an aspect.

The politician in a democratic society is a man who makes a living by winning elections. This rather simple and obvious observation seems to have escaped the early students of government. To quote an American aphorism: "In order to be a great Senator, one must, first of all, be a Senator." In other words, those people whom we elect to office are there because they are good at being elected. This characteristic of periodic re-assessment makes them similar in many ways to the businessman. Just as a businessman designs, let us say, the latest automobile so as to attract customers, the politician selects policies with the idea that his customer, the voter, will reward him in the next election. No one considers this activity as absolutely wicked, but it is, in general, not an exercise in the application of some high-level moral principle. Politicians and businessmen will sometimes pay a price (lost constituent support) in order to do what they think is good, but on the whole they can be expected to act in such a way as to maximise their own well-being in terms of re-election prospects. Stated in different language, the politician as businessman pursues policies which he thinks the people want because he hopes they will reward him with their votes. To say that the voters actually rule under this scheme is not a bad approximation. Nor is this from the standpoint of democracy particularly undesirable.

Politics and the Information Problem

In considering the consequences of this simple view of government, there is one special problem: economists have based their predictions on the notion that purchasers in the market are perfectly informed.[10] Unfortunately, in

10. The reason may be the development of the mathematical theory of perfect competition in which if you assume that people are perfectly informed, the mathematics is easier than if you assume they have the kind of information they really do have. The more modern theory of economics argues that people accumulate information as long as the value of more information will exceed its cost. However, the decision about collecting information is made at a time when they do not know the value of additional information in terms of what advantages it would provide.

the case of politics the information problem is much worse than it is in the market. Consider the following example of individual behavioural incentives in a private market choice. In purchasing an automobile I invest a certain amount of time and resources in learning about new cars, for the simple reason that I know a mistake will directly affect me, my wallet, convenience, and comfort.

But, when voting for the president of the United States, my vote will be one of 70 million cast and is highly unlikely to affect the final outcome of the election. This realisation can be expected to affect the valuation which I place on my vote and the resources that I will invest to collect information to make a "correct" choice. This means that politicians trying to select policies that will attract voters know that the voters will put much less energy into trying to make a correct choice than they would when purchasing an automobile or some other item whose shortcomings and advantages will accrue to them alone. The voters are, therefore, likely to be badly informed and may favour a politician or policies that are directly contrary to their interest. From the standpoint of the individual candidate, what is important is what the people want given their perception of the value of their vote on the outcome and the cost of becoming informed, *not* what they would want if they were better informed.

The same is true for designers of automobiles, but they know that their customers will be, if not perfectly informed, at least better informed than the voter. Putting it briefly, I get a positive return on additional information when I am buying a car because it will improve my choice. Frequent and costly repairs and the inconvenience of being stranded on a cold and lonely highway waiting for a tow truck are in my self-interest to avoid. Automobile designers know this, and hence design cars with the intention of attracting reasonably informed customers. But when I vote I am aware that my vote will have almost no effect on the kind of policies I shall get. This result occurs because the policies and politicians chosen will be determined to a much greater extent by the votes of other people. Politicians once again know this, and hence attempt to design policies which will attract ill-informed voters.

This limited information on general topics contrasts with the much greater knowledge most people have about specific policies. Consider the following examples: farmers know a great deal about farm subsidies and acreage limitations (in the United States and in Europe); workers and management are well-informed about import restrictions on goods which directly compete with those they manufacture. This asymmetrical information bias leads to the emergence of special-interest groups and encourages politicians to pay attention to them.

Democratic versus Non-democratic Government

It is important to issue a special note of warning. In this *Primer* we will discuss at length the defects of the government in a democratic process; however, it does not mean that we know a better way to deal with these problems. Air pollution is normally handled ineffectively by the government, but whatever one can say about the defects of the air quality management controls that now exist, they *may* be better than leaving it to the market. Further experimentation with non-democratic forms of government indicates that they produce outcomes which are less desirable than democracy. As a consequence, we have a form of government which is far from what we would really like, but until a new and better one is invented, we had better keep the one we have despite its shortcomings. Nevertheless, it is true that we should be fully aware of the difficulties and inefficiencies that are to be expected from the government. The objective of this *Primer* is more limited: We ask, what is public choice and what difference does public choice make in understanding democratic processes?

Leaving Everything to the Market?

Are students of public choice different and, if so, why? To begin, we might ask why we have government at all. The market produces many things with remarkable efficiency, but why not have the market take over everything, as recommended by economists such as Murray Rothbard (1926–1995)? The *standard* answer to this argument goes back to Hume, but in modern times it is associated with the names of economists such as A. C. Pigou (1877–1959) and Paul A. Samuelson (Nobel laureate in Economics, 1970). The problem is essentially technological. The market requires some system of property rights under which individuals are allocated power over various aspects of the real world. Individuals holding "property" see opportunities for improving their well-being by various types of agreements with each other (as well as, of course, their individual labour), and enter into agreements, thus achieving improvements in their well-being. Unfortunately, under any known allocation of property rights, it will occasionally occur that the number of people who must agree is very large and, further (and this is a very important qualification), that the particular group which must agree is not given at the outset of the analysis.

The importance of the last criterion is fundamental. If we propose to establish a new corporation and sell stock on the stock market, we may require the concurrence of a very large number of people (buyers, sellers of other stock, regulators). But the number of people we require is a small part of all potential investors, and hence the people who will become stockholders are not prespecified. If, on the other hand, we are proposing to improve police protection in Tucson or London, the number of people who are directly concerned is determined at the outset. If we permit individuals to decide whether they will pay for the police department, and given the technological conditions under which additional police protection is delivered, we would anticipate that very little police protection would be purchased. The only way out of this dilemma, assuming we have complete private property, would be to arrange a unanimous agreement under which each of us put a certain amount of money up in return for the agreement of all the others. Clearly the bargaining costs would be immense. The role of government, under the modern view, is to permit us to gain this type of an advantage, to enter into this kind of an agreement—*without* requiring unanimity, and hence obtain much lower bargaining costs.

The Costs and Benefits of Government

It will immediately be obvious that, without unanimous agreement, we must have some other method of making decisions, and it may clearly impose costs upon at least some members of the community. Thus, we would adopt government decision-making only if we anticipated that the costs to us of the bargaining eliminated are higher than the potential of being victimised by whatever decision process we choose. In this sense, government becomes a market surrogate for obtaining economic profit in areas where bargaining is costly. Looked at in this way, there is no obvious reason why the "public interest" must be served by the government, but one can at least imagine that decision-making processes could be designed such that an outcome in a sense equivalent to the classical public interest might be achieved. It would, in other words, be somewhat like market provision. In both cases, it could be argued that the system provided something which most people would want, simply because the motivating force of the organisation is individual desires.

The student of public choice, in dealing with the government, does not expect that it will efficiently achieve the "classical goals" of government. It does not follow that it cannot efficiently achieve *other* goals or, indeed, that with appropriate redesign, it might not achieve *some* of the classical goals, such as efficient enforcement of the law against assault and battery. Indeed, we can find many cases in which that goal of government has been carried out quite efficiently in the past or in the present. Washington, D.C., in 1911, had safe streets, as does Zurich today.[11]

Government and the Pursuit of Private Interests

We must accept that in government, as in any form of commerce, people will pursue their private interests, and they will achieve goals which are reasonably closely related to those of company stockholders or of citizens only if it is in their private interest to do so. The primacy of private interest is not inconsistent with the observation that most people, in addition to pursuing their private interests, have some charitable instincts, some tendency to help others, and to engage in various morally correct activities.

However, the evidence seems fairly strong that those motives other than the pursuit of private interests are not ones on which we can depend for the achievement of long-continued efficient performance. Consider two groups, federal judges and college professors. Both groups have been granted substantially guaranteed employment with no risk of being fired. In both cases, there are a great many who take advantage of this, not to maximise the production of truth, truthful research, or correct decisions, but to maximise their enjoyment of leisure. There are tenured professors and judges who work hard; but, in both cases, the average is fairly low.[12]

11. The 1911 date comes from the fact that the morning paper reported the death, as the result of a daylight mugging incident directly in front of her home, of a very elderly socialite, Gladys H. Werlich, who first moved to that address in 1911. (*Washington Post*, 21 January 1976, p. A1.)

12. No authority is needed with respect to college professors, but for a discussion of federal judges' work habits, see G. Tullock, "On the Efficient Organization of Trials," *Kyklos* 28,

Most traditional students of political science would regard such remarks as not only wrong but wicked. Indeed, it is possible that such statements about federal judges are illegal in the sense that, in theory, one could be held in contempt of court for having made them, regardless of the ability to prove their truth. But the different attitude towards government which arises from public choice does have major effects on our views on what policies government should undertake or can carry out. In particular, it makes us much less ambitious about relying on government to provide certain services. No student of public choice would feel that the establishment of a national health service in the United States would mean that the doctors would work devotedly to improve the health of the citizens. We should anticipate that, unless a very carefully designed incentive system is set up, many doctors will tend to behave rather as the British doctors have.

Public Choice and Policy Choices

Unfortunately, few students of public choice have integrated their studies of public choice into their choice of policy. Public choice is a relatively recent intellectual endeavour and most of us are subject to a great deal of advice and information about policy which comes from non–public choice sources. Further, most of us are (at least to some extent) allied with political forces, the main strength of which comes from influences aside from public choice economists.

Of course, we are far from unanimous agreement about every policy, even in those activities where public choice would be relevant. Some students of public choice try to change public choice to fit their prior conceptions, rather than *vice versa.* An example which impresses me is the continued defence of simple majority voting as a standard method of making decisions.

But so much for cases where public choice has not been integrated into the policy views of its students. Where are the areas where it has been integrated? One is simply a lack of enthusiasm for government as a solution to problems. The view that government is the automatic perfect solution to innumerable

---

Fasc. 4, 1975, pp. 745–62; see also comments by McChesney, and Ordover and Weitzman and my reply in *Kyklos*, Fasc. 30, 1977, pp. 517–19. Also "Public Decisions as Public Goods," *Journal of Political Economy*, July/August 1971, pp. 913–18.

problems no longer exists. Not very long ago, the simple proof that the economy did not function perfectly was regarded as an adequate reason for governmental action. Today, we start from the knowledge that the government also does not function perfectly and make a selection between two imperfect operational devices in terms of their relative perfection and certain other characteristics, such as the distributional effect of government programmes.

Market Imperfection and Government Imperfections

This change, although it originated in the public choice field, has now spread through economics as a whole. A deep-seated feeling that government is imperfect carries with it two consequences. The *first* is that imperfections in the market process do not necessarily call for government intervention; the *second* is a desire to see if we cannot do something about government processes which might conceivably improve their efficiency (discussed in Chapter 7).

Public choice students are more likely than students of the older approaches to political matters to be in favour of shifting reliance from the government sector to the market sector. However, we must not make a mistake which is the converse of the one criticised above: that the government performs certain functions poorly does not, in and of itself, prove that the market would do better. That government and market alternatives should be compared on the same basis is a strength of public choice. As it happens, I believe there are clear cases for privatisation; but my arguments for it would have to involve a comparison of the likely inefficiency of private services with the existing inefficiency of the public services. Arguments of this sort, in which a theory is compared with a functioning entity, are always difficult.

There are many areas where the government has been called in to supplement the activity of the private market by regulation—for example, the Interstate Commerce Commission and the Federal Trade Commission in the United States. However, it has only quite recently been appreciated that such regulatory agencies might make the market work less well. It is certainly true that the market for transportation in the days when the railroad was the basic method of surface transportation worked badly in many respects. If public choice had been in existence in those days, however, I imagine that there would have been at least a few academics testifying before Congress that government cartelisation of the industry was likely to be even more imperfect.

The principal proponents of deregulation in recent years have not in general been public choice economists, but a number of them have been subject to a strong public choice influence. It is certainly true that students of public choice are apt to be in the forefront of those who want to critically examine existing regulatory agencies or proposals for further regulation.

The Design of Government

Enough has been said about the areas where public choice leads to what might be called "a lack of enthusiasm" for the governmental solution. Let us now turn to the design of government itself and how the student of public choice might view it. Traditional political science was to a very large extent devoted to the study of democracy and discussed various forms of government, to a large extent in terms of how "democratic" they were. Since there was no clear agreement on what "democratic" meant, these discussions tended not to get very far. In any event, it is interesting that the idea that whatever democracy was, it was the be-all and end-all of government seems not to have been questioned until very recently. Now, partly because of the existence of the public choice paradigm, it is possible to discuss market alternatives to government in a serious and scientific way.

Another area where public choice has been important is in decisions on the location and optimal size of government units. By location, in this case, I am thinking not of geographic location but location on the hierarchy of scale. Most public choice students are in favour of much more decentralisation of government than was characteristic of the intellectuals interested in politics even 20 years ago. The development of techniques which make it possible, at least in theory, to determine what is an optimal government unit has been an important reason for this development.

The realisation that we can adjust sizes of government to fit our needs has led to another development, the very local government. I live in a collective called the Sunshine Mountain Ridge Association in the state of Arizona, where the 400 other householders (voters in this area) engage in all sorts of collective activity which traditionally would have been left to private citizens. We jointly plant trees and shrubs, regulate other gardening efforts, and the paint of the exterior of our houses. This, as readers will realise, is an illustration of a type of intervention in private life which must be expected when activities are collectivised and planned. Nevertheless, although there is clearly a cost here, there is an advantage, too. I have some control over the physical appearance of my neighbours' houses as they have over mine, and we are able to produce a better general effect than if we had not collectivised these activities in order to internalise externalities.

The Behaviour of Government Officials

A final area where knowledge of public choice has an effect on people's views about policy concerns the behaviour of government officials. The student of public choice is unlikely to believe that government officials are overly concerned with the public interest. Since they operate in an area where information is very poor (and the proof that the voters' information on political issues would be poor was one of the first achievements of the public choice theory), deception is much more likely to be a paying tactic than it is in the market-place. Therefore, one would anticipate more dishonesty in government. Indeed, granted that government officials are the only people who can check on the dishonesty of government officials, the problem of curing dishonesty in government involves an infinite regress. Private businessmen, who deal with better informed consumers than do politicians, are also subject to surveillance by public officials who, dishonest though some may be, very commonly have no personal motive to protect a particular private businessman. The amount of dishonesty which has turned up in private business in spite of these inspections gives a rough idea of the almost complete uniformity of dishonesty in politics.

Having little confidence in politicians and depending upon the electoral process to discipline them, insofar as they are disciplined, is the appropriate attitude and it leads to some feelings of cynicism about election campaigns. Moreover, there are problems of defining honesty or dishonesty. The politician who sells his decision in Congress for votes is not obviously in better moral shape than the politician who sells it for cash. Nevertheless, the first act is not strictly speaking illegal.

If this gives the public choice student a rather cool attitude towards political enthusiasms associated with particular candidates, his attitude towards the professional bureaucracy is equally cool but technically more complex. The view that the individual bureaucrat is not attempting to maximise the "public interest" very vigorously but is attempting to maximise his own utility just as vigorously as you and I has been held for a very long time by most people in the backs of their minds. But bringing it into formal theory is a public choice accomplishment. So far this revelation has not had much impact on any real-world government, but policy implications are regularly drawn from it by public choice students. One particular conclusion is the feeling that it is undesirable to have monopolistic government bureaus. Since almost all previous discussion of government efficiency had been dominated by a desire to eliminate "duplication," the change is very radical indeed.

Contracting Out

The desire that there be a number of government bureaus whose performance can be compared by the legislative body is a new theme in policy which has emerged from public choice. Subordinate to this theme are two more radical variants. The first is the suggestion that many government activities can be contracted out instead of run by government agencies. This would be particularly easy if we did not have a monopoly structure and the government agency were broken up into a number of small units and contracted out unit by unit. Thus, we would not contract out the Navy, but we might contract out individual aircraft carriers. By this line of reasoning, it would not be of immense importance whether the holder of the contract for the USS *Enterprise* was the West Point Alumni Association or the US Postal Service. As long as they had to bid competitively, they would be under pressure. Of course, it would be important that the holder of the contract on the USS *Enterprise* did not have contracts on all the other naval vessels.

This proposal is not so radical in application as it is in theory, since governments already contract out various services. In the United States, highways are normally built by contracting out and then maintained by collective bureaucratic organisations. There seems no reason for the distinction. Similarly, for many years the Air Force purchased all its ordnance, whereas the Army and the Navy manufactured their own. Again, there seems no reason for the distinction. The most complicated and technically difficult parts of military activity seem to be contracted out, whilst routine activities are retained for direct government control.[13]

13. The famous U-2 was piloted by an employee of Lockheed Aircraft, not by an Air Force officer. For a long period our early-warning network in the far north was a subsidiary of the American Telephone and Telegraph Company, with only a very few military officers compelled to live in these frigid and unpleasant surroundings for supervisory purposes.

Most public choice students would be more radical in their proposals for contracting out and, in particular, would favour competition, whether from separate government agencies or separate private companies. However, though a competitive market works better than a non-competitive market, if the people purchasing the goods are government bureaucrats, it may not work particularly well. The US military external procurement industry is, I believe, massively more efficient than what remains of the direct military production of its own material. Unfortunately, this is not saying a great deal. Large-scale inefficiencies remain, probably because the purchasing agencies are bureaucracies sheltered against duplication and with an incentive structure such that for any given purchasing agent, the more money he spends the better off he is.

Summary

To sum up, the difference between a public choice student and a non-student of this relatively new discipline in policy matters is very largely a difference in attitude which arises from his knowledge of public choice. Much traditional reasoning has turned on totally unrealistic ideas about the efficiency of government. The student of public choice will not think that government is systematically engaged in maximising the public interest, but assumes that its officials are attempting to maximise their own private interests. In this, of course, they are like managers of, for example, United States Steel. The public choice student will feel that both in the private market and in the government sector there are institutions which tend to lead individuals maximising their own interests to, at least to some extent, provide goods for other people as a byproduct. In neither case is the institutional structure so designed that perfection is obtained. Unfortunately, much previous analysis has implicitly assumed that perfection was obtained in the government sector. The public choice student knows that it is not, and that insight affects his policy views. He is also aware of a number of possible improvements in the structure of government. Thus, his ideas of policy are apt to be different both in the fact that he is less enthusiastic about government and that among the policy considerations he is willing to consider (and may be devoted to) are structural changes in government.

PART 2

WHAT SHOULD GOVERNMENT DO?

MOSQUITO ABATEMENT

In Illinois where I was born, and indeed in most of the two American continents, the common mosquito is a major pest.[1] The American Indians adapted to this pest by developing immunity, and the early settlers, by swearing. In the nineteenth century and the early twentieth century, however, a method of protecting oneself from the mosquito when indoors was developed: the window and door screen. With the discovery that the mosquito was not only a pest but a carrier of a number of fairly nasty diseases, more radical methods of control were adopted in some areas. The construction of the Panama Canal vitally depended upon an extensive program for limiting the number of malaria-carrying mosquitoes and keeping the workers on the canal within screened areas so that they were unlikely to be bitten by even the few mosquitoes that remained. In the more temperate zones of the United States, malaria and yellow fever were a less serious menace, but the mosquito was still a nuisance. As a result, in a number of communities, notably Chicago, programs were instituted in the 1920's and 1930's to reduce the number of mosquitoes by attacks on their breeding areas. These programs in general were modeled on those that had been developed in Panama, but were not as extensive. The reduction in the number of mosquitoes from these programs was relatively small but meaningful.

With the development of DDT during World War II, a much cheaper way of reducing the mosquito population became available, and many communities hired aircraft in the years after World War II to spray areas with DDT. Recently this spraying has become much less common, partially as a result of a realization that DDT has other effects on the natural environment than the reduction of the mosquitoes and that some of these other effects may be quite undesirable, and partially as a result of the adoption of home air-conditioning. A person living in an air-conditioned house is unlikely to spend anywhere near as much time exposed to mosquitoes in the summer as a person living in a non-air-conditioned house. As a consequence, the amount of aerial spraying of DDT has been reduced considerably in recent years, and a num-

Reprinted, with permission, from *Private Wants, Public Means: An Economic Analysis of the Desirable Scope of Government* (New York and London: Basic Books, 1970), 3–28.

1. Actually the common mosquito is a popular name, not a biological name. Quite a number of species of the same general type of insect are involved.

ber of other techniques that are both less effective in dealing with mosquitoes and more expensive have been adopted, but on a smaller scale.

The reader may wonder why a book on government should begin with a technological discussion of a minor local problem. The reason is simple. Almost all of the problems involved in decisions as to what activities should be undertaken by the government are found in this simple example. Furthermore, there is nothing in the way of a traditional solution to this problem. One of the great problems in talking about the new discoveries in the field of social cost, externalities, and the economics of the government sector is that most people have been thoroughly indoctrinated with the existing tradition. Those who have not learned the orthodox tradition normally learn some particularly strong attack on it, which is in many ways just another tradition. Thus a discussion of government activities runs into a barrier of strongly held ideas. If we discuss mosquito abatement, however, we normally find a complete absence of these traditions or antitraditions and hence we can deal with the problem with less emotional difficulty. Since recent developments in economics make it possible to rethink almost all of our basic ideas in this field and place them on a sounder basis, our avoidance of "conditioned reactions" is vital.[2] The first steps in this rethinking will be outlined in this book. I must confess, however, that much of the material in the book will not be original. Still, what I have to say will seem new, and perhaps strange, to that 99.99 per cent of the population who have not been keeping up with recent developments in the rather arcane fields of welfare economics and public finance. Thus, the use of an example that is free from emotional and traditional overtones seems desirable.

To return, then, to the mosquitoes, let us assume that we are in 1952 (and, as we will discover reading through this book, the specific technology in any given time is a highly important matter in deciding whether a given activity should be handled by the government, by private enterprise, by the central government, by the local government, or perhaps should be simply left completely untouched) and that we are living in a small town in Iowa where the mosquito problem is serious. Presumably we already have screens on our houses. However, since we go outdoors fairly frequently in the summer, mosquitoes are a serious problem to us. There are several ways for us to deal with the problem of mosquitoes. First, of course, we could reduce the

2. It does not follow from the fact that we rethink them that the conclusions we eventually reach will be radically different from the tradition. The rethinking in fact will indicate that a good portion of the tradition is correct.

amount of time we spend outdoors, and everyone who lives in an area where mosquitoes are prevalent does indeed do this. Second, there were as of 1952 certain creams and greases that could be placed on exposed skin areas to repel mosquitoes. Unfortunately, these preparations also tended to keep people away because they gave off a peculiar odor. Nevertheless, for anyone who had to go into the woods or along a stream, the use of these creams was a sensible precaution. Third, we could undertake a spraying campaign in our own backyard. We could buy a suitable insect spray in a local supermarket and spray our backyard and perhaps spray a little into our neighbor's yard. This spray would generally reduce the number of mosquitoes in the area, partly by killing the ones that were there at the time of the spraying and partly because a residuum of the spray was left on the vegetation, and mosquitoes landing on the residuum might be killed. Nevertheless, the last method would be an expensive and inefficient way of reducing the number of mosquitoes in an immediate vicinity. It was used, however, particularly by people who were planning garden parties.

Another method of mosquito abatement was available, however. For a small sum of approximately fifty dollars, an airplane could be chartered to spray an entire town with DDT, which would produce considerable mosquito abatement. More frequent spraying would lead to more deaths of mosquitoes. The situation is illustrated in Figure 1. For an individual, the demand for mosquito abatement is shown by the slanting line. If he chooses the hand spray method, then the line marked one dollar will indicate the cost of killing one unit of mosquitoes in his yard. The individual will choose to purchase A units, and his total cost is represented by the rectangle to the left of A. The individual would not be interested in hiring an airplane because he can obtain any amount of mosquito abatement in his own yard more cheaply by hand spraying than by spraying from the air.

The situation changes radically, however, if the individual joins together with the other citizens of the town to hire the airplane. If there are 1,000 citizens in the town, the cost to each one for mosquito abatement in his backyard falls to five cents a unit and the total amount consumed would rise to C. Under these circumstances, the entire mosquito abatement demand would be met by air spraying rather than hand spraying because, once again, this particular technological method is strictly dominant.[3]

3. In actual practice, the demand may be for spraying at certain times, and an individual who is having a garden party several days after the last spraying may also engage in hand spraying. We need not bother with this complication.

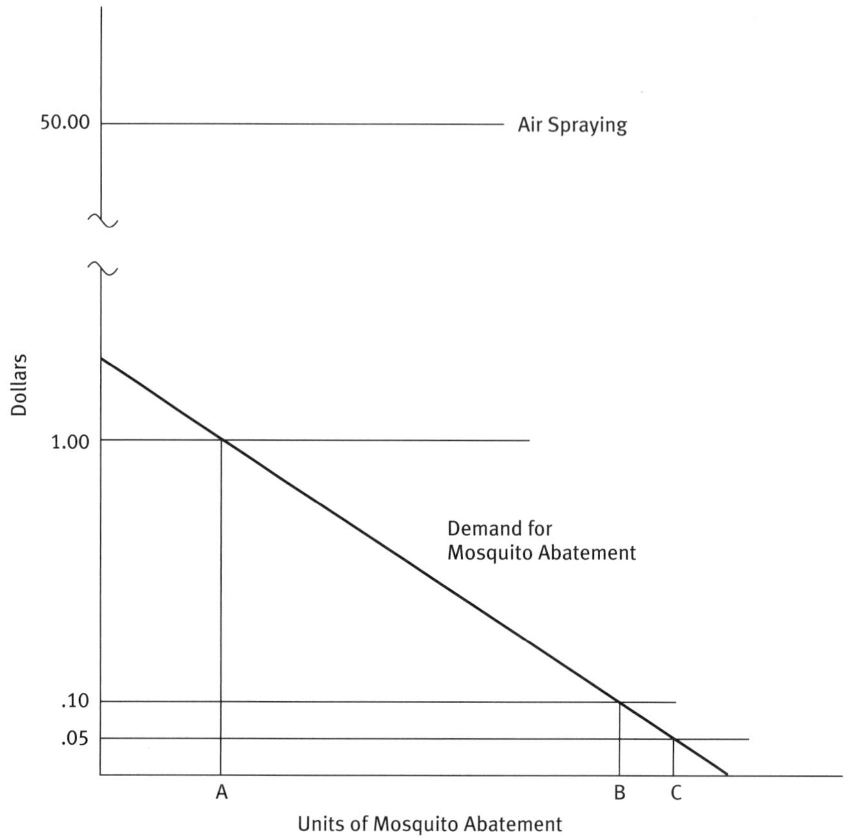

FIGURE 1
Individual choice of mosquito abatement

Clearly, at these prices, if the individual were given a choice he would prefer C mosquito abatement by air spraying to A units produced by hand spraying. Thus one could present a good argument for the collective provision of mosquito abatement. Suppose, however, that instead of a government agency undertaking mosquito abatement, a private effort is made to induce various individuals to contribute money to charter the airplane. Under these circumstances, the cost of chartering an airplane depends upon the number of people who have contributed. If only 500 people are willing to contribute, then the cost of the mosquito abatement by air (per unit) is ten cents and they would then choose to purchase the amount B.

Assuming that this voluntary method of mosquito abatement is adopted, the individual would be sensible not to make the payment. If he is not a member of the group making the payment, he receives the mosquito abatement free. If, on the other hand, he decides to make his payment, and we assume that the amount of money he puts in is then invested in purchasing additional aircraft time for the whole city, he then faces a purchase price for mosquito abatement in his yard of fifty dollars a unit. This price is clearly far above the amount that he wishes to pay. The general discussion of the bargaining problems that would arise if we attempted to handle problems of this sort through voluntary provision will be deferred until a later chapter. It is unlikely, however, that individuals would be willing to make a voluntary contribution. Normally only a government could provide the airplane spraying.[4]

Of course, the possibility always exists that some individual may believe that he is influential enough so that everyone else will copy his action. If this individual feels this way he would logically become a member of the group that plans to charter the airplane. Clearly, however, not everybody can entertain such delusions of grandeur. Hence, if voluntary renting of the airplane were suggested, the bulk of the community would be unwilling to make payments. We thus have what appears to be a fairly unambiguous argument for a governmental agency compelling the citizens of this small town to pay for the chartering of an airplane. The citizens themselves would be better off under this arrangement and would presumably favor it.

It has been, however, an implicit assumption in the discussion so far that each citizen has exactly the same demand for mosquito abatement. Presumably, this is not true and indicates that a decision must be made as to how much mosquito abatement should be purchased. In order to consider this decision, let us now examine Figure 2 in which the demand curves for mosquito abatement of three citizens (Mr. A, Mr. B, and Mr. C) are shown. Note that if there is no decision to charter an airplane, the three individuals will simply purchase different numbers of units of mosquito abatement through the use of the hand spray: Mr. A purchasing a′ units, Mr. B purchasing b′ units, and Mr. C purchasing c′ units.

If, however, the citizens decide to rent an airplane and engage in collective provision of mosquito abatement, then a decision must be made as to how much mosquito abatement should be purchased. The three individuals have

4. Sometimes informal pressures can function very much like a government. As a general rule, however, human experience seems to indicate that informal pressure is not sufficient and we normally use governmental coercion in such cases.

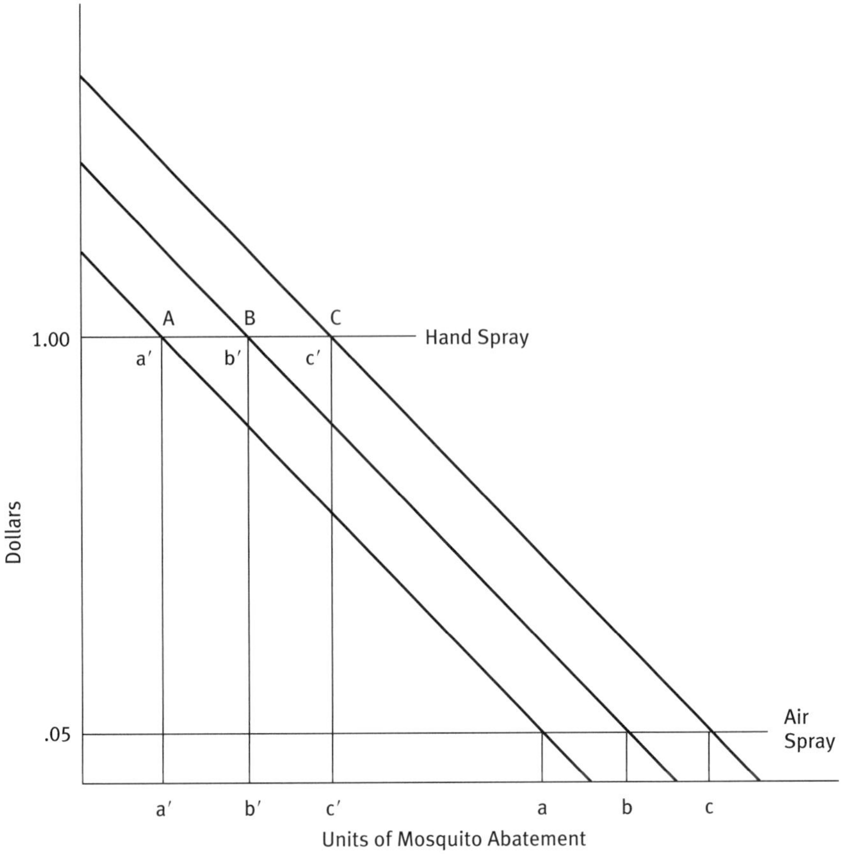

FIGURE 2
Mosquito abatement with majority vote

three different ideas regarding the amount of abatement—represented by a, b, and c on the diagram. This example is carefully constructed so that their preferences on this particular point would be what is known as "single peaked."[5] If we consider ourselves as dealing with only a three-man community that makes decisions by a majority vote (and this particular type of situation presents arguments for doing this), then we would predict that the three men would purchase the amount b of mosquito abatement. Thus, Mr. A and Mr. C have failed to obtain their optimum amount of mosquito abatement.

5. See Duncan Black, *The Theory of Committees and Elections* (Cambridge: Cambridge University Press, 1958).

It does not follow, of course, from the fact that the individuals could make a perfect adjustment of how much mosquito abatement they wish to purchase if they use hand spray. In most cases they must anticipate that they will not get their first choice of quantity if the government provides the spraying, and that hand spraying is superior. It merely follows that in collective action a cost is involved that should be considered. Assuming again that we have our society of 1,000 people, I would compare my likely purchase of spray with what I thought was the likely outcome of the voting process in terms of the amount that would be obtained by collective provision. I would anticipate that the amount provided collectively would not turn out to be exactly the amount that I wanted. I presume that in areas where mosquitoes are prevalent most people would choose the collective provision. Note, however, that this means that they are choosing a less than optimal arrangement of the resource by their own preference ordering. In a sense, an externality is imposed upon them by the choice of the collective decision process; they will no longer be able to make an ideal adjustment.

We have, however, imposed a further unrealistic assumption by assuming that the only way of obtaining collective mosquito abatement is through airplane spraying. This method, in fact, is not even common today and never was the only one used, although at one time it was widely thought to be the cheapest. If we include the possibility of mosquito abatement by other methods, then the simple single-peaked structure that we put into this system disappears and the end product is likely to be more complicated. It is also likely that the individual will find the outcome further from his own optima and therefore the use of collective decision techniques involves a greater cost to the individual. It still, of course, does not follow that collective decision-making is inferior to private decision-making, and, once again, I presume that most people who live in areas where mosquitoes are prevalent would prefer collective mosquito abatement. I am not arguing against collective decision-making, but am simply pointing out that like market decision-making, it also has a cost. In each case we must weigh the cost against the benefit, and in the particular case we are now discussing, I think we would all agree that the benefit is greater than the cost.

It should be noted, however, that for some people in the community, the cost of this type of collective mosquito abatement was great. Let us suppose that a genuine American Indian with his inherited immunity to mosquito bites lives in the community. Presumably he would not voluntarily purchase mosquito abatement and would regard the necessity of paying taxes to purchase mosquito abatement under collective decision-making as an unmitigated wrong. In his case the choice of the collective decision-making process rather than private decision-making process is clearly undesirable. As a general rule, people whose personal preferences are markedly unconventional or markedly different from those of the community are likely to be injured by collective decision-making procedures. Fortunately, for most people concerning most issues, our preferences are not so radically different from the norm as to cause collective decision-making to be necessarily inferior.

As another example, we may assume that at the time we conducted our mental experiment, one member of the community had read Rachel Carson's *The Silent Spring*. He would regard the aerial spraying of the town as positively dangerous, a creator of illth. Thus he would be opposed to it and would obtain considerable dissatisfaction from the spraying even if he did not have to pay for it himself. He may, however, be strongly in favor of mosquito abatement by other methods. Once again, we are faced with someone who would object strenuously to the use of collective methods. The costs of collective as against private provision characteristically depend upon two things: the preference of the people making the decisions and the available technology. Frequently, for people with unusual preferences, costs of public provision of facilities are extremely great. If everybody has similar preferences, technology may make collective provision inefficient. The working out of the details of these relationships will fill many chapters in the latter part of this book.

The reader may well be interested in whether simple majority voting is the most efficient way of achieving a decision as to the amount of air spraying to be used in a particular case. This is an interesting and important question, but will not be discussed greatly in this book. The reason is not that I object to talking about it but that I have already talked about it a great deal in other books and probably will continue to talk about it in still further books.[6] For the time being we can simply say that if we assume that individuals have relatively similar preference intensities or that preference intensities are randomly distributed, then the single-peak preference curve and simple majority voting lead to what can reasonably be described as a "good" outcome. If we do not make these assumptions, more complicated arrangements are desirable. This book will not discuss these more complicated arrangements.

6. Gordon Tullock, *The Calculus of Consent*, with James M. Buchanan (Ann Arbor: University of Michigan Press, 1962), and *Toward a Mathematics of Politics* (Ann Arbor: University of Michigan Press, 1966).

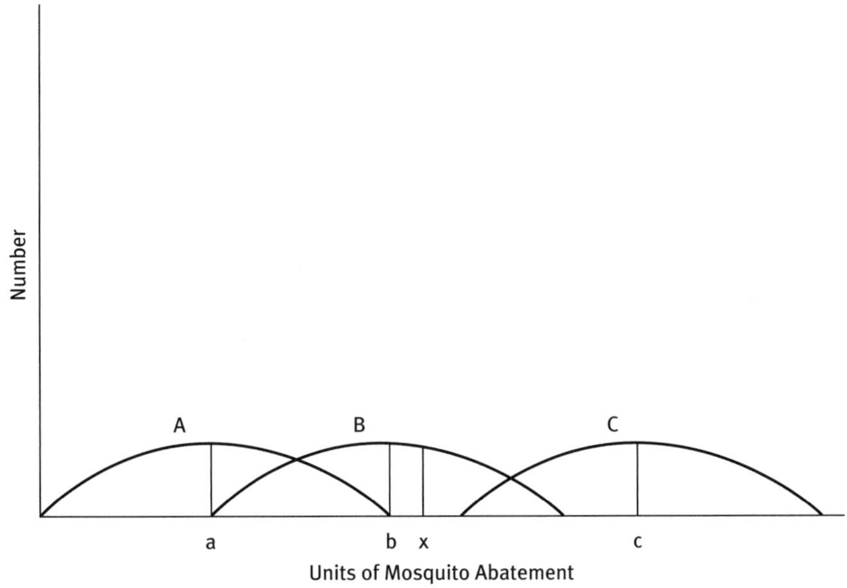

FIGURE 3
Distribution of preferences on mosquito abatement

We can, however, say *something* about desirable political arrangements for our mosquito abatement program. As a beginning, we may inquire as to what is the ideal size of the government unit to deal with this program. First, we should note the limits that are placed upon this method by the technology of aircraft spraying. In order to be efficient in abating mosquitoes over our small town, the aircraft should spray the entire town and certain nearby mosquito breeding areas. An effort to spray half of the town would give much less than half the protection; it would be a bad bargain. Therefore, the minimum size of a government unit that decides to hire the airplane should be our small town in the Middle West.

We may, however, inquire whether this size is also the optimum. For this purpose, let us turn to Figure 3. On the horizontal axis of Figure 3, we have once again drawn in the units of mosquito abatement. Then on the vertical axis we have shown the number of people who have as their optimum any particular amount of mosquito abatement. Our method is a type of shorthand compression of one of Duncan Black's sets of single-peak preference curves. We have drawn in the optima collections for three different communities (A, B, and C). It will be noted that each of these has a somewhat different distribution of optima, which could result from different technological conditions—for example, community C may be located close to a swamp—or to simple differences in taste.

In any event, we would anticipate that different communities would not have identical preferences. For any individual community it can be demonstrated that the midpoint in the preference distribution is the "policy" that comes closest to optimizing the preferences of the entire community under our assumptions. Thus, the individual communities could select the amounts of spraying shown by a, b, and c. If the communities join together and all vote on a standard amount of spraying, however, they would end up at point x. For all three communities, this would be less satisfactory than the optima for their individual community, although it would be the best policy to be followed assuming we must choose a uniform policy for the three communities.[7] Thus, a substantial loss is involved in combining the three communities into one for purposes of making decisions on mosquito abatement. The optimal size of the collective unit for this decision would be the individual community.

In part, this conclusion is a result of the available technology. It is possible that a large metropolis (such as Chicago) would find that the technologically optimal area would be small enough so that subsections of the metropolis could efficiently vote themselves on the amount of spraying. This problem necessarily involves detailed technological investigations.

Rather than having all of the communities joining together to vote on a single level of spraying for all of them, they could form a large group of communities that would then select different amounts of spraying for each individual community. If this large unit determined the amount of spraying for each individual unit by conducting a local plebiscite, there would be no objection to this procedure but also no obvious reason for the existence of the large unit. If, on the other hand, the entire unit voted on a complex plan involving different levels of spraying in different communities, one would anticipate that the outcome may be highly nonoptimal. First, there is no obvious reason why the citizens of community C should be well informed about the needs of community A. Insofar as their votes have any effect on the

7. For a general proof see Yoram Barzel, "Two Propositions on the Optimal Level of Producing Collective Goods," *Public Choice*, 6 (Spring 1969): 31–37.

amount of spraying that will be undertaken in community A, at best, this is the addition of random noise to the decision process and generally tends to lower its efficiency.

More important, however, there is no strong reason to believe that the communities will have a totally altruistic approach to these problems. Surely a proposal under which communities A and B tax community C for the purpose of spraying themselves would be a continuing danger. If we look at real-world politics, we can observe that this type of situation is quite common. It does not take the form of straightforward exploitation of one community in all cases, although such examples can be found. More normally, it takes the form of logrolling in which all communities receive some spraying, and, in fact, the general level of spraying granted the assumptions we have made, would be way above the optima that the individual communities would select for themselves.[8] This again would be a substantial inefficiency. Thus, it would appear that the lowest cost method is to let the communities determine how much spraying they want for themselves. In other words, the optimal collective unit is the small city.

We can, however, turn to another matter here. It may seem tedious for each small community to vote yearly on mosquito abatement. It is not clear why we feel this way. We are never particularly concerned about the possibility that individuals will spend too much time making private decisions. If private mosquito abatement were used in these communities, each individual would have decided for himself whether he needed a new can of spray and whether to go out in the yard and spray. It is not exactly obvious why we should be disturbed by the prospect that he would have somewhat the same amount of decision-making time involved in deciding whether or not the city should have an airplane for the same purpose.

It may be that the reason we attempt to economize on decision-making efforts for collective decisions and not on private decisions is simply that our present mechanisms for making collective decisions are complex and inconvenient. Going to the polls to cast a vote on an issue is in many ways an expensive process. If this is the only reason we worry, then technology is rapidly coming to our rescue. In a few years it will be quite possible for everyone to attach a device to his telephone that permits him to express his opinions

8. See Gordon Tullock, "Problems of Majority Voting," *Journal of Political Economy*, 67, no. 6 (June 1956): 571–79.

on any issue. If the only reason we attempt to economize on the time spent in voting is that present-day methods of voting are quite inconvenient, this matter will shortly be a matter of past history.[9]

Still, under present circumstances, we do attempt to economize on the number of votes in individual communities. Our usual method is to have the votes cast on a collection of issues at a single time rather than on a single issue. For example, we may vote on an individual or a board to make decisions for the small community. In this case, the voting decisions are made on a complex of different matters. First, the candidates presumably will have made statements as to what they propose to do and we can choose the one that seems most desirable to us; second, we will be interested in the personality of the individuals concerned. In the real world this personal interest is apt to be rather wide. Whether Mrs. Jones or Mrs. Smith is the more attractive woman may have considerable influence on whether Mr. Jones or Mr. Smith is elected. In any event, if we cast our votes in such a way that each vote affects a number of issues, some of which concern the personalities of the candidates, we can anticipate that we will have considerably poorer adjustment in the decision on mosquito spraying than if we had a specific vote on that particular issue.

This is so for several reasons; first, there is the noise effect. I can communicate less information to the "government" by a single vote covering eight or nine issues than by eight or nine separate votes. I should anticipate, therefore, that the government will be less closely attuned to my desires. To some extent this is offset by the possibility of logrolling if the vote is made on a collection of issues. The individual candidates make up a "platform" appealing to different people, which permits them to take into account the intensity of individual preferences. Thus, I may find myself selecting a candidate whose views on the amount of mosquito spraying are quite radically different from my own because I like his views on other matters. My voting for this candidate will reduce my degree of satisfaction from mosquito spraying, although it may improve my degree of satisfaction with the activities of the town government as a whole.

The second reason one may anticipate poorer adjustment in the amount of mosquito spraying if mosquito spraying is voted on together with a number of other issues is, simply, that it is a harder choice to make. I cannot think

9. See James C. Miller, III, "A Program for Direct and Proxy Voting in the Legislative Process," *Public Choice*, 7 (Fall 1969): 107–13.

of the matter in relatively simple terms, but must consider it in terms of interrelation with a number of different issues. Since the matter is not very important, I may be well advised not to think much about it and to accept a poor decision as opposed to using much energy in an attempt to reach a good decision.

Some *bona fide* political theories argue that we should leave decisions on such matters to a government servant. Theoreticians differ as to whether the servant is to be elected, selected by examination, or appointed by a divine king. What we should note here is that if we are simply leaving the decision to someone who is selected on other characteristics, then we are accepting a fairly large random variable in the decision on mosquito abatement. Under these circumstances we would anticipate that the amount of mosquito spraying would be more deviant from that of the individual than if the decision were made by simple majority voting.

It does not follow from these costs incurred by deviating from a simple majority vote on the amount of mosquito spraying that we should not so deviate. The reduction in cost that can come from reducing the number of votes that individuals must undertake is a real one, and it should be balanced against the additional cost imposed by other methods of making decisions. Here we have what amounts to an empirical problem, and a problem that has not yet been subject to any substantial empirical research. It does, however, appear to be a researchable problem, and we can hope that such research will give us a better idea of how many issues we should vote on directly and how many we should deal with in clusters.

So far, we have been discussing the problem of mosquito abatement as it existed about ten years ago. Since that time considerable technological change has taken place. Let us confine ourselves to considering only those technological changes that have indicated that the simple airplane spraying of DDT is not desirable. It has been realized that a large number of secondary costs result from this operation and that these secondary costs may well be much in excess of the benefits derived. As a result, the technology of mosquito abatement now no longer depends mainly on this extremely cheap method. We need not go into the more complicated and more expensive methods that are now in general use; it is perfectly possible that tomorrow someone will invent another, and better, method. We can simply note that present methods are expensive and inquire what effect this would have on our decision.

The first possible effect of the increase in the expense of mosquito abatement by collective measures may be that the unit cost of a given amount of mosquito abatement would be equal or higher if one uses the collective methods than if one restricts mosquito abatement to the private use of sprays in one's own backyard. In this easy case, the proper decision, of course, would be to completely abandon all collective efforts to reduce mosquitoes and let individuals make their own decisions.[10] The second possibility (also very easy) is that mosquito abatement either by public or by private means may become so expensive that it would no longer be desired. Once again, the proper solution is to have no public program, and we would anticipate that there would be no private abatement either. Both of these are easy problems and in both cases we need go no further with our analysis.

The interesting question, however, is what we would do if the use of various public means for reducing the mosquito population (let us say spraying oil on the breeding ponds) is still a less expensive method of obtaining a certain amount of mosquito abatement than is private spraying, but that the difference is small. This situation is illustrated in Figure 4. We assume that methods of mosquito abatement by collective means exist and these are efficient enough so that if all members of the community were compelled to contribute the cost of purchasing one unit of mosquito abatement, the cost would be ninety-five cents per head; whereas a private purchase of one unit of mosquito abatement would remain at one dollar. If we consider only Mr. B whose demand curve is shown on the diagram, clearly collective provisions would be desirable. He would be better off purchasing x units of mosquito abatement at ninety-five cents instead of purchasing b units at one dollar, which is his market economy alternative. His net benefit is measured by the areas shaded horizontally and slanting to the left in Figure 4.

If, however, we consider a community consisting of three members

10. Conceivably, it may be possible to purchase the mosquito spraying devices for the individual household more economically if the city bought them than if the individual did. Under these circumstances, collective provision of the individual sprays could (if the saving in money was large enough) be justified on exactly the same reasoning as airplane spraying. It would also be at least theoretically possible for the community to purchase the mosquito spray and then distribute it to the households, even if there was no economy involved. This would have the disadvantage that if every household were given the same amount, it would mean that most households were not in appropriate adjustment. Any effort on the part of the government to guess the demands for mosquito abatement of the individual citizens and provide them with a number of bug bombs and presumably a tax bill proportionate to their demand would most assuredly be abortive.

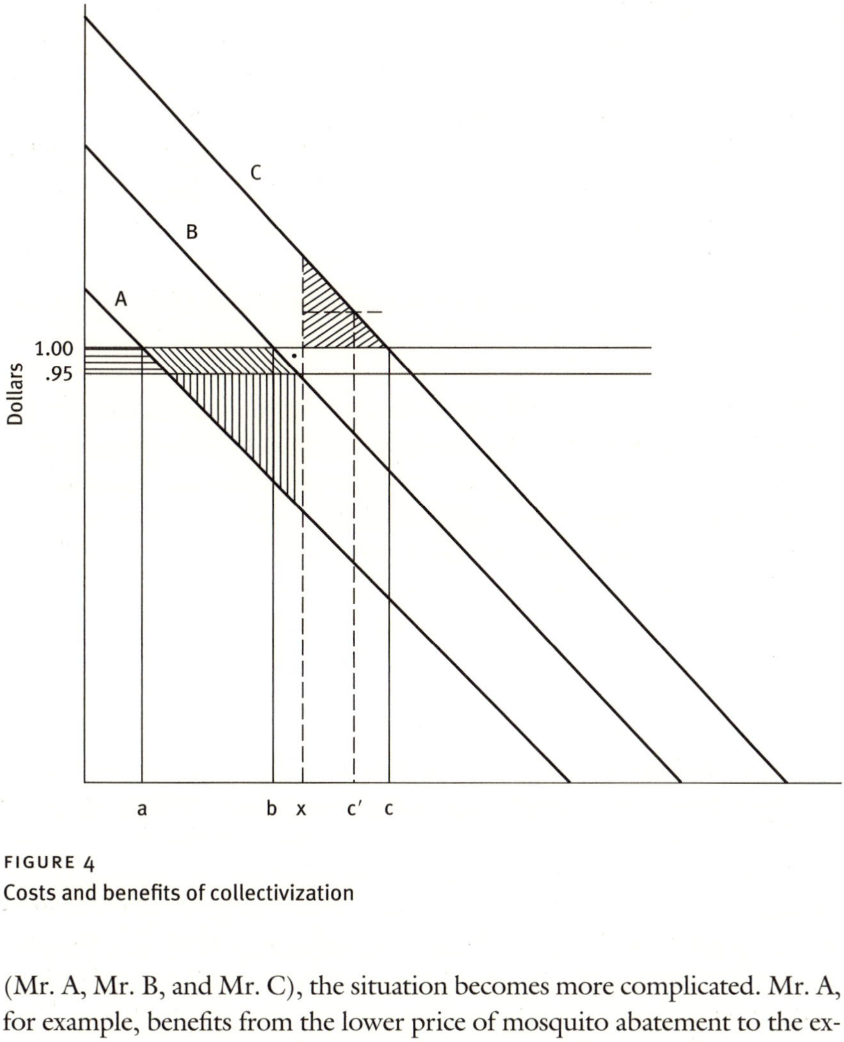

FIGURE 4
Costs and benefits of collectivization

(Mr. A, Mr. B, and Mr. C), the situation becomes more complicated. Mr. A, for example, benefits from the lower price of mosquito abatement to the extent of the horizontally shaded trapezoid to the left. He is injured by having to buy more mosquito abatement than he wants to the extent of the vertically shaded triangle. He is in a worse position with collective provision than he would be with individual provision. Naturally, this simply reflects where we have chosen to draw his demand line, but we will be able to discuss the subject in a more general way after we have considered this example. Mr. C is affected in a somewhat more ambiguous way. His gross gain is the gross gain of Mr. B plus the dotted triangle. However, he suffers a loss to the extent of the triangle shaded by lines slanting to the right by not being able to purchase mosquito abatement privately. This loss will only be suffered if it is not possible for him (for technological or legal reasons) to supplement the public provision at the same cost as he could have previously bought mosquito abatement privately. If the public provision of mosquito abatement actually reduced the cost of additional mosquito abatement (which is conceivable), he may make an additional profit. If the public provision made private supplements rather inefficient (which I imagine is the common case), then Mr. C would face a supply curve somewhat similar to the horizontal dashed line and would purchase c′ − x mosquito abatement privately. The gross cost to him of the new arrangement then would be the trapezoid lying between the horizontal dashed line and the one-dollar line. If this were a smaller area than the rectangle to the left of the new supply quantity, he would gain in net terms.

Let us turn to the question of whether it would be desirable to undertake public provision of the mosquito abatement for this small three-person community. If the provision of public abatement injures both A and C and benefits B, then the welfare economist would inquire whether B is able to compensate A and C for their injury. If (and this is also quite possible) the provision benefits both B and C but injures A, then of course it is more likely that compensation can be paid. Unfortunately, with public goods and with the quantity of public goods set by voting, or any other collective process, compensation becomes almost impossible in the real world.

Under these circumstances we will be unable to find out the amount of the compensation. Mr. A probably has not given much thought to how much would be required to compensate him for x mosquito abatement and the resulting taxes. If asked to give thought to this rather strange problem, he has absolutely no motive to correctly interpret his own feelings. This would be even more obvious if we were dealing not with our small three-man community but a larger unit. In the three-man community, A might feel that too large a claim for damages on his part may prevent the whole project. Thus, there would be some limit to how much he could exaggerate his loss. Similarly, B and C even if they benefit would probably find difficulty in placing a monetary value on their benefit and have substantially no motive to do so accurately.

As a general principle, attempting to get voters to compensate each other for their individual losses is not a feasible political proposition. Thus, we cannot use the traditional welfare method of making a direct payment from the people who gain to the people who were injured. There is, however, another and rather debatable tool in the welfare economist's toolbox. Some (but by no means all) welfare economists would argue that if we could compute that the payment would be possible, then it is not necessary to make the payment. Under this line of reasoning, if there is a computed net social benefit, we do not need to concern ourselves with the way in which it is distributed. This method of applying the Paretian criterion is highly controversial and I do not wish to endorse it here. There is, however, a variant on it which is clearly respectable.

According to this variant, if we anticipate making a large number of decisions in the future, and if we cannot tell who will benefit and who will be injured by any one of these collective decisions, but can anticipate that most members of the society will find themselves benefited sometimes and injured sometimes, then the rule of simply computing whether there is a net benefit or not and using that rule for all of these decisions would probably give to each individual in society a positive discounted future income stream. Applying this routine to our present problem, we may find that there was a net benefit for society as a whole.[11] Whether we would or would not depends on the particular values of various parameters and the preference functions of the individuals.

It could be said under this argument that if we found a "net gain," we could undertake the collective provision of mosquito abatement without worrying about the fact that some people (particularly Mr. A) are injured. Mr. A is injured, Mr. B is benefited, and depending on the particular parameters of the problem, Mr. C may be either benefited or injured. This transfer is clearly not something we would positively favor, particularly since the members of society who are interested in restricting the consumption of any particular public good are apt to be the poorer members. Thus, the income transfers we are now talking about are apt to be transfers from the poor to the better off. Poor Mr. A is made worse off, middle-class Mr. B is benefited, and upper-class Mr. C may gain or lose. Still this is not an absolute argument against collective mosquito abatement. Surely if the computed gain was very large, we would favor collective provision.

One further conclusion may be drawn from our discussion thus far. If collective provision of some good and private provision can be combined (that is, if the private provision can be used to supplement the public provision) there is an argument for reducing public provision. Mr. A can do nothing about the taxes that he must pay for x amount of mosquito abatement. If, on

11. For further discussion of this matter see Buchanan and Tullock, *The Calculus of Consent.*

the other hand, the community provided only b, it would be possible for Mr. C to supplement this amount to some extent by private purchase. Thus, in cases of this sort we should provide somewhat less of the public good than otherwise, because it is easier to add additional units privately than it is to evade paying taxes. In general, the larger the cost savings, the more likely it is that we would choose collective provision; the more similar the different individuals' demand curves, the better the collective alternative.

The basic parameters that have guided the decision between collective and private provision of mosquito abatement have been essentially technological. It is, therefore, sensible to pause briefly and inquire exactly as to the nature of technological superiority of collective provision in this case. At first glance one may think that it was simply an example of an ordinary scale economy, but this is clearly not so. General Motors has surely exhausted all the scale economies that are available in the manufacture of automobiles, yet we find no need for collective provision here. General Motors can sell its cars to people scattered all over the United States without worrying very much about whether the next-door neighbor of any given purchaser of a Chevrolet owns a Ford.

If we look at the detailed problems of mosquito abatement, we would also notice no significant scale economies. The private companies that manufacture the bug bombs for private mosquito abatement are probably characteristically considerably larger than are the companies that provide aerial spraying. Furthermore, the community of 1,000 that we are talking about is not a very large economic unit, and it is normally not large enough to be capable of providing the spraying itself. The community will characteristically turn to a private contract sprayer. This private concern, if it is an ordinary one in this business, will not only spray cities but will also spray or dust individual farms, mainly for pests other than mosquitoes. Thus, some individual citizens (farmers) are able to purchase this good, which for the small city we have been talking about becomes a collective purchase. Furthermore, the small city is not large enough to exhaust the economies of scale in a traditional sense.

The special characteristic of the aerial spraying of mosquito abatement is that it is generally impossible to spray economically on one city lot at a time. For economy, it is necessary to spray a fairly large area partly because the plane must fly from its airport to the place where it releases the spray and partly because the characteristics of the spray are such that it is apt to spread to several surrounding house lots. If only one householder is paying for it, the others will receive a "free ride." The problem, then, is geographical contiguity. As we continue, in the remainder of this book, we will find that geographical contiguity is a basic characteristic of almost all of the problems to which we will turn our attention. The distinction between an economy of scale that can be obtained only if the customers are located next door to each other, and an economy of scale that can be obtained without this type of contiguity, will be basic for our analysis. This is, of course, why these effects are so often called "spillovers," or "neighborhood effects."

PROPERTY, CONTRACT, AND THE STATE

A traditional scholar may be quite surprised by my beginning a discussion of the desirable role of the state with the topic of mosquito abatement. In a sense this surprise was my motive in so starting. The traditional approach does not seem relevant in discussing mosquito abatement and new methods are clearly needed. Furthermore, mosquito abatement is a particularly good example for introducing the newer techniques that have been developed in this field. The more general application of these newer techniques is the subject of this book. Today part of our society is market controlled and part is government controlled. This mixture has developed mostly without any scientific study of the desirability of placing any particular portion of the economy under market or government control. It simply developed in this way because the scientific tools for investigating the problem were discovered only very recently. In fact, this book will be the first attempt to make a *general* application of these newly discovered techniques to the problem of the scope of government.[1]

The new approach to government involves two strands, both discovered relatively recently. The first of these is "social cost, externality, and public goods," dating back to Pigou's *Economics of Welfare*.[2] The second, the application of economic analysis to the functioning of the government itself, is even more recent. Considering these two strands in combination is more recent still. Considering these two different lines of research and their interaction, and using them to determine the desirable scope of governmental and private action seems worthwhile.

It should be noted that in the present state of our knowledge it is impossible to reach final conclusions as to the exact portion of our society that should be governmental and that portion that should be market controlled.

Reprinted, with permission, from *Private Wants, Public Means: An Economic Analysis of the Desirable Scope of Government* (New York and London: Basic Books, 1970), 29–54.

1. Richard A. Musgrave in his classic book, *The Theory of Public Finance* (New York: McGraw-Hill, Inc., 1959), aimed at much the same objective. Unfortunately much of the research developed after he wrote his book. Hence his book suffered from "prematurity."

2. Arthur C. Pigou, *The Economics of Welfare*, 4th ed. (London: The Macmillan Company, 1938).

The field is new, and we need to perform empirical research to develop certain parameters that we do not now know. Until this research is done, no one can say with certainty exactly what should be left to the market and what should be undertaken by the government. Thus, to a considerable extent, this book will develop a theoretical structure to which it is hoped empirical research will eventually add an element of definiteness and precision that will make it possible for us to make decisions about the real world. In practice, I will express my particular views as to what parameters should be in some cases and thus draw actual conclusions. The reader should, however, accept this as simply an expression of personal prejudice on the part of the author, and an effort to make the book less dry than it would be if it were entirely theoretical. These conclusions in general are not of any high degree of scientific value. The analytical techniques used, however, do seem to be sufficiently developed so that we can be fairly confident of them. Our problem in this area is not that our analytical techniques are poor, but that we have not yet accumulated the empirical information necessary to apply them.

It will not have escaped the reader that I have mentioned only two sectors of the economy: the private market and the government controlled portions. Most economies include a number of other economic areas, charity and nonprofit activity, for example, or intrafamily relations. The boundary between these areas and the areas controlled by the market and the government is as important as the problem discussed in this book, but, I have very little to contribute on the subject. Research in these areas is relatively new and undeveloped. These sectors are less easily controlled by governmental policy than is the boundary between the government sector and the private sector. Nevertheless, a complete theory would also require a careful treatment of these areas. Unfortunately, we will have to wait a number of years for the theoretical and practical developments that will make it possible to produce a picture of society in which these additional areas are treated along with the government sector and the market sector.

The newer method of dealing with the market-government problem involves one philosophical change in our approach to government. In the Middle Ages, it was widely believed that both the economic side of life and the political side aimed at higher, transcendental goals. Since the time of Adam Smith, economists have, on the whole, assumed that the purpose of the economic sector was simply to carry out the desires of various individuals. These individuals might, of course, have desires that are not of a "selfish" nature; they might be interested in charity, glorifying Buddha, or a holy war. Nevertheless, the analytical technique used individual preferences and inquired as to how these preferences could be "maximized."

Most theorists of the state, however, retained the older view. The state was seen as a method of reaching some "higher goal," such as the "public interest," rather than simply a way of "maximizing" the preference schedules of individuals. Perhaps the reason for this was simply that most of the states in history have been despotisms of one sort or another, and maximizing the preference schedule of the despot did not seem a very desirable goal to the philosopher. For those of us who live in a democracy, this problem does not arise. Recent studies of politics, mainly by economists, have transferred Adam Smith's basic idea to the political sphere.[3] There are several reasons for the change, one of which, of course, is simply that the economists are accustomed to using this set of tools. More respectable, however, is the fact that it is very difficult to see why we should be interested in a higher goal unless we have some way of determining what the appropriate "higher goal" is. If the higher goal is somehow given to us, let us say in a book that we believe to be sacred, and does not require a detailed interpretation, then we could aim at maximizing that goal. In the real world, however, these higher goals invariably turn up as statements made by human beings; other human beings favor other higher goals. Such statements are, in a real sense, simply statements by these individuals of their preferences if we define preferences as widely as the economist characteristically does.

Here, however, I must say one thing in order to be completely candid. It is my opinion that most human beings are (except within their families) to a very large extent interested in fairly narrow selfish goals. Note that I do not say solely so interested. Clearly, most people have some charitable impulses and some interest in things other than mere personal aggrandizement. The point I am making is simply that the resources they are willing to invest in these goals are customarily very much less than the amount they are willing to invest to reach straightforward selfish goals. The problem is an extremely difficult one, but I have attempted a little empirical research in the strength of individuals' charitable impulses. If we measure the strength of people's

3. It should be noted that Adam Smith himself did not create the distinction. The development of different philosophical approaches to economics and political science is a later development. See Nathan Rosenberg, "Some Institutional Aspects of the Wealth of Nations," *Journal of Political Economy*, 68 (December 1960): 57–70.

charitable impulses or devotion to higher goals by what they say, the result would indicate a relatively selfless population. If, on the other hand, we inquire how much people are actually willing to sacrifice for these goals, all the admittedly rather poor measures that I have been able to develop thus far indicate that the amount is small.[4] Furthermore, the individual is not more charitably inclined in the political sphere than he is in the private sphere. Private individuals do make gifts to charity, but these gifts usually are only a small part of their income. The same individual acting as a voter will customarily vote for "welfare programs" that benefit people for whom he feels charitable impulses. Again, however, the amount of the national budget that he is willing to allocate in this way is relatively small.

This analysis is somewhat obscured by modern budgetary accounting in which a very large share of the government's income will customarily be allocated to "welfare." If we examine this expenditure, we normally find that the bulk of it goes to people who are by no means poor. It seems likely that what actually happens is that the welfare expenditure is largely obtained by political pressure applied by its recipients. Mr. A may be interested in voting for a candidate who proposes to improve the well-being of the poor, but he is even more interested in voting for a candidate who proposes to improve his own well-being. The candidate who is able to combine these two and who announces a program that he says will benefit the poor, but also benefits Mr. A (and very likely benefits Mr. A much more than the poor) will get his vote. It is indeed even possible that no charitable impulses at all are expressed in voting. The entire aid that the poor do obtain, and they do no doubt obtain such aid, may be the result of the fact that they themselves can vote and, selfishly, vote for aid to themselves.

There are various bits of evidence that this last view might be the correct one. In most Western societies the poor actually do not receive any great amount of aid from the state. The bulk of the welfare program is expended for people who are well above the bottom 20 per cent in income, and the bottom 20 per cent remain in poor condition. Second, those people who are poor but do not have votes characteristically do very badly. The obvious case of this, of course, is those people who are aided only by foreign aid programs. Here we have a clear case of charity with the recipient not being permitted to vote. Most countries are not willing to invest much of the national income

4. For measures, see Thomas R. Ireland and David B. Johnson, *The Economics of Charity*, ed. G. Tullock (Blacksburg, Va.: Center for Study of Public Choice, 1970).

in this activity, although the poor in foreign countries are characteristically much poorer than the poor who have the vote inside the national boundaries of the Western democracies. Another example, which is of interest perhaps only to Americans, is the pay scale of draftees in the United States Army. The people who are drafted into the Army very commonly cannot vote because they are too young, and they are given a very low rate of pay. Seventy-one thousand military "heads of families" were, in fact, officially classified as living in poverty in 1966.[5] Thus we have a government that is allegedly engaged in a "War on Poverty" and yet that is paying some extremely important employees less than what it itself maintains is the minimum amount that any American should receive. It seems likely that the political reason for this action is that people are really not very charitable and that soldiers, many of whom do not have the right to vote, are unable to exert political pressures to obtain increased income for themselves. If so, this would be an illustration of the basically noncharitable nature of most governmental welfare expenditures.

This, however, has been a digression into what I consider the shape of people's preferences to be. I could be quite wrong, and it would still not invalidate much of the discussion in this book. As a matter of fact, the specific problem of the redistribution of income will be dealt with only in a chapter near the end of the book, and the earlier chapters will deal solely with cases in which government might adopt some policy, such as mosquito abatement, without much concern for its possible distributive effects.

To return, then, to our main theme, it will be assumed that the state (like the market) has no goal "higher" than the carrying out of the desires of the people who are "within" it. Our analysis will be similar to that used by ordinary economists in that we will in general not worry about what the preferences of the individuals are. Some concrete examples will be used to illustrate various theoretical positions, and in these concrete examples I will assume various popular preferences. In general, my assumptions as to people's preferences will not raise many objections, but it must be admitted they are assumptions, and we would need further empirical evidence to be certain they are true or false. The main reason for making these assumptions is that it is somewhat easier to discuss these matters in terms of a specific problem than in purely abstract terms. A secondary objective will be to indicate the general outlines of what, given our present state of knowledge, would seem to be the

5. Personal correspondence from Lucy Cifuentes, OS-ASPE Economist.

type of activity for which government organization is desirable and that type of activity for which government is undesirable. The latter is decidedly a state of the arts objective. We can hope that with time and with further research we will have better results. Nevertheless, it is sensible to use the best information you have.

We find ourselves, then, in the same world the economist has lived in for a very long time. We have a great many people with a great many diverse desires. In order to obtain the economies from division of labor and large-scale production, individuals will not be given exactly what they want in every respect. Stating the matter more precisely, they can, if they wish, consume a candy bar that is made exactly to their specifications provided they are willing to pay an extremely high price for it. As a result of mass production, it is possible to produce cars that are not exactly adjusted to each consumer's taste, but that rather closely approximate a large number of consumers' tastes at much less than the cost of producing a set of individually designed cars. We observe that generally the consumer prefers to pay the lower cost for a car that is not exactly to his taste rather than, let us say, $200,000 for a car designed especially for him. We regard the lower priced car as actually meeting his preferences better than the higher priced car because we include the price among the factors that determine his preference.

The same problem arises in government. The government will not normally provide exactly what each voter wants because it would be too expensive to do so. The voter would prefer a somewhat standardized product at a lower price to one costing more but being fitted exactly to his requirements. It is, however, unfortunately true that we can anticipate a good deal more uniformity in government-supplied goods than in private goods because the individual in voting must of necessity vote for the entire community and cannot make an individual choice. If he votes for a standard provision for the whole community, he will receive a standard commodity. If, instead of a standard provision for the whole community, a complex mixture of various amounts and types of consumption for different members of the community is offered for political decision, then his vote will determine not only his own consumption, but also the consumption of other people. Similarly, his consumption will be almost entirely determined by other people's votes. Under the circumstances, we would anticipate that he would have less accurate adjustment of his consumption to his desires than in the market.

This situation does not indicate that we should not use government provision. It simply is one of the costs in government provision that must be set off against the costs in market provision. Other special costs are also involved in governmental provision. The average person buying on the market is not very well informed about the products and services that he buys. He is, however, characteristically much better informed than he is about the political alternatives for which he votes.[6] Furthermore, there seems to be nothing much that can be done about this difference. It is almost certain that our present methods of choice in the two fields lead to this differential in information.

It should, however, be pointed out that although it is inevitable that the individual in making a political choice will be less well informed than the individual making a market choice, and hence is more likely to be fooled or defrauded, the difference does not have to be as large as it is under present institutional arrangements. The recent investigation of political theory indicates that a great deal of our present political structure is inefficient simply because it is badly designed. It is something that just grew up, that came to us by tradition, and was never really thought out. We can make great improvement in its design and hence increase the desirable scope of governmental as opposed to private action. Speaking analogically, if the market in producing a particular line of services is 50 per cent efficient, and the government is 20 per cent efficient, we would choose the market. If, however, it is possible to raise government efficiency to 60 per cent, we would choose the government. It should not, of course, be overlooked that it may also be possible to improve the efficiency of the market.

Let us now end our discussion of general philosophy and turn to technical problems. First, we must consider an old problem—that of property. Let us begin by considering our remote caveman ancestors who apparently invented the concept of property.[7] An individual caveman, perhaps, would think of putting up a hut in order to obtain shelter from the rain. If, once he put up the hut, anyone else could occupy it, or alternatively anyone could pull it down because they wanted to use the wood for a fire, it is unlikely that the individual would invest much in building the hut. If, on the other hand, the man who builds the hut is given complete control of the hut from that time on, so that he can prevent any others from occupying it and/or tearing it

6. See Gordon Tullock, *Toward a Mathematics of Politics* (Ann Arbor: University of Michigan Press, 1966), chaps. 7, 8.

7. It can be argued that property is much older than the human race. It is certainly true that a great many nonhuman species, particularly birds, are real estate "owners." The issue of biological "property," however, is still to some extent an unsolved one and I would like to leave it aside.

down for firewood, then the incentives for producing such a hut are much greater.

It might be thought that the institution of private property would help the man who built the hut but injure everyone else. This is clearly true if we are only considering an existing hut. The man who built the hut is in a better position if he is "given property rights," which means complete disposition over the future of the hut, but surely his fellow tribesmen would be better off if they were given freedom to use it themselves.[8] If, however, we consider a general rule giving anyone who builds a hut the right to retain exclusive control over that hut, then this institution will substantially benefit everyone.

On the vertical axis of Figure 1, the net cost of the services of a hut to an individual measured in hours of work is shown. On the horizontal axis is shown the benefit he derives from them. The slanting line is the usual demand curve, in this case the demand for the services of the hut. Line A represents the cost of obtaining units of hut services assuming that there is no property institution, and line B shows the cost if there is property in huts. Note that the difference between line A and line B is not a difference in the cost of building the hut, which we assume is the same, but it is a difference, in essence, in the return on the investment. If I put one hour of my time into building a hut under the circumstances in which there is no property in huts, I can assume that as a result I will merely obtain the right to share the hut with other people until such time as someone needing wood for a fire pulls it down. Thus, although the hut is not very expensive to build, the hut services that I derive may be quite expensive. If, on the other hand, there is a property institution, putting one hour into building a hut gives me something that I can exclusively occupy, and gives me insurance that it will last as long as it does not fall down or I do not decide to tear it down. Under the first set of institutions, I choose a amount of hut, and under the second, I choose b amount of hut.

Note that under the nonproperty set of institutions, the individual would have some possibility of obtaining hut services from huts built by other persons. Presumably, the amount would be very low since the only incentive for building a new hut, which you would promptly have to share with everyone else in the tribe, would be that huts were scarce enough so that your right to, let us say, a one-tenth share in a hut for two weeks was worth more than the labor of building the hut.

8. This is basically what is meant by property rights—control.

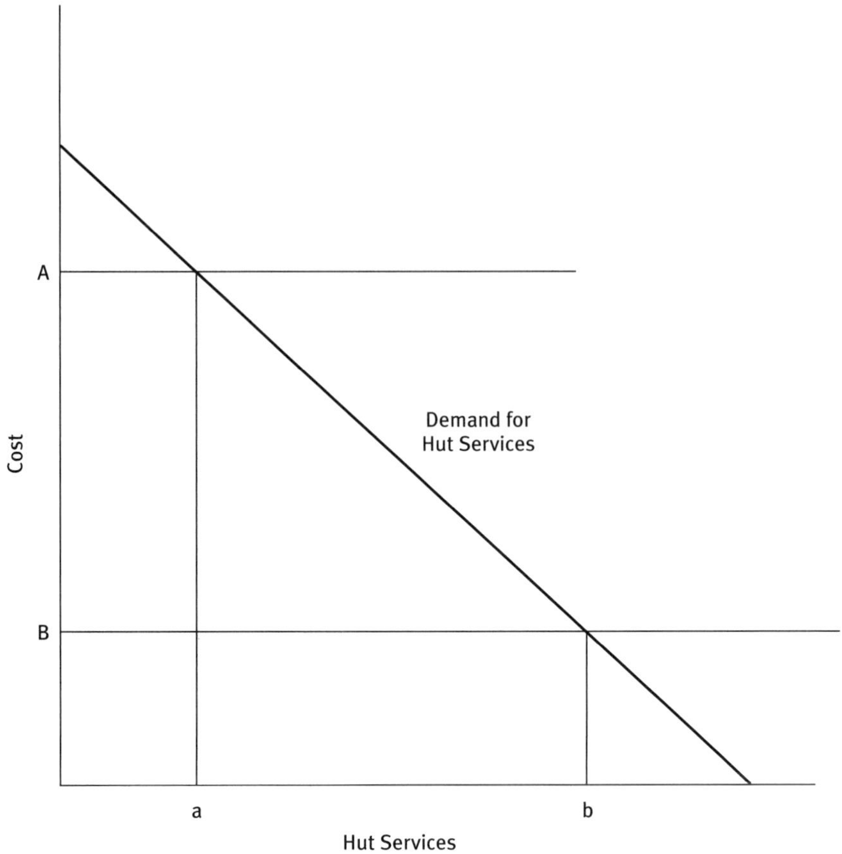

FIGURE 1
Demand with and without property institutions

In choosing between an individual opportunity set in which people are permitted to build huts for which they have permanent "ownership" or a set in which this institution does not exist, an individual would presumably prefer the first alternative simply because the existence of owned huts does not prevent the building of nonowned huts. In other words, he has greater freedom under these circumstances. However, we can go beyond this; we might consider two sets of institutions, one in which if you build a hut you own it whether you want to or not, and another in which you cannot own the hut. With this pair of institutions, it seems likely that the individual would prefer the ownership set, although judgment as to the shape of preference curves is required. Fortunately, it is a judgment with which I think very few people will quarrel. In a society in which anyone may tear down any hut for use as firewood, the individual would gain some benefit from the occasional construction of a hut by one of his neighbors, perhaps during a heavy rainstorm, thus simplifying both his shelter problems (because he could get into the hut) and his firewood problems later. Presumably, however, this would in most cases be a small benefit, much smaller than the benefit he could obtain from building a permanent hut himself.

The above description is the classical justification for property rights. It tells us that "property" is a desirable institution but it does not in and of itself tell us much about the desirable structure of this institution. Suppose, for example, that a primitive tribe has discovered fire. A man who has built a hut might be quite perturbed by someone else building a hut next door to his because the danger of the hut burning down is doubled. An accidental fire might occur in either of the two huts and spread to the other. Under these circumstances, I would be subject to an "externality" from a neighbor building a hut very close to mine. This is a "negative" externality; however, a possible "positive" externality might counterbalance it. The men of the Stone Age no doubt found the protection from marauders (human and animal) that came from having a large number of huts built very close together a benefit that more than outweighed the increased danger of fire. There would be an optimum location.

Externalities are innumerable and omnipresent. My choice of a necktie affects people I meet and therefore exerts an externality. If I choose to advocate or publicly oppose black power, this will affect the behavior of our society to some extent. If I vote for a politician because I think he will do something for me, the actions of that politician with regard to those who voted against him are, in essence, externalities. Returning to more characteristic economic areas, a factory that produces smoke involves an externality; the dumping of waste into water is an externality; loud noises are clearly an example of externality; and driving a car produces a large number of externalities ranging from the danger of life and limb to other people on the highways to the production of air pollution. Positive externalities are equally common. I may arrange my garden in such a way as to improve the view from my neighbor's house. Similarly, if I build a particularly attractive building for some purpose, this generates positive externalities for people passing by. The advance of science and technology creates massive positive externalities as well as the negative ones that are so often mentioned in the press. It should be noted that positive externalities can cause great deviation from the optimum because they are not extended as far as they would be if the beneficiary's interest were taken into account.

In addition to the danger of fire and the need for protection, cavemen may well have believed that some supernatural phenomenon made it important that all of the huts in the village have their doors facing north. If the doors were not all facing the north, then the hunting pole star would be annoyed. From our standpoint, this is fantasy, but if we consider their utility, they would feel injured by the construction of a hut with its door facing the south. What, then, can they do? The first suggestion is that an individual might simply pay his neighbors to choose a location for their huts that maximizes his utility. Note that this payment could either be positive, that is, he could give them a stone axe, or it could be negative—he could tell them that if they did not build their houses in the way he wished, he would smash their heads with the stone axe. In either event, he changes the choice situation that they face in such a way that they are more likely to choose as he wishes. We may examine this question in a very preliminary way with the aid of Figure 2. Assume that Gurt has a hut located somewhere and that Trug is thinking of building another hut due south of Gurt's hut. The only question remaining is how far away Trug's hut will be. Gurt would prefer to have the hut at point G, and his preference slopes away from that point in both directions as

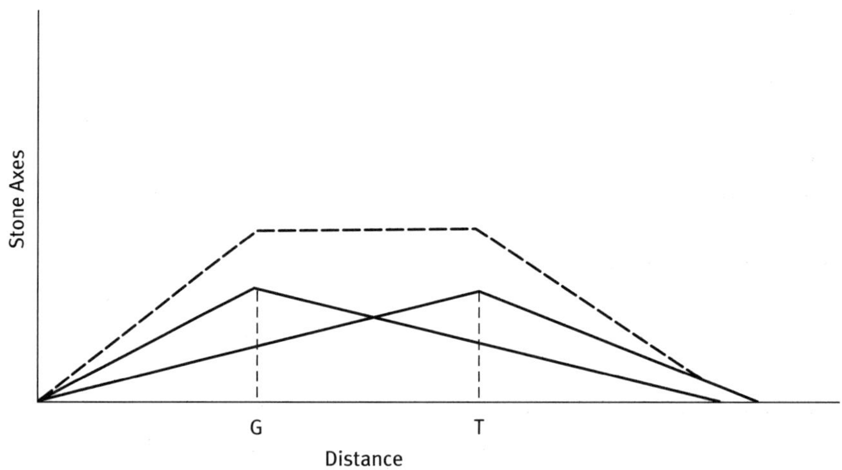

FIGURE 2
Preferences as a function of distance between two huts

shown by the line. We have shown the preferences in cardinal terms by inquiring how many stone axes Gurt would give to have the hut built at any given distance. If it is to be located very far away, he will pay nothing. Similarly, Trug has preferences as to the location of the hut and he would prefer to build it at point T. Here, again, his preferences slope away on both sides, and we have drawn in the number of axes he would be willing to pay for the "right" to put his hut at various distances from Gurt's hut.

These payments, according to the famous Coase theorem, are invertible. If Gurt would be willing to pay two axes to have Trug put his hut at point G, then two axes is also the price that he would be willing to take for permitting Trug to build it two miles away if Gurt had complete control of the location. Similarly, Trug would be happy to take two axes to build it well away from his optimum location. We can, in a sense, sum the two curves; that is, we can obtain the number of stone axes that the two people would pay jointly to build Trug's hut at some particular point, this sum being shown by the upper line. Note that this line is flat between points G and T, which simply indicates that I have drawn the original lines to make this phenomenon occur. If this were a traditional economic problem, we would probably predict that the hut would be built somewhere between points G and T and that there would be some compensation paid by one party or the other as the result of the bargaining. The exact location would have no welfare connotation. Unfortunately, as shall be seen in the next chapter on bargaining, such things are not simple. Nevertheless, we can use this very simple apparatus for our present purposes; note that if the two parties bargain, it is likely that the outcome will be better for both of them than if they do not. That is, contract is a way of reducing externalities.

Indeed, if it were not for the problems involved in bargaining, a contract would be a solution for all problems of externalities. Abstracting from bargaining problems, the optimum will always be reached by a system of freely arranged exchanges, provided of course that we are not concerned with income distribution. Unfortunately, the bargaining problem does exist and therefore this type of solution is not generally available. It should be kept clearly in mind, however, that private bargains are a major method of reducing or eliminating externalities. It should also be noted, as in the case of Figure 2, that it makes very little difference who is given the right to make the initial decision; if in the diagram Gurt had the complete right to determine where anyone else's hut was to be located, then Trug would have to pay him in order to move the hut away from point G. On the other hand, if Trug had the complete right to choose where to put the hut, then Gurt would have to pay him to move it away from point T. The location of the hut, however, would not be *very much* affected by this fact.[9]

In the real world we frequently observe private arrangements to reduce externalities. If I may give a rather extreme example, in the city of Orlando, where my mother used to live, a real estate man bought a plot of land intending to erect a commercial building on it. This would have required a change in the zoning code, which he thought would be easily obtained. In Orlando, Florida, as in most parts of the United States, the zoning code can be changed as a general rule only if the bulk of the neighboring property holders approve, and in this case they did not.

This annoyed the real estate man, who then built a most peculiar apartment house on the plot. It was not modern architecture; it was cheap architecture with a piebald paint job. Having this unsightly building, which needless to say was also poorly finished inside, he then proceeded to rent space in it to the most disreputable families he could find.

The result was quite amusing to those who did not live near it, and extremely annoying to the people who did. It was not a violation of the building code. The outcome, I suppose, was predictable. A number of neighbors joined together and bought the lot and apartment building from the realtor at a price that was found to be quite profitable to him. He had deliberately generated a negative externality that was eliminated by private contract. Note that in this case the externality was revenge for an externality generated by his neighbors who had used the local government to restrict his use of his land. Whether the outcome was or was not optimal was something about which I refuse to make a statement.

Further examples can easily be discovered. Last year I taught at Rice University, and as part of my teaching contract, the university required me to perform a few modest services, such as giving an occasional public lecture, which was designed to generate externalities of a positive nature for their

9. Note the *very much*. The bargaining process may be affected by the point at which it begins. Secondly, the decision as to who has the power to make the initial decision and therefore must be bribed is in itself a decision about the distribution of wealth in the society. Since Gurt and Trug have different tastes, the decision that one or the other will have a larger amount of wealth should lead to somewhat different allocations. It is customary to leave these second order effects aside. This custom will be followed here, but the reader is at least warned that they exist.

principal customers, the students. This is a private contract. Similarly, I lived in an apartment building that enforced a variety of rules to prevent the individual apartment holders from annoying each other. On a more serious level, a very large number of economic enterprises involve "internalizing" externalities by private contract.

Fortunately, or unfortunately, according to your point of view, bargaining costs are not zero. In many cases the bargaining costs are so high that in ordinary speech we would say that bargains were impossible. We turn, therefore, to some type of collective decision-making process; that is, some arrangement under which individuals are compelled to carry out the wish of others. Thus we finally come to the role of the state, and this role superficially appears to be a very modest one—that of reducing the costs of bargaining. The reducing of bargaining costs may not be terribly dignified, but it is a matter of great practical importance in the world, and the states that perform this function tend to be very major and important parts of our society.

Suppose that each of the inhabitants of our Stone Age village had preferences as to the location of the other huts in the village. These preferences, we may assume, are not absolutely identical, although all may feel that if any hut is built with its door pointing south, this will injure the hunting for the entire village. If there were a general effort on the part of everyone to engage in bargaining with all the other people as to the location of all their huts, we could anticipate a tremendous amount of negotiation and bargaining, and no real prospect of a satisfactory outcome. Once again, if we look at the modern world we find this even more obvious.

Strictly speaking, nothing except bargaining costs prevents me from making an arrangement with a large number of other people under which we may privately build a network of roads. But when we say that nothing except bargaining costs prevents this type of action, we immediately realize how extreme these bargaining costs would be. The proposal that we replace governmental roads with an agreement to build roads privately is literally absurd. The full reason for its absurdity, however, oddly enough has only recently been discovered.

Activities of this type were traditionally handled by the government, and there was a realization that private persons could not undertake them, but it was not known that the reason private persons could not undertake them was simply that the bargaining costs would be excessive. There would be no way of assuring agreement within a finite amount of time. The development of government eliminates this problem. The outstanding characteristic of government is that we do not have to obtain everyone's agreement. Somebody makes a decision and then "pains and penalties" are applied to people who refuse to carry it out. These penalties have been different in different periods of history—at one time, boiling in oil, today perhaps something as minor as seizing a small part of a checking account. Furthermore, the government decision process itself has varied tremendously.

Probably, the most common governments under which human beings have lived have been despotisms. Characteristically these have not been benevolent despotisms, but disorderly and decidedly unbenevolent organizations. Nevertheless, if we observe history we see that most people much preferred to live under an inefficient and oppressive despotism to living with no government at all. This fact is an indication of the importance of the suppression of externalities and bargaining costs by even a very poor government.

We can, then, imagine Gurt and his fellow villagers deciding to establish a government that will issue rules on the location of the huts. Here we have two problems: (1) the nature of the government and (2) the nature of the rules that it issues. For the first problem, the nature of the government, we would expect from anthropological information about present-day tribes that the village would have some kind of chief who would usually seek advice from the other members of the village. This scheme, no doubt, would be better than having no government, but let us assume that our primitive community is in some respects very modern and that it reaches its decisions by a formal process of collective decision-making. It could vote on the decisions directly or it could elect some kind of council or even an individual to make the decisions. We need not consider here the question of whether each individual will have one and only one vote. In the real world this is, of course, a tremendously important problem; but for our purposes this decision is exogenous. For convenience we will normally consider a situation in which each individual has only one vote. Most of our reasoning, however, can be readily extended to other possible ways of voting.

The second problem is what kind of hut location rules the village (however it is constituted) should establish. Until very recently there were a considerable number of people who believed that the optimal way of running any economic organization (and house building certainly is an economic organization) was detailed regulation from the center. Clearly, this *could* indeed completely eliminate all externalities. As was demonstrated in the last chapter, however, a whole series of other problems was raised because individual preferences are subordinated to the collective decision. If you wish to optimize your own future utility stream, you would not want *all* of your decisions externally controlled, whether by majority voting or a benevolent authority.

In general this belief in detailed regulation has ceased to be a major intellectual influence in recent times, not because of the arguments that I presented in the last chapter, but because of a gradual realization that the detailed regulation is (with our present mental and physical equipment) impossible.[10] The advent of Liebermanism in the Soviet Union is simply one of the many chains of evidence that centralized planning does not seem to work. Furthermore, even if we looked at highly planned activities (for example, the Soviet Union before Liebermanism or the interior organization of some part of the government bureaucracy), we find a considerable use of decisions made outside the central planning office and "quasi-property."

If we look at any large governmental office, we find that the office furniture and a good deal of the office equipment are not kept in good order by detailed regulations. Such detailed regulations may exist, but the basic dependence is put upon what Alchian has named "quasi-property." I have been issued a desk and a chair by my university. If I am careless and scar the top of my desk by pulling things that have sharp undersurfaces across it, they will not fine me. They will simply leave me in "possession" of the same desk. Thus, I am motivated to be careful. This is an example of the sort of use of quasi-property that is common even in the most centralized and most highly controlled organizations.

Another, and more important, single subdivision of this same phenomenon, is the fact that in almost all large organizations, the head of any given office is given a good deal of discretion in dealing with various things within his area of control, and the restrictions on his decisions are not entirely in terms of general regulations, but partly in terms of making him continue to live with that office. These are examples of the use of quasi-property in the most centralized organizations. Today most people do not think that a high degree of centralization is desirable. Much of the recent efforts to improve the efficiency of government (particularly in the United States and particularly in the Department of Defense) have been attempts to create a decentralized process that functions somewhat like a market process although within a bureaucratic context.

10. It is possible, although I think unlikely, that we may be developing an apparatus that would make such detailed controls possible in the future.

But, be that as it may, most systems do have a mixture of property, government, and contract. The mixture is usually extremely subtle. For example, what is meant by property is characteristically a governmental decision. In fact, the government may be said to do more reducing of externalities by maintaining a law of property than by all its other activities put together. Similarly, it is sometimes very hard to see the difference between a contract and a government. The private corporation is clearly the result of a contract, a group of people entering into an agreement to conduct an enterprise.[11] They further agree to use some form of elective process to appoint the actual managers and give these managers control of the resources of the enterprise. It will be noted that if we just give the word "enterprise" a somewhat wider meaning, this description would fit Rousseau's theory of the state. It would also, I may say, fit my own theory of the state.

The corporation usually makes most of its decisions by a method other than unanimous consent. Exactly what method is used varies from time to time, from place to place, and from corporation to corporation, but clearly the decision-making process is not one of agreement by all interested parties. This permits much greater efficiency than requiring complete agreement and is the major reason why the corporate form of enterprise is adopted. We can find many other cases where individuals choose to voluntarily subject themselves to decisions over which they do not have a veto. Any club will serve as an example. Universities normally have rather obscure decision processes, but it is clear that total agreement is not necessary.

What, then, is the difference between a government and a corporation? The answer to this question is simply that we have grown accustomed to calling one particular type of collective organization a government. Characteristically, there is one collective apparatus in society that is more powerful than any other and that can, if it comes to a battle, win over others. This apparatus we call the government. It should be emphasized, however, that the difference between this organization and a general contract is less than one might suppose.[12] Although it seems to me the difference between a corporation and the government is not as great as has perhaps been traditionally described, it still is true that there is much to be said for separately discussing

11. Although in most cases the contract is closely regulated by the state, this is not necessary. There have been instances in which corporations have existed without corporation laws.

12. See Thomas Ireland, "The Rationale of Revolt," *Papers on Non-Market Decision Making*, 3 (Fall 1967): 49–66.

the institutions of property, contract, and government. At the border, of course, it may be hard to tell in which of these areas any given institution should be classified. The government, for example, enforces contracts and both defines and enforces the laws of real property. Fortunately, for the purposes of this book, a precise distinction between these three spheres is not necessary. Most of the externality reducing institutions discussed will very clearly fall in one or the other of these three general areas and for those that do not thus classify themselves, the distinction will not be of much importance.

This book, then, will approach the classical problem of the scope of government from a modern angle. What should be controlled by the state and what should be controlled by private individuals either through contract or by themselves? In general, our method will be to contrast the externality cost to be expected through private action with the cost to be expected from government action. We will seek that combination of government and private action that optimizes the future discounted income stream of members of society. Unfortunately, this approach is new and a great deal of empirical information necessary to make definite decisions is as yet unavailable. Thus, in many places the statements about the real world in this book are simply the conjectures of a reasonably well-informed observer. It is my hope that in a few more years it will be possible to replace these conjectures with carefully collected empirical data.

BARGAINING

Personally, I have always disliked bargaining and have been poor at doing it. This statement sounds peculiar coming from a man who at one time was an expert on China, but it is nevertheless true. It seems only candid to make this admission before I begin my discussion of bargaining so that the reader may be warned that I am an unsympathetic critic. I think, however, that the theoretical tools now available in economics are adequate and that my personal feelings are unlikely to result in any great distortion.

In an oriental bazaar, the shopkeeper will usually begin by asking a price somewhat higher than he actually hopes to get, but after some chaffering he and his customer will reach an agreement on the price and quantity. Economists have represented this situation by the standard Edgeworth box and have argued that the eventual outcome will be "efficient." This, of course, ignores the investment of resources in bargaining (an investment that I always object to). *Ex post* the parties would always be better off if they had reached the same agreement without investing resources in the bargaining. Furthermore, there may be enough friction in the process so that the neat economist's contract locus is not always reached. Nevertheless, this apparatus is clearly a reasonable approximation of reality.

Let us, however, consider a case in which there are externalities. Mr. Smith and Mr. Brown live next door to each other. Both of them have gardens and each can see the other's garden from his windows. If Mr. Brown put more resources into his garden, the view from Mr. Smith's dining room would be improved. The standard externality argument is shown in Figure 1. Mr. Smith has a demand curve for rosebushes in his own yard; Mr. Brown also has a demand for rosebushes in Mr. Smith's yard. These are illustrated in Figure 1, as is the cost of rosebushes (one dollar each). Now if Mr. Smith simply chooses the number of rosebushes he would wish to put in his yard, he will purchase quantity A. Mr. Brown, however, who also obtains some satisfaction from the roses, has a demand curve for rosebushes in Mr. Smith's yard, and if we add these two demand curves, we have a total demand curve. Point B, which is the global optimum number of rosebushes, can quite readily be obtained if Mr. Brown is willing to pay a subsidy equivalent to the

Reprinted, with permission, from *Private Wants, Public Means: An Economic Analysis of the Desirable Scope of Government* (New York and London: Basic Books, 1970), 55–70.

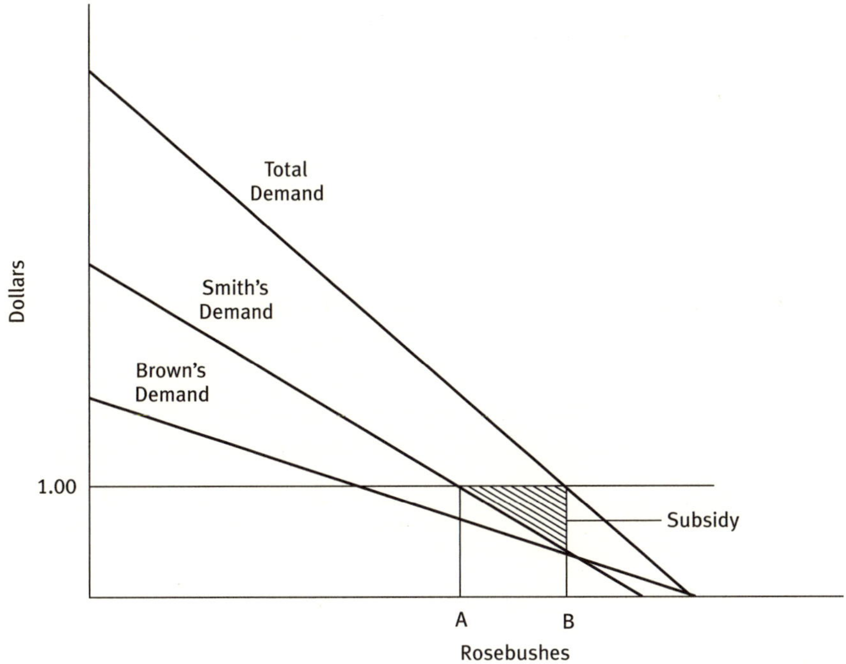

FIGURE 1
Individual and social demand for rosebushes

marked triangle in return for Mr. Smith's planting the additional roses. The subsidy would be less than the gain for Mr. Brown, which is, of course, the area between A and B and under Mr. Brown's demand curve. Thus, both Mr. Brown and Mr. Smith could be better off by moving to quantity B with the making of a suitable payment by Mr. Brown to Mr. Smith.

In the real world, for various reasons, we do not observe such transactions frequently. One reason that certainly has some real importance is that gardeners may regard gardening as a competitive sport; although the view from Mr. Brown's dining room window would be more beautiful if Mr. Smith had more rosebushes, he actually prefers a view that permits him to feel superior to Mr. Smith. Although I am sure that this kind of jealous feeling exists, I do not believe it is universal, which leads us to the question of why this type of bargaining is not more common.

Through the use of Figure 2, we can develop an explanation for the absence of such bargaining. On the horizontal axis, I have placed the number

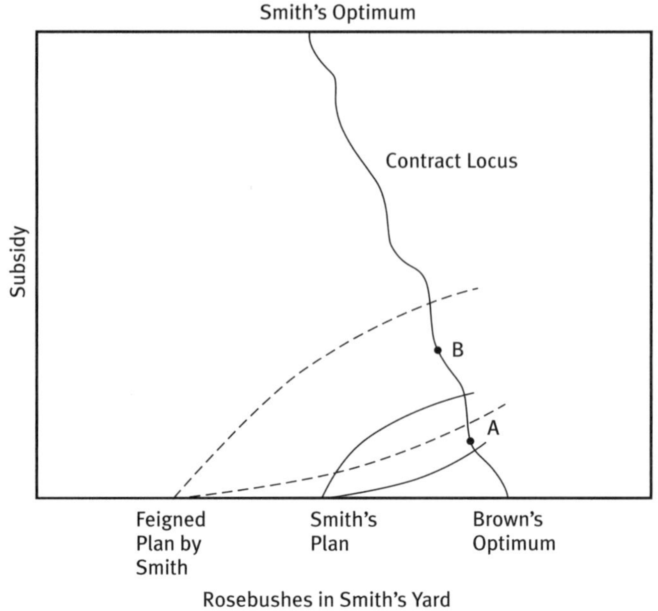

FIGURE 2
Bargaining on the reduction of an externality

of rosebushes in Mr. Smith's yard. Mr. Smith, acting independently, would choose the quantity indicated by "Smith's plan." Mr. Brown, however, could pay him a subsidy, which is shown by the vertical axis. If we consider the optima on this two-dimensional plane, Mr. Brown would prefer to have Mr. Smith put in more rosebushes voluntarily; so Mr. Brown's optimum is shown on the lower boundary to the right of Mr. Smith's plan. Mr. Smith, on the other hand, would prefer to put in the number of rosebushes, ignoring income effects, he originally planned and to also receive a large transfer payment from Mr. Brown. Thus, his optimum is at the top of the diagram. Note that the upper boundary on the subsidy that is shown in Figure 2 is there simply for convenience. There is no natural law limiting the size of the payment that could be made.

If we regard this diagram as a conventional bargain, we can then draw the indifference curves of Mr. Smith and Mr. Brown through Mr. Smith's plan, and bargaining between the two parties would then proceed until they reach some point on the contract locus such as A. If the "play" begins with

Mr. Smith truthfully stating his plan, then there is no reason why this kind of bargaining should not occur. In the real world, however, Mr. Brown has no way of knowing Mr. Smith's actual plan. Thus, Mr. Smith could choose to announce the "feigned plan." The indifference curves through this are the dotted lines. The result of the bargaining might be that Mr. Brown would end up in a position like that of Point B, which is substantially worse than if he had never contemplated a subsidy.[1]

Under these circumstances, on the whole, Mr. Brown is unwise to begin negotiations, since the end product is likely to be that he will be worse off than he would have been if he had done nothing. Thus, not only does Mr. Brown waste his resources in the bargaining process, he may actually reduce his ultimate degree of satisfaction. This is, of course, not inevitable. He can make a gain, but clearly the situation is quite different from that of traditional bargaining in which the individuals each know the other's location at the start, and there is no doubt that they will move in the general direction of an improvement for each of them. The possibility open to Mr. Smith in our example of concealing his initial position, while Mr. Brown's initial position cannot, strictly speaking, be concealed, makes this type of bargaining highly one-sided and may lead to significant injury to Mr. Brown.[2]

In the real world we sometimes observe payments of one sort or another being made to change the gardening arrangements next door. If these happen intermittently so that they cannot be anticipated, they may be reasonably successful. Perfect adjustment, of course, is not to be expected. As a simple example, Mr. Brown might one day come to Mr. Smith and say that he had been able to buy a half-dozen rosebushes at a great bargain and he only wanted three of them for his yard. He might then ask if Mr. Smith would like the other three. Probably Mr. Smith would accept the gift. If Mr. Brown did this regularly, however, Mr. Smith would begin planning his own purchase

1. If Mr. Smith were to announce that his basic program was to plant the number of rosebushes shown at the feigned plan, then he would in a sense be presenting Mr. Brown with a set of indifference curves for which the contract locus would be farther to the left than the one I have drawn in. The bargaining might proceed to this contract locus instead of to the real one. But it seems likely that having reached this feigned contract locus, the parties could then go on to the real contract locus.

2. It would not, of course, be possible for Mr. Smith to know exactly where Mr. Brown's optimum was, but he could safely assume that it was on the horizontal axis and to the right of his own.

of rosebushes in anticipation of a gift and Mr. Brown would be worse off than if he had not provided the subsidy.

But with the clear possibility of gains to both Mr. Brown and Mr. Smith, we should carefully consider whether there may not be some method of avoiding these bargaining problems. For example, if Mr. Brown were to compute the exact value to him of each rosebush in Mr. Smith's yard and agree to pay Mr. Smith that amount, then the rosebushes would clearly be installed to exactly the optimal amount. Unfortunately, from Mr. Brown's point of view, it could amount to a large subsidy to Mr. Smith and he would presumably regard the net outcome as being worse than if he had done nothing. This loss would occur in spite of the fact that on the *incremental* rosebushes his payment would exactly balance his gains.[3]

Another possibility for Mr. Brown would be to make an estimate of what he thinks Mr. Smith will do and then offer a payment for rosebushes beyond that point. The problem, of course, is that Mr. Smith would have a strong motive to give the appearance of putting in fewer rosebushes than he actually intended. Once again, we can readily imagine a situation in which Mr. Brown was worse off than he was before.

Altogether the possibilities of mutual gains through this type of bargaining seem poor. It is possible, however, that there is an arrangement that would help both parties. Let us suppose that Mr. Smith is also interested in the number of rosebushes in Mr. Brown's yard, which is surely not inconceivable. One can imagine an arrangement between Mr. Smith and Mr. Brown under which each of them agrees to pay, let us say, 10 per cent of the cost of planting rosebushes in the other's yard. If the two parties had a similar taste for rosebushes, there would be substantially no change in their wealth, but there would be a change in the marginal conditions under which they purchased rosebushes. Each would buy more rosebushes, and the appearance of the two yards would be more pleasing.

As far as I know, there are no examples of this kind of bargaining in the world. Perhaps one of the reasons for this is that the end product would certainly not be on the contract locus. Some kind of "rough and ready" system under which each party receives the same amount of subsidy would probably

3. See M. I. Kamien, N. L. Schwartz, and F. T. Dolbear, "Asymmetry Between Bribes and Charges," *Water Resources Research*, 2, no. 1 (1966): 147–57. A comment by Gordon Tullock together with a reply by Kamien, Schwartz, and Dolbear are printed in *Water Resources Research*, 2, no. 4 (1966): 854–55, 856–57.

be necessary, and this would most assuredly deviate from the theoretical optimum. A second, and probably more important, reason may be that people feel that the benefits are not worth the time, and a third possibility is that people just have not thought of it. We tend to forget that there is such a thing as technological progress in contracts. People discover new ways of making agreements, and over a period of time we obtain considerable benefit from this sort of technological progress.

The possibility of implicit bargains of this type with a different institutional structure will be studied later in this book. For the moment, let us simply note that they do not often occur and that an externality in which one party wishes to change the behavior of a second party by the payment of subsidies leads to a bargaining problem of extraordinary difficulty. The problems are twofold. First, Mr. Brown is attempting to change Mr. Smith's behavior without any positive information as to what Mr. Smith's behavior would be if Mr. Brown did not make his attempt to change it. Mr. Smith has an advantage in the bargaining and Mr. Brown may not wish to enter into a process of bargaining that will quite possibly put him in a worse position than he would have been if he had never suggested the bargaining. The second, and more basic, problem is once again the problem of contiguity. In ordinary bargaining we know what the other party's reservation price is because we know what competing offers are available on the market. These offers give us a fairly good measure as to what we can expect from the man we are dealing with. In this case there is only one person living just north of Mr. Brown. This contiguity characteristic, the delimitation of the bargaining to one specific person or to a small contiguous group, is an important factor in the bargaining difficulties in this case. When we turn to multiple party bargaining, we will find once again that contiguity is a basic and major problem. If we could somehow shuffle pieces of real estate around, it would make a tremendous improvement in the functioning of both our market economy and that part of the economy that must be dealt with politically.

Perhaps we should note that the advantage that theoretically can be obtained from an agreement between Mr. Brown and Mr. Smith could, also theoretically, be obtained through a government agency that placed a suitable tax on Mr. Brown and used the money to subsidize Mr. Smith. Unfortunately, again, there seems to be no way in which we can obtain the necessary information to make the proper adjustment. Mr. Smith would have no motive for correctly informing the government agency of his initial position. Mr. Brown, on the other hand, may wish to obtain profits on the deal and thus also misrepresents his preference curves. All that the government could hope for would be some kind of rule of thumb, which might well be better than what we would, in practice, obtain in the market, but would not be a perfect solution and would not obtain the total profit that can be made in theory from the situation shown in Figure 1. Here the bargaining problems are such that it is impossible for either the political or the market process to reach the theoretically optimal solution. Whether the market process or the political process would reach the best solution is a matter on which one can have opinions but no real knowledge in the present state of the world.

The real bargaining problem occurs when there are considerable numbers of people whose agreement is necessary. Once again, contiguity is the important problem because it necessitates dealing with a specified group of people. The problem that would arise if General Motors decided that it wished to buy up *all* of the shares of stock now outstanding in public hands is that they are held by a designated group of people. Every year General Motors sells automobiles to a group of people that is larger than its stockholders, but not having a designated group to deal with it finds this relatively easy. Generally, it is easier to sell to 10,000 people out of 1 million than it is to sell to 10,000 people out of 10,000. Indeed, it is probably easier to sell something to 10,000 persons out of 1 million than to 100 out of 100. In a normal "take over bid" in the stock market, the people buying control of the corporation reduce their total potential profit by not attempting to buy all of the stock. Their offer will be to buy at a specified price provided, let us say, that at least 85 per cent of the stock is tendered to them. They are aware of the fact that this gives the holders of 15 per cent of the stock a "free ride," but they are also aware that attempting to get all the stock would make the deal impossible.

Most cases in which governmental action is called for, however, are cases of contiguity because a certain designated group of people must be dealt with who live, own property, or work next to each other. The typical externality is "geographic." Let us begin our analysis of this problem with a matter that is not often a governmental activity by supposing that there is a tract of land now being used for housing on the outskirts of an American city. Assume further that there are forty people who have houses on the land with lots of varying sizes and characteristics. Let us also assume that at the moment the total real estate value of the lots on which these houses exist is approximately $100,000, and the houses themselves are valuable enough so that the value of the whole area (in its present use) is around $500,000, and that the location is very suitable for the establishment of a shopping center. If all of the lots are placed together in one unit, it is highly probable that the real estate alone can be sold to a developer for a price of $1 million. I should say that there is nothing even modestly improbable about this example.

Here we have a problem in what is called "assembly" of property. If these various individual plots can be grouped into one unit, they are much more valuable than if they are kept separate. Assembly of property is an extremely difficult and costly business. Most specialists in the field would look at the problem I have stated above and simply say that it was impossible to obtain this potential profit of $500,000. By this they would mean, in essence, that the bargaining costs would be considerably in excess of $500,000.

Now, why would an experienced man in this trade feel that it would be impossible to purchase these homes at well above their current market value? The answer is, of course, the bargaining problem; but in order to understand it let us look into the situation of one individual house owner. If he agrees to sell his property to the organization that is attempting to assemble the plot at a price above its value to him, he makes a profit. But in this case (at least theoretically) a much larger profit is available. He is in the position of a monopolist holding an essential resource. If he refuses to sell his plot of land, then the entire deal cannot go through. Let us assume that the property that he holds has a current sale value as a single lot of $20,000 and that the remaining people hold property with a current sale value (again not assembled) of $480,000. If the owner of this single plot gives his permission, the value of the entire property is raised by $500,000. His consent to the organization of the plots in one holding is in fact an asset, which, if he refuses to sell, can inflict an opportunity cost of $500,000 on the other parties.

The real estate developers have a good reason for not paying our individual owner of the lot $500,000; the reason being that every single householder there is in approximately the same position. We have a situation in which any one of these people (if he holds out long enough) could reasonably assume that he will obtain a very large advantage over the others. Although no one would really anticipate making the full amount, it would be true that the individuals who held out longest, who were least cooperative with the people trying to assemble the land, and who showed the least interest in getting their land into the assembled group, would make the most money. It is a situation in which the potential payoff is extremely high for obstructive tactics. With a considerable number of people on the plot, one can assume a good many of them will realize this fact and will be obstructive.

Furthermore, it should be noted that the payoff for obstructiveness increases as time goes by. As the people who are attempting to assemble the plot pick up options on individual pieces of property, the amount of their investment increases and the probability they will be willing to abandon the entire matter is lessened; the likelihood that any remaining property owner's consent will be decisive also increases to some extent. The individual who holds out to the end might conceivably make the full amount, $500,000, even if the people buying the options have been paying large fees up to this point. The reason is simply that at the very end the individual's decision does make a difference of $500,000 to the buyer, and hence these people might be willing to pay it. One would also anticipate that the holders of the other pieces of real estate might be willing to make payments to him if the company assembling the property is not. Granted that the operation must take time, it is perfectly possible that the total payments made by the people who are trying to assemble the property will greatly exceed the value of the plot, although at any given time, their estimate of returns on future expenditures is positive.

As I have said, with the number of people I have chosen to use in my example, most real estate assemblers would not be willing to undertake this particular operation. They probably would be quite willing to undertake it if the profit were as large as this and the number of people whose consent was needed was much smaller, but in general, if the number of individual owners is large, it is impossible to assemble land. This is part of the theoretical justification of the federal government's urban renewal program. It is argued that various areas of "deteriorated" property in the downtown areas of American cities cannot be revived by private persons. The reason, according to this argument, is that no individual would be motivated to improve the building on his property because the dilapidated buildings on adjoining property would make it impossible for him to rent or sell his property at a reasonable price. Thus, what is needed is a large plot of land that can be renovated at a single time.

If this argument is correct, the plot of land once assembled would be worth more than it was when disassembled because it is possible to avoid these externality effects. The impossibility of assembling the plot by private bargaining for the reasons outlined above is accepted, and it is therefore proposed that the government use its power of condemnation to force people to sell at what is normally called a "fair price," but that is usually (not always) a price that is somewhat above the market value. Clearly, there is nothing wrong with this argument. It is perfectly possible, although there have been a number of investigations in recent years that would seem to indicate that empirically the situation called for is not very common. It would seem that people are not as concerned with the appearance of buildings on neighboring plots of land as had been thought, so that the externality is smaller. Nevertheless, it is clear that a case can be made and regardless of whether or not we are in favor of urban renewal, it fits our specifications for government action.

One can continue to find innumerable other cases in which it is perfectly clear that individual activity on one piece of property may create externalities (positive or negative) for people on the next piece of property and hence where the bargaining difficulties would be very great. The obvious case for this, of course, is national defense. In general it is impossible for someone who sets up an antimissile defense for a house in a city in which I am living to avoid giving me protection even if I do not choose to pay for it. Thus, the bargaining problem here would involve the entire population of the city, and it is extremely unlikely that it could be solved by voluntary contract.

The importance of these bargaining problems for the justification of government activity is, I take it, now clear. The externalities that governmental activities are mainly aimed at eliminating could be effectively eliminated by private bargaining, if it were not for the extreme difficulty involved in bargaining.[4] We do not turn to private bargains because of the extreme difficulty in bargaining in this area. The bargains would be extremely costly, and would take tremendous amounts of time, and to all practical intents and purposes can be said to be impossible. The pure theorist, of course, will insist that if one waited an infinite amount of time and were willing to invest vast resources into active bargaining, some agreement would eventually be reached.

Note, however, that there is a cost to government action. Bargaining will eventually reach the contract locus or the Paretian frontier; governmental activity will not. In fact, as we will demonstrate in Chapter 5, there is every reason to believe that governmental adjustment will characteristically be far from perfect. Thus, we would normally wish to impose upon parties a certain amount of bargaining, rather than the use of governmental activities, simply because the bargaining will ultimately reach a conclusion that is superior to the government outcome. If the bargaining costs involved rise above some point (a point that at the moment we can not accurately specify but with further research we may know very well), then government becomes a more desirable way of dealing with the problem than does the private market.

The choice is one between two instrumentalities both of which have con-

4. I am, as I mentioned before, deferring problems of income equalization until a later chapter.

siderable error, noise, and inefficiency inherent in them. We choose between two imperfect instrumentalities and thus must face much the same situation as the mechanical engineer who must choose the power for a new ship. Since no engine is perfect, he chooses the one that, for the particular use concerned, is least inefficient. We will be doing the same. There is no reason why we should be particularly unhappy about this, but it is the choice between imperfect instruments rather than, as is sometimes suggested, the abandonment of an imperfect instrument, the market, for a perfect instrument, the government. The situation is rather analogical to the second law of thermodynamics, a general proof that no perfect machine can ever be produced. In any event, this book accepts the absence of a perfect institutional solution.

Bargaining costs are not only important as a reason for government action but they are also important in government action. If we observe any functioning government unit, we will always observe a great deal of bargaining between different parts of it, and between it and the general polity, whether this general polity consists of the voters or a central organization, as in the Soviet Union. This bargaining is also subject to the same costs as private bargaining, that is, it moves toward a contract locus that is a superior situation for the parties, and it may be impossible to attain that locus within a finite amount of time.

In the particular case of government action, we characteristically have a situation whereby compensation is extremely difficult to arrange. Let us suppose that we have a simple majority voting rule and that the parties are not all equally intense about their views on some particular subject and/or we do not have single-peak preference curves with respect to this subject. Under these circumstances, side payments in cash would be the economist's normal prescription. The people who are injured would then be paid off, and some citizens would benefit. As we have emphasized before, there is no reason why the individual should tell other people his attitude in such detail that we can compute the amount of side payments to make. Bargaining would be necessary under highly unfavorable conditions. The government could not compensate the people who are injured by its actions in any reasonably efficient way simply because extreme bargaining problems would be involved in determining how much compensation should be paid. Thus bargaining costs are both a reason for government and one of the reasons why it will never be perfectly efficient.

EXTERNALITIES AND ALL THAT

The usual case of an externality in economic texts is a contract between two persons that will have some effect on a third person. I purchase a necktie; the salesman will seldom if ever see me wearing it and hence is not likely to be offended if I have bad taste, and I am presumably perfectly happy with the necktie (which I also will seldom see when I am wearing it). Those people who may see me and find it offensive, however, have no way of expressing their opinions at the time of the transaction. Note, however, that this is merely a standard example. If I were to make the necktie myself out of materials that I had raised with my own hands, only one person would be involved, but the effect on other persons would be the same or, perhaps, worse. Thus we would have an externality in this case, too. Similarly, there might be more than two parties to the original transaction. As long as one person who is affected is left out of the group whose consent is necessary, there is an externality.

The problem that most economists have examined in their analyses of externalities has been the quantity of something or other purchased, not the exact specifications. Thus, you will find little discussion of the possibility that I might buy a red necktie, whereas I should buy a gray one. This tradition in the analysis of externalities is harmless since any qualitative problem can be converted into several quantitative problems. Thus, if I am intending to purchase a red necktie, and you would rather that I purchase a gray one, you can say that I am overinvesting in red neckties and underinvesting in gray neckties, and that it is the quantity of red neckties, that is, one, and quantity of gray neckties, that is, zero, which I am purchasing that disturbs you. This is simply a different way of expressing the same thing. Since this analysis of externalities is convenient, we will use it for the bulk of this book.

Externalities can arise from either action or failure to take action. The analytical tools needed to deal with an externality fortunately are such that action and inaction are easily handled with the same apparatus. Indeed, as a general rule, even the number of people involved in the externality is not of much significance in the analysis.

Let us begin with the classical case of the smoking chimney and tempo-

Reprinted, with permission, from *Private Wants, Public Means: An Economic Analysis of the Desirable Scope of Government* (New York and London: Basic Books, 1970), 71–95.

rarily assume there are only two people concerned: the factory owner whose chimney smokes and the next-door neighbor who likes to air her laundry on a line and finds that the smoke makes it dirty. Under these circumstances it has been demonstrated that, distributional matters aside, it makes very little difference what the initial situation is. Let us suppose, for example, that the law provides that factories may make as much smoke as they wish. Under these circumstances, the housewife would be motivated to offer a payment to the manufacturer to reduce his smoke emission. If the reduction of smoke by one unit was less costly to the manufacturer than the benefit conferred on the housewife, the amount that she offered him would be sufficient for him to reduce his smoke production until such time as the marginal cost to the housewife and cost to the manufacturer were equal. Similarly, if the law provides that the factory may not emit smoke without the permission of the housewife, the manufacturer could purchase the housewife's permission to emit smoke until such time as he reached the point where the two costs were once again in equilibrium. One would anticipate exactly the same amount of smoke from both of these institutional arrangements.

Since, however, this problem involves an effort by one individual to modify the behavior of another, the bargaining problems discussed in the two-party case at the end of Chapter 3 would be relevant here also. The manufacturer and the housewife would attempt to deceive each other as to their initial position in the bargaining game. In this respect, the housewife is at some disadvantage, because it is perfectly clear that her ideal is zero smoke. It would not be obvious to the housewife how much smoke the factory would emit if no payment were made, and hence the manufacturer may be able to deceive her in the bargaining process. She *might* end up worse off than she would have been if she had made no payment at all.[1] On the other hand, if the housewife is given the right to exact a payment from the factory owner for emitting smoke and the factory is already in existence, she may designate her price for emitting smoke high enough so as to extract the full rent on the existing factory from the manufacturer. Clearly he cannot operate the factory without emitting at least a certain amount of smoke from his smokestack and by prohibiting him from operating until he made a suitable transfer to her,

1. M. I. Kamien, N. L. Schwartz, and F. T. Dolbear, "Asymmetry Between Bribes and Changes," *Water Resources Research*, 2, no. 1 (1966): 147–57. A comment by Gordon Tullock together with a reply by Kamien, Schwartz, and Dolbear are printed in *Water Resources Research*, 2, no. 4 (1966): 854–55.

the housewife could extract quite large amounts of money from him. It should be noted, however, that she will be best off if the factory produces at the point where the injury inflicted on her by the last unit of smoke is equal to the marginal cost of smoke reduction to the manufacturer. At this point she can obtain the largest total transfer from the factory owner. If the housewife has certain long-term goals, that is, an interest in attracting other industries to operate near her home, she might not extort this additional transfer from the factory owner.

If we wish to achieve theoretical perfection, this case presents a special difficulty. Not only is it necessary that the factory owner be charged for the smoke he emits, it is essential that the housewife somehow have her income vary with the amount of smoke damage. Suppose, for example, that we compute the cost to the housewife of each unit of smoke and place a tax on the factory owner of that amount, with the result that the factory owner reduces his production of smoke to the point where his marginal cost and that of the housewife exactly match. We do not, however, pay this tax that we have collected to the housewife. Under these circumstances, she would still find that there was a substantial smoke nuisance and might decide to purchase a dryer that she would not otherwise have wanted. This would mean that she would be suffering something in the way of an excess burden from the smoke emitted by the factory and hence society would still be receiving some injury from the smoke. Only if the housewife is subsidized to compensate her for the smoke injury do we obtain total optima.

Nevertheless, it may well be that a tax on the smoke without any payments to the householders would be a desirable social institution. The government must obtain money from some source, and the excess burden associated with the failure to pay the subsidy to the householder may be less than the excess burden obtained from other types of revenue devices.

In practice, of course, there is no reason to believe that a democratically selected tax would match the margins in the way we have been specifying thus far. It presumably would be higher or lower than the ideal tax depending upon the voting process. Nevertheless, a tax (even a rather badly calculated tax) may result in improvements. We must, however, keep in mind that a tax on the smoke may do considerably more harm than good. Once again the problem is not that of eliminating the externality by transferring the activities of the government, but that of comparing the inefficiency that arises from the externality in the market process with the inefficiency that arises from the decision procedures used in the government.

The inefficiency that can come through government can arise from a number of causes, most of which are to be discussed in Chapter 5. There is, however, one example that is a pure externality and, therefore, is best discussed here. Let us suppose that the factory produces smoke that blows over a fairly wide area. If the governmental unit that is to make the decisions on the factory's emission of smoke is exactly coextensive with this area, then all of the externality will be internalized to that district. The amount of smoke injury suffered by different pieces of property will vary, however, and the particular restrictions that will optimize the situation for one householder will not optimize for another. As we have pointed out before, compensation within the political process is not possible here, so it is likely that the outcome will be nonoptimal for this reason alone. There are, of course, a large number of other reasons, but even if we assume that all of the householders are perfectly informed and have some method of expressing their opinion that is free from defects, we would still anticipate that the tax placed upon the emission of smoke would be too heavy from the standpoint of some of the householders and too light from the standpoint of others. This is a fairly straightforward cost arising out of the political process.

The point of this short discussion of externalities, however, is not to deal with this specific problem, but with a more general example of the same thing. Let us suppose that the jurisdiction within which the factory is located does not encompass the entire area in which the smoke damage occurs. The individuals voting to establish an appropriate tax rate on the factory would have two objectives in mind. First, they would prefer, insofar as possible, to transfer income from the factory owner (and his customers) to themselves. This is, of course, a characteristic of substantially all political taxation schemes. Second, they would be interested in adjusting the production of smoke in the factory to the point where the marginal costs of introducing further smoke reducing procedures is the same as the marginal cost from additional smoke. This is the point at which they, granting that they are obtaining maximum practical transfers from the factory owner, will find their well-being optimized. Note, however, that there is no reason why the citizens of this district should take into account the well-being of people outside the district who would also suffer smoke damage. Therefore, the total smoke damage cost will not be "internalized," and the factory will emit more smoke than it should.

Let us, however, take the opposite case. Suppose that the governmental unit having jurisdiction over the factory is markedly larger than the area in which the smoke damage occurs. Under these circumstances, a considerable number of voters in the district will suffer no smoke damage at all. For them the tax will simply transfer resources from the factory owner to themselves. Clearly, they can place a higher tax on the factory owner without driving him out of business if he is permitted to emit more smoke. Since the smoke does not damage them, and since they have at least some influence over the political apparatus, one would anticipate a tax so arranged as to lead once again to a larger amount of smoke generation than is socially optimal.

Logrolling, of course, could eliminate this effect. It would give the people who lived closest to the smokestacks a disproportionate weight in deciding on restrictions. Unfortunately, here again there is no reason to believe that the social optimum would be achieved. The degree to which the externality is reduced, which may, of course, be more or less than the optimal amount, is extremely sensitive to the specific political arrangement that is used to deal with it. It is difficult to comprehend how a political organization could be motivated to establish the optimal size and organization of a political subunit to deal with an externality problem. Hence, it is likely that externality problems will be dealt with by political organizations that will normally not be ideal for dealing with the particular problem. Thus we can anticipate that some pure economic externality will remain even if we ignore the problems of political efficiency.

In pure theory the citizens who live close to the mill could join together and pay their more distant neighbors enough so that the voters would adjust the amount of smoke emitted by the factory and the tax collected from the factory to the social optimum. Once again this involves a highly unlikely bargaining process within the political process. Thus, perfect adjustment requires that the political area that makes the adjustment be exactly the same size as the area of the externality. But most externalities do not have a clear cut border; they do not inflict a five-dollar a year damage on every house out to some line and then zero. Thus, this is essentially an impossible requirement. The fact that most externalities gradually taper off so that the cost is different to different people means that any democratic process will almost certainly put an inappropriate level of taxation on the externality. The converse, of course, applies in those cases of externality that generate benefits rather than inflict injuries.

Note that there is no argument here that the government may not be able to produce a better outcome than the market. The point is simply that the government does not produce a perfect outcome. It is even possible to imagine circumstances where there is a very substantial externality, but where government activity would lead to a worse outcome than the market.

There has been a general tendency to ignore the externalities generated by the governmental process itself. These externalities can be classified in two categories. The first is the injury inflicted on me as a citizen of a state because the state does something I dislike. Let us say that I am deeply antagonistic to the Vietnam War; I object to the war itself and to paying taxes to support it. Nevertheless, I find myself being compelled to participate. There are economists who say that this is not a true externality and there is no point in bandying words. They can call it by some other name if they wish, but I would be happier if I could prevent this situation from arising. The second type of externality arises because the government is engaging in some activity or failing to engage in activity that affects people outside its jurisdiction. It is fairly certain, for example, that the inhabitants of North Vietnam found the presence of large numbers of American aircraft flying over their country and dropping bombs a very, very prominent example of a negative externality. The cases mentioned previously in which the amount of coal smoke generated was inappropriate because the area of the governmental unit was inappropriate are simply milder examples of the same phenomenon.

Our present discussion involves only negative externalities, that is, externalities that inflict injury. This is not because they are the most important. On the contrary, I suspect that the so-called positive externalities are more important in the present-day world than the negative externalities, but the latter happen to be somewhat easier to handle analytically and anything that can be said about them may be transferred to positive externalities. The externalities I would like to discuss now are the so-called reciprocal externalities, which occur when A's activities affect B, and B's activities affect A. The factory chimney and the housewife are clearly an asymmetrical case. If we think of a number of people living in a community, all of whom burn soft coal and all of whom hang their laundry outdoors to dry, we have a case of reciprocal externality. Each individual would find that his laundry was cleaner if the amount of smoke he emitted was reduced. If he could persuade his neighbors to reduce their emission of smoke without reducing his own, he would be better off than if he was also compelled to reduce his own smoke emission, but normally this is not a politically feasible solution.

Situations that give rise to this kind of reciprocal externality are endemic in the present-day world. Probably the most conspicuous example is traffic congestion. If I decide to travel southwest on the Southwest Freeway between the hours of five and six in the evening, or to travel northeast on the same freeway between the hours of eight-thirty and nine-thirty in the morning, I will take into account the private costs of making this trip. One of these costs is that I will make a comparatively slow trip because of the number of other cars on the highway. Unfortunately, there are a number of other costs, which, if I am rational, I will not consider. The presence of my car on the highway increases congestion and therefore inflicts costs on the other people also on the highway. I have a choice, for example, between driving from my office to the Post Oak section at four o'clock in the afternoon or at five-thirty. I know that I will make a much quicker and more convenient trip at four than at five-thirty, but it will be inconvenient in other ways. Let us say that the benefit to me in terms of reduced wear and tear on my nerves of driving at four as opposed to five-thirty is two dollars, but the other inconveniences of leaving my office early would be worth two dollars and fifty cents to me. Under these circumstances, I would wait until five-thirty to begin my trip, but it may well be that the cost inflicted on other people by the presence of my car on the highway at that time is as much as fifty dollars to one hundred dollars. Thus, I am ignoring an externality and inflicting very substantial injury on other people.

Note, however, that all of the other people on the highway at five-thirty are doing the same.[2] Under these circumstances we have an interesting situation in which a tax on everyone can make everyone better off. Let us suppose that the city of Houston established toll booths at the entries of the highways and charged a fee of one dollar for driving west on the freeway between the hours of four-thirty and six o'clock. This means that the number of people driving on the throughway at that time will be reduced. If I switch times and drive at four, the people actually on the highway will in net be benefited by the tax. Those people who do not drive on the highway are not benefited by the tax. In fact they suffer an excess burden, but it is probable that they are compensated for this by the government revenues derived from the tax. Thus we have what appears to be black magic: the people who actually pay the tax are not in any way injured by it; in fact, they achieve a substantial benefit. Even ignoring the revenue derived, by paying the tax and using the highway in an uncongested state, they are better off than they would

2. There may, of course, be some individual on the highway for whom the advantage of driving at that particular time is great enough so that even socially he is justified in driving at that time. I rather doubt it, but it is possible.

be if they did not pay the tax and had to face the congestion. The only people who are injured are those who do not pay the tax. Clearly, their injury cannot exceed one dollar and should be much less. As an even more magical example, John Moore has examined the situation that would arise if all of the users of the highway simply reduced their consumption of it as a response to a tax. In this case there are no people who actually stop using the highway, and therefore there is no excess burden. Every single person can be directly benefited under these circumstances by a suitably chosen tax.[3]

Although the case of reciprocal externality is usually discussed in terms of many persons, that is, congestion problems, it can arise with two people or a very small group. The reader will recall the case of two adjacent houses, with each owner interested in the number of rosebushes in the backyard of the other. Under these circumstances, it *may* be possible for the two parties to benefit themselves by entering into an agreement that eliminates the reciprocal effect of their choice of what they plant in their garden. As a result of bargaining problems, they can never hope to reach perfect adjustment, but nevertheless they may be able to effect a positive improvement in their welfare. In our previous example, each agreed to pay 10 per cent of the cost of rosebushes placed in the other's yard.

Nevertheless, the common case of reciprocal externalities is one that involves a large number of people. Moreover, reciprocal externality is, in general, the situation that will arise if some particular service can be provided cheaply if it is provided for an entire geographical area, and is extremely expensive if the individuals attempt to provide it by themselves. Our mosquito abatement project will serve as an example. Other examples are national defense and police. In each of these cases, there is no reason why a person would not hire his own services except that there are contiguity-scale economies that make this extremely inefficient.[4] I can, for example, hire a private police-

3. See "Congestion and Welfare—Comment," John Moore, *The Economic Journal*, 78 (March 1968): 157–65.

4. In general, these cases are discussed under the rubric of "public goods." A public good is defined as one that can be consumed by one person without any reduction in the quantities available to others. Thus my consumption of national defense does not reduce your consumption. In fact, they are simply extreme and rather special cases of an externality. Furthermore, they are not necessarily publicly provided. A private television station is a similar example. It would be fantastically expensive to provide the type of entertainment that is obtained on television for a single user, but it is relatively economical if a large number of people share the services of the same station.

man to pass in front of my house as often as, or more often than, the city police do. It is also by no means impossible for me to spend part of my fortune on arms to protect myself against foreign enemies. In both cases, however, on the whole it is unlikely that I will obtain anywhere near as good results with this activity as does the government.

Furthermore, in all of these cases, it is highly likely that an individual who chooses not to protect himself in this way would find himself benefited to some extent by the protection purchased by his neighbors. If I hire a police patrol that will pass in front of my house (let us say) seven times a week at random intervals, and the police patrol observes a suspicious character three houses down from mine, that patrol would be protecting me rather poorly if it did not stop and question him. On the other hand, if it does stop and question the suspicious character, it is extending protection to people who have not paid for its service. Therefore, there is no obvious reason why my neighbor should choose to invest in protection if I am doing so.[5]

This is an example of the prisoner's dilemma. Let us say that hiring a police force having a reasonable degree of efficiency would cost each individual ten dollars a year. If I refuse to contribute my yearly allotment, I will receive almost as much protection as if I did make the contribution. The problem is identical to that of the mosquito abatement program. Clearly the difference in my police protection will be only very slightly affected by my ten-dollar investment, and I would, on the whole, be wiser not to pay. On the other hand, if everybody made this calculation, we would have no police force and thus would all be worse off than if each paid the ten dollars. Therefore, we join together and form a police force that has as one of its duties coercing people into paying the ten dollars. All of us are better off, although our freedom has been restricted.

The problem is simply a special case of a reciprocal externality. Gains can be made by collective arrangement for some particular service. It should be noted that the necessity for collective control of this particular service does not mean that it must be directly provided by a governmental body. A great

5. Theoretically, it would be possible for this situation to be remedied by keeping a list of people in the vicinity who are and who are not protected, and permitting professional criminals to prey on those who are not protected. The reason that this would work, however, is not that it solves the externality problem but simply that the costs of being unprotected would be so high that one could predict that no one would choose to not pay. The amount of protection that should be given and its spatial arrangement would still be matters that could not be determined in this simple way.

deal of "governmental" activity is actually provided by private companies by contract or purchase. One of the suburbs of Houston has entered into a contract under which a private company provides its police force. More commonly, many small governmental units have entered into contracts with other governmental units under which the second governmental unit provides some service for the first in return for a fee. At the moment, we do not have any adequate criterion for the types of activity that should be provided directly by the government and the types that should be obtained by contract. The analogous problem in private industry, whether a company should buy or make components, is also extremely difficult.

A fairly good theoretical rule emerges for the types of "goods" that the government should purchase for its citizens. Stated more concretely, we have good arguments for the existence of a collective body that levies taxes in order to provide police protection. At the moment we have no arguments for the police force being provided through the direct hiring of individuals as policemen by the government, instead of entering into a contract with another governmental unit or a private corporation to provide the police force as a unit.[6] The fact that we do not now have a theory in this area does not, of course, indicate that none exists or that there is no reason why the entire government should not be contracted out to private persons. All we can actually say is that at the moment we do not know the answer.

To return to the pure problem of externality, generally speaking it is a matter of some importance that the externality be fully understood and the institutions designed to deal with it be carefully designed. For example, let us consider the factory with the smoking chimney. Suppose further that the householders in attempting to deal with the smoking chimney, instead of placing a gauge in the chimney and taxing the factory in terms of how much smoke it emits, taxed the output of the factory. Mistakes of this sort may not seem very likely, but as a matter of fact, on a somewhat more subtle level they can and do occur. Under these circumstances, the factory owner would usually reduce production, but the social optimum would be almost impossible to reach.[7] The factory owner is not impelled to invest his resources to reduce

6. Needless to say, in such contracting arrangements it would be necessary to avoid the prospect of a monopoly supplier. Normally this would cause no great difficulty. See Harold Demsetz, "Why Regulate Utilities?" *Journal of Law and Economics*, 11 (April 1968): 55–65.

7. There are special circumstances in which a tax of this sort might both restrict output and increase smoke. I doubt that these special circumstances are likely to be met in the real world, but the theoretical possibility should be kept in mind.

smoke emission but to restrict production as a whole. From the standpoint of the people who are attempting to adjust the output of smoke, this is not a completely irrelevant objective since restriction of production will normally reduce smoke. It is, however, a situation in which the adjustment is only indirectly relevant to the problem. The ultimate outcome presumably would be social waste; probably less than the original smoking chimney, but conceivably more.

An even more perverse effect can be obtained if some externality is produced in a joint production function with something else that has no external effects and a mistake is made in attempting to correct the problem. James Buchanan and I presented a case of this type in "Public and Private Interaction under Reciprocal Externality."[8] Contagious diseases produce an externality in that the individual who is ill may pass the illness on. As a general rule, individuals can deal with contagious disease in two ways. They can have themselves inoculated against it, and they can undergo medical treatment if they catch the disease. Reduction of contagion and reduction of the risk to other people largely depend on the former, since most diseases are contagious before they become serious enough for the person who has contracted a disease to realize that he should see a doctor. In present-day circumstances he is unlikely to pass the disease on while under medical supervision.

Thus, the inoculation reduces the likelihood that the individual who is inoculated will become ill and also reduces the likelihood of other people becoming ill. The individual presumably will not take the second effect into account, and therefore an externality is present. Governmental action can readily be supported in this case. Let us suppose, however, that the government makes a mistake. It provides free hospitalization for people who are ill instead of subsidizing inoculations. With the cost of the disease reduced, the individual will be less inclined to become inoculated against the disease and hence is more likely to catch the disease and pass it on. Thus, the result of what is probably a sizable governmental expenditure in the form of a subsidy is actually an increase in the externality.

Once again, the problem is not that governmental action is not called for but that the action chosen has been badly calculated. It is quite possible for a government aiming at reducing an externality to worsen matters, but the fact that the government can make errors in this area is nothing remarkable. Governments, like other organizations, make many errors. The only moral

8. *The Public Economy of Urban Communities*, ed. Julius Margolis (Washington, D.C.: Resources for the Future, Inc., 1965), pp. 52–74.

that can be drawn from the possibility of errors is that we should be careful; we should do more research into externalities, and be very careful in applying what we already know. This is the kind of standard advice that is offered in every field and is always sensible, but has nothing specific to do with externalities.

It might be noted, however, that one aspect of this advice can be said to have an indirect bearing on the externality problem. Research, including research into externalities, is an externality-generating activity by itself. If I increase the amount of knowledge that exists in the world, it is probable that many people will benefit in addition to myself; I am creating a favorable externality. Thus, externality economics teaches us that it is desirable to stimulate further research into externality economics. Since patents are not available in this area, a system of lump sum prizes to encourage research might be sensible.

Thus far, I have confined myself fairly closely to what might be called a standard discussion of the economics of externality, and I have avoided the voluminous literature dealing with special problems. Covering all of the many difficult, complicated details would require a much longer book. Furthermore, it seems to me that, except for people who propose to become specialists in this particular branch of economics, a detailed knowledge of these complications is not necessary. Thus, I do not intend to comprehensively cover all of the problems that have been raised in this new and really quite difficult field of economics. Nevertheless, it does seem sensible to outline some of the more important of these special problems. The first is not regarded as an externality by all economists. I do not wish to quarrel about words and, therefore, if my reader prefers not to regard the problem I am about to discuss as an example of an externality but as an example of something else, this is perfectly all right with me. It is, however, something that should be kept in mind when considering social policy.

If the government decides to spend money on anything, including an activity that might reduce an externality, it must first obtain that money. Economists long ago noted that when the government obtains money through a tax, unless the tax is the little-used head tax, there will be a burden imposed upon the society in addition to the cost of the tax itself. This so-called excess burden comes from the fact that the members of the society will not only pay their tax but they will adjust their behavior to some extent in order to reduce their tax burden. There is some cost to society imposed by this adjustment process as well as by the tax, so the net cost of the tax to the taxpayer is somewhat greater than the amount that the government collects. Thus, if the government is considering reducing an externality by a subsidy, it must first make careful calculations in which the cost of the excess burden is included. This, again, is merely a warning to be careful.

There is, however, another conclusion that can be drawn from the reasoning just given. Suppose the government is able to reduce an externality-generating activity by taxing it. Under these circumstances, the tax modifies behavior in the desired direction and at the same time provides revenue that can be used to pay for another government service. This means that the government can abandon another tax and hence that there is a gain as a result of the elimination of the excess burden of this tax.[9] If there is a choice between a tax and a subsidy, one would normally choose the tax.

Perfect adjustment frequently requires both a tax and a subsidy. Since we can hardly expect perfect adjustment, granted the imperfections of the governmental decision processes, this does not seem to be a matter of much importance. Some deviation from the optimum will occur, but it is likely to be small compared to the deviation from the optimum found in any event. Furthermore, the elimination of the excess burden on what would otherwise be taxed might well be much larger than the benefit from the subsidy.

This proposition is a partial modification of the existing orthodoxy. It has been demonstrated by Ronald Coase that it makes no difference to the ultimate outcome whether a subsidy is paid or a tax is levied.[10] The different effect on the revenue obtained by the government, however, is a relevant, if not the only consideration.

Another and more conventional problem in connection with externality is the problem of "Pareto relevance" introduced by Buchanan and Stubblebine.[11] Suppose that my neighbor builds a house that offends me. I would be willing to pay as much as $500 to him if he would paint it another color. He, on the other hand, is quite happy with the present color and would not be willing to change it for less than $2,000. Here we clearly have a significant

9. See Gordon Tullock, "Excess Benefit," *Water Resources Research*, 2nd Quarter (1967), 643–44.

10. Ronald Coase, "The Problem of Social Costs," *Journal of Law and Economics*, 3 (1960): 1–44. See also Kamien, Schwartz, and Dolbear, *Water Resources Research*, pp. 147–57, and Tullock, *Water Resources Research*, pp. 854–55.

11. "Externality," *Economica* (1962), p. 371, reprinted in *Readings in Welfare Economics*, ed. Kenneth J. Arrow and Tibor Scitovsky (Homewood, Ill.: Richard D. Irwin, 1969), p. 199.

externality. I am suffering sizable externality costs. Nevertheless, the arrangement under which the color remains unchanged is optimal. If my preferences were much stronger, and his much weaker; if I were willing to pay $2,000 to have it repainted, and he would be willing to change it for $500, then the situation would not be Pareto optimal, but presumably we could reach an agreement.[12]

A large number of externalities are of this sort. An individual is undertaking an activity that causes pain to others or fails to provide a positive gain that other people could otherwise obtain, but the satisfaction he receives from the activity is greater than the injury or lack of gain to other people. In such cases nothing should be done. Mishan in *The Costs of Economic Growth* points out that there may be an income distribution effect.[13] Suppose I build a house on the top of a hill, and someone then buys the plot down the hill from me and proposes to build a house on it that is tall enough so that it will cut off my view. I find this objectionable. If I am wealthy, it is rather likely that I will place a higher cash value on the damage to my view than I would if I were poor. Similarly, if the man who buys the property is wealthy, he is apt to place a higher cash value on abandoning his plan for a tall house. Thus, the outcome to some extent is determined by the relative wealth of the two parties.

This is no criticism of the normal method of computing the gain from eliminating externalities. If we approve of the current distribution of wealth in society, we are not concerned that the wealthy man is able to consume more than the poor man. There seems no reason why this should not apply to views and tall houses. If, on the other hand, we are not happy with the present distribution of wealth in society, we should do something about it directly. Once we have obtained a distribution that meets our requirements, we should not concern ourselves as to the particular ways in which people spend their money.

Another minor problem might be called the inertia effect. Considering the situation in which my neighbor is proposing to build a house that might damage my view, the amount that I would be willing to pay him to prevent his taking action after he has decided to build the house would not be enough

12. Note, however, the bargaining problem first introduced in the case of the rosebushes. It might or might not be an obstacle to adjustment in this case.

13. Edward Mishan, *The Costs of Economic Growth* (New York: Frederick A. Praeger, Inc., 1967).

to restrain him. However, before he had made any decision on the matter, the same payment might have led him to agree to not even plan a tall building. One can elaborate this into a problem in which it makes a difference who is to pay whom. Thus, my neighbor plans to do something that will inconvenience me in some way. I might be willing to pay him $500 not to do it, whereas the minimum amount for which he would be willing to give up his rights was $600. On the other hand, if the legal situation were such that I had an original legal right to prevent him from doing it, it might well be that he would not be willing to pay me more than (let us say) $450 for my giving up the right, while I might demand $550. This type of inertia might exist in some transactions, but I doubt that it would be common. In any event, it is difficult to see the difference. If this inertia exists, then the outcome would still be Pareto optimal, although it would, of course, be different than if there were no inertia.

A final special case of something that can be treated like an externality (although we need not call it that) is a natural monopoly. A natural monopoly is an industry with decreasing cost; that is, a larger enterprise will be able to charge lower prices than a smaller enterprise even though perhaps it earns larger profits. Under these circumstances, a free market will lead to the expansion of some enterprises and the extinction of others until either the cost of additional production by each enterprise begins to rise or until the entire market is supplied by one company. There is a great deal of debate as to whether there are many genuine examples of such industries. If we find such a situation, however, competition is impossible in the long run. Under these circumstances, it is possible for government action to improve the functioning of the economy. Unfortunately, we must emphasize it is only possible. Our experience with agencies such as the Interstate Commerce Commission would seem to indicate that government intervention will normally worsen the economy.

This experience, however, may once again simply indicate that we should improve the efficiency of the government. Government operation of a natural monopoly will perhaps not benefit the economy. It is extremely difficult to tell whether an enterprise with declining costs is actually operating efficiently or not. If the enterprise is under instructions from its owners, that is, the state, not to extort the maximum monopoly profit that can be obtained, that becomes almost impossible. The same problem exists in the case of a regulated monopoly except that in this situation we can predict with a great deal of certainty that the company will not operate efficiently and will, in fact, have much higher costs than is desirable. Still, our bad experience may indicate inept management rather than anything inherent in the nature of things.

Note, however, that if we begin looking for examples of a natural monopoly, we find only a few. If we are in a country that has a high tariff barrier protecting a particular industry, it may well be that that industry is a natural monopoly in that country. Under these circumstances, a repeal of the tariff, rather than government operation, would be the proper remedy. Most other cases are situations in which, for one reason or another, it is inconvenient for several companies to operate in the same area. Electric power production is perhaps the commonest example of this situation, although it is by no means obvious that it would be impossible to have competitive distribution of power.[14] In these cases, and there are many others that may be cited, there is always a question of whether it is indeed inconvenient for several units to operate in one area. Some economists have argued that such things as milk provision and the collection of refuse are natural monopolies. If this were so, then one would anticipate that in any area in which the government does not provide these services, only one private company would operate. This is not, however, what actually occurs. Apparently the cost of having several milk wagons operate on a given street is in fact quite modest.

Note, however, that this particular natural monopoly problem is really quite similar to that of the public good. We have an activity that can be most effectively provided (if the natural monopoly argument is true) for a given region by one particular enterprise. The problem is one of contiguity. The benefits of mass production are obtained without much difficulty by General

14. In the wholesale market, electricity is in fact purchased and sold in a competitive manner in the United States. The monopolies are in the retail distribution of the electricity. We will discuss the possibility of having very small governmental units covering only one or two city blocks. Such a governmental unit that took the trouble to buy its own wiring system and basic transformer (a very modest investment) could presumably purchase its electricity competitively or perhaps could even install a small diesel set. At the moment it is illegal to even experiment with this kind of thing or any other competition in provision of electricity. Here we have a case in which the laws compel a legal monopoly today, but the laws are justified by the argument that it is a natural monopoly. If it is a natural monopoly, it is hard to see why repeal of the laws would be in any way undesirable. If it is not a natural monopoly, the repeal of the laws would reveal that fact. Here we have an opportunity for social experimentation. The reader interested in further discussion of the matter should read Harold Demsetz's "Why Regulate Utilities?" *Journal of Law and Economics*, p. 55.

Motors, a monster organization in a fairly competitive market. In electricity provision, police services, and possibly fire prevention there are economies of scale that can be obtained in production, and it is believed that efficiency requires that contiguous areas be served by the same source of supply.[15]

As an example, in most communities of the United States there are a number of taxi companies and, although subject to price regulation by the city, they are highly competitive. In Los Angeles, however, the city council, in its wisdom, has given each of the taxi companies a monopoly on originating trips in a particular area. This has created a situation in which vast inefficiency exists but clearly the motive was to increase efficiency, producing a more efficient way of allocating taxis. The fact remains, however, that an artificial contiguity was created. Any individual customer is compelled to deal with a given taxi company, and yet the Los Angeles city government cannot understand why rates are high and service is poor. Obviously, here is a case in which contiguity was produced by an unwise law and has greatly reduced the efficiency of the economy. Unfortunately, there are many cases in which the contiguity is not artificial but is a part of the nature of things.

It will be noticed that in all of the examples given, the externality is, in essence, a characteristic of the technology. One can imagine changes in technology that would eliminate the externality. Thus, as we have already noted, any statement as to what the government should or should not do is merely a statement about the present. Changes in the way we do things and improvements in technology of all sorts may well mean that the government should discontinue something it is now doing or begin doing something it is not. The old simple certainties under which one could produce a list of activities that were suitable for governmental activity have ended. The economics of externality are undeniably a scientific advance, but equally undeniably they are going to make life rather more uncertain.

15. Fire prevention originally started in the United States with a number of competing fire engines paid for essentially by insurance companies. It is by no means obvious that the change to the present system benefits anyone except the insurance companies, who no longer have to support the system directly.

THE COSTS OF GOVERNMENT

In this chapter we shall list the various costs of governmental action. We must begin by again emphasizing that the fact that there are costs attached to government is not a criticism of government. If we could improve the functioning of government, of course, we would greatly increase the number of functions allocated to it. Nevertheless, if we are to determine whether a given activity should be entrusted to the market, to governmental control, or to some combination of the two, we must have some idea of the costs and benefits associated with each of these institutions. We have already dealt with externalities, or the costs of the market, and now we will discuss the costs that governmental action may impose in order to learn the other part of the equation.

If we consider externalities, we find that they are large in some areas and small in others, although there are practically no areas in which they are zero. The same is true of costs of government. They are large sometimes and small elsewhere, and practically are never zero. I should like, however, to express a personal opinion that the reader may think is mere prejudice. In my opinion, many of the costs now associated with governmental action simply reflect poor design. It is my opinion that the largest single area for reform in our present society is the government itself, particularly the federal government. If we wish to improve our well-being, raise our standard of living, and improve the "quality of life," our first priority should be a drastic reform of government. Large improvements can be made in this area with correspondingly large benefits.

But this is the subject of other research and other books; let us now turn to the costs that government may impose upon individuals. Strictly speaking, we should use the Paretian apparatus. We could inquire whether those who would benefit from transferring some activity to the governmental sphere would be able to compensate those who were injured, or vice versa. This is, of course, the correct rule assuming that we are not, at the moment, talking about income distribution. Most economists would accept the results as being decisive. In this chapter, however, we will not perform this computation but simply discuss the government cost side. Later when we apply our line of

Reprinted, with permission, from *Private Wants, Public Means: An Economic Analysis of the Desirable Scope of Government* (New York and London: Basic Books, 1970), 96–128.

FIGURE 1
Quantity of a governmental activity

reasoning to specific areas, we will consider whether compensation would be possible for transfers from the private to the public sector. It should be noted that, in general, we will be able to make only qualitative judgments. The empirical data are not yet available for a definitive answer to most of these problems.

Turning, then, to the costs of government; the first such cost is one we have already discussed, the fact that the governmental decision will characteristically not be the optimum decision for any given voter. The individual voter must make an estimate as to what the governmental decision is likely to be and thus decide from his standpoint whether governmental activity is better or worse than private activity. It is clear, however, that there will be a great many voters for whom the governmental decision will be nonoptimal and for these voters, there is a cost (even though the cost may well be less than the cost generated by externalities in the private market). In Figure 1, on the horizontal axis (which is all there is to this figure) is shown the amount of a typical governmental activity that could be undertaken. Let us begin by assuming that a simple majority vote is held to determine the desired amount of activity by the government. If we assume that the voters are randomly distributed along the continuum and that their preference intensities are either equal or randomly distributed, then a simple majority voting process will reach the same point as would be reached if the parties were permitted to bargain for an infinite period of time and finally decide after side-payments how much the government would do.[1]

In other words, under these circumstances simple majority voting will achieve a solution that is equivalent to the Paretian process except for distribution. An individual would have some costs as a result of the fact that his preference is not the majority voting outcome, point A. In practice, of course, he will not be compensated for the reasons we discussed in Chapter 1. If we permitted people not only to vote on the exact amount of the gov-

1. In the next few pages a number of conclusions about the political process will be presented that are based on reasoning contained in James M. Buchanan and Gordon Tullock, *The Calculus of Consent* (Ann Arbor: University of Michigan Press, 1962).

ernment provision but also to seek compensation, we would face an impossible bargaining problem. Hence the individual faces a straightforward uncompensated loss as a result of the governmental action. It is, of course, only inappropriate from his standpoint, rather than from the standpoint of the total group, but theoretically one can compute the average cost that individuals would suffer. In order to make such computations, we would have to make some assumptions of the distribution of the people and the amount to which they are injured by the lack of optimality in the quantity of goods purchased. Instead of making these computations, which would be of little use to us unless they were based upon empirical knowledge that we do not have, let us inquire as to the change in these costs from varying political arrangements.

First, suppose we simply divided the population affected by this governmental activity into two randomly selected samples. What effect would this have? Presumably, if these two samples are large, the midpoints of their distributions, and therefore, the points they would choose by majority voting, would be very close together and very close to point A on our diagram. Nevertheless, they would not be identical. Furthermore, the sample whose optima lay to the right of point A would have more people in it whose optimum lay to the right, and the sample whose optimum lay to the left of point A would have more people whose optima lay to the left. The result of this would be that the average distance of the individuals from the collective decision controlling them would be reduced. Probably with larger samples, this would be a tiny effect, but continuing the subdividing we would get small samples. These small samples would have considerable variance, and this effect would become quite significant. Ultimately, of course, we would have one person in each area and in that event, there would be perfect adjustment.[2] All of this is, once again, to make the point made in the first chapter. In general, the larger the governmental unit the less likely it is that any individual will have his preferences perfectly satisfied. This factor must, of course, be set off against the externality that may be best dealt with by a fairly large governmental unit.

We do not, however, have to select our sample in a random way. Suppose, for example, there were some way of pulling out a sample of about 20 per cent that was heavily skewed toward the left end. If we did this, we would then be able to have two collective decision processes producing two differ-

2. See Yoram Barzel, "Two Propositions on the Optimum Level of Producing Collective Goods," *Public Choice*, 6 (Spring 1969): 31–37.

ent outcomes, one shown at point C, and another shown at point B. This would materially improve the satisfaction of the parties and government cost would be less.

The obvious example, of course, is the use of geographically limited local governments. Characteristically, each small area is indeed somewhat different in its needs from other small areas and hence the division of the government into small jurisdictions is desirable,[3] insofar as it can be done without raising significant externality problems. We need not, however, confine ourselves to this particular method of dividing government. It may be possible to cut out some functional activity rather than cutting out a geographical area. The average private club is an example of this since it provides some type of public good that its members value more than does society in general. Whether this public good is a golf course, flying field, or simply an opportunity for discussion, the fact remains that there is an improvement in the organization of society as a result of the existence of this particular private organization. There are a great many similar specialized boards which control various types of activities. Normally these are, in fact, controlled by the participants in the activity. Unfortunately, in the real world these boards are often mainly concerned with strengthening the cartel power of their members.

Another possible example that has occurred to me would be a special governmental agency to control highways.[4] In the United States, the highways are largely self-supporting, being paid for by gasoline taxes. Thus an arrangement under which the decisions as to the use of highways, construction of new highways, and highway regulations were determined by a special elective body in which only (let us say) automobile owners were permitted to vote might produce an improved allocation of resources, although, of course, it may not. Still, it seems an idea worthy of further consideration.

Note that it is possible only because both the taxes and the benefits accrue to the same people. If we permitted one small group of people to decide how much was to be spent in a given area, but collected the taxes from the population at large, we would then be creating a governmental externality. Unfortunately, such things are also quite common in the present world. They are

3. See Vincent Ostrom, "Operational Federalism: Organization for the Provision of Public Services in the American Federal System," *Public Choice*, 6 (Spring 1969): 1–17, and Gordon Tullock, "Federalism: Problems of Scale," *Public Choice*, 6 (Spring 1969): 19–29.

4. This would not necessarily be a single national organization; a number of local organizations would be possible.

intriguing because they are almost perfect examples of private externalities although they exist in the governmental sphere. Their further discussion must, however, be deferred.

If we examine the type of acts that are passed by Congress or the administrative decisions made by governments, we observe that most of them do not deal with matters that concern the whole population. Characteristically, they involve the expenditure of government funds for the benefit of a fairly small part of the population. Note that this is not said in a critical spirit. Of necessity, the decision to build a road network will be composed of a large number of individual decisions to build each part of it. Each one of these partial decisions to build or to improve a short length of road will primarily benefit only a small portion of the population. Nevertheless, the population as a whole has a real interest in the existence of the entire road network. The same can be said for a large number of other governmental activities.

It must, of course, be admitted that there are a considerable number in any government's list of activities that should never be undertaken. Tulsa, Oklahoma, is now advertising itself as the world's newest port. Unfortunately, this claim is perfectly true. A group of adroit congressmen have succeeded in maneuvering the federal government into dredging a nine-foot channel to Tulsa. Clearly, this is an activity whose benefits are confined to an *extremely* small group of people.

But let us confine ourselves to activities that it is reasonably clear that the government should undertake (such as road repair and extension of the road network). In Figure 2 the preferences of the population are shown with respect to a particular road repair project. Since this road by definition directly serves only a limited area, the bulk of the population has little interest in its being repaired and is aware of the fact that they will pay in taxes for the repair. Their interest, then, is to keep the road in an economical state of disrepair. They are aware of the fact that the economy of the country is to some extent affected by this road, but they feel, quite correctly, that the effect on them is very small compared to the tax cost. The people who live on the road, on the other hand (who will, after all, pay only a small part of the cost of repairing it if it is repaired out of general funds), in general would like to have it repaired, and their preferences are shown at the far right of the diagram in the small hump. If this matter is put to a simple majority vote, we would end up at point B or somewhere to its left. In this case, however, this is not a Pareto optimal decision. The people who have a desire to have the road repaired could, most assuredly, compensate the others for the movement to the

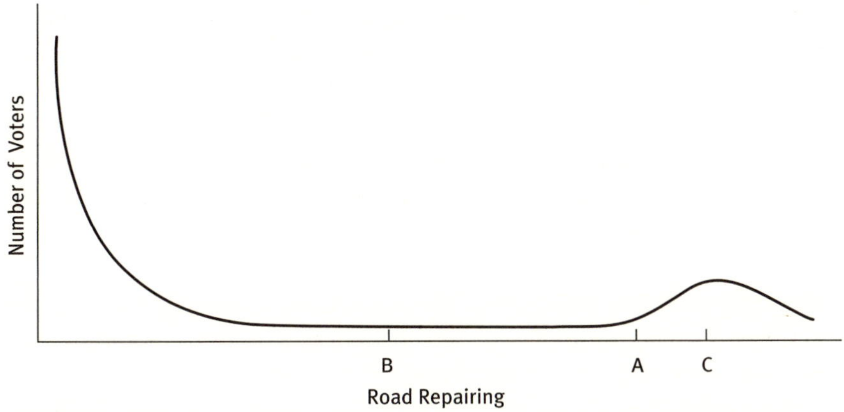

FIGURE 2
Distribution of optima with respect to the quantity of some governmental activity

right. The reason for this is that their interest in the road repair is much more intense than is the interest of the remainder of the voters in the rather small increase in their taxes. The result of computing what would be the optimal bargaining point would be some point such as point A on the continuum.

If we have logrolling, or if we have a central government that makes up programs in general that have the effect of implicit logrolling, then it is likely that the road will be repaired; hence, the institution of logrolling does improve the general satisfaction of the community. Unfortunately, if we have simple majority voting, the amount of repair work put in on the road under these circumstances would be considerably greater than the optimal outcome, the amount C in fact. Under these circumstances, simple majority voting, if taken on each individual issue, leads to point B that probably is hardly (if at all) better than market provision of road services, and logrolling leads to C, which is clearly very much better than market provision.[5] Under either of these assumptions, majority voting does not work as well as it does where the voters are relatively evenly distributed both in intensity and in location along the issue dimension.

Here we have an area in which we could hope for institutional reform. If the number of votes required to cause the road to be repaired is raised from a simple majority to a somewhat higher number, let us say two-thirds, the

5. The reasoning upon which this conclusion and those immediately following are based may be found in Buchanan and Tullock, *The Calculus of Consent*.

logrolling process will continue to work, but the eventual outcome will be moved closer to point A, which is the Pareto optimal outcome. Thus the cost to the individual as a result of placing this particular activity under government control would be less under qualified majority rule. Furthermore, this would mean that various governmental activities, which would be best to leave in private hands under simple majority voting, would be suitable objects for collectivization if we were using something like a two-thirds or three-quarters voting rule. The increase in the required majority by reducing the costs of collective provision of the activity in question would make the collective provision more efficient and hence in these cases would make it desirable to switch from private provision.

In situations such as those shown on Figure 2, there may, however, be another and indeed superior available procedure. Governments have, like Topsy, just grown, but radical institutional revision may still be possible. As a first approximation, let us assume that the tax structure is changed so that when a road is repaired the entire cost of repairing that road falls on the people who live close to it. Under these circumstances, we could set up a separate constituency to vote on the tax and road repair project alone, and they would make their choice considering that all the cost falls upon themselves. This would lead them to want less road repairing than if they can induce someone else to pay the bulk of the cost, and we could use simple majority voting, perhaps, to achieve the optimal result. The problems are obvious, such as the problem of actually defining the area that is to vote, the fact that road repairing and road extension projects are not really continuous over large areas. It is notable that in many parts of the United States at any event, small local government districts with jurisdiction only over certain specialized problems (mosquito abatement is one) have been established. Whether they are the right size and, therefore, produce the most efficient output is something on which I cannot offer any judgment. Here, again, research is needed.

But most economists reading the above paragraph would immediately object that it is not just the people who live right near a given road who have an interest in having it repaired. The voters at the left end of the spectrum want some money spent on the repair of the road, and are aware of the fact that the road network as a whole benefits them. There is again a simple procedure that is available. Let us suppose that the central government under the control of the mass of voters simply subsidizes the local road repair projects. It offers, let us say, to pay half the cost and then permits the local governmental agencies to choose which roads they will repair and how much they will spend.

This clearly is a case in which we are using the standard Pigovian method of subsidy to deal with an externality. This method is widely used. The federal government, for example, is obtaining the construction of an interstate highway system by paying 90 per cent of the cost, but many of the decisions as to where the highway will be built are left to the local authorities who put up the other 10 per cent.

The last example indicates the danger of this type of arrangement. It is fairly clear that the 90 per cent of the cost is vastly in excess of the amount that should be offered for the improvement of roads in a restricted area. Here we have a case in which a mechanism that theoretically seems sensible has been used in such a way that it probably causes substantial diseconomies.[6] The fact, however, does not mean that correct calculations to prevent this result are impossible. The problem is that it is, at present, impossible to design a voting procedure that would produce the correct division between state, central, and local governments.

This discussion of logrolling may impress the reader as not being realistic. We do not often observe individual voters engaging in logrolling—that is done mainly by the representatives in the legislature. We observe direct logrolling only in rare town meetings. There is, of course, something similar to logrolling in party platforms.[7] This criticism is both correct and slightly misleading. We can consider how the government would work if the individual voter had more direct control over it. The fact that he does not have this degree of control over what the government does surely results in a reduction of his satisfaction. If we observe an individual purchasing things in the market, we see that he is able to make direct decisions on a great number of different issues. His decision whether to buy apples or oranges and the quantity of each is made several times a week during the course of a year. In the course of the average year, the individual makes something on the order of 15,000 to 20,000 buying decisions. If we turn to the political sphere, however, we find that the individual characteristically makes very few decisions. Surely this must lead to inefficiency in governmental maximization of his utility function.

6. These diseconomies are not as great as you might think, because as a matter of fact the federal government sometimes refuses to provide the money. Granted the situation in which the federal government has put itself by adopting a 90 per cent subsidy, this is very wise.

7. See my *Entrepreneurial Politics*, Thomas Jefferson Center Monograph #5, University of Virginia.

We can imagine a situation in which an individual entered into a contract with a department store, with the store agreeing to provide the individual with all his needs for a year in return for some initial price—this contract to be renewable from year to year but not changeable during the year. Clearly, this would greatly reduce the individual's satisfaction. This is more or less what we do in government. The individual must choose between two monstrous packages of services every time he votes instead of choosing in an incremental manner from a large number of small packages as he does in the market. The inefficiency is clear, and unfortunately it is not very obvious that a great deal can be done about it, although the situation is more the result of historical accident than of careful design.

There seem to be three basic reasons why we make rather few political choices through the voting process in contrast to the number of economic choices we make in the market. The first of these is simply an obsolete political theory. The second is the fact that voting has traditionally been generally more of a bothersome procedure than purchasing, and hence, people have economized on the number of votes they will cast; and the third is that the information problems that occur in voting are not as severe in the market.

The founding fathers were at one with the rest of the world in believing in a theory of politics that can best be described as aristocratic. It has often been said that they based their work on Montesquieu's misunderstanding of the British Constitution. The theory, however, dates back to Aristotle. In this view, individuals select the best people from the community who then go to a central place and form the government. The individual is not thought of as registering direct preferences on government action, but only as selecting a superior individual who will participate in the government. Under this theory, frequent or detailed elections would not be required. In its pure form, this theory is no longer held by anyone, but in discussing political matters with traditional students of political science, or indeed with most people who have thought about this matter and become accustomed to traditional literature, I have always found they still retain elements of "The Old Belief." To them government is not, like the market, simply a mechanism to obtain our preferences, insofar as possible; it has some higher goal.

I must say that in my discussions with these people I have never been able to find out exactly what this higher goal is.[8] Furthermore, these people themselves recognize differences of opinion as to what these higher goals should

8. Those who are of religious inclination are sometimes able to specify higher goals in terms of whatever particular religion they happen to believe in.

be. Nevertheless, it *is* clear that simply satisfying the individual is not the objective they have in mind. The government is supposed to do things that are good for the individual, not things that the individual wants. Now if we assume that somehow or other governments do have information on what is "good for" the individual, and that they act on it, then the individual himself would find that his preferences are not maximized in the short run, although in the long run they might be. He would have to make a decision as to whether he wanted whatever he wanted now, or whether he proposed to submit to the judgment of someone else who might give a better long run level of satisfaction.[9]

If the individual is not convinced that these people actually know more about what will please him than he does himself, then clearly he will suffer a cost from a government that is organized, not to give him what he wants, but to give him what someone thinks he "should" want. The exact size of this cost would depend on the difference between the individual's preference function and the objectives of the government. There is little that can be said in general except that there is surely no reason to believe that a government that is not attempting to maximize individual satisfaction will, in fact, do so as a by-product. It would seem on the whole that an individual given his choice between market activity and governmental activity would wish to submit relatively little of his life to governmental activity if the government is not, even theoretically, functioning as an apparatus for carrying out individual desires in some aggregative form.

In practice, of course, democratic governments are not attempting to impose higher values.[10] In practice, politicians are the people we elect to office in a democracy, and normally, as part of their campaign, they make promises as to what policies they will carry out. Furthermore, once they are elected, they normally want to be reelected, and hence in choosing their policies, politicians pay careful attention to the preferences of the voters. As we shall see, information problems may lead them to do things that the bulk of the voters may dislike. Their intention, however, is not to impose some higher values on the voter, but to get reelected.

9. Here, again, there is some oversimplification. Many of these people apparently do not really think that what is good for people is what gives them satisfaction even in the long run. Some sort of higher goal, higher, that is, than the happiness of the people, is apparently somewhat cloudily present.

10. Nondemocratic governments may very well be engaged in this. It must be remembered that only a few of the people who have lived in the world have lived under democracies.

The theory that government should not maximize individual preferences or should not try to act as a preference aggregating system can be described as a normative theory. One can say that this is what one would like the government to do, but one cannot say that this is what the governments in democracies actually do. Governments in democracies characteristically are attempting to do things that they think will get them reelected and this means that they must pay careful attention to the preference functions of their citizens. Thus, the individual who wants his preference maximized can feel fairly confident that if some activity is transferred from the private sphere to the government sphere, the government will not simply try to impose its own preference. The government will be engaged in an effort to determine what will gain the most votes and will count his vote among those it wishes to gain. This may not in all cases be of much help to him, but it is better than a government that is trying to reach some goal different from that of the voter.

The previous line of reasoning, I suspect, will strike most economists as being simple and obvious, and they will wonder why I have spent so much time on it. The political scientist, on the other hand, will probably feel that what I am saying is absurd. My last academic appointment was a joint one at both the Political Science and Economics departments at Rice University. I found a complete difference in attitude in my colleagues in these two areas. The political scientists always assured me that I was wrong—that the point of government was not simply to do what the people want. In fact, they thought this would be an inferior objective of government. I was, however, unable to discover exactly what the government was supposed to do, if this was not its objective. "The integrative function" or the "authoritative allocation of values" seem to be slogans with little content, but I may just not be understanding them. In any event, I am compelled to proceed on my present state of information, although I must admit it may be imperfect in this respect.

But if the people who design most modern governments did not operate on the theory that the government was attempting to maximize individual preferences, this is not a reason for not using this theory. If we do follow it, we should consider the possibility of increasing the number of occasions on which individuals are enabled to affect the political order in the direction of their preferences. Our system of competing department stores that provided goods on a yearly contract to everyone would clearly be improved if the contract were shortened to six months or, for that matter, if smaller stores handling rather different lines of business were created and if each individual was permitted to enter into contracts with more than one store. Eventually, of course, if we kept breaking the contracts up into smaller and smaller units, we would reach our present market arrangement. There seems to be no reason why we could not similarly reduce the choice unit in politics, although the information problems, which are to be discussed shortly, place stringent limitations on the amount of such division that can be undertaken in politics.

Before discussing the possibility of having individuals more frequently express their preferences through the vote, perhaps as frequently as in Switzerland, the mechanical problems of voting should be mentioned. The standard method of voting that we have inherited from our ancestors involves the individual's going to a location designated by the authorities, which is frequently not conveniently located and seldom within a few feet of his home or business, and there expressing his opinion by casting a vote. The entire procedure is fairly time consuming. Furthermore, the government itself is put to a considerable expense in maintaining the election machinery. There is no one, as there is in the private market, who has a positive material motive to make the choice process easier or more convenient, and hence we do not have the convenience of transaction that exists in the commercial market. Under modern circumstances, or to be more exact, under the circumstances that will occur in a year or so, this degree of inconvenience is clearly unnecessary. There is no intrinsic reason why the telephone system and computers could not be linked to permit anyone who wished to vote to do so in his own home or place of business.

James C. Miller has worked out a system under which individuals could exercise a great degree of direct supervision over government by casting direct votes, or alternatively if they wished, could designate representatives in the legislature to vote for them. At the moment the system would be rather expensive but if the electronics industry continues to progress, it should become fairly inexpensive in the next five to ten years.[11] Thus, the physical inconvenience of present-day voting is unnecessary. It could be made inexpensive for the voter, and the voting apparatus itself, now a complex and inefficient set of election judges and guards, could be replaced by a computer. With the costs of voting reduced, the voting process could obviously be used to greater advantage. Clearly, in this situation purely mechanical governmental reform is desirable. The present degree of aggregation of voting must lead

11. James C. Miller, III, "A Program for Direct and Proxy Voting in the Legislative Process," *Public Choice*, 7 (Fall 1969): 49–66.

to a lower level of satisfaction than could be obtained if the individual were given an opportunity to express his opinion in a more finely structured way. The techniques are available and they should be implemented.

Nevertheless, if we are talking about current costs of government, the individual is faced with a situation in which he has relatively little control over governmental activity simply because he votes fairly rarely. When he does vote, he normally votes on a highly aggregated bundle of issues, which must be considered when one compares the market with the government. At the moment, then, we would anticipate that individuals would choose market provision over government provision in those circumstances in which they would make the opposite choice if the voting process were reformed.

A large number of elections on a large number of issues would probably be quite a considerable trial for the voter, but in his capacity as customer in the private market, the voter is not required to make decisions on matters in which he does not wish to decide. He can simply refrain from going into the store. Similarly, the existence of a large number of issues on which the voter was permitted to express his preference but not compelled to do so, might well work out the same way. The individual would choose to vote on those issues that he thought might sufficiently affect his interest so that it would be worth the effort to cast the vote and leave the others to his representative. Thus, we may have a large number of votes with relatively few people voting directly at each election. Given perfect information, there is no reason why this process would not work perfectly. As we shall see when we discuss the information limitations that actually exist in the political area, it is possible that this system would work out very badly indeed. Still, it should be remembered that every individual voter does not have to vote in every individual election and, hence, multiplying the number of elections does not necessarily produce an increase in cost for the voter.

In regard to the information problem, however, we find ourselves faced with much greater difficulties. It is possible that the information situation in politics can be improved, but it is fairly clear that voter information will always be much poorer than the information possessed by customers in the market. Unfortunately, we cannot express the exact importance of this relative ignorance. All we know is that this particular difficulty does exist in the political sphere, at least in democracies, and that it should be taken into account. It is possible that empirical research might eventually achieve a measure of this phenomenon, but at the moment we have no such data.

If we consider what empirical work has been done in this area, however, we find extraordinary evidence of ignorance in the political field. Voters who do not know the name of their congressmen are common, and ignorance of the stands taken by the parties on major issues is even more common. Furthermore, the information that people do obtain is largely a by-product of entertainment. Conversation, for example, is a major source of political information-gathering. The traditional response of students of politics to the obvious ignorance of the voters has been to lecture the voters on their duty to learn more. There is no evidence that this has had any great effect, and recently students, beginning with Anthony Downs, have realized that the individual voter has actually behaved quite rationally in not acquiring much information.[12]

The reasons for this can be easily understood if we refer to our small Iowa community of 1,000 making a decision on the level of collective mosquito abatement. The individual voter will be aware (if he is rational) of the fact that the odds are heavily against his being the median voter. If this is so, if he does not learn much about the issue and inaccurately specifies his preference in the voting process, it will have no effect on the outcome unless he makes a gigantic error and actually votes on the other side of the median from his "true position." Even in this case he will cause only a slight change in the outcome; he will move the median by one voter. If the voter suspects that he himself might be the median voter and hence that his preference would determine the outcome, an error on his part would only make a slight difference.

The voter in this case would rationally set off the cost of improving his information against the likely effect that that information will have on the outcome of the election. If the individual is considering purchasing something at a given cost, he is motivated to investigate the qualities of the thing he is purchasing to an extent that discounts the value of an erroneous choice to him. If he is participating in a collective decision process, however, he must further discount the value of the item by the weight of his own contribution to the decision. For further information on this subject, the reader is referred to my book *Toward a Mathematics of Politics.*[13] The outcome of the

12. Anthony Downs, *An Economic Theory of Democracy* (New York: Harper & Row Publishers, Inc., 1958).

13. Gordon Tullock, *Toward a Mathematics of Politics* (Ann Arbor: University of Michigan Press, 1966), chaps. 7, 8.

reasoning is simply that the voter will spend less resources in obtaining information on political issues than on private purchases. Furthermore, this difference can be extremely great. Lastly, this theoretical prediction is abundantly confirmed by empirical investigations.

From the economist's standpoint, however, there might appear to be a strong argument against what I have just been saying. The slogan *de gustibus non est disputandum* has been an important one for a long time, and it might appear that all that the political process should be expected to do is give the voter what he wants regardless of his state of information. Although we do not greatly concern ourselves with his state of information in the marketplace, economists have almost always felt that measures to improve information are desirable. Government acts requiring accurate labeling or requiring organizations to make certain information public have normally been supported by economists. When they have been objected to, the objections have normally taken the form of claiming not that there are no benefits, but that the costs associated with them are greater than the benefits.

Theoretically, we can see that we do concern ourselves with information in spite of the slogan *chacun à son goût* by considering the possibility of a tax on information. Suppose, for example, that people were taxed a specific amount per minute of time spent obtaining information on the purchase of major items. Disregarding the difficulty of administering such a tax, I suppose that economists would agree that this tax would have a substantial excess burden. Furthermore, this excess burden must take the form of reducing the efficiency of the purchasing process, in spite of the fact that the individuals buy whatever car, radio, or other item that they want. Thus, in this case, we are interested in the quality of their expressed preferences.

This mystery, insofar as it is a mystery, is easily explained. Individuals, in fact, have preferences for different qualities of products. The investigation that they undertake in the marketplace is to help them determine whether a particular product or service will provide them with what they want. The more energy they expend in their investigations, the greater is the likelihood that the ultimate purchase will be satisfactory to them. The individual theoretically makes continuous estimates as to whether the additional satisfaction from improving his purchase by acquiring more information is equal to the cost to him of acquiring that additional information. This cost to a large extent is the delay in making the purchase. He continues to acquire information until the margins meet, and then he buys.

In the political marketplace the problem is that the amount of information that one would normally acquire is usually extremely small. If my decision on the amount that should be purchased will only have a tiny and probably insignificant effect on the amount that I do purchase through a collective procedure, it is likely that I will invest relatively little time and effort in becoming well informed. Thus, I will normally make a much poorer adjustment to my basic preferences than I would in the market. People in the real world clearly behave this way. Furthermore, the political parties and candidates seem to be aware of this and plan their arguments to the voter in terms of a relatively ignorant audience. There seem to be three basic political "platforms." One is an effort by the candidate to impress people that he is indeed a nice fellow, which is probably the major single political activity of most candidates. The canvassing in England and the more elaborate campaign methods normally used in the United States where the constituencies are larger both have this as their major objective.

A second "argument" that is very widely used in most political systems is an effort to get voters who have no preference at all to vote for their candidate simply by asking them to do so. Stephen Shadegg's *How to Win an Election* is a clear and direct statement of this technique by a man who has had great experience in organizing elections.[14] The issues are also discussed by the candidates because there are various people who are interested in specific issues. Normally, however, the people who are interested in the issues are only interested in one or two issues that directly concern them. The minority of the populace who are interested in all of the issues, the intellectuals, are not only a minority but as far as we can see they do not significantly change their position from election to election and hence are not likely to be affected by a discussion of the issues. Once again, I have discussed these matters in greater detail in *Toward a Mathematics of Politics.*[15]

The costs inflicted upon us by this relatively poor information in the political process must be great. We can now turn to the question of what can be done about it. There seem to be several possibilities. Preaching has been widely tried by political scientists and has had little effect. A second possibility would be an effort to introduce fair labeling laws into the political area of

14. Stephen C. Shadegg, *How to Win an Election* (New York: Taplinger Publishing Co., 1964).

15. Gordon Tullock, *Toward a Mathematics of Politics*, chaps. 7, 8.

the type now in effect in the commercial area. The problems connected with these laws are extreme—they are not so much technical problems in the pure sense as they are problems that are raised by the fact that the politicians themselves would, of necessity, enforce these laws. One would worry about the prospect of the party in power using these laws to damage its opponents.[16] Nevertheless, it seems that there should be some experimentation carried out along these lines. Individuals are not totally uninterested in obtaining information on political matters; they just have a very slight interest. Under these circumstances, compelling people to provide information may have much more effect than it would have in the market. But this is merely a suggestion; I cannot be sure that it would be of any great use. In any event, it is a palliative and does not cure the problem as a whole.

Another prospect would be to eliminate the present strong social pressure to vote. It is likely that if these pressures were reduced, the total number of people voting would decline, and the people who stopped voting would, on the whole, be the less informed. I do not know how much this would improve the situation, but it surely should have at least some helpful effect. The person who voluntarily chose not to invest his resources in going to the polls would also likely be the person who had chosen not to invest resources in becoming informed. Thus our rather elaborate indoctrination in the schools and the public opinion molding activities at election periods for the purpose of getting out the vote are probably counterproductive.

As mentioned before, the fact that the voter is badly informed means that the optimum detail in voting choices is not likely to involve as much differentiation as that observed in market choice. It still seems likely, however, that at least some additional differentiation would be desirable. Furthermore, it might make the information problem easier for the voter. It may be easier to make up one's mind on ten different votes, each of which governs 10 per cent of government activity, than it is to make a decision on only a single vote that covers the entire scope of governmental activity. Lastly, if the division of the activity covered by the individual elections involved more use of local governmental agencies, then the voter actually has a net reduction in his total decision load. If highways are decided upon by a national agency upon which we vote, then each individual must decide how many highways are to be built

16. Treason doth never prosper; what's the reason?
Why if it prosper, none dare call it treason.
Sir John Harington, *Epigrams, of Treason*

all over the United States. If, on the other hand, highway expenditures are chosen locally, he will make decisions only about the local highways. Surely the latter is likely to be a more informed decision. This factor would, as is usual when we talk of the cost of government, have to be laid off against the externalities that could be brought under control if we had a national or indeed world government building our highways.

There is one way in which one can conceive of government services being provided where the individual voter-customer would have the same incentives to obtain information as he does in the market. Americans move a great deal; the average family moves from one city to another every five years. Characteristically this move will involve, among other things, a consideration of the governmental services that are obtainable in the various localities. In fact, in the area surrounding large cities, movements from one area to another are not infrequently caused by differences in governmental services. Superior schools, in particular, are likely to attract families to a given suburb.

Clearly, the individual in "purchasing" government by deciding where to live is in much the same position as the individual who is buying a car. His decision is controlling, and hence, he is motivated to obtain information. Thus, if we could somehow arrange a competitive market in governments, we would anticipate that the information problems we have been discussing would be greatly reduced. Something of this sort actually does exist in the United States, and I suspect, in other countries. Unfortunately, for a variety of reasons, it is not very well developed and is probably doomed to remain permanently relatively undeveloped.

There are two aspects to the "competitive provision of government." The first is private provision of a limited collection of "governmental" services. There are now a number of private enterprises that establish communities in which a great many potential externalities have been internalized by the management. Characteristically, they do not provide the total scope of governmental services and thus do not produce totally competitive governments. It is an interesting, but as far as I know, completely unexplored, question as to whether or not one might extend this idea so that private corporations provided the total of governmental services for some particular area. The dangers are obvious, but it is not by any means certain that they could not be overcome. In any event, at the moment these organizations (which will be discussed in more detail later) are a relatively minor and modest feature of the political landscape. Normally, they provide only a small part of the services that would ordinarily be provided by government.

The second area in which governmental competition exists is the previously mentioned suburban area surrounding a large city, where a large number of communities may be found in which individuals make choices among these communities. The reason that this competitive market in governmental services does not function like a private competitive market is that the individual "enterprises" are not run by profit maximizing entrepreneurs. Once an individual moves into a community he becomes a voter, and the voters in the communities behave very much like voters elsewhere. Thus, although the individual makes his initial choice of the community in which he lives in much the same way as he makes his choice of a car, he is choosing among communities that are run by relatively inattentive voters. Furthermore, the motives that may lead the voters in some particular community to favor desirable political institutions in order to attract immigrants from other communities, are not very strong.

Thus, although the individual moving into a suburban community makes a choice that is as well informed as his market choices, the communities themselves are not managed by people who are vigorously attempting to increase the number of "customers" they receive. In consequence, this "market" works badly. Nevertheless, anyone who has lived in a large metropolitan area will realize that this factor (the tendency of people to move in and out of communities depending upon the line of services offered) does exert some pressure for increased efficiency. Here, again, it might be possible to reorganize government so that individual choices would be of greater importance. Unfortunately, I can offer no present ideas as to how this can be done, but it does not seem to be totally beyond the mind of man.

In most discussions of the costs of government, bureaucracy is emphasized. Complaints about bureaucracy in government are an omnipresent feature of modern life and such complaints are in general justified. Clearly, most modern governments are appallingly badly organized. If we are considering placing a particular activity under governmental control, we should, of course, take into account the fact that this means expanding an already swollen bureaucracy, and that the particular activity we are placing under governmental control will probably be handled in much the same way as the Post Office.

But it is reasonable to ask whether this cost is necessary. It is certainly true that today we have vast and inefficient bureaucracies. Is there no way of producing more efficient bureaucracies? If we could organize the government in a more efficient way, presumably we would wish to entrust more activities to it because its cost would be less. Before discussing the possibilities of improvement, we might inquire briefly why it is that General Motors, a very large organization, seems to have less difficulty with its bureaucracy than does the smaller government Post Office. First, we must note that it is not true that General Motors has absolutely no difficulty; in fact, anyone who has had contact with large corporations is aware of the fact that bureaucracy is also a real problem there. It is, however, a lesser problem. There is now a beginning of serious research into internal organization of large hierarchal structures of which any bureaucracy is an example. From this research it would appear that the difficulties that most Western nations have with their governmental bureaucracy to a very large extent simply represent poor design, whereas the types of difficulties that are faced by General Motors are, to a considerable extent, the minimum residual that can be obtained with good design. There are, however, as we shall see, certain special problems that would perhaps make governmental bureaucracy less efficient in any event.

The problem faced by any designer of a bureaucracy is that he must employ human beings to act as his bureaucrats, and they have individual objectives that are not necessarily those that would be desired by the organizer of the bureaucracy. The larger the bureaucracy and the less it is possible to reduce its objectives to some single numerical measure such as profit, the more likely it is that the individual bureaucrats will be able to follow their individual preferences rather than the preferences of the "organization." Thus, reduction in size and increasingly detailed specification of what is wanted from the bureaucracy will normally help. In this connection, William Niskanen, who has had many years of experience in attempting to improve the efficiency of one particularly large bureaucracy, the Department of Defense, has suggested various methods whereby one might impose upon segments of the gigantic bureaucracy somewhat similar conditions as those faced by segments of General Motors.[17] These proposals are at the moment tentative, and I do not think anyone (certainly not Niskanen) regards them as more than suggestions for research. But they do indicate that a possibility of drastic reform in bureaucracy does exist and that, therefore, great improvements in the functioning of government might be possible. Again, such improvements would make it sensible to entrust a greater portion of our society to government hands instead of to the market.

17. William Niskanen, "The Peculiar Economics of Bureaucracy," *American Economic Review*, 58, no. 2 (May 1968): 293–305.

There appears, however, to be one very serious problem in connection with governmental bureaucracies as opposed to private bureaucracies, at least in a democracy. Characteristically, in a democracy, minorities who are deeply concerned with a given issue have disproportionate influence. Unfortunately, the bureaucrats themselves are such an intense minority, and they are interested in the expansion of their power and financial base. Thus, they are able to, in part, specify that one of the objectives toward which any governmental enterprise will aim is the benefiting of its employees. Indeed, in numerous cases, it would appear that benefits to the employees and to the private companies that supply the given segment of the bureaucracy are the principal "goods" generated by the organization.

This means that many programs do not really achieve very much in the way of meeting their ostensible objectives. At the time that I write this book, the United States government has for a number of years been engaging in something known as the "War on Poverty," which has involved the spending of large sums of money to allegedly help the poor. It is notable, however, that the help that the poor have actually received from these programs is really quite modest.[18] It apparently costs about $15,000 to $20,000 a year per person to set up a program that will train a poor person to occupy a job in which he might receive, after a number of years, a yearly salary of $3,000 to $4,000. The seepage into the bureaucratic morass (and, it must be admitted, into paying off local politicians) is much greater than the nominal impact of the program. Clearly, one of the major reasons for this is that the bureaucrats vote. They are an intense minority who are able to convert many bureaucracies from agencies aimed at defending the country, suppressing crime, and helping the poor into agencies whose principal output is providing amenities for bureaucrats and for whom the defense of the country, repression of crime, and aid to the poor are somewhat of a by-product.

But here again, we come up against the economist's motto, *de gustibus non est disputandum*. If what the voters want is employment for themselves, as bureaucrats, then why not? The answer to this question would appear to be that most of us would not in fact be interested in setting up a bureaucracy ostensibly for the purpose of helping the poor if its principal real effect would be merely to employ a number of bureaucrats at above the market wages, with very little help to the poor. If our choice is leaving the poor to the tender

18. In the trade, the phenomenon is known as "feeding the sparrows by feeding the horses."

mercies of private charity, or placing them in the hands of a bureaucracy, which, in fact, will pay little attention to the poor and very much attention to its own private gain, we might well choose the private charity even if we thought the private charity was basically quite inadequate. In other words, it may be that the fact that bureaucrats are able to distort agencies into instrumentalities for supporting themselves would mean that the cost of establishing such agencies would be vastly in excess of the benefits for any but the bureaucrats.

This is speculation, however, and we cannot be sure how large the effect of this type of bureaucratic activity is. It should be noted that theoretically there is a fairly simple and straightforward remedy. We could deprive the bureaucrats, their families, government suppliers, indeed anyone who obtains a significant portion of his income from dealing with the government, of the vote. Radical as this proposal may seem, it is hard to offer any very strong argument against it. The bureaucrats are such a large part of our population that it is unlikely that their attitudes toward political matters are greatly different from those of the population as a whole, if we abstract out only their attitude toward their own bureau's expansion and their own salary. They should be simply a very large random sample. If this is so, then the only difference resulting from the abolition of the vote of bureaucrats would be that the bureaucrat's interests would not be pushed by a particular pressure group of voters.

Since the bureaucrats would obtain the full market value of their services without this type of pressure (because they cannot be hired if they are not paid as much as they can obtain elsewhere) this would not harm them unless they are now receiving more than the full value of their services. It seems difficult to argue that bureaucrats should receive more than the value of their services. Thus, it would seem to be difficult to produce any valid argument against depriving bureaucrats of the vote. Needless to say, I do not anticipate that this logical difficulty will significantly impede criticism of this portion of my book.

In this chapter, we have reviewed many distinct and fairly sizable costs of governmental action. In the previous chapter we covered externalities that made it certain that private activities in many areas would have greater costs. In every case, the problem that we face when deciding whether some activity shall be market or governmental is the minimization of these costs, or stating the same thing in opposite terms, the maximization of the benefit. Clearly, neither method is perfect, and clearly, we are choosing between two techniques that will produce less than if we lived in a perfect world. There is no reason to be terribly upset about this; most institutions and devices we use lack theoretical perfection.

Finally, it should be noted that although improvements in market organization are rather hard to find today, there are a great many improvements possible in governmental activities. Even though we may now regard the costs of governmental activities as being excessive with respect to some activity, it is possible that with improved governmental design we could reduce the governmental cost and hence make it desirable to shift this activity from the private to the public sector. Still, as things exist today, it would appear that there are a great many activities presently being carried on by governmental agencies that could reasonably be shifted to the market sphere.

REMEDIES

This chapter examines the various remedies that can be applied when externalities exist; the following chapters then consider specific problems in which we can apply our newly acquired knowledge. It must be remembered, of course, that selecting a suitable institution to deal with an externality, in a sense is playing God. In the real world, these decisions are likely to be made either by governments or by businessmen. Neither is free from error; mistakes are made. Furthermore, the decision-making processes used in democratic governments ensure a suboptimal outcome. Nevertheless, we should consider what can be done on the assumption that we can make a perfect choice of institutions. Later we can examine the institutions of the real world and make recommendations that are not totally unrealistic.

Let me begin by describing three institutional arrangements that I think are not normally considered by economists. The first of these is exemplified by Belvedere Park where I spent most of my summers as a boy. About fifty years before I was born, some people (living mainly in the town of Belvedere, Illinois) had purchased a plot of land on Lake Geneva in southern Wisconsin. The plot was about 500 feet wide and almost a mile long with the 500-foot frontage on the lake and the other end on what, at that time, was the only available access road. It was a very attractive piece of real estate. Lake Geneva is a beautiful lake, and the tract was not only wooded throughout, but a small stream began about 1,000 feet from the lake and wound entirely within the strip (receiving numerous small tributaries) down to the lake.

The owners of the land formed a corporation. Each building lot carried with it a share of the corporation. These lots were placed in two lines along the side of the strip from very close to the lake shore to about the headwaters of the small stream. Thus, the owner of each of these lots (about forty) not only had the right to build a house on his particular lot, but also had considerable influence on the environment in which that building would stand.[1] By the time that I became old enough to notice Belvedere Park at all, this institution had been in existence for a fairly long period of time and had developed into what one might call a climax form. Naturally, I did not realize that

Reprinted, with permission, from *Private Wants, Public Means: An Economic Analysis of the Desirable Scope of Government* (New York and London: Basic Books, 1970), 129–57.

1. There were some restrictions on the type of building that could be constructed.

there was anything particularly remarkable about this organization, and unfortunately as a child I did not observe it carefully enough so that I can be absolutely certain that everything I relate here is true. Nevertheless, I think that this is an accurate account.

As I have said, the houses were arranged along the edge of the tracts in two long lines at right angles to the shore of the lake. The lots nearest to the lake were the most valuable and had been sold at correspondingly higher original sale prices. In general, the quality of the houses tended to decline as one went farther away from the lake. Nevertheless, each householder held a share of the stock, and by the time I arrived on the scene there had been some concentration of ownership. Several people owned more than one house and therefore had several votes. Thus, as in most corporations, there was weighted voting. In general, the houses were located on very small plots, not because they were particularly crowded, but because a center strip about 350 feet wide was maintained as a park. This center strip, which contained practically all of the main stream, although not of its tributaries, was gardened by park personnel. They mowed the lawns of the house lots, although gardening around the houses was done by the individual householder. My grandmother, who owned the cottage in which I used to spend my summers, was very proud of the rare ferns that she had coaxed into growing directly under the front porch of her cottage. She also was able to raise watercress in a small tributary stream that was one of the boundaries of her lot.

Since the park had first been formed, another road had been built much closer to the lake than the original road so that the park now consisted of two tracts on either side of the new road. All of the cottages were located between the lake and the road. On the other side of the road there were some tennis courts, a number of garages, an open-air parking lot, and a rather large club building that had once been used for social purposes and was still intermittently used for this purpose at the time I was there. Basically, however, during my childhood, the clubhouse was a place where boats were stored and where the children could play on rainy days. It performed both of these functions admirably. The long strip of woodland leading up to the other road was also, of course, a place where the children could amuse themselves.

Basically, however, most of the children's play and indeed most of the social activities of the camp in general revolved around the lakefront where the camp maintained two small piers for rowboats and one large pier for swimming. A resident of the camp had built a rather elaborate diving float, and this was anchored off the pier. Another resident had, with the permission of the camp council, built a small private pier to accommodate his speed boat. This small private pier was also available to anyone who wanted to use it for swimming or fishing. All of these piers had to be dismantled in the fall, stored, and then rebuilt in the spring. This was, of course, done by the camp.

The waterfront as a whole was owned collectively by the camp. It was the custom around Lake Geneva for all pieces of property on the waterfront to maintain footpaths about ten or fifteen feet from the shore. This meant that it was possible for energetic members to walk completely around the lake, a distance of about twenty miles. Some public utilities were provided in the camp, but in a rather unusual way. An access road from the main road had been built by the park and was kept in good condition. There were continual problems about the parking rules with respect to this access road. As a general rule, the continual small changes in the parking regulations were motivated by the fact that the road was really too narrow for permanent parking but that almost everyone found it convenient to park their car in front of their house to load and unload. Attempts at developing a set of rules that would permit people to load and unload from their cars but would not result in so many cars being stopped on the road that traffic was impossible led, as I suppose was predictable, to a long series of petty bickerings and petty changes in the rules.

Electricity was provided by a local private utility. Individual householders purchased their electricity directly but the corporation was responsible for ensuring that the utility did not place its poles down the central park. The electricity was delivered by poles running along the property line behind the houses, and hence did not affect the pleasant appearance of the camp. Water was, oddly enough, an individual matter left to each householder. When I was a small boy, rams in the main stream were the principal source of water with each house having its own ram. Gradually, as I grew older, these rams were replaced by electric pumps. I can recall to this day the chorus of a dozen rams in the stream in front of my grandmother's house. Their replacement by electric pumps was, no doubt, efficient but a very distinct reduction of a positive externality.

Sewage was, in general, also privately provided, with the cottages each having a private septic tank. The corporation was, of course, very much interested in the possibility of contamination of householder A's spring by waste from householder B's septic tank, and engaged in fairly close supervision of the location and design of the septic tanks. There was, oddly enough, another small collective enterprise in the camp. About eight of the cottages that were near the lake had built a very large joint septic tank. This small additional corporation was apparently handled quietly on a cooperative basis by the houses that had provided it. My grandmother's house was not one of them, and therefore I know very little about this institution.

The camp itself provided substantially all local governmental services. Since it was occupied only during the summer when students would normally be on vacation, schooling was not provided. What little police protection was needed was obtained by arranging for one of the men in the camp to be a deputy sheriff equipped with a badge and a gun. So far as I know, neither of these two items was ever used. Substantially, there was no fire protection except insofar as the local water supplies were quite sizable. Furthermore, the camp provided certain other "public services." For example, on the Fourth of July the camp purchased and set off an elaborate display of fireworks. Various other social activities were organized by the entire camp or by small groups of people within the camp. The formal government of the immediate area appeared only as an exploiter. A small village located about a mile from the camp had arranged to hold all of its elections in the winter when the camp would be empty. It then annexed a sizable portion of the shoreline of Lake Geneva, including Belvedere Park, and taxed this area for its own benefit. We, of course, received the general benefits of the state and national government.

The intriguing feature of this institution, from the standpoint of present-day economics, is the very neat way in which it internalized a very large number of externalities that we normally either think of as problems that cannot be solved or as political issues. Furthermore, it is of considerable interest that the particular services that were collectively provided by this "voluntary government" were in many ways quite different from those that are traditional. Perhaps as a holdover from my boyhood experience in this area, I tend to think that if there were very small governmental units (of which more is said in the latter part of this chapter) collective gardening might become much more common than it is today. The problem of the rosebushes that we have now discussed several times could be relatively easily dealt with if all the people in a given small neighborhood were organized in some kind of collective entity.

But let me turn to my second institutional arrangement. Once again, and this will also be true of my third, it is an institution with which I have had considerable personal contact. It is, in fact, the apartment house in which I formerly lived (2016 Main, Houston, Texas). This large apartment house also had as one of its major objectives the internalization of a large collection of externalities. In the first place, the owners had designed the apartment house in such a way that the walls, if not completely soundproof, were sufficiently close to that objective so that we did not annoy our neighbors even if we made quite a bit of noise in our apartments. Second, they had provided us with an elaborate set of communal facilities for our use. There was an extremely handsome entry foyer, for example, which was not only attractive but was used also for various social events. Social life, in general, was actively organized by the management of the apartment house. Free coffee and rolls were provided on Sunday morning to all tenants, and a hostess was provided who made strong efforts to promote "socialization" among the tenants. Furthermore, the management had made arrangements so that there would be a coffee shop, a small store that sold food and incidentals, and even a barber shop and a nightclub on the premises. I am sure all of these things operated at a loss, but the management apparently believed that providing these special services to their tenants increased the value of the property as a whole.

Needless to say, the management at 2016 Main also provided a large number of other services. Indoor parking space, maid service if you wanted it, and laundry facilities through both an office of a local laundry and dry cleaning establishment and coin-operated washing and drying equipment on the premises. There was a ceramics course available for those who wished to take it, and a recreation room in which people could hold parties. The management also made arrangements for regular bridge sessions in order to promote social relations among its tenants, and an art show was recently held.

Altogether, 2016 Main is another example of the internalization of externalities. It is, in fact, a rather small example. The same kind of thing on a much larger scale is now becoming common in the United States, in which designed communities owned by one landlord and having a population of 30,000 people are not unknown. Generally speaking, such communities find that the necessity of paying taxes for a number of governmental services, whether or not they themselves provide these services, makes it impossible for them to provide a full line of such services. Nevertheless, they do internalize a number of externalities that are not internalized in the ordinary community and probably could do an excellent job of providing many of these governmental services.

To anticipate some discussion mentioned later in the book, one of the objectives of the urban renewal program in the United States is the creation of the possibility for this type of internalization of externalities. Land that is now divided into a number of small plots is condemned by the government and then resold as a unit to someone who will develop it as a whole. The program has not worked very well, but this seems to be a case of bad management, and not an inherent characteristic.[2]

My third institutional system is one I observed while I was in China, but in fact in variant forms it is characteristic of the whole of Asia from, roughly speaking, Persia to the northern boundary of Manchuria.[3] In China the bulk of the population are farmers who live in the country. Traditionally they were organized in small, basically self-governing, villages, which combined with a centralized despotism—for the higher level of government has apparently arisen from what Karl Wittfogel refers to as "declining marginal returns on administration."[4] These local communities were, of course, creatures of the despotic central government and had to be responsive to its wishes, but central government was relatively weak in China. Central government was not greatly concerned about such matters as the placement of a road in a village, the location of a school, or the amount of tax to be raised for *local* facilities. Consequently, these small, self-governing local governments in fact have had a very high degree of autonomy.

The interesting feature of this institution is that these small village organizations (which do not really seem to be much different from the organizations existing in New England) were retained for large cities. A large city in China is legally simply a unit of the same sort as a similar population unit would have in the countryside. There are varying numbers of small neighborhoods that have similar powers and the same type of self-government as they would have if they were villages in the countryside. Such neighborhoods are then grouped into circuits and counties in the same way they would be if they were in the countryside. Under the old imperial government, for example, the city of Peking was legally about 3,000 villages grouped into three counties. Thus, the Chinese attitude is that local matters should be dealt

2. The program at the moment is in disrepute in the United States, because it does seem to have been used to a very large extent for the purpose of removing Negro communities from places where they are inconvenient from the standpoint of the whites. The title "Negro Removal" has been given to the program by a great many people of liberal bent.

3. Perhaps I should say *was* characteristic. It may be in the process of complete destruction today. In my opinion this will be a most unfortunate example of *The Cost of Economic Growth*, Edward J. Mishan (New York: Frederick A. Praeger, Inc., 1967).

4. Karl Wittfogel, *Oriental Despotism* (New Haven: Yale University Press, 1954).

with locally; and by locally they mean by some small group of people, not by the city of Peking acting as a whole. They would not quarrel with the statement that there are a number of matters that cannot be dealt with at this level, but they realize that there are a number that can be.

Once again, this general institution spreads over much of Asia and is also found in India and Indonesia. In the cities there are little clusters, which, perhaps without any legal recognition at all, are to a considerable extent self-governing. Needless to say, their powers are never so impressive as to significantly reduce the control of the central government, but they do provide a method of dealing with many local problems at the local level. It seems to me that this is an institution that we could well copy in the Western world. If areas of a few blocks were permitted to establish their own little governmental agency to take care of such matters as street cleaning, and perhaps the purchase of public utilities in the wholesale market, as well as doing some supplementary gardening, and controlling the entire range of things that Mishan refers to as "amenities," it seems to me that many externalities could be eliminated.

Such local governments have a further advantage such as that found in some communities in the United States even though we do not have these very small "village" organizations in our cities. That advantage is the possibility of moving if one dislikes the government of a particular community. Thus, it is possible to develop decentralized communities catering to different tastes. In general, the smaller such communities are, the better they would be able to cater to specialized tastes but the fewer externalities they would be able to internalize. On the other hand, in a massive city such as New York, it would seem reasonable that not only would there be organizations dealing with the problems of a few blocks, but also larger subdivisions dealing with larger problems.

As far as I can see from the examination of public opinion polls, Harlem, for example, would be much better governed if the inhabitants had control over a great range of the public services they now receive. It seems certain that they would acquire an all-Black police force, but it seems equally certain that this all-Black police force would then proceed to establish law and order in areas where the present police force does not. Furthermore, the issue of police brutality would not arise. The people who are now most injured by the state of public order in Harlem are the inhabitants of Harlem, and the public opinion data indicate that they are fully aware of this.

It is probably the racial overtones of the problem that have led a great many people in the United States to turn toward the development of neighborhood governments within the present cities. It would, indeed, benefit the Negro communities in such places as New York and Chicago, but we should not assume that that is its principal advantage. It also seems likely that, in general, these Negro communities themselves are large enough so that a great many services should be controlled at a smaller, or "block" level. Obviously, communities that are all white or that have some other ethnic coloration would also be better governed if there were neighborhood control of a number of problems. It should be emphasized again that these very small local governments would not only be able to carry on some of the present-day activities in a way that is more in accord with local preferences, but it seems likely that they would also be able to undertake various additional activities.

The cities of New York and Houston, for example, must, to a considerable extent, provide the same service throughout the city, which means that for many activities it would be wiser for an individual to keep complete control himself rather than to transfer control to such a large organization. If he were given the alternative of transferring control to a small organization, close to his own interest and in which his own vote is actually a significant matter, he might well find that further services should be transferred to collective control. I have mentioned gardening and mowing lawns, and it does seem to me that these are particularly obvious examples.

Note that the use of small governmental units would not make it particularly difficult to obtain the advantages of normal economies of scale. There is no reason why these small governmental units should not enter into contracts with larger agencies to provide specialized service as is now done, for example, by many small cities in Los Angeles County. The problem here, of course, is one of what we have called contiguity rather than the economies of scale. When there are only economies of scale, when a large producer can produce more cheaply than a small producer, there is no reason why a very small local community should not purchase from the large producer. When, however, efficient production requires that the large areas all receive exactly the same service from exactly the same producer, then we have the contiguity problem, a special type of externality, and it is no longer possible to obtain economies by contract. It may still be possible, however, for a group of small governmental units to organize a cooperative to provide the services. Nevertheless, as the number of small units increases, the bargaining problems also increase, and it becomes more difficult to attain voluntary agreement. It must be noted, however, that our experience with the suburbs would seem to indicate that the very elaborate and complex governmental arrangements providing specialized services can be negotiated among large numbers of small governmental units.

The existence of many small governmental units provides an opportunity for a wide diversity of services and hence for a good deal more satisfaction for the citizens who are permitted to choose from among these services, but it is unlikely that this wide diversity will be fully utilized as long as the individual units are democratic. As stated previously, there are a number of reasons why voters are unlikely to bother to thoroughly inform themselves. Furthermore, the voters have only relatively weak motives for attempting to attract other people into their district or to prevent people from leaving it. Thus, they are unlikely to attempt to produce a specialized set of municipal services in order to attract people into the area. A private corporation that somehow had control of the government might be motivated to produce a combination of services that was considerably different from the standard set in order to appeal to a minority. Thus, the provision of a wide diversity of services by local governments probably is not possible under present institutions. It would seem desirable to experiment by permitting individual companies to provide the full range of government services in small areas in order to make possible this greater diversity. As long as the areas were small and anyone could move out of them, there does not seem to be any obvious reason why such experiments would endanger anyone's rights.

Another problem raised by the use of small governmental units, or indeed, by any method of eliminating externalities that does not take in the entire solar system, is the boundary between units. Insofar as two adjacent governmental units are dealing with the same externality in much the same way, it may well be that the boundary between the two communities will have no observable effects. If, however, the two communities decide to deal with a problem differently (one, for example, by deciding it doesn't want to worry about mosquitoes and the other by having a highly active mosquito abatement program), then there will be externalities at the border of the units. The cost of these externalities certainly should be considered and weighed against the advantages of obtaining a degree of mosquito abatement that is in close accord with the desires of the people who are in each of the governmental units. One does not wish to internalize all externalities. A finite possibility exists that some person from Afghanistan will meet you and be offended by your clothing. This externality could only be dealt with by giving the

Afghans some control over your choice of shirts. Most people would agree that in this case the externality is of less importance than the preferences of the "local unit."

This discussion has been merely a cursory examination of three institutional arrangements that should be given greater consideration. Let us now turn to an examination of the technical methods of reducing externalities. In general, if I feel that someone is causing me external costs or that by altering his behavior he could provide me with greater external economies than I now receive, I have two methods of influencing his action. The first of these is to attempt to arrange some kind of agreement with him on a private basis, the second is to attempt to manipulate the government into action. My choice between these two methods will normally involve a judgment on my part as to their cost and benefit. A second question that I must consider is exactly what kind of change I want in order to alter his behavior. I might, for example, want to have him completely desist from doing something or I might simply be interested in his paying me compensation for doing it. There are, as we shall see later, many different ways in which such problems can be dealt with.

Let us, however, begin by considering the private or governmental choice. Traditionally, I think, governmental action was distinguished from private action on the grounds that governmental action is backed by force and private action characteristically is not. Recently, some scholars have been distinguishing between collective action and private action in terms of the decision process. Private action, in this view, requires unanimous assent; collective action is based upon a decision process other than that requiring unanimous agreement. Either of these definitions raises problems. I can, for example, hire a private police force that will make use of force to protect my property as many people have done. In using the force definition, it is difficult to decide whether this is a government or private act.

I prefer the distinction based on the presence or absence of a requirement of unanimous assent; but with this definition, a great many things that are normally referred to as private, that is, corporations, are called collective. For the remainder of the chapter, however, let us ignore these difficult problems and follow common practice.

Turning then to the actual procedures that may be used, the simplest way of dealing with an externality is to make some change in the property arrangements. Suppose that my neighbor is proposing to construct a building that will cut off my view. I can approach him and offer to pay him a sum of money to give me the air rights over his plot; that is, to sell me that part of his "landholding" that is more than thirty feet above the surface. He can then no longer build a building at that level without my permission. The property that he holds has been transferred in part to me. Approximately the same situation can be handled in another way. I could pay my neighbor to add a covenant to his deed not to erect a building more than thirty feet high and provide that this covenant will remain in the deed in future sales of the property to other persons.

This type of covenant, restricting the use of property, is common, and frequently complex and detailed. Residential property in particular is likely to be subject to such covenants for the purpose of usually preventing the generation of negative externalities on neighboring property. This widespread activity is the most common single method of reducing the number of short-range externalities. As far as I know, it has not been thoroughly studied by economists, but it surely would repay a good deal of serious research.

As we have noted a number of times before, bargaining is extremely difficult if a number of persons are involved. Thus, if an externality is evident that affects a number of people and/or is generated by a number of people, it is unlikely that we will be able to enter into such a private bargain. In this case, I might rationally attempt to lobby the government into doing something about the matter. The government remedy might, however, also be a modification of property rights. One of the normal activities of government is to define and enforce property rights, although it can, of course, change these property definitions.

An obvious example of this modification would be the development of setback rules in our larger cities. The early builders of skyscrapers held rather literally to the view that they owned all the space over their land and simply built skyscrapers that covered the entire surface of the ground. Anyone who has visited Wall Street in New York City is aware of the rather gloomy effect of this type of architecture.

Eventually the city government, in essence, confiscated part of the airspace above any plot of land in New York. Setback rules were enacted that made it impossible for the owner of property in New York to build an extremely tall building on all of his property. He must taper his building inwardly at the upper floors in order to avoid cutting off light and air from his neighbors. These laws clearly altered what the individual owned. They redefined property in an effort to reduce the generation of negative externalities by a person on his neighbor's property. Since the externality was reciprocal, it is quite probable that the restriction actually increased the value of the real estate involved.

Zoning restrictions are, of course, another obvious example, but consider also the building lines in most cities. In most residential areas, each street has a specified building line past which owners are prohibited from building houses farther forward on their lots. The object of the prohibition, of course, is to provide sizable front lawns and thus generate a pleasant effect. It is a clear example of regulating "gardening" in order to produce a positive externality. The prospects for reducing externalities by changing property laws are apparently almost infinite. The unitization of oil pools is one example, but there are many others. Our present property laws have largely developed through historical accretion, and there is no strong reason to believe that they are anywhere near optimal. Changes in the law may well be desirable.

There are, however, two disadvantages to any proposal for government changes of property laws. The first of these, of course, is that the mere discussion of such changes generates externalities. If I purchase a piece of property and do not know whether or not the government may make radical changes in the bundle of rights that I have purchased, I incur a substantial risk from that uncertainty. Minimizing this risk would appear to be something that would be a desirable reduction of externalities. In general, this can be done if any change in property rights requires condemnation proceedings with payment of full compensation. Any change in the law of property that reduces externalities will confer more benefits than its cost, and hence there is always a theoretical possibility of fully compensating everyone injured and at the same time making a profit. Compensation, then, should normally be required.[5]

The second problem is that if we turn to the government as an instrument for changing people's property rules, then the voters may make use of the government instrumentality not only to change property rules but also to transfer resources to themselves. For example, the setback laws in New York City were simply enacted. No compensation was paid to the owners who found that their rights had been to some extent restricted, nor was a tax placed on the beneficiaries. It was a transfer of assets among the owners of real estate. It should, then, be kept in mind that a governmental agency that has been called into some area in order to reduce externalities may, in fact, do more. It may well be more interested in transferring income to powerfully

5. Another technique, suggested by Mishan, is simply to provide that the law take effect, say, seven years in the future. The present value of the change would be slight, and everyone would have seven years in which to adjust.

situated political groups and perhaps actually create further externalities if there is some political advantage to be gained.

As has already been pointed out, there is no reason to believe that the government will choose an optimal policy with respect to the externality. Presumably the decision processes will produce an outcome which may very well be better than that obtained in the market. It may, however, be worse. As was pointed out in the first chapter, if the members of the community have relatively similar tastes and the externality is a large one, it is likely that government action will improve matters. If tastes are widely varying and the externality is a small one, it is likely that governmental action will be worse than market provision. In any given case, we could theoretically make precise calculations, predict the outcome under governmental and private provision, and then decide which of the two institutional sets was better. It is unfortunate, but true, that such calculations have almost never been undertaken.

A second method that can be used to deal with an externality is a rule regulating the action of some person or persons. It may be noted that there is a gray area between the first method, the change of property definition, and the second method of rules. A provision that I may not do something on my property could well be described either as a rule restricting my action or as changing the nature of my title to the property. The reason for mentioning the rule process is not because I want to make any subtle distinction here, but because there are a number of rules that reduce externalities and that do not seem to be very closely connected to any property institution.

Many American cities, for example, require that dog owners inoculate their dogs against rabies. It is difficult, although not impossible, to describe this as a modification of the property laws. Requiring individuals to undertake actions that will produce positive externalities for others or reduce negative externalities is common in the world at large. In many parts of the world, the streets are kept clean by requiring the householders to clean that part of the street in front of their house. Many laws also prohibit people from engaging in conduct that would be offensive to the rest of the community. There are minimum standards in the amount of clothing worn in public, and even, to some extent, on the stage. Loud noises at certain times are prohibited, and individuals are under a positive duty to take care to avoid inflicting injury on others.

It is my general impression that this particular way of reducing externalities is less likely to be significant in highly prosperous communities than it is in poorer communities. Still, this is merely my impression and one should not assume without further evidence that as we become more prosperous, this particular method of reducing externalities will be used less frequently. There are, in fact, many economists who feel that this is a growing, rather than a shrinking, field of action.

All of the examples mentioned thus far of the control of individual action in order to reduce externalities have involved the government. As a matter of fact, governmental controls are the largest example of this category, unless we wish to include contracts of employment as examples. Assuming that we do not wish to include such contracts, then this particular method of reducing externalities is relatively rare in the private sector. One can, however, cite some examples. Frequently, when an individual sells a business to someone else, he also agrees that he will not start a new, competing business for a specified term of years. This is clearly an effort to reduce an externality. Easements may contain requirements that the person holding the property subject to the easement take positive action with respect to it. For example, my sister and her husband have recently purchased a plot of land, the only access to which is across the land of another individual. They have been granted an easement across this other land in return for their agreeing to build and maintain a road that will be used by both themselves and the other owner.

Nevertheless, again excepting contracts of employment, I do not think there are very many cases in which the externalities are eliminated by private agreements that simply require a person to do something. Thus, this particular method of reducing externalities is mainly characteristic of governments. In this it is unique. All of the other methods we will discuss are as commonly found in private agreements as they are in government action. It is also unique in that it probably is more subject to abuse for political reasons than any other method of reducing externalities. The cost to the government of compelling an individual to do something or preventing him from doing something is normally very low. Furthermore, the activities to which the government objects are frequently only under certain circumstances externality generating. Suppose, for example, I enjoy drinking myself into a drunken stupor. As long as I do this quietly at home, it disturbs no one. If, however, I choose to drive to the store for another bottle of whiskey (let us say, my fourth for the evening) I am generating a decided externality. In this particular case, our laws recognize the problem and there is substantially no legal restriction on private drunkenness. The laws prohibit drunken driving and public drunkenness. With respect to some drugs, however, this is not so; marijuana and heroin, for example, are illegal even when they do not affect behavior outside the home.

The various restrictions on sexual irregularities are further examples of this method. An individual may well be deeply offended by the knowledge that there is a brothel next door to him. In this sense, the brothel is generating a negative externality for him. If, however, none of the people who are offended by the existence of the brothel discovers that it exists, it generates no negative externality. Nevertheless, our laws do not prohibit brothels whose existence is known to puritans; they prohibit all brothels. Thus, this effort to reduce an externality has been improperly drafted, presumably because the operators of the brothels find themselves in politically difficult positions.

Thus far we have been concerned with the provision of definite rules for controlling conduct. It is also possible to reduce externalities by establishing administrative controls. Instead of Mr. A's activities being controlled by a definite rule, whether contractual or legal, he may be placed under a duty to carry out regulations or administrative orders from an individual or organization in order to reduce the same externality. The fact that almost a quarter of all American retail trade today is organized in this way is a fairly clear example of an externality-reducing activity. Let us, for example, consider the Howard Johnson's "chain." Individual Howard Johnson restaurants are mostly owned by private entrepreneurs who usually live in the same area as the restaurant. The restaurants are, however, all of the same architectural pattern and offer substantially identical menus. This requires that the individual restaurant be subject to careful supervision from the central Howard Johnson organization, and, in fact, the individual restaurant owner pays a substantial fee for this supervision.

Clearly the owner of an individual Howard Johnson restaurant does not benefit greatly from this supervision of his own restaurant. He does receive technical advice that probably improves his efficiency, but he would probably be better off if he could slightly reduce the standards of his restaurant and thus obtain a favorable externality from the advertising effect of the other Howard Johnson restaurants operating at a slightly higher quality level. The reason for the detailed regulation is simply to make this reduction of quality impossible. The bulk of Howard Johnson's customers are people driving from one place to another who are not familiar with the local restaurants. They do know, however, almost exactly what they will find at a Howard Johnson. Thus, the behavior of one Howard Johnson restaurant administered by detailed regulation will affect the others, and the internalization of this externality and the provision to the traveler of a highly standardized fare are a valuable service to the customer.

Similar detailed regulation by governmental agencies is not infrequent.

For various reasons, at least in the United States, this has not worked out very well. The governmental agencies seem, after a while, to either become hopelessly stodgy and old-fashioned or to develop into organizations that, in essence, operate a cartel for the industry they are allegedly regulating. Sometimes both of these results occur, but the fact that our experience indicates that the government does not do well in this role does not mean that it cannot do so. Neither does it mean that we should not try to improve the efficiency of the governmental agencies conducting it.

But let us proceed to analyze further methods of reducing externalities. The method that I should like to discuss next consists of setting up an organization to provide a service. Here, again, we find that examples of private organizations of this sort are nearly as common as governmental organizations. Earlier I discussed the organization of Belvedere Park, and a great many large apartment buildings or large real estate developments of any sort involve an organization providing special services to its members. When I was a boy I worked as a caddymaster at a golf course, which was owned jointly by the people who had purchased lots in a subdivision lying around the course. It generated significant externalities for its owners. Farmington Country Club, just outside Charlottesville, Virginia, is a spectacular example of this particular way of generating externalities through a golf course. In this case the collectivity is the corporation that originally sold the Farmington lots to the present owners. With great commercial acumen they have been able to time the sale of lots and the changes and additions to the golf course so that they continuously bring new pieces of property into the market in extremely attractive environments. It has been profitable for the owners, and the people who have purchased the property in the country club area also seem to be satisfied with their bargain.

On a smaller scale, arrangements of this sort are frequently found among business organizations. Two or three corporations who need a specialized service will form a special corporation for that purpose. Dow-Corning, for example, was set up by a chemical company and a glass company to deal with a special line of products that involved technologies lying between the lines of the two companies. Dow-Corning has expanded and is now one of the hundred largest corporations in the United States. This was an effort to internalize certain externalities in the research and production capacities of the two corporations. On a smaller scale, trade associations are examples of private persons joining together to set up a special organization that can obtain certain external benefits for them.

In this area, also are found a large portion of the activities of existing governments. The police force is a good example. The government organizes something that proceeds to generate favorable externalities or to eliminate negative externalities (depending upon how you wish to state it) for a great many people. The highway system, national defense, and the weather bureau are other examples. Indeed one can make a list involving a very large part of the activities of both local and national governments as coming under this heading. Here again we have the usual set of problems as to whether or not in a given case a government would provide a better "product" than the private market, and, again, this is a matter of careful calculation.

One special problem should also be briefly discussed. If several people observe an externality and feel that an organization should be established to deal with it, they can either set up the organization themselves or they can contract with someone else to provide the necessary service. Furthermore, they are not confronted with the choice of contracting out the entire organization or setting up an entire organization themselves. They may contract out various parts of it. For example, most roads in the United States are produced by private companies. However, a great deal of the road maintenance is done directly by the government.

Similarly, if we consider private agreements in which an externality is internalized through an organization, we sometimes observe that this is done by contracting it out. The building in which I formerly lived (2016 Main), for example, obtains a number of economies of scale in mechanical maintenance by hiring other specialized corporations to carry out maintenance activities. These specialized corporations obtain their economies of scale by having a large number of similar customers. The choice for 2016 Main between joining together with a large number of other apartment buildings and setting up a special organization that hires plumbers or entering into contract with a company that provides plumbing for them as a unit is clearly the traditional management problem of whether a company should make or buy a component. The same holds true for the government.

As anyone who has read the managerial literature will realize, this is frequently (although not always) an extremely difficult problem and once again little can be said about it in a general way. Careful individual calculations should be made, and it should be emphasized, however, that tradition is not a good guide. Many activities were initially undertaken by the government on its own, rather than by contract. It does not follow that this procedure is efficient. For example, the different branches of the armed services have completely different policies relative to the procurement of weapons: the Army tries to produce everything itself, the Air Force tries to contract out everything, and the Navy has an intermediate position on these matters. There is no evidence that this difference represents any difference in technology; it appears simply to be a result of tradition. What we need is careful calculations and decisions in terms of efficiency in which we should be very careful not to be misled by the dead hand of the past.

The final method of dealing with externalities is one that is relatively little used but that, in recent years, has attracted attention because it appears to be the most efficient way of dealing with a large range of externalities. This method involves changing the prices that the individual enterprise faces by a system of taxes and/or subsidies. We have already discussed this method in connection with a number of individual cases, but it is worthwhile repeating it again. Suppose, for example, that there are a number of companies engaged in dumping polluted waste into a river. Instead of establishing a set of standards for the amount of such waste these companies can put into the river, we tax them. It becomes expensive for them to pollute the river, and they reduce the pollution. Furthermore, this solution permits each individual company to adjust the amount of its pollution to its cost structure. By an appropriate choice of the tax, we can obtain whatever amount of total pollution we wish for the river, while not interfering with the individual company management. This appears to be the most efficient method of pollution control.

Similarly, in an activity that generates positive externalities, we can cause individuals to increase their production by giving them subsidies. To return again to the subject of individual gardens, which surely do create positive externalities for neighbors, a program under which people were subsidized to the extent of (shall we say) one-third of the cost of any flowering bush that they plant in their garden, would lead to an increase in the number of flowering bushes and hence to the "internalization" of the externality. Generally speaking, economists have thought that this method is the most efficient way of dealing with a wide range of externalities, but as I stated previously there do not seem to be a vast number of examples of this method in the real world. The wonderfully conceived organization for controlling the Ruhr River basin is perhaps the best illustration.[6]

An excellent example of this type of subsidy in the private sector is advertising by those enterprises in which the retail unit is a separate business from the manufacturer. If a local Plymouth agency decides to lease a billboard to advertise its wares, it will not only increase its own business but it is likely to

6. Allen Kneese, *Water Pollution: Economic Aspects and Research Needs* (Baltimore: Johns Hopkins University Press, 1962).

some extent to increase the business of all other Plymouth dealers as well. Thus, the externality can be dealt with by subsidization. By any one of a very large number of techniques, the central manufacturer will subsidize local advertising. This is a simple way of internalizing an externality.

In this method, we also have problems in deciding what a governmental agency is likely to do. The subsidy or tax on the externality-generating activity will, unless it is greatly excessive, normally improve the situation over what it was prior to the imposition of the subsidy or tax, but it is difficult to understand why a government would choose the optimal tax or subsidy. My efforts to determine what would happen in a voting context, in which the individuals are both the payers of the subsidy through a tax and the recipients of a subsidy in the sense that a positive externality-generating commodity that they normally purchase will be subsidized, have led to a complicated individual decision process. There does not seem to be anything about this decision process that would lead to the conclusion that the majority voting outcome would be close to the optimum. Other decision-making procedures seem to be equally unlikely to achieve the optimal adjustment. Since there is a real danger of overtaxation or oversubsidization, it would seem desirable to carry this particular research much further and to obtain fairly definite ideas as to whether or not the governmental decision process may be likely to lead to a situation that is worse than no subsidization at all. Note, however, that it would appear that these investigations are merely a precaution. One would assume that in most cases a modest subsidy or a modest tax would benefit matters. The fact that it would not reach the optimum is unfortunate, but we live in an imperfect world.

This chapter has been devoted to a discussion of the methods of reducing externalities. In the first part, we discussed some organizational methods that are not normally, I think, carefully considered by economists who investigate this problem, and in the second part, we listed the technical possibilities. Clearly, we have a wide range of available methods, and clearly the one that should be applied in any given case is not necessarily an easy decision. We do, however, have a fair margin for error in those cases in which we are dealing with a large externality. If the externality is sizable, then although we would like to choose the best possible way of dealing with it, we can still benefit from dealing with it by a rather ineptly chosen tool. In general, the larger the externality, the less care we need in choosing the tool. Although we can obtain a benefit from even somewhat inept externality reduction, we will obtain a greater benefit if we are able to more efficiently design the externality-reducing activity.

THE SOCIAL COSTS OF REDUCING SOCIAL COST

During much of my career as a sort-of economist I have been a specialist on social cost. During the first part of this career, I continuously told people (and muttered to myself) that there were vast profits to be made in our society by reducing a number of obvious social costs. In recent years I find myself warning people (and muttering to myself) that, quite commonly, action taken to reduce these social costs turns out to be worse than doing nothing. It is my personal experience, in changing from an advocate of expanded government to an opponent of specific government action, that prompted this discussion.

If the government engages in an unwise action, it does not indicate that without government action the situation would have been ideal. Indeed, it seems undeniable that very large profits are available to our society from carefully calculated government action in a wide variety of areas where there are large social costs. I perceive the problem to be simply that the government is apt to impose social costs rather than to eliminate them.

Since it is not possible to talk about everything at once, I propose to omit from this discussion certain serious problems which democratic action can raise. The first of these is the Arrow problem, which is the prospect that democracy actually produces random results due to problems of aggregating preferences. I shall assume throughout this discussion that the voting process produces an outcome which is, on the whole, in accord with majority preferences and that terrible mathematical problems associated with democracy do not exist.

Secondly, I shall assume that the bureaucratic problems discussed in Niskanen's *Bureaucracy and Representative Government* have somehow been solved or, perhaps, are not real.[1] Using a simple maximizing model of the bureaucrat and looking at the type of institutional structure we have in our federal government, Niskanen argues that the profits from establishing a

Reprinted, with permission, from *Managing the Commons*, ed. Garrett Hardin and John Baden (San Francisco: W. H. Freeman, 1976), 147–56.

1. William A. Niskanen, *Bureaucracy and Representative Government* (Chicago: Aldine-Atherton, 1971).

government activity are apt to be entirely consumed in the expansion of the bureaucracy itself. Thus, in equilibrium, in the Niskanen model, the society would be indifferent to maintaining the bureaucracy at the size it reaches or abolishing it. The entire profit of eliminating some social costs would be eaten up in the cost of supporting additional bureaucrats. Niskanen's arguments for the frequency of this phenomenon are fairly powerful, but here I simply assume that it does not occur.

In 1949, I was in North China. The country was backward, as it had been for a long time, and as it is today; furthermore, it was also disturbed by civil war. Nevertheless, the doctors there maintained that their medical practice was better than that currently in use in the United States. Their argument was that various new drugs were not permitted for general use in the United States because these drugs had not yet been approved by the appropriate federal authorities, but they were widely available in China.

Let us temporarily assume that these Chinese physicians were completely correct in their evaluation of the situation. Here was a case in which the federal government of the United States was attempting to reduce certain private costs—the prospect that in purchasing a product for my own use, I might find that I had been misinformed about its effects. But this action was generating what we must concede was a social cost, specifically, a government rule that reduced the availability of certain medicines in the United States. The government was taking action which, in this case, created a social cost where none existed before.

Obviously, this particular effect has been greatly magnified by the recent expansion of government control in medicine. It is clear that people who live outside the United States have certain advantages over us. They are able to purchase newly developed drugs immediately, rather than waiting the nine months or more that it takes to get government approval for sale in the United States. Furthermore, the cost of obtaining approval for sale has surely led to a reduction in total research for new medicines.

Note that my discussion so far does not indicate that these provisions prohibiting the sale of new drugs until they have been tested to the satisfaction of the federal government are, on balance, causing additional deaths. New drugs are, indeed, dangerous, although it should be noted that we have better technical advice in the purchase of drugs than in the purchase of any other single commodity. Restricting general use of such drugs reduces unexpected patient reactions, and this may be more important than the rise in death rate and the retarding of medical research that come from wide usage of such drugs. My point here is simply that the individual cost that is reduced through this particular bit of government action is clearly offset by a social cost.

An even better example of this phenomenon is the development of automobiles so designed that passengers are less likely to be killed in accidents. Clearly, this reduces the private danger to the driver and his passengers while it increases the social danger, as the driver of such a car presumably uses fewer resources in attempting to avoid accidents. If we were interested in actually reducing the social cost of automobile accidents—their externality component—we would go exactly opposite to the direction being taken by Ralph Nader. We would require that every car be equipped with a dagger mounted in the hub of a steering wheel pointing toward the chest of the driver; this would surely be a good device for reducing the likelihood that the driver would be killed through someone else's fault in an automobile accident. In a less radical vein, lowering the speed limits and enforcing them very vigorously sharply reduces the social cost of accidents but at the cost of imposing private inconvenience on individuals. Thus, we inflict a private cost in the sense that we compel the individual to purchase safety devices which he would rather not purchase in order to reduce the possibility that he will be killed and, thereby, increase the likelihood that other people will be killed.

Note that I have not argued that either of these policies is, in and of itself, undesirable. It may be that probable death rates would be higher under a system in which any type of medicine could be freely prescribed by a physician than under a system in which most new medicines are not generally available before very thorough testing. Similarly, the laws which make it impossible to buy a new car without a number of life-protecting devices built into it may, indeed, reduce the overall death rate from automobile accidents. In each case, however, the result is to generate a social cost in a fairly pure form. No social cost is eliminated.

Let me, however, return to my basic subject, namely, the effects that may be expected from efforts to reduce cost in a democracy. A recent problem in the generation of atomic energy is a simple example. There have been a number of sensational public claims that the Atomic Energy Commission has set its limits for radiation emission much too high. As a result, the AEC, although denying a response to pressures, has sharply lowered these limits. The result is, by any criteria including simple minimization of radiation with no other cost considered, highly uneconomical. If the cost of meeting these new standards were put simply as a tax on the atomic energy generation industry, with the returns used to reduce exposures to medical X-rays, then radiation exposure for the average American would decrease greatly. Furthermore, although the data are meager, it appears likely that replacement of a fossil fuel generating plant by an atomic energy plant, under present technology, would reduce the effective national death rate because the current atomic plants produce fewer dangerous contaminants in the air than do the fossil plants.

In fact, of course, the data on which all of these decisions are made are extremely incomplete. It seems likely that the best use of funds in this area would be to finance a search for better data and to defer further decisions based on present data. Nevertheless, on the basis of the data now available, it appears that the Atomic Energy Commission was not only wrong, it was pathologically wrong; and it is clear that the decision was the result of what we may call democratic factors.

These examples are by no means unusual. Indeed, something like this is the norm in government attempts to reduce social costs. Why may such behavior be expected in a democracy? Let us begin by taking Pigou's well-known example of the smoking chimney, which has become traditional in discussions of social costs. Suppose we have a factory chimney that smokes, and living around it are a number of people who dry their washing on an outside line. These householders suffer loss from the soot that accumulates on their clothing, but they cannot, individually, enter into an agreement with the factory owner because of the free-rider problem. Each individual could reasonably suppose that any payment which he might make to the factory owner to reduce smoke emission would have only a trivial effect on the total amount of smoke which fell on his laundry. Thus, even though the damage suffered by the householders may be much greater than the benefit obtained by the factory owner, no private bargains will be made. This is, of course, a motive for the householders to organize and form a uniform bargaining coalition; but, obviously it is less costly and certainly easier for the individual householder to stay outside of this bargaining coalition and enjoy its profits without making any payment. Under the circumstances, nothing is done, and we turn, following the traditional line of reasoning, to governmental control.

Given the possibility of governmental intervention, each individual votes on the issue of smoke emission, and since the government will use coercion to require all people to carry out whatever decision is made by its democratic processes, no individual has any motive to conceal his preferences in this voting procedure. Therefore, according to this traditional line of reasoning, one should anticipate that this problem would be handled better by a democracy than by free-market activity.

This line of reasoning is unexceptionable as far as it goes, but the problem of information is not considered. The decision as to how much the factory smoke should be restricted, or what particular method should be used to restrict it—for example, by a tax on smoke emissions—is a technical problem, but not a terribly difficult one. Should the individual voter take the trouble to become informed on these matters? Traditional reasoning indicates clearly that the voters should not bother. Just as each householder would find that his individual benefits from a payment to the factory owner are very small, so any time spent on gathering information would mainly benefit other people.

Indeed, the case is much stronger. I have not specified any particular voting model for the government of this community, but if the number of citizens exceeds about one hundred, in almost any voting scheme several propositions would be true. If the individual improves his information and hence changes the criterion by which he would vote, the odds are great that this change would have no effect whatsoever on the outcome; or if it does, the effect would be extremely small. Under the circumstances, the benefits of improved information are practically nil, and the individual would probably not bother to seek it. Hence, the free-rider problem returns. In the market with externalities, the individual can be a free rider in the sense that he does not make payments. In governmental dealing with externalities, the individual can be a free rider in the sense that he acquires no information, and therefore, his decisions are uninformed.

I began this discussion with examples of restrictions on the purchase of medicine and automobiles without certain safety devices. These examples were selected with malice aforethought. In each case, the advocates of these plans have argued that individuals are not well enough informed to make sensible decisions. In the case of medicine, the individual characteristically first selects an expert advisor and then purchases the medicine on the advice of this expert. The only argument for restrictions is that the individual may injure himself because he is inadequately informed. Note, however, that it is the individual himself who bears the full cost of any such injury. Surely he would be motivated to acquire information for making this decision more strongly than he is motivated to acquire adequate information whether or not to have a seat belt in his car. It must be assumed that he is not motivated to acquire information as to how he should cast his vote or to write his congressman on a particular issue.

Now it might be thought that all of this is a matter of little importance. The individual presumably has some preferences about smoke, which he can simply express by voting, leaving to others the problem of how those decisions shall be implemented. However, this attributes to the government apparatus some intellectual capabilities which it does not have, but let us defer that matter for the moment. The present question is simply whether the individual knows his own preferences well enough to cast an informed vote.

I presume that most people object to industrial smoke. The issue confronting the voters in this small hypothetical community, however, is not whether they object to the smoke, but how strongly they feel this preference. How much are they willing to sacrifice to reduce smoke emission? Thus, the individual voter, if he were to cast an informed vote, would have to go through an elaborate mental process in which he determined how much he would be willing to pay for various reductions in smoke level. Most people are not accustomed to this kind of thinking, and, moreover, the gain to each voter from undertaking it is virtually nil. Once again, we suspect that voters would prefer not to engage in this type of thinking.

If the voter does undertake any such an analysis, however, he is likely to look upon the problem as one of obtaining not an optimum allocation of resources, but a transfer of wealth from the factory owner to himself. Hence, he is not particularly motivated to reach the correct conclusion. The situation is one in which the voter has substantially no motive to examine his preferences with any care, but if he does, he is likely to ask the wrong question.

In practice, of course, there may be offsetting public goods. The reduction in the factory smoke by legislation may reduce the likelihood of new factories settling in the area, and lead to lower average wages. Here again, the individual is offsetting two different considerations, both of which are fairly complicated; there is no reason why he should devote any energy to reaching the correct conclusion.

Before going further with my analysis of democracy, I should like to deal briefly with an alternative theory of social cost elimination which I think is quite widely held, although it is not usually articulated. According to this theory, the people do not actually make basic decisions, either by direct voting or by voting for politicians who make the decisions in terms of their expected benefits. Instead, civil servants make the basic decisions. Further, these civil servants are not deeply influenced by political factors. Indeed, they are a quite unusual group of people. Instead of being primarily concerned with their own careers and only secondarily interested in such matters as the public interest, they are a wise and objective group of people. These paragons, then, reach the correct conclusions because they are wise and devoted to the public interest.

Such decisions are, of course, superior to market decisions. It will be noted, however, that there is no evidence that civil servants are one whit different from the rest of us. One can always "solve" any government problem by assuming a person or group is both devoted to the public interest and intelligent. For example, we could assume that all businessmen are devoted to the public interest, and hence would never generate externalities except when it is in the national interest to do so. In the real world, however, the central problem is to design institutions that produce general benefits, even though each person is primarily interested in his personal well being rather than the public interest. If we do, indeed, find exceptional individuals like those described above, it would be sensible to discontinue democracy and simply put them in complete charge of the government. I doubt that we are going to find such paragons in the near future.

To return to my main theme, I believe I have demonstrated that the voters are characteristically ill-informed when voting on reducing social costs. Furthermore, their primary concern is with wealth transferred to themselves, rather than with social cost efficiency. Logically, this would mean that a democratic government would be inefficient in reducing social costs. What type of behavior could we expect in such a government?

First, individuals would make their decisions not through careful thought or study, but as a result of information which came to them casually. Fad and fashion would be of tremendous importance. No one can look at the real world without realizing that this prediction has been fulfilled.

Subsequently, we would anticipate that media personalities and other people in a position to influence the current intellectual fashions would be of great importance in determining action taken in any given area. This would mean that individuals in television broadcasting, journalism, and so on could find their personal power and position in society improved by the expansion of government activity. Hence, these people might well be in favor of greater government activity in this area.

It is also conceivable that private corporations would develop fairly elaborate procedures set up for the sole purpose of influencing the media and, consequently, public opinion. Thus we could predict the modern phenomenon of the corporate president selected because he is thought to be able to present a good image for the company rather than because he is efficient. Other factors also contribute to the selection of such men, so the existence of corporate presidents of this sort cannot be used as evidence for our hypothesis.

A government official, whether a civil servant or a politician, would also favor further government programs for purely selfish reasons. Washington, D.C., has recently blossomed forth with a number of very expensive restaurants, in which a single meal may cost $50. It is clear that these restaurants are not supported by the native rich of Washington, because there are none, nor are they supported by civil servants and congressmen, few of whom can afford such a bill. Who, then, does support them? A vice president of General Dynamics—who happens to live in Washington and who has been named to his position not because he is an engineer, but because he knows 8 congressmen and 27 civil servants—is the characteristic customer. Further, these specialists on government manipulation do not, in general, take each other to lunch at these restaurants. The people they take to lunch are newspapermen, TV reporters, civil servants, etc.

Although I believe most American high-ranking civil servants are still unbribable in cash, they do find their living standards increased somewhat owing to their positions. Under the circumstances, it is easy to see why civil servants should be interested in expanding the power of the government to regulate (although they also have other good reasons for this particular bias). Also, it is fairly certain that major corporations are not wasting money when they establish Washington offices; they do indeed influence government policy in their own interests.

Thus, we could expect that the voters' lack of information and thought would lead both to an increased importance of fashion and other fluctuating influences, and to the manipulation of the system by various interest groups. Probably civil servants and the media are the most powerful special interest groups.

In order to discuss another characteristic resulting from lack of voter information, let me go back to one of the problems which was fashionable among intellectuals before ecology became the all-encompassing rage: fluoridation of water. Normally, when the question of whether water should be fluoridated was put to the voters, anti-fluoridation organizations staged a campaign and won. After a good deal of name-calling, some serious research was undertaken and an explanation for the vote was discovered. The pro-fluoridation people argued that a child who drinks fluoridated water throughout his childhood will have fewer cavities in his teeth than one who does not. In general, the reduction of cavities was proportional to the length of time the child drank the water; hence, delaying introduction of fluoridation by two or three years would result in only a fairly small change in what is, after all, a fairly small health problem for most children. The anti-fluoridation people, on the other hand, had much more spectacular charges, alleging, for example, that fluoridation caused cancer. Both sides produced technical specialists to argue their points, and the average voter was not able to choose between the competing technical experts.

The cost of delaying fluoridation was, even by the claims of its advocates, not very great. The cost of introducing fluoridation, on the other hand, according to the claims of its opponents, could be very great indeed. Under these circumstances, the voter chose to play safe.

We have observed the same behavior in a number of social cost problems in the United States. On one side is the utility president who argues that unless he is permitted to begin construction of a new generating plant within three years there will be power shortages at certain times of the year. On the other side are people who maintain that construction of the utility plant will cause fairly spectacular and serious damage. The voter is unable to determine the relative expertise of the specialists on each side and, hence, chooses to play safe by voting against the construction. We can hardly blame the voter for this conclusion, assuming that he has no motive to become informed and that (particularly in this case) becoming well informed would be quite difficult. Decisions of this sort lead to optimum allocation of resources only by accident. However, a large number of such decisions are being made today, and it is likely that the cost to our society will be quite great.

I must say, in this case, I do not have very much to offer as a solution. It is certainly true that social costs exist and are important and that the market in general will not deal with them adequately. The problem is that the government also deals with them badly. In essence, the market has a systematic bias toward producing certain kinds of "bads," and while the government has no such calculable bias, it does have a systematic tendency to take ill-judged action.

Under the circumstances, there is one very obvious recommendation. Government action should be resorted to only when the social cost emanating from the market is quite great. The level of efficiency of government action is apt to be low, and the possibility of damage through erratic, ill-informed decisions is great. The situation is like that of a person who was ill in 1700 and considering whether or not to call the doctor. The best rule was to call the doctor only if the person was *very* ill. The doctor, using the medical technology of the day, clearly brought with him a real chance of death from his treatment. Unless the possibility of death from the disease itself was greater, one was best advised not to call the doctor.

I have another recommendation which should occur almost immediately to any scholar, but, so far as I know, has not been proposed by anyone else. We should try to invent a new form of government. Democracy is at least 2500 years old and probably older. It was developed by a group of very primitive people and was not the result of a great deal of careful thought. In general, with the advance of science we anticipate that we will be able to replace old devices and institutions with new inventions. One would therefore assume that a great many people are searching for a better form of government than democracy. This assumption is directly contrary to fact.

As far as I know, the strongest argument for democracy is Winston Churchill's statement "democracy is the worst of all possible forms of government, except those others that have been tried out from time to time." No one really regards democracy as highly efficient; the fact that it is better than despotism or consulting the augurs is surely extremely modest praise. I think we should begin an effort to invent something better. I myself have been trying to think of a better form of government for some time, and I must confess that I have failed totally. This does not mean that it is impossible. Democracy is not a holy institution, but a mechanism for achieving some fairly prosaic goals. It does not appear to be a very efficient mechanism. Under the circumstances, I can think of few more important fields for research than looking for something better.

PART 3

THE VOTE MOTIVE

An Essay in the Economics of Politics

I. Economics and Politics

The economic view of politics has usually been associated with Marxist thinking. This *Paper* uses a totally different method of analysis. Section I is a brief introduction to and summary of work done long after Marx, the bulk since 1960, to apply essentially economic tools to the analysis of political behaviour.

Adam Smith, the founder of scientific economics, was a philosopher by profession and interested in many subjects. Although his great contribution was in what we now call economics, he taught in other subjects, including politics. During the 19th century, however, the interest of his followers and economists generally narrowed, and until very recently they largely confined themselves to the study of what is now generally referred to as economics, the analysis of the system of production and distribution. Most economists thus studied the functioning of the market. But there were exceptions: some were interested in the functioning of a centrally planned economy. Others were concerned with the government as a provider of goods and services, and as a tax collector. Characteristically, their branch of economics was referred to as public finance, and, in practice, until very recently, it concerned itself mainly with problems of taxation.

Most people think the largest single use of traditional economics in the public sector is "macro-economics"—the economics of unemployment and inflation on a national scale. Although economists were to some extent interested in macro-economics from the very beginning, there was a very large concentration of interest in it from about 1940 to about 1970. In recent years there has also been a lot of application of economics to detailed studies of individual government policies. It seems that economists can provide a good deal of guidance, although seldom final decisions, for such problems as the optimal mix of fighter planes, the number and distribution of hospital beds, etc. This *Paper* is not relevant to any of these traditional concerns of economics. In a way it is antagonistic to them.

Reprinted, with permission. Hobart paperback no. 9 (London: Institute of Economic Affairs, 1976), 1–58.

THE BENEVOLENT DESPOT—AND THE END OF ILLUSION

In all such applications of economics, the economist has been concerned with determining an optimal government policy, granted certain objectives, for example, low unemployment, moderate inflation, or defence at the lowest cost. The new economics approach to politics, which was substantially developed at the University of Virginia in Charlottesville, Virginia, is the analysis of the functioning of government itself, i.e. the process by which government makes decisions. In a sense, the traditional economists had what might be called the "benevolent despot" model of the political order. They have thought their duty was to determine the optimal policy and recommend it to the government, which would adopt it and faithfully carry it out.

Economists in the USA and lately in Europe who are now analysing politics, and indeed the political scientists now rapidly learning economics in order to apply the same tools, have no such illusions. They are characteristically interested in improving the efficiency of the government and have no objections to advising on, say, the internal organisation of the post office; but their primary research is the internal working of government itself, not its output. Government is seen as an apparatus, like the market, by which people attempt to achieve their goals. Instead of assuming that government aims at some particular goal—say, the most health per pound of expenditure—and then calculating how it should be achieved, students in this newly established economics of politics assume that all the individuals in government aim at raising their own utility, that is, serve their own interests within certain institutional limits, and then inquire what policies they can be expected to pursue.

Insofar as the new economists suggest improvements, they are normally structural improvements in government. Most of the students in the subject would, for example, favour a much more decentralised government. Although in a small minority, I favour a two-thirds rather than a simple majority in Parliament for most legislation. Forms of government and voting systems were not the kind of problem with which traditional economists dealt. A few years ago they would have been very doubtful whether economic tools could be used to analyse either the functions of government or electoral systems.

ENTER THE POLITICAL SCIENTISTS

Although the new approach to politics originated among economists, before it was very old it also attracted political scientists. Both groups found it was necessary for them to do a good deal of study in the other discipline in order to use economic methods on traditionally political problems. The intellectual retooling was perhaps a little more severe for the political scientists than for the economists, but both had much to learn.

As the editor of *Public Choice*,[1] the journal of the "movement," I can testify that about 45 per cent of the members of the Public Choice Society are economists, about 45 per cent political scientists, and the remainder are drawn from other subjects such as philosophy and sociology.[2] Today it is not possible to tell whether the author of an article using economic tools in political science was originally an economist or a political scientist. Indeed, economists from the Virginia Polytechnic Institute or political scientists from the University of Rochester in the State of New York (the two strongest centres of the new work) may study from much the same books, although with a different concentration. Most, however, are scholars who started out in one of the two subjects and have been attracted into the inter-disciplinary work by what they (and I) see as a better explanation of politics than can be obtained from either economics or political science alone.

To date, the work has been theoretical and there has been relatively little empirical testing. This does not reflect an aversion to empirical work. Theories must be invented before they can be tested, and new theories frequently are hard to test. The appropriate data have not yet been collected, and in some cases new statistical methods are necessary. Yet there has been enough empirical testing to confirm the general structure of the new theory.

To give but a few examples, recent issues of *Public Choice* have included articles on "A Clear Test of Rational Voting," "Information and Voting: An Empirical Note," "An Economic Analysis of Government Ownership and Regulation: Theory and the Evidence from the Electric Power In-

1. Subscriptions to *Public Choice* are $11 per year, including membership of the Public Choice Society; student subscriptions are $5.50 and institutional subscriptions $25.00. Foreign subscribers should add $1.50. *Public Choice* is for the specialist reader.

2. The current president is a sociologist; previous presidents have been split about evenly between economists and political scientists.

dustry," and "A Description and Explanation of Citizen Participation in the Canadian Municipality."[3]

ETHICS IN POLITICAL CONDUCT

It is unfortunate but true that the economic approach to politics raises ethical issues. Much of traditional political science was devoted to determining the morally correct policy to be followed in a given inquiry. This kind of issue will not be much discussed here, not because I object to morally correct policies, or even that I do not have views on what policies are morally correct, but because people differ about what is morally correct. And some 2,000 years of debate in the Christian era does not seem to have had much effect on this difference. It does not follow, of course, that the morally correct policies cannot be produced, but it does indicate that, on the whole, we are not likely in the near future to reach general agreement on the morality of egalitarian policies, or the death penalty for murder, or "just" war versus pacificism, etc. It therefore seems sensible to at least try another approach. Economics has sometimes been claimed to be amoral, although its defenders normally say that giving people what they want seems morally right. The new economic approach to political science can be subjected to the same criticism and defended in the same way.

The economic approach to political problems—like the economic approach to the more traditional economic problems—is not in any sense immoral in itself. Democratic political structures are examined in terms of how well they can be expected to get for the people what they really want. Some social scientists regard this as a low objective, and feel that government should give the people what they *should* want. Normally academics or politicians who hold this view are quite willing to lay down exactly what the people should have. I frequently feel that other people would be better off if, instead

3. Jeffrey W. Smith, "A Clear Test of Rational Voting," *Public Choice*, No. 23, Fall 1975, pp. 55–67; Robert Tollison, Mark Crain, and Paul Pautler, "Information and Voting: An Empirical Note," *Public Choice*, No. 24, Winter 1975, pp. 43–50; Louis De Alessi, "An Economic Analysis of Government Ownership and Regulation: Theory and Evidence from the Electric Power Industry," *Public Choice*, No. 19, Fall 1974, pp. 1–42; and Mark Sproule-Jones, "A Description and Explanation of Citizen Participation in a Canadian Municipality," *Public Choice*, No. 17, Spring 1974, pp. 73–83.

of doing as they wished, they followed my advice; but in a democracy there is not much we can do about imposing our view upon the people. They will vote to obtain what they want, not what we think they should want.

VOTERS AND CUSTOMERS: CHOOSING THE BEST BARGAIN

Voters and customers are essentially the same people. Mr. Smith buys and votes; he is the same man in the supermarket and in the voting booth. There is no strong reason to believe his behaviour is radically different in the two environments. We assume that in both he will choose the product or candidate he thinks is the best bargain for him.

Although it seems very modest, this indeed is a very radical—even if obvious—assumption. For decades, the bulk of political science has been based on the assumption that government aims at higher goals than individuals aim at in the market. The voter is sometimes assumed to be aiming at achieving "the public interest," the man in the shop his "private interest." Is this true? Is he Jekyll and Hyde?

The private market provides all sorts of opportunities for people who wish to sacrifice their well-being for the benefit of others. There is an immense collection of private charities to which they can contribute money or time.[4] But they do not put a very large part of their income, time, etc., into them. People are interested in the well-being of others, but, except for the immediate members of their families, less intensely than in their own well-being. As a result of empirical research, I once concluded that the average human being is about 95 per cent selfish in the narrow meaning of the term. Of course, many are less selfish (and many are more).

TALKING AND ACTING: ACADEMICS AND GROCERS

There is a sharp contrast between the way people act and the way they talk. It is particularly striking among academics, where discussion of the desirability of making sacrifices for others, striving for abstract moral goals, and

4. *The Economics of Charity*, Readings No. 12, IEA, 1974, discusses charitable giving in Britain and the USA. My contribution there analysed the functioning in practice of government redistribution in a democracy.

in general living a highly virtuous life, is combined with behaviour which is not one whit less selfish than that of the average grocer.

The intellectual history of this fascinating subject is that up to about 250 years ago most discussion of economics was based on the assumption that businessmen were, or at least should be, trying to do their "social" duty: there was "the just price" and various moral duties the business community was supposed to perform. One of the great achievements of the late English Enlightenment (in particular of Adam Smith) was the realisation that we in economics did not have to make this assumption. Accepting that most in business are there most of the time to make money, even if they then give part of it to charity, permits more accurate analysis of their behaviour than supposing they are attempting to achieve "the just price." Further, in practice the behaviour of the businessman is morally quite respectable, if not saintly. In the course of the pursuit of his private profit, he produces values for other people and, with improved institutions, can be led to produce even more.

POLITICIANS/CIVIL SERVANTS AND LESSER MORTALS

On the whole, we would hope the same would be true with politics. There is certainly not much difference between politicians and civil servants on the one hand and the rest of us. A businessman who has been very successful as head of a large firm may change his job to head of a Department of government, but there is no reason to believe his basic character has changed. The conditions under which he operates change, and this should have led to some change in his behaviour, but he is essentially the same man.

In addition to being a government employee as a university professor at a state institution, I am also on the board of directors of a small company in Iowa.[5] As far as I can see introspectively, there is no difference in my character when sitting with my fellow directors and when carrying out my duties as a university professor. The conditions under which I operate are, of course, somewhat different, and hence my behaviour is not identical; but basically I am the same man.

Both the market and democratic government are institutional structures through which the bulk of us, as customers or as voters, try to achieve our goals. The bulk of us also, as producers, find ourselves employed either in the

5. Dodger Products, Eldora, Iowa: we have about 150 employees.

private or the government sector; and most of us in both are also primarily seeking personal goals. As a general proposition, we shall achieve the well-being of society for the most part only if there is some private benefit for us in taking action to that end. Once again, let me emphasise that almost everyone is to some extent interested in the well-being of others and in various abstract goals, like the "public interest." Almost everyone is, in practice, willing to make some (usually rather modest) sacrifices to those ends. This is true, however, just as much of people in private as in government employment.

The difference between government and private employment is simply that the limitations within which the individual operates differ. In general the constraints put upon people's behaviour in the market are more "efficient" than those in government, with the result that individuals in the market are more likely to serve someone else's well-being when they seek to serve their own than they are in government (pp. 27–28). Indeed, one of the objects of the economic approach to politics is to invent reforms that would raise the "efficiency" of government closer to that of the private market.

This short *Paper*, written mainly for the newcomer to economics and the general reader, cannot cover the entire work of a large number of scholars who have been working in the subject for 10 years or more. My outline sketch of the basic argument assumes that if the reader is interested he will turn to the "Note on Reading"(p. 57) for a guide to further material. I shall try to avoid the mathematics which is a prominent feature of the new work. My object is to introduce the subject to people who are not familiar with it. I hope specialists who read the *Paper* will recommend it to their students and to their colleagues in other subjects as an introduction to a still relatively new but rapidly developing branch of economics that is yielding new insights into the working of government.

II. Why Government?

Among modern social scientists there are devout believers in a centrally-controlled economy who would regard the title of this section as expressing bias. They feel that it is the market, not the government, that must be justified. I should, therefore, say at once that I propose to demonstrate that part of society should be left to the market and part dealt with by government. Since this *Paper* deals with the economics of government rather than the market, it seems sensible to explain why some functions should be controlled by government rather than why some should be controlled by the market; but this is merely a matter of style and not of substance. Readers who wish to assume that government is the norm and the market should be adopted only when there are special reasons for it will find the reasoning fits this approach.[6]

THE DAWN OF "EXTERNALITIES"

David Hume began the discussion of "externalities." As an example he used a meadow[7] which was badly drained and the value of which could be increased by drainage by much more than the cost. If the meadow is owned by one man, there is no problem. He drains it and takes the profit. If the meadow happens to lie across the property of two people, they can agree between themselves about the division of the cost and profit of drainage. If many people own pieces of the meadow, agreement becomes extremely difficult. Each person is aware that if he does not contribute to the drainage, his abstention only very slightly reduces the resources available. Further, he will get his share of the benefit at no cost. Individuals are therefore sensible to engage in hard bargaining about their participation in the project and so no agreement may be reached and the meadow may remain undrained.

There are only 20 people or so in Hume's meadow; in government activities there may be millions. Until the Second World War, London was noted for its pea-soup fogs and pulmonary disease. The cause was soft-coal fires. If everyone switched to other fuels, everyone would benefit; but no individual could benefit *himself* noticeably by stopping, because the reduction in the total amount of coal smoke put into the atmosphere when *he* switched to electric or gas fires was insignificant. A private agreement in which everybody stopped using coal fires would therefore have been impossible.

6. In London in the 1930s there was a debate between Professors William Hutt and Abba Lerner on capitalism *versus* socialism. Hutt argued that everything should be done by the market except those activities which are better handled by government. Lerner argued that everything should be done by government except those activities better done by the market. The approaches were from the opposite extremes, but both indicated much the same policies in the government/market mix.

7. David Hume, *A Treatise of Human Nature* (1740), ed. L. A. Selby-Bigge, Clarendon Press, Oxford, 1960, p. 538.

Hume recommended, in these circumstances, the use of government.[8] Even if the individuals could not agree among themselves on who was to put up what sum of money for draining the meadow and who was to get what parts of the profit, they might have been able to agree to let this decision be made in a more or less automatic way or by an agency thought to be "impartial." The agency would not have perfect knowledge about the situation of the individuals, and hence its decisions would be, in a sense, inferior to those from bargaining *if* it worked perfectly.

The decision to adopt a collective method would not be because the outcome is thought superior but because it guarantees an outcome at all. The collectivity can *coerce* the individuals into giving up their private bargaining strategies and accepting an imposed solution, which, although not perfect, could be better than no solution at all. This reasoning is particularly obvious in the London coal-fire problem. Clearly nothing could be done by purely private action; the only alternative was a collective solution through government. It should be noted, however, that the government solution was by no means perfectly fitted to the desires of various individuals. Thus, there was inefficiency in the government solution, although much less than if the problem had been left unsolved.

"EXTERNALITIES" AND GOVERNMENT

These effects are called "externalities" in economics. We may have a set of property institutions such that some of the effects of the activity (or inactivity) of a few people are apt to fall on many. The smoking chimney is a classic example. In these circumstances, the people normally cannot come together to bargain on the methods and costs of abatement of the smoke, drainage of the meadow, or the innumerable other objects which governments satisfy. They therefore turn to a collective instrument which performs the function with some (although not impressive) efficiency.

There is nothing in the analysis so far about the "public interest." Some governmental activities (such as an adequate police force) are so broadly beneficial that one can reasonably refer to them as being "in the public interest." But even here "the public interest" is simply the sum of the private in-

8. David Hume, *ibid.*

terests. I would rather not be burgled, mugged, murdered, or subject to embezzlement and fraud, and I presume the same is true of the reader. These desires are just as "selfish" as my wish for a pay rise.

There is no reason to believe that government reaches perfect solutions either. The number of cases where economists have argued that the market is imperfect and *therefore* recommended that government should deal with the problem is very large. The British economist A. C. Pigou and the American Professor Paul Samuelson both made this error. They *assumed* that government reaches a perfect solution.[9] No one really believes this, but economists frequently recommend government action simply because the private market creates externalities, and hence is not likely to function perfectly. This is clearly a mistake; we should compare the likely errors of both in the real world and use the institution which will cause less inefficiency, whether government or the market.

Where there are large externalities we would anticipate that the private market would not do well. This is called "market failure" in the technical-economic literature. We must then consider whether the governmental process will do better, or less imperfectly. There is a legend of a Roman emperor who, being asked to judge a contest between two singers, heard only the first and gave the prize to the second, assuming he could not be worse. This is not an optimal selection procedure. We must ask: what are the defects *in practice* of the governmental process compared with the defects of the market?

DEFECTS OF GOVERNMENT: PUBLIC GOODS—ALL OR NOTHING

The defects (and the advantages) of government provision are discussed later. A few can be dealt with here. The first defect is simply that government, of necessity, buys a single quantity of any "public good." When I buy something in the private marketplace, I can decide *how much* of it I want. If I club together with my neighbours to buy a public service, I have to accept the quantity decided upon by the majority (or other) rule in the collective decision process of representative democracy.

9. A. C. Pigou, *The Economics of Welfare*, 4th Edn., Macmillan, London, 1938; Paul A. Samuelson, *Economics: An Introductory Analysis*, 3rd Edn., McGraw-Hill, New York, 1955, pp. 271–72.

I may prefer to pay somewhat higher taxes and have a larger police force with the concomitant lower crime rate; you may prefer a lower tax rate, a smaller police force, and a higher crime rate. If it were possible to buy police efficiently in the private market[10] (I do not believe it is), we could each have our optimal quantity. If it must be bought collectively, however, we have to reach a compromise, which may be your optimum, my optimum, or in between; but in any event we will not have our individual optimum, as we would if we bought in the private market.

A second disadvantage is that some people simply dislike uniformity, regardless of quantity or quality. They would not wish to receive the same quantity or quality of services as other people, even if by coincidence it happened to be that which they would choose themselves. This may be a fairly small cost, but it is not negligible.

Since government activity imposes costs in this sense, it does not follow that we should not use the government for some activities. There are also costs in the use of the market process. We must measure and compare the costs in both, and choose the institution which, for the purpose at hand, is the more efficient. To make this decision rationally, we have to consider externalities or other defects in the private market, and the conditions that lead to inefficiency in government provision. We listen to *both* the opera singers and choose the one with the fewer defects. An engineer choosing between a diesel engine and a steam turbine knows that neither of them is perfectly efficient and, for some purposes, one works better than the other. That neither institution is perfect is no argument for not making a choice, but it is an argument for careful calculation of *all* effects, good and bad. The whole point of the new economic analysis of politics is that it makes these calculations easier, more complete, and more accurate.

CHANGING CHOICE BETWEEN MARKET AND GOVERNMENT

There is no reason why the choice between government and market should be permanent or unchanging. Technological changes could increase the externalities where they had previously been low or, perhaps, make it easier for government to produce a good solution. In either event, this would

10. [In *Theft in the Market*, Hobart Paper No. 60, IEA, 1974, Dr. R. L. Carter argues that *some* police services could be bought privately, e.g. cash-carrying and other manned security services and detailed advice on crime prevention.—ED.]

argue for transferring a service previously provided through the market to the government. On the other hand, a sharp fall in the externalities, or a development which made it harder for government to make an optimal decision, would both be arguments for transferring an activity from government to the private market. In a well-functioning polity, activities which had been private 100 years ago would not necessarily be private now, and activities which had been conducted by government 100 years ago would not necessarily still be governmental now, except by coincidence.

As the size and general vigour of human civilisation grows, it has more harmful effects on the environment. A small community surrounded by wilderness can afford to dump all its waste into a stream, while collecting all its drinking water upriver from the dumping point. As the population around the stream increases, this procedure becomes costly. Since government's method of dealing with the problem will not be perfect, it is not sensible to introduce government until the pollution in the stream becomes considerable. Eventually we would reach a stage where the potential costs from inept government action would be less than the current cost from the pollution. Governmental control would then become preferable.

I am an avid reader of science fiction. Suppose someone invents a small, compact, and inexpensive household and industrial waste dispenser which will convert all the waste at very low cost into saleable fertiliser. Since this is a superior system, households and industries begin switching to it from their traditional methods of waste disposal. After a while, the continued existence of the (local) government agency for refuse collection will inflict more costs on society than the little pollution that would be dumped into the stream if the agency were abolished. At that time, the activity should be shifted back to the private market.

My waste disposal device may never be produced, but technological improvement may often call for reduced governmental control. Immediately after the Second World War, when new television stations were being started in the United States, there was a strong likelihood that they would interfere with one another; their watching areas overlapped on the same wavelength. The regulatory institution chosen to deal with the problem was the Federal Communications Commission (FCC), which had been performing the same function for radio. It did an outstandingly bad job of allocating and policing the TV wavelengths. The result is that Americans have markedly less choice of TV programmes than they could have, and that choice is warped by the FCC's eccentric ideas of TV programming. Yet, while many would prefer better regulation,[11] no one has argued that broadcast TV should not be regulated.

Another way of propagating a TV signal is by cable. There is no reason whatsoever why it should be regulated nationally, but the FCC does regulate it and there is no doubt that its regulation retarded the rate of growth of cable television. The original application of the FCC to TV wavelength allocation was sensible, if not optimal. With the development of new cable technology, the market should have replaced government. Unfortunately, our institutions have not yet been adapted to the changed conditions. And that in itself—the resistance to winding down government even when it has been made out-of-date—is an aspect of the economics of politics (pp. 26–40).

Once again, this is simply an example. There are many services in which government is less harmful than the market, and many where the market is less harmful than government. We should seek an optimal combination by carefully offsetting the costs in one instrument against those in the other.

III. Voting as a Means of Collective Control

(*The diagrams and accompanying text may be skipped by readers who prefer to follow the argument in words. The main conclusions are stated at the end of the Chapter, pp. 24–25.*—ED.)

We now examine the functioning of government through the eyes of an economist. We deal only with democracy because it is only in democracies that this kind of subject can be studied and because we know more about them than about despotic forms of government. This is not a judgement that democracy is more important than despotic government. Throughout substantially the whole of history the bulk of the world's population has lived under dictatorships of one sort or another. Nevertheless democracy is the system in the UK and the USA, and the only method of obtaining popular control of government that has been tried.[12]

11. One other regulatory technique would have been simply to sell the wavelengths on the open market.

12. To keep the discussion suitable for a reader without much mathematics, I omit the very difficult problems raised by the so-called "paradox of voting," which suggests the possibility that no voting rule produces stable results. Since these problems are not only abstract and

The simplest form of democracy is what we may call the town meeting. It was used by most of the ancient Greek city-states, and it is to this day used by some cantons in Switzerland and by some local governments in the United States.[13] The use of referenda, which are rare in Britain but common in Switzerland and moderately common in the United States, is similar. In most of the democratic countries, the town meeting form of "direct" government has been replaced by "indirect" representative democracy—a very complicated system.

THE MEDIAN VOTER THEOREM

For simplicity, assume a small community in which the basic decisions are taken by direct vote of the citizens. A possible issue is the amount of police services. In Figure 1, the horizontal axis shows various possible expenditures on police services from zero to 1 million. The individual voter, Mr A, will take into account both the costs of possibly being a victim of crime and the tax cost of maintaining the police services. As the police force is expanded, he is less likely to be a victim of crime, but his tax bill will go up. At first, as we move above zero, his total satisfaction increases as we enlarge the police force, because the gain he receives from a reduced crime rate is more than the cost to him of the taxes. Eventually, however, as the police force grows larger and larger and his tax bill swells proportionately, he reaches the point where he feels that any more police service is not worth its cost. For Mr A in Figure 1, this is at A.

The inverted V with its point at A is a graphic way of representing A's relative satisfaction with various police budgets.[14] Two other voters, Mr B and

---

mathematically difficult but currently the subject of considerable research, leaving them to the specialists seems a sensible approach. It is possible that a new discovery in the economics of politics will invalidate not only this section but, indeed, the whole idea of democratic government! Riker and Ordeshook, cited in the "Note on Further Reading"(p. 57), discuss the subject.

13. Sometimes in the form of "town meetings," as in the State of New Hampshire.

14. For mathematical purists it should be emphasised that the vertical dimension of Figure 1 is an ordinal rather than a cardinal dimension. All the lines show is that as Mr A moves from A in either direction, his satisfaction declines continuously. We do not have to say anything about the speed of decline. These lines could be quite irregular, instead of straight, without affecting the reasoning that will follow. The absolute height of the peak also means nothing.

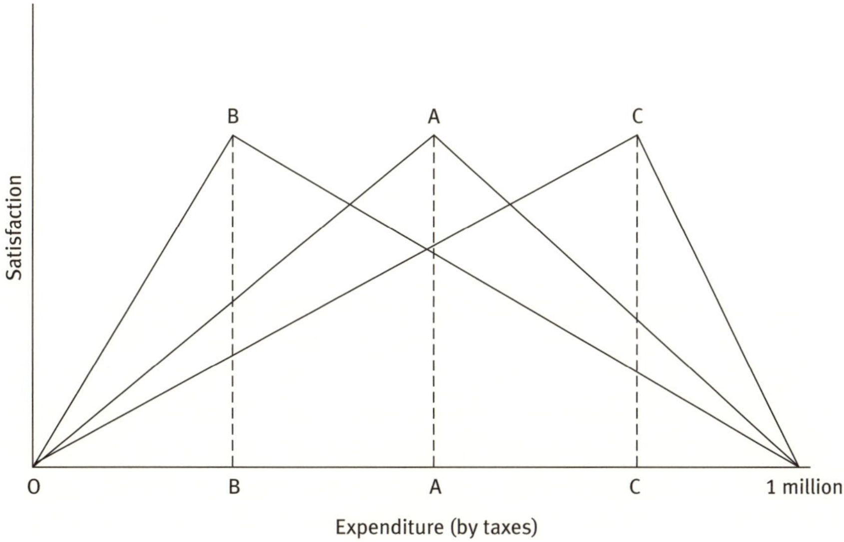

FIGURE 1
Collective control by voting (police services)

Mr C, appear on the horizontal axis with an optimum expenditure for each. Suppose our community, Messrs A, B, and C, makes decisions by direct voting in open assembly.[15] It is obvious that the median voter, Mr A, will achieve his optimal preference. If A's police budget is placed against any larger police budget, i.e. some point to the right of A, both A and B will be opposed to the change, and only C at the most will favour it. Thus, there will be a majority for point A. The same line of reasoning applies for any lower budget than A.

This simple proposition is the so-called median voter[16] theorem, which simply states that if a number of voters with different views on an issue choose by majority voting, the outcome will be the optimum of the median voter. This theorem is immediately applicable to any odd number of voters; and for large even numbers of voters the slight inaccuracy generated by the possibility of a tie is insignificant.

15. I assume here simple majority voting. It is by no means obvious that this system is optimal. Indeed, one of the more interesting aspects of the economics of public choice is the investigation of optimal voting rules or constitutions. The interested reader will find it discussed in J. M. Buchanan and Gordon Tullock, *The Calculus of Consent*, University of Michigan Press, Ann Arbor, 1962 (2nd Edn., 1965).

16. The median voter is midway in the total range (according to opinion on the policy).

This result may seem trivial. On the contrary, it has turned out to have surprisingly powerful predictive value. A good deal of empirical research, primarily in the United States, has been built upon this model, which has been found of great value in predicting[17] the size of school budgets, government policies on conservation, etc.[18]

The median voter model is eminently "positive" (or what economists used to call behaviourist): it simply predicts what the outcome will be, i.e. how people will behave, without making "normative" statements about its desirability or undesirability. Some political theorists, sociologists, and others tend to feel it is undesirable that the average man gets his way; but in a democracy he frequently does. In considering whether a voting scheme which chooses the median option is desirable or not, we should first notice that, strictly speaking, it does not pass the test of what economists call Pareto optimality. It could be that Mr B feels much more strongly about the issue than either A or C, and hence that some point between B and A would be "better" than A. This issue is dealt with at pages 41–55.

If the voters have roughly the same intensity of feeling, or if they are randomly distributed, so that people at the left of the midpoint have about as many who feel strongly as people at the right, and assuming that the location of the optima is roughly symmetrical, the median voter preference will be the point of minimum disappointment, i.e. which inflicts the least aggregate dissatisfaction upon society as a whole. The point cannot be proved rigorously without mathematics, but it is intuitively obvious for our three-voter society in Figure 1. As you move left from point A, for example, the satisfaction of B rises but the satisfaction of both A and C falls. On the average, then, this should lead to a fall-off in satisfaction over the group as a whole, although of course with a small number of voters, such as three, none of us would be very happy with taking a statistical approach.

Let us temporarily ignore the "welfare" impact of this model and attempt to see what we can deduce from it about real-world politics. To make it easier to deal with more realistic problems, we can convert our diagram to another form. In Figure 2, the vertical axis represents the number of vot-

17. By building econometric models around this idea.

18. Political parties regularly attempt to stay near the centre of the distribution of voters for this reason. Perhaps the strongest recent public statement of this was President Gerald Ford's remark: "We are going to stay in the middle." (*Washington Post*, 10 August, 1975, p. 1.)

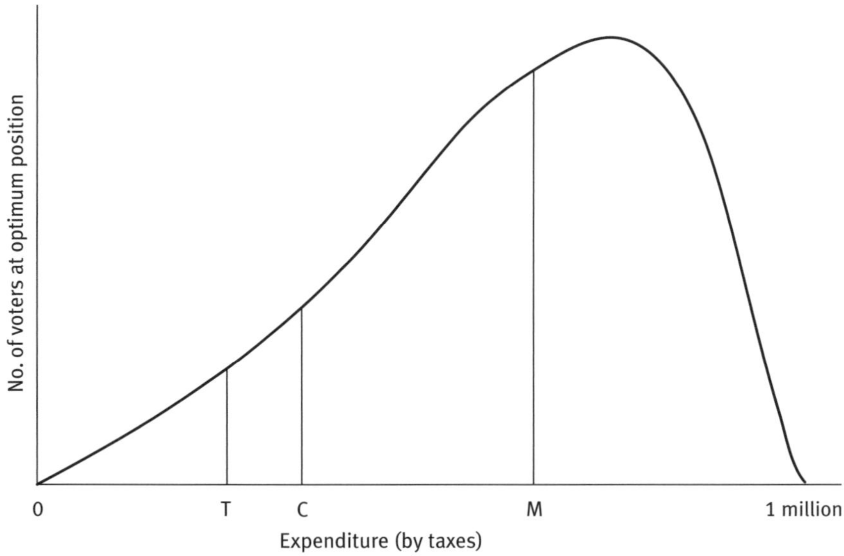

FIGURE 2
Many voters (police services)

ers who have their optimum at any given appropriation level for police services.[19]

Although the reasoning in this section will not be affected by the shape of the distribution of voters, this is because we assume the voter always votes for the alternative from among any two that are put up to vote which is closest to his optimum. If we assume voters sometimes do not vote at all, or they are confused when two choices are too close together, the distribution of the voters becomes important. These problems require more mathematics. They do not, however, raise any difficulties in principle for the type of model we will use here. I have inserted the median voter at point M on Figure 2; there are as many voters to his left as to his right. The median voter is not at the high point of the distribution and, indeed, would not be unless the distribution happened to be a perfectly normal bell-shaped curve.

19. I have drawn this line in as a somewhat skewed normal curve, but nothing much follows from this. For the reasoning to be used in most of the remainder of this section, the reader can draw in any curve he wishes, although it will be necessary to adjust the rest of the diagram to conform. For theoretical research, I usually recommend the use of a flat horizontal line, i.e. the assumption that there are as many people at one point on the issue dimension as at another.

TENDENCY TO MEDIAN "CONSENSUS"

It is relatively rare in modern democracies for government to depend on direct votes of the citizens for the bulk of their decisions. The two-party system with disciplined parties, however, works much the same way. If the parties would rather be elected than beaten, and they choose their policies accordingly, they would attempt to take the position of the median voter, because that assures them of success against any other policy taken by the other party. In practice, of course, we observe that in most two-party democracies the parties are very close together and near the dead centre of opinion.

Once again, this decision of the parties can be criticised, but the party managers, in seeking re-election and choosing their policies accordingly, are creating what advocates of democracy are supposed to favour, i.e. government in which the will of the people counts—heavily.

If there are more than two parties in the legislature or, as in the United States, party discipline is lacking, the median preference model will apply within the legislature itself, with the median individual party (in a multiparty system) or legislator (in the American system) dominating. Congressmen in the United States attempt to follow policies in the legislature which will please the median voter in their constituencies, with the result that the median congressman is not too far from the median voter of the country as a whole.

Politicians, like everyone else, make mistakes and on occasion will adopt policies far from the optimum of the median voter. Suppose Mrs Margaret Thatcher makes a mistake and comes out for a very small police budget, with its accompanying high crime rate, taking position T in Figure 2. Mr James Callaghan will not take the median position at M, but will move over in the general direction of her position, taking up position C. In these circumstances both parties are offering the voters less police protection and a higher crime rate than the median voter wants. Yet this response to the Conservative Party's initial error will maximise votes for the Labour Party.

Normally we expect politicians to be reasonably skilful, and hence to adopt positions close to the preferences of the median voter. But this result applies only with two parties. If there are three, and the voting process is like the one used in Britain and the United States, i.e. the candidate with the largest number of votes wins, regardless of how small the win, "models" of the sort we have been discussing do not predict any stable outcome. It is possible to compute an optimal strategy for a given party, granted the other two have taken a known stand; but we cannot predict the location of the three parties. By complicating the model a little we can easily accommodate three or more parties. I shall first use a more complicated model, to deal with a two-party rather than a three-party situation.

TWO-PARTY SYSTEM

Figure 3 shows on one axis expenditures on police forces and on the other axis the expenditure on the fire brigade. The individual citizen-taxpayer who benefits from both the police and the fire services, but has to pay for them, has an optimal combination of police expenditures, fire expenditures, and the tax (in Figure 3 it is at O). At this stage we assume that the individual, in choosing between two budgets which cover both police and fire services, will choose that closer to his optimum. For example, he would prefer A to B. In

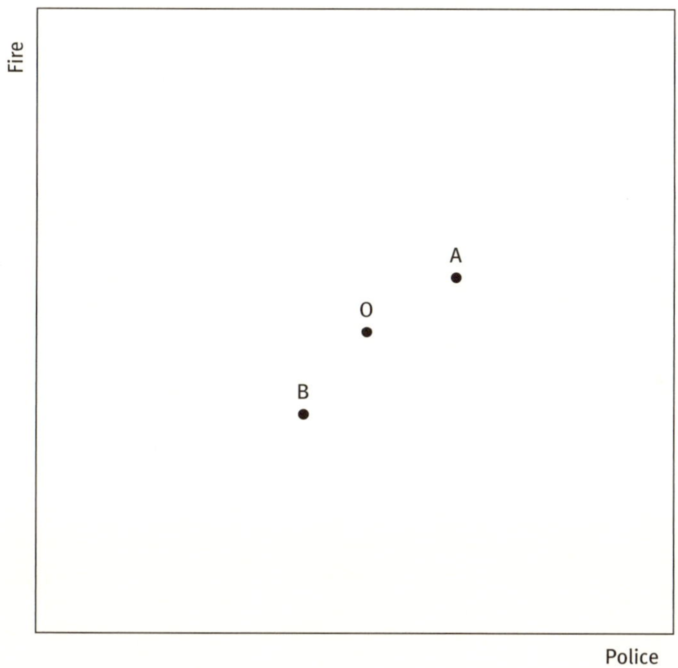

FIGURE 3
Joint decision on fire and police services

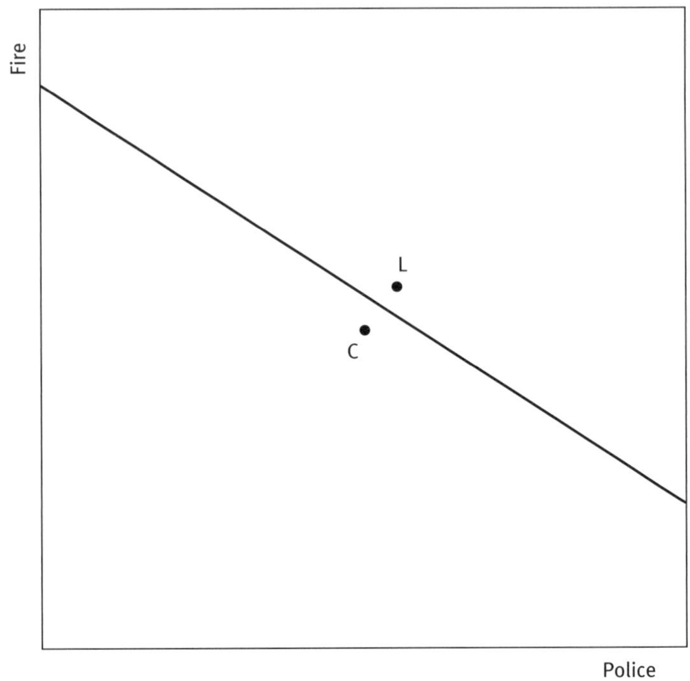

FIGURE 4
Fire and police services with two parties

these circumstances, if we place all of the optima on a figure such as Figure 3, then, if we want to find whether A or B would attract a majority of the votes, we can do so very easily by dividing the space into those parts that are closer to A and those parts that are closer to B, and then count the number of optima in each.

If there are many voters, we would not insert the points, but use a method of showing their total distribution, such as contour lines. (I assume the voters are evenly distributed over the space, because it makes the reasoning easier. The same conclusions can be reached with a more realistic distribution of voter optima, but it requires advanced algebra.)

Figure 4 is an example. I have marked the two "policies," L (say, Labour) and C (say, Conservative). The straight line slanting across the diagram is halfway between the two points and perpendicular to an imaginary line connecting them, and hence divides points closer to L from those closer to C. (If drawn correctly, it exactly bisects the issue space.)

This is a two-dimensional analogue of the median preference theorem described above (p. 14) and can be rigorously proved, as indeed it can be proved for any number of dimensions. We would anticipate that the two parties would be found close together near the centre of the distribution of the voters, and that they would split the voters about 50-50 unless one of them had made a mistake and wandered off from the centre, with the result that the other, by moving in his direction, had succeeded in obtaining more than a majority.

THREE-PARTY SYSTEM: POLARISING PARTY WINGS?

The major advantage of using a two-dimensional diagram is that it permits us to discuss more than two parties. Suppose, now, that there are three parties and that we follow the voting system in the United States and Britain under which the party with the most votes wins the election, regardless of whether it has a majority over the other two parties.[20] At first glance, it might appear that the three parties would cluster at the middle in order to attract the most votes, just as two parties tend to be very close together. This is not so. In Figure 5 the location of three parties is shown by the little triangle of dots, and the voters who favour the one closest to their optima are divided among them. What happens if one of the parties moves a little away? Assume that the lower of the three parties moves to the position shown by the X. We can now determine the number of voters who are closer to X than either of the two parties who have not changed their location, and this is shown by the dotted line. The party which moved away from the middle lost votes in the centre of the distribution, but picked up votes around the edge (represented by the shaded areas), and the net result for this move was a gain.

It is not true, of course, that as the parties move out they continue to gain. After a while they move far enough out so that the losses balance the gains from a movement farther out, and the three parties establish equilibrium in

20. The situation in the United States and Britain is somewhat complicated because this rule applies only in individual constituencies. At our present level of abstraction, this raises no difficulty. The use of the continental-type of proportional representation, however, is rather more elegant conceptually and rather more readily analysed.

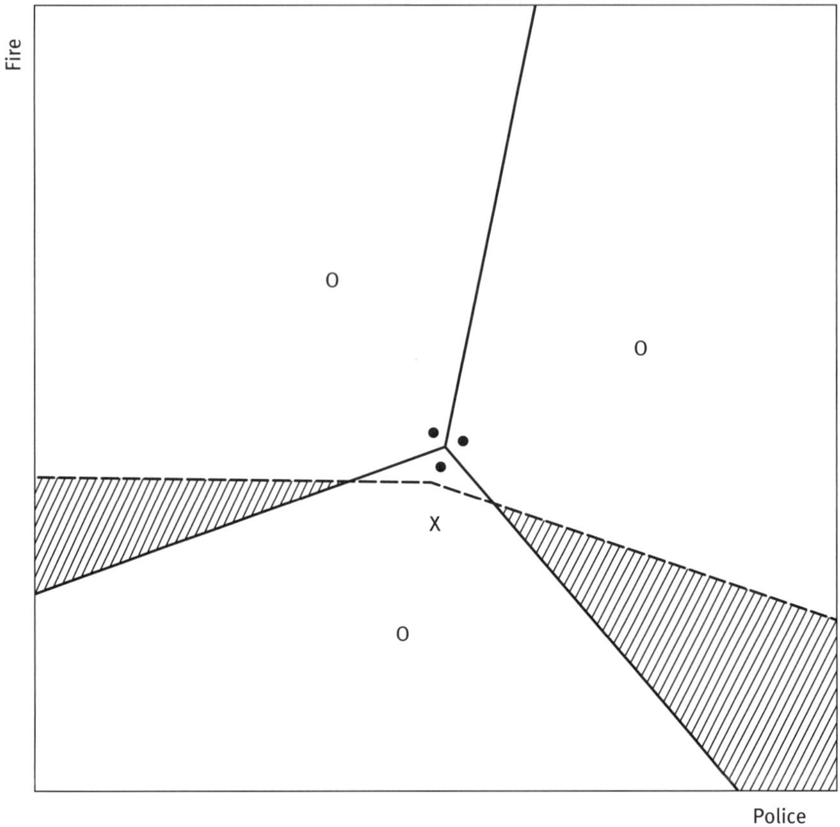

FIGURE 5
Choice of fire and police services with three parties

locations roughly like the three Os in Figure 5. Thus, one anticipates that the parties in a two-party system would be very close together but that there would be considerable difference between them in a three- (or more) party system. This is what we observe in the real world. It may be that the present situation in Britain, in which the Liberal Party has been reviving and regional parties have developed, means that there will be more difference between the two main (and smaller) parties than in the past. Indeed the current internal developments of sharpening differences between wings or groups within both the Conservative and Labour parties may represent a movement in this direction.

Whatever can be said about the future policies of political parties in Britain, it can be said for certain about a three- (or more) party system that it requires a good deal more skill on the part of the party leaders, and mistakes are much easier to make. In a two-party system there is a simple operational rule for the politician: find out what the other party is doing and take a position very close to it in the popular direction. With a three-party system, nothing so simple exists. Difficult decisions must be made and frequent errors are to be expected.

THE VOTER'S INTEREST: ONE MAIN ISSUE

So far I have been assuming that the voters are equally interested in all issues, i.e. as you move away from their optimum point in any direction, they are equally disappointed. In the real world, voters frequently are much more interested in one issue than another: housing, taxation, freedom, overseas aid, etc. In these circumstances, the job of the politician is somewhat more difficult than we have shown here. Anyone who has observed real politicians in action sees how they solve the problem. They try to give to minority groups with strong preferences in one item, say agriculture, favourable treatment in it, and then hope that the group will accept relatively unfavourable treatment in other issues where its feelings are less intense. Analysing this problem in models of the sort developed here is not difficult, but it requires more than two dimensions (which means we should have to proceed from geometry to multi-dimensional algebra).

The rules deduced for the situation in which all the voters are equally interested in all the issues continue to apply if we consider it from the standpoint of the politician himself. He should select that point in the issue space (Figures 4 and 5) which will attract the largest number of voters: if there are only two parties, we will find him selecting positions very close together; if more than two, the parties will be farther apart.

POWER—OR THE PUBLIC INTEREST?

This analysis of the politician's tactics indicates simply that he is attempting to be re-elected to office, not that he is attempting to maximise the public interest. We think this situation is realistic, and, in particular, that politicians trying to be re-elected are more likely to be re-elected than those who are not. Goldwater, McGovern, and Enoch Powell demonstrate the fate of politicians with strong policy ideals who try to persuade the voters of their truth. Although all three have had considerable national attention, none has risen to supreme power. Wilson, Nixon, Johnson, and Heath are examples of politicians who reached the top, and we doubt that anyone will claim they are highly motivated by devotion to a consistent set of policies. It is true they normally talk in terms of policies, but the policies they favour changed depending on where political support was to be found.

There is no reason why we should be disturbed by this phenomenon. The market operates by providing a structure in which individuals who simply want to make money end up by producing motor-cars that people want. Similarly, democracy operates so that politicians who simply want to hold public office end up by doing things the people want. Perhaps the people are badly informed in their choice of policies, but all a democracy can really guarantee is popular control, and politicians whose motives and methods we have analysed do give the people control.

IV. Bureaucracy

Bureaucrats are like other men. This proposition sounds very simple and straightforward, but the consequences are a radical departure from orthodox economic theory.

If bureaucrats are ordinary men, they will make most of (not all) their decisions in terms of what benefits them, not society as a whole. Like other men, they may occasionally sacrifice their own well-being for the wider good, but we should expect this to be exceptional behaviour.

Most of the existing literature on the machinery of government assumes that, when an activity is delegated to a bureaucrat, he will either carry out the rules and regulations or will make decisions in the public interest regardless of whether it benefits him or not. We do not make this assumption about businessmen. We do not make it about consumers in the market. I see no reason why we should make it about bureaucrats.

BUREAUCRATS AND BUSINESSMEN

A businessman, in an environment that is reasonably competitive and without severe externalities, will normally make a decision which is more or less in accord with the well-being of society, but not because he is consciously *aiming* at the public good. His general aim is simply to make as much money as he can,[21] and he makes the most by doing what is in the social interest. The bureaucrat will also do what is in the social interest if the constraints to which he is subject are such that his own personal interest is identical to the social interest.

The theory of bureaucracy should be based upon the assumption that bureaucrats are as self-seeking as businessmen, and it should concern itself with the design of constraints which will make the bureaucrats' self-interest identical with the interests of society. We should not expect the identity to be perfect—we do not have perfection in the market—but we should expect at least a high correlation. Unfortunately it is harder to arrange such high correlation in a bureaucratic context than in the market (pp. 28–30). To return to the main theme of this *Paper*, since we have no perfect solution we must choose among imperfect instrumentalities. What, then, are the imperfections of the bureaucratic process?

BUREAUCRATS AND ELECTED REPRESENTATIVES

In most modern countries, an immense number of decisions are taken by bureaucrats. They are supposedly in accord with the decisions of the elected representatives in democracies (or of the dictator in despotisms); but often the influence of these representatives is in practice modest. Indeed there seems now to be developing a mystique under which the bureaucrats are not even supposed to be under the control of elected officials. One of the criticisms of President Nixon during the Watergate affair was that he was trying to bring the bureaucrats under his control. The view that many decisions should be separated from political control by being put solely under the control of bureaucrats (sometimes in that oldest branch of the bureaucracy, the judiciary) is wide-spread.

21. In practice, and especially in the short run, this general long-run objective may be qualified by other purposes: a wish to avoid antagonising colleagues, staff, trade-union organisers, suppliers, customers; to gain power or prestige or influence with government; etc. Economists allow for non-monetary objectives. As Alfred Marshall put it, economists suppose only that men try to maximise their *net* (monetary less non-monetary) advantages.

MOTIVES OF BUREAUCRATS

What does happen in a bureaucracy? What are the motivations of bureaucrats? Like everyone else, bureaucrats presumably try to improve their own utility. Their utility, again like everyone else's, is partly based upon their immediate ability to consume goods and partly on their appreciation of good things happening to other people. In other words, they are partly selfish and partly public-interested.

In most business activities, the approximation that the businessman is trying to maximise his money income turns out to work rather well, although seldom perfectly. In the bureaucracy, we would like a somewhat similar approximation. If we look over aims in which a bureaucrat might be interested, we can begin by listing those which are of primary concern to him: his salary, his conditions of work—office furniture, etc. (strictly apportioned according to rank in most bureaucracies), his power over other people, his public respect and reputation. In addition to these self-regarding values, let us assume he is also interested in the public good and consciously wants to accomplish something in his job. We can easily think of circumstances in which the two would be in clear conflict. Mr James Smith, for example, is due for promotion to department head, a job which will lead in due course to his becoming Sir James; but Mr Charles Brown is the best man for the job. It is, on the whole, doubtful whether Mr Smith will bring that truth firmly to the attention of his superiors.

On the other hand, we can easily find circumstances where Mr Smith would, for purely *selfish* reasons, be motivated to serve the interest of society. If we assume in this example that he is much abler than Mr Brown, his *selfish* motives would point in the correct direction.

(One of the advantages of the simple profit-maximising assumption in business is that it permits us to assume a single "maximand" and make calculations. If we consider the businessman as maximising his utility—Marshall's net advantages—we no longer have as easy a problem. His utility is, to him, a simple "function" which he can maximise; but, to us as outsiders, what is observed is a number of different elements, such as his income, respect in his profession, the beauty of his secretary, other aspects of his office, etc. We would have to work out a complex function of all those variables and then attempt to maximise it; and this complex function would have to be identical to the one he uses in utility maximising. In general, economists have abandoned this problem, and assume a simple, single goal: the profit. The loss in accuracy is fortunately slight.)

WHAT DOES THE BUREAUCRAT TRY TO MAXIMISE?

Is there a similar maximand we can use for bureaucracies? The answer is, unfortunately, "No," if we want to be completely general. Bureaucrats tend to maximise different collections of activity. But it is true that if we confine ourselves to the type of bureaucracy found in most Western countries, there is a "not bad" approximation: *size*.

As a general rule, a bureaucrat will find that his possibilities for promotion increase, his power, influence, and public respect improve, and even the physical conditions of his office improve, if the bureaucracy in which he works expands. This proposition is fairly general. Almost any bureaucrat gains at least something if the *whole* bureaucracy expands. He gains more, however, if *his* Ministry expands, and more yet if the *sub*-division in which he is employed expands.

I have confined this proposition to *most* bureaucracies in *modern Western democracies*. It is not necessarily true of all these bureaucracies, or of bureaucracies in other political systems. The real issue here is whether the reward structure in the bureaucracy is such that people gain when their burden expands. This is not necessarily true everywhere. Further, there is one important limitation on profit-maximisation which also applies to size-maximisation for bureaucrats: in general, people do not like hard work!

A bureaucrat ordered to do research on, say, improving the bid process for North Sea oil is presumably not totally uninterested in discovering a better method of letting the bids; but he is apt to give more consideration to the opportunity this project gives him to expand the size of his office, and hence improve his probability of promotion, prestige, etc. However, it is by no means certain that he will work hard to achieve either of these goals. Indeed, in the pathological case, he will devote the bulk of this time to essentially leisure activities (some of which, like reading history or solving crosswords, may be located in his office), and time he devotes to work will be solely devoted to an effort to expand his office with no concern at all for its ostensible object. In the more normal non-pathological case, although he may not engage in what we would normally refer to as hard work, he will devote a good deal of attention both to improving the bid process and to using the project to expand his office.

Assume the bureaucrats are simply attempting to maximise the size of their bureaucracies and leave aside, for the time being, their desire to consume leisure (technically described as "shirking" in the management literature). Economists have gone a long way with their simple, one-argument "utility function" for businessmen (profit-maximisation); if we cannot get as far with our one-argument utility function for bureaucrats (size-maximisation), at least we should make some progress.

IMPROVING THE BUREAUCRACY

One way of improving the size of a bureaucracy is to do a good enough job so that people want more of the activity it is producing. The famous Liverpool Bath would no doubt have continued to function indefinitely, and might even have had a number of additional employees and a promotion for its head, had they been able to make it attractive enough to capture a large number of customers. It does not seem likely that they would have succeeded, but undeniably there are many cases in which individual bureaucrats, whose simple motive is to expand the size of their bureaucracy, are motivated—at least to some extent—to improve efficiency and provide good service.

To examine the matter a little more formally, assume that a government activity, say police protection, is produced at constant cost, represented by the horizontal line on Figure 6. The demand for it (DD) should slant downward as in Figure 6, and can be thought of as a demand of the citizenry, or of the higher level of government, i.e. the legislature or, perhaps, of the cabinet.

The usual way of organising and supplying the police is to create a series of regional monopolies, all the police in, say, Liverpool being organised under one control. It has its own decision-making process and its own ends (although much writing on administration implicitly assumes otherwise).[22]

If it were somehow possible to buy police services competitively, individuals buying it and competing companies supplying it, the optimum amount would be obtained at point O, the cost would be the rectangle below and to the left of point O, and the consumer surplus generated for the citizenry shown by the triangle DOC.

If we assume the citizenry continue to buy police services independently

22. Two classical sources are Leonard D. White, *Introduction to the Study of Public Administration*, Macmillan, New York, 1948; and William E. Mosher, J. Donald Kingsley, and O. Glenn Stahl, *Public Personnel Administration*, 3rd Edn., Harper and Brothers, New York, 1950. For the same attitude in military administration, J. D. Hittle, *The Military Staff: Its History and Development*, Military Service Publishing Co., Harrisburg, Pa., 1949. This attitude may be found widely spread through the literature; for an example, Mike Royko, *Boss: Richard J. Daley of Chicago*, New American Library, New York, 1971.

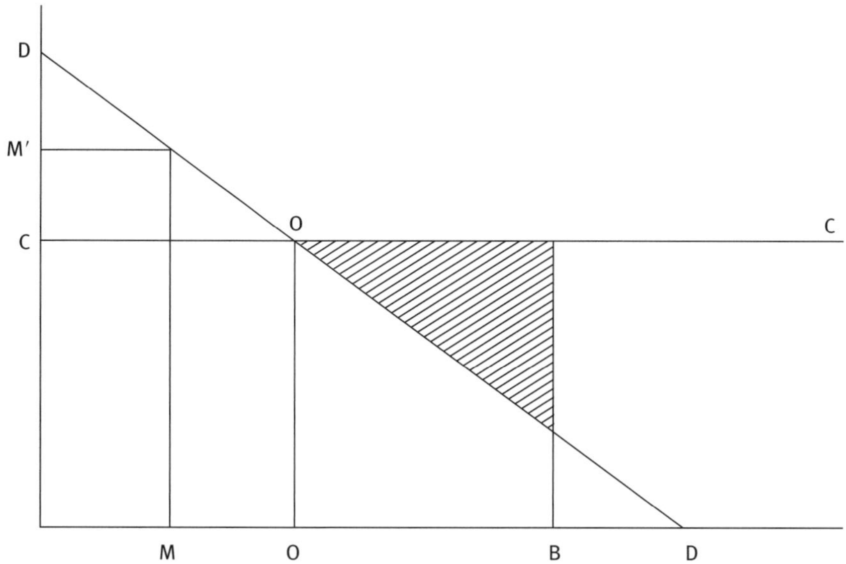

FIGURE 6
Supply and demand for police services

(we are assuming this is technologically feasible), but they are supplied by a profit-maximising monopoly, it would provide M units of police service at a price of M′, and make a profit equivalent to the rectangle above the cost line and to the left of line M. There would still be some consumer surplus, but clearly the consumers would be in a much worse situation than with competitive suppliers.

Let us now more realistically assume that the individuals are not purchasing the police services as individuals but through a governmental agency which has a demand for police services derived from the demand of the individual citizens. The supplier is also a monopoly: there is only one police force in Liverpool; and let us assume that the police attempt to maximise the size of their bureaucracy. What is the likely outcome?

SINGLE BUYER V. SINGLE SELLER

First, we have a monopsony (single buyer) against monopoly (single seller), and this is always a difficult situation for economists to analyse. What would happen if one or the other of the two had everything his own way? If the legislature is in complete control of the situation and has a perfect idea of the cost structure facing the police, they could offer the rectangle left of and below O to the police in return for the police producing O amount of police protection, and we would have the same solution as in free competition.

If the police have everything on their side, which means they are able to conceal their own cost from the legislature, they can misrepresent the cost of providing various amounts of police services, and the legislature will not be able to discover their true "production function." We then get a most extraordinary situation. The police will provide B police services and charge the amount of the rectangle under the cost line and to the left of B. This means that for the marginal police services they are charging more than they receive and there is a net social waste shown by the shaded triangle. They are able to get away with this, however, because the size of the shaded triangle is the same as DOC. As a perfectly discriminating monopolist always will, they have squeezed out the entire consumer surplus, but have spent it on providing additional police services.

How do we reach this conclusion? The police department is not assumed to be profit-maximising (it is not possible for the policemen simply to pocket any profit they make), but they are benefited in various ways by the expansion in the size of the force. Since we assume that they are exploiting the demand curve to the maximum, they are also maximising their size by this socially wasteful expansion.

This situation is the ultimate result which could be expected if the bureaucracy worked hard at expanding its budget and was able to exploit the full monopoly gains in all-or-nothing bargaining from the legislature. The taxpayer would be indifferent between the existing police force and no police force at all, which, of course, also makes possible much lower taxes. It seems doubtful whether any existing bureaucracy has reached this position. Many bureaucracies, from the standpoint of the citizen-taxpayers as a whole, may be beyond this point; but that is because they are satisfying the demands of some persistent and voluble minority. In these circumstances, a true demand curve would be that of the minority and, once again, I doubt whether many real-world bureaucracies have succeeded in exploiting their monopoly positions to the full.

There are a number of reasons why bureaucracies would not be able to reach this goal with any degree of regularity. First, and obviously, the legislature or purchaser of the services from the bureaucracy characteristically has at least some information about the production function of the bureaucracy and is not subject to what we might call "complete" exploitation. Secondly, since the members of the bureaucracy among other things want leisure, they are unlikely to put in the concentration and hard work required to exploit the legislature to the theoretical maximum.

Ironically, the desire for leisure—what we normally call laziness—has a net benefit for society. Suppose the individuals in the bureaucracy work hard enough to get only 80 per cent of what they could if they devoted full force to achieving it. The cost level line in the diagram would be adjusted upward to indicate that you have to hire more policemen to get a given amount of protection. This clearly would be a disadvantage for the taxpayer-citizen. On the other hand, the bureaucracy in negotiating with the legislature would not get all of the welfare triangle; it would leave 20 per cent of it to the citizen. The citizen would therefore derive some benefit from the service, although if the policemen were energetic and hard-working in both "policing" and exploiting the legislature, the consumer surplus would be entirely consumed in producing "efficiently" police services not worth their cost. The citizen-taxpayer is better off with lazy servants than with diligent ones here, but this results simply because the diligent ones will use their diligence to extract surplus value from the taxpayer.

ODDS WITH THE BUREAUCRACY

Does the bureaucracy in practice extort its entire theoretically possible gain from the legislature? This is the classic monopoly-against-monopsony problem, and economists normally say it is insoluble. But there are good reasons for believing the odds will be heavily on the side of the bureaucracy. It will have a good idea of the legislative demand for its services, which is essentially derived from the voters' demand. The bureaucracy has access to the newspapers, television, etc., and therefore has a good idea of the popular demand. In the circumstances, the legislature is not able to keep its demand curve a secret.

These factors are exaggerated by two special characteristics of governmental demand. First, most government demands are organised by special interest pressure groups, like the farmers, who normally are intimately connected with the bureaucracy which will carry out the policy, the Ministry of Agriculture, which, in turn, is therefore very well informed about the political pressures that can be brought to bear upon Parliament and the government. Secondly, a good part of the demand for bureaucratic services comes not from the people who will *receive* them but from those who will be paid to *supply* them. The bureaucrat who works for the Minister of Agriculture, or the policeman who works for the chief constable, is also a voter. In voting, he (and his family) have two demands for their bureaucracy's service. First, they, like other citizens, gain whatever benefits it generates; but, secondly, they gain privately from the payments made to them.[23]

They are part of the demand for their own services, and a particularly important part. They combine very good information about their bureau with strong motivation. And, indeed, they seem to represent a larger percentage of the voting population than of the total population, because they are more likely to vote. Rough estimates in the United States indicate that about one out of five Americans derives his support from a government job in the family, but about one out of four voters does so.

If the bureaucracy has a good idea of the demand for the service, the government has difficulty determining the cost of providing it. In general, the only source of such information is the bureaucracy, which is apt not only to say that economies are impossible but also, if economies are imposed, to act so as to maximise their cost instead of attempting to do the best job it can in the new circumstances.

BUREAUCRATS RESIST "CUTS" BY SUPERIOR KNOWLEDGE

Three examples readily come to mind. The first occurred when I was serving on the council of the American Political Science Association. We were in one of the budget crises which afflict learned societies from time to time. The APSA maintains in Washington, D.C., a large office, engaged in not too well defined activities. It was suggested that one of the ways we could escape from our budget problem was to reduce expenses in this office. The permanent secretary of the society, who had been responsible for building up the office after he was appointed, immediately said that "Yes, that could be

23. This, of course, assumes that the payment to them is higher than their opportunity cost, not a very radical assumption in most modern governments. At the time this *Paper* was under preparation, the city of New York, as a result of a fiscal crisis, was talking of firing 10,000 policemen. The police officers' union prepared and circulated to tourists a pamphlet entitled "Scare City," warning against the dangers of visiting New York City if the police force were reduced—an effort to manipulate the demand for their services.

done"; it would be possible for him to lay off two or three of the employees in the subscription service branch, i.e. those who took care of seeing to it that everyone got their *American Political Science Review, P.S.*, and other documents circulated to members. The result clearly would be that members were inconvenienced. He did not suggest that any of the "policy officials" might be dispensed with, although it was never clear what the bulk of them were doing.

My second example involves the Federal Customs Service. Its budget was reduced. The civil servant in charge laid off every Customs Inspector in the United States but not one person in any other part of the Customs Service. This was too extreme, and he was transferred in a burst of unfavourable publicity; but he was not fired.

The third case, more recent, concerns newspaper reports that the Immigration Service is deliberately investing its resources in office staff rather than in Inspectors to make it necessary for Congress to increase its budget.

This kind of behaviour is common with bureaucracies; and, in general, congressmen have found it difficult to prevent. Professor William Niskanen, whose book *Bureaucracy and Representative Government*[24] rigorously develops the size-maximising principle, spent most of his life in the Department of Defense, attempting to improve its efficiency before writing about it as an economist. Immediately after writing the book, he moved to a higher-level agency, the Office of Management and Budget, the general control agency of the United States government, and found that there, too, it was impossible for him to outmanoeuvre the bureaucrats because they simply knew more about their departments than he did.

SOLUTIONS: MORE INFORMATION?—REDUCING BUREAU MONOPOLY?

What can be done? First, an attempt to develop expertise at the upper layer is required to which the whole development of cost-benefit analysis is directed. More information would help, but it is not obviously going to lead to much improvement. What is needed is some way of lowering the bargaining potential of the monopoly bureaus.

24. Aldine-Atherton, New York, 1971; the argument is summarised in *Bureaucracy: Servant or Master?* Hobart Paperback No. 5, IEA, 1973.

In the marketplace we do not try to discover the cost structure of companies from whom we buy products or services. All we do is compare the prices and services offered by organisations and choose the one that suits us best. The existence of a monopoly, of course, makes it hard for us to do this, and we tend to feel disadvantaged. Is there some way in which we could provide for Parliament or Congress the same ability to select the lowest price rather than putting upon it the burden of determining the operating efficiency of the bureaucracy? The answer, fortunately, is that such possibilities often exist, and as far as we can tell they improve efficiency.

First, although most government services are produced under monopoly conditions, some are produced with varying degrees of competition. It is very hard to get measures of efficiency, but something can be done. Examining the data,[25] we find that the least efficient bureaus are those which have perfect monopolies.

Second, where, although the individual bureau has a monopoly in one area, several bureaus operate in different areas, the legislature can at least compare cost curves. The police forces, which in both the United States and Britain are organised as a series of local monopolies (except for privately-supplied police services) rather than as a national service, are an example. There are, of course, many others, such as refuse-collection, fire-fighting, education, sewerage, etc.

Third, still more efficient are government bureaus which provide a service that is also supplied by private companies. Waste removal in the United States, for example, is sometimes a government activity and sometimes carried out by private companies charging a contract fee. So far as we can tell, the government bureaus, although not as efficient as the private companies (as measured by price and service), are nevertheless markedly more efficient than government bureaus which do not face private competition.

Government bureaus, even in this final negative situation, are almost never as efficient as private companies in a competitive industry.[26]

The question of the efficiency of private industry in monopolistic situations, of course, is not at issue here, since no one (so far as I know) regards this as a particularly desirable organisation of the economy. The reason is simple (Figure 6). If one company protected by a high tariff has a monopoly

25. Thomas E. Borcherding (ed.), *Budgets and Bureaucrats: The Origins of Government Growth*, Duke University Press, Durham, N.C., forthcoming 1976.

26. *Ibid.*

in motor-car production in its home market, the demand curve is for motor-cars in total. If there are two companies, the motorist who is thinking whether or not to buy a car also has the alternative of buying it from the other company. Similarly with a bureaucracy: the more the competition, the more it is forced to produce close to the optimum output and productive efficiency one would anticipate in a competitive industry.

INTRODUCING COMPETITION INTO THE BUREAUCRACY

(a) Competition Within Bureaus Can we introduce competition into bureaucracy? First, we could simply stop enacting cartel legislation. Most "efficiency" studies of government[27] have attempted to root out competition (called "duplication"). In the United States' automobile market, not only is General Motors "duplicated" by Ford, Chrysler, and American Motors, but a lot of odd foreigners like British Leyland, Fiat, Volkswagen, and Toyota are also "duplicating activity." Wouldn't we be much more efficient if we abolished "duplication"?

The absurdity of this proposition would not in any way be reduced if we substituted a government service for production of motor-cars. In the United States, highways are characteristically constructed by a large number of private companies. Their repair and maintenance, however, are normally done by monopolistic government enterprises. In some areas—Blacksburg, Virginia, where I live, is an example—a good deal of the maintenance is let out on bids to competing private companies. We pay lower repair prices than we would if a monopolistic agency were doing all the repairing. Furthermore, the competing companies ready and willing to replace bureaucracies in other cities and counties also make the road repair bureaucracies there careful about prices.

Thus one way of increasing the competitiveness of government services is simply to contract them out. Many services are contracted out in various

27. This tradition has been maintained consistently. A very thorough example is the multi-volumed Hoover Report prepared by former President Herbert Hoover for former President Harry S. Truman immediately after the Second World War, and the almost equally voluminous Ash Report prepared for former President Richard M. Nixon by Roy Ash, formerly the president of a large corporation and, after completing the report, Chief of the Office of Management and Budget. Both reports may be obtained from the US Government Printing Office, Washington, D.C.

places in the world. The entire line of public utilities—telephone, telegraph, radio and television transmission, water supply, sewage removal, electricity, and gas—are sometimes provided privately and sometimes publicly. Usually the private companies are given some kind of a government monopoly, which sharply reduces their efficiency; but sometimes one or more of the utilities are generated by competing private companies. It is not obvious that this arrangement is ideal, but it would certainly be worth careful investigation. The mere act of looking into this possibility would probably lead to very sharp improvements in efficiency in the corresponding government agencies.

There are also many other government activities which can be performed by private agencies on contract. Fire protection is, in general, a government activity, but for some obscure reason a private fire protection industry has developed in the state of Arizona. The private fire protection companies enter into contracts with the smaller cities to provide them with fire protection, and also offer their services to private individuals. Comparative studies[28] seem to indicate that the private companies provide fire protection for about *half* the cost of public fire departments serving similar communities. Further, the private companies—tiny though they are—have been the cutting edge of scientific progress in the fire protection industry. They have invented an entirely new technology which, granted the extraordinarily small funds they have for research, is a remarkable achievement. This technology is beginning to spread through the United States government fire departments, but only very slowly, since there are few fire commissioners who really want to cut their budgets in half.

(b) Competition Between Bureaus A second way to impose competition on bureaucracies is to retain bureaucratic control but permit competition within it. The area served by a bureaucracy might simply be divided into smaller areas with separate budgets. It would help efficiency if Parliament made a habit of changing the geographic scope of the small bureaucracies handling, say, police protection. If, for example, the Commander in charge of division I seems to have done better one year than the Commander in charge of neighbouring division II, 15 per cent of II might be added to I, the Commander

28. A popular account of this phenomenon is William C. Wooldridge, *Uncle Sam, the Monopoly Man*, Arlington House, New Rochelle, N.Y., 1970, pp. 124–27. For a more scholarly account, Roger Ahlbrandt, "Efficiency in the Provision of Fire Services," *Public Choice*, No. 16, Fall 1973, pp. 1–15.

of I promoted, and the Commander of II reduced. In the following year, at the very least a good deal of thought on methods of improving efficiency by both might be expected. Perhaps the 15 per cent could be shifted back at the end of the next year.

SMALL-SCALE EXPERIMENTS DESIRABLE

So far we have gone from analysis to a set of reforms which may seem extremely radical. It is generally not desirable to adopt radical proposals instantly for a large and important organisation. Experimentation on a small scale would seem to be called for. The proponents in Britain of the voucher method of financing school education are a good example.[29] Although they are convinced it is the best method, they are not proposing that the education system be revolutionised, but that well-conceived experiments be undertaken to obtain more information and to find whether their proposals are as attractive in practice as they appear to be in theory. The reforms for bureaucracy (pp. 36–39) should be handled in a similar manner. They can be tried in a local area and, if they work, expanded. As may not have escaped the reader, I think they would work.

V. Logrolling

The word "logrolling" is a fairly unusual one in the American version of English and seems unknown in the English version. Its meaning is very simple: I agree to vote for something you want in return for your agreeing to vote for something I want. It is also a very common phenomenon in a democratic political system; indeed, it usually dominates the process of selecting policy although it is concealed from public view.

Logrolling is frequently thought to be wicked and, indeed, is against the law in many democracies. The laws against logrolling (probably passed in part through logrolling) have substantially no effect on the functioning of democracy in countries which have adopted them. At best, they make it necessary to carry on the logrolling in a somewhat indirect and hidden way, which probably reduces its efficiency to some extent. Nevertheless, most people

29. I understand that Kent County Council is the pioneer in studying the feasibility of voucher experimentation.

when first told about logrolling feel it is undesirable, yet they normally do not respond in this way if it is explained with a little tact.

A BRITISH EXAMPLE

I once attended a meeting where there were several British MPs. One, of outstanding personal ability and with an academic background, seemed a good man to ask about the institutions in Britain. When I put the matter to him, he denied flatly that there was any logrolling; and, after my efforts to explain my hypothesis on how it was done, he denied this was so. Shortly thereafter, he made a public speech in which he explained how he was working to get his party to support a certain policy. The description was 100 per cent logrolling; as he put it, "I attend committee meetings and vote on things I don't care about at all in order to get the people who really are interested in those subjects to attend my meeting. And then I hold up their hands when it comes to a vote." The latter, of course, was an exaggeration.

This MP had simply been trained in one theoretical description of how politics works and then learned how politics works in practice. Since there was no reason for him to put these two ideas together, he had not done so. When I, a visiting specialist in the economics of politics, asked questions about British procedure, he answered quite truthfully in accordance with the theory he had *learned*. When he was explaining what he himself *did*, he again truthfully explained, but was not aware of the divergence. It was not until after his public meeting, when I raised the issue, that he realised there was any contradiction between the two positions.

LOGROLLING IN LABOUR AND CONSERVATIVE POLITICS

My friend the MP was typical. Most people who deny the existence of logrolling in what we may call the theoretical context either engage in it or expect that their representatives will engage in it in practice. The "social contract" in Britain, for example, if one accepts the Labour Party and trade union description of it, involves an exchange of redistributional policies for union support. Union support is supposed to take the form of not making too large wage demands, but it is nevertheless a policy swap. But I have seen no public claims that it is immoral. It is sometimes said it will not work, or that it is fraudulent in the sense that neither party really intends that it shall work. This is quite different from saying that the social contract would be immoral even if it were completely successful.

Recent Conservative Party politics raises something like the same issue. Mrs Thatcher promptly introduced into her shadow cabinet a number of people who had opposed her when running for the leadership. She also quickly moderated her political position so that she would acquire more votes, and hence have a better chance of applying her policy. The various factions of the Conservative Party who will now back Mrs Thatcher are clearly going to find themselves, if the Conservatives should form a government, required to vote in Parliament for some policies they do not like in return for receiving others they do like but to which other groups in the party object.

All of this is perfectly normal, not only for British politics but for democratic politics in general. Indeed it is also normal for non-democratic politics, although we know less about them, and hence it is not so clear there. In all democracies I know of there is both public criticism of logrolling as immoral, as well as the widespread use of it in making government decisions.

EXPLICIT OR IMPLICIT LOGROLLING: A US "MODEL"

Logrolling is usually classified as either explicit or implicit. Explicit logrolling is more common in the United States than in Britain, but it is a little easier to explain if we begin with an explicit "model" and then proceed to an implicit "model." So, although this *Paper* is to be published in Britain, let me begin with the American Congress rather than the British Parliament, and simplify matters by assuming there is only one legislative house.

If we examine the day-to-day process of government in a democracy (or, indeed, a non-democratic government), we observe that most of the activities have differential impact: they affect some people more than others. A proposal to change the tax law will have more effect on some citizens than on others. Almost all expenditure decisions affect some citizens more than others. Even simple changes in the criminal law are usually of differential effect.

These observations are not necessarily obvious to the casual observer. "The public works budget," "the military appropriation," "the health programme" appear to have wide scope if we think of the whole programme at once. In practice, detailed decisions must be made, such as where to run a dual carriage highway (which makes a lot of difference to many people because of the effect on the value of their homes), which weapons system the armed forces will purchase, and where new hospitals will be built.

These policies can be dealt with by establishing general rules. But the details become important to special groups and, in any event, democracies do not seem to be able to stick to general rules. Referring them to non-political officials may be a solution, provided they are convinced the elected officials will not take their performance into account when deciding on such matters as departmental appropriations.

DIFFERENTIAL IMPACT OF POLITICAL DECISIONS

We cannot avoid such differential impact of decisions (although we can avoid *thinking* about it). But it is not obviously undesirable. Suppose all government acts were decided by direct majority vote, with all individuals voting on them. Some of the smaller Swiss cantons come very close to this system. Suppose there is a project which would benefit one city, say Durham, very much and which would have a relatively modest cost to the national taxpayers. If Durham were unique, i.e. if there were no other city which could receive a major benefit at modest cost to the national taxpayers, we might feel that the nation should not make this gift to them. But in the real world, such situations are common. There are many opportunities for investment in public facilities in local areas for which the cost is less than the benefit. If they are to be paid for from the national exchequer, however, and if they are voted on individually, they would most assuredly fail.

Suppose the benefit to Durham would be £100 million and the tax cost is £1 per head for all UK voters. If we put it up to a direct vote, the voters in Durham, facing a very favourable "trade-off" of a £1 expenditure against a large return, would presumably vote for it. The taxpayers in the rest of the UK, facing a cost of £1 which does not benefit them at all, would surely vote against it. And the project would be lost. We deal with these problems by setting up a kind of bargain, explicit or implicit, in which Durham gets its project and a lot of other cities get theirs.

In the United States Congress, this bargain is fairly open and above board. The bulk of the negotiations take place in committees, cloakrooms, and congressional offices, but there is no secret about what is going on. In the traditional "pork-barrel" area of public works, suppose we are 20 years in the past and President Eisenhower has decided that dual carriage highways be built in various parts of the United States to improve highway transportation. They are to be paid for (as indeed they were) by a tax on the gasoline consumed by *all* drivers—not only those who drive on the dual carriage highways.

In these circumstances, a given community is best off if it has one of the interstate roads running through it, but it must also pay for interstate roads built in other parts of the country. One would anticipate that the congressional delegation from, say, Pennsylvania would, on the whole, favour interstate highways in Pennsylvania and, to some extent, those outside; but, generally speaking, they would not be interested in taxing the inhabitants of Pennsylvania to build "interstates" 3,000 miles away in California. In the event, Eisenhower met this problem by implicit logrolling, rather than explicit. But it is a nice example to explain *ex*plicit logrolling also; so let us discuss it as *if* it had been decided by explicit logrolling, and then switch to explain implicit logrolling.[30]

EXPLICIT (OPEN) LOGROLLING

If the congressional delegation from Pennsylvania is interested in getting its interstate highway through, it goes to the delegation from Illinois and offers to vote for "interstates" in Illinois if they will vote for "interstates" in Pennsylvania. It makes the same kind of trade (exchange, swap) with Texas, New York, etc., until it gets a majority of the congressmen willing to vote for "interstates" in Pennsylvania. We now have the "interstates" being built in Pennsylvania and a number of other states have the Pennsylvania delegation's promise to vote for their highways. The delegation from, say, Illinois already have the Pennsylvania vote and require others. They seek out, say, California, Oregon, Florida, etc., until they also compile a majority.

There is no reason in this type of (explicit) logrolling why the coalition that votes for the Illinois roads should be the same as for Pennsylvania. Indeed, we would anticipate that almost all the states would be able to build up this kind of coalition simply because a state that seemed to be on the verge of being left out could offer exceptionally good terms. It could, for example,

30. A study of the way in which the highway system has adjusted itself to the political reality is Ann F. Friedlander, *The Interstate Highway System: A Study in Public Investment*, North Holland Publishing Co., Amsterdam, 1965.

take somewhat fewer miles of road in its own state, and hence impose a lower tax on citizens in other states, or it could "sweeten" the bargain by promising to vote for something else of special interest to another state in addition to their roads. The end-product should be an "interstate" network spreading all over the United States in a way which fairly uniformly reflected the number of voters in each state.

Although this was not the way the interstate was laid out in the United States, the nationalestrassen in Switzerland are being built almost entirely in this way: by explicit logrolling. This is why nationalestrassen are highly disconnected. It is necessary to give at least a few miles of divided highway to mountain cantons, such as Chur, if their support is to be obtained for the nationalestrassen running through heavy-density areas such as the plateau between Lake Geneva and Lake Konstanz.

IMPLICIT ("SECRET") LOGROLLING

In the United States the interstate system was built by a special form of implicit logrolling. A professor at Harvard, who had been deeply involved in negotiating the interstate bill when on leave as a government official, read a book[31] which discusses logrolling on return to Harvard. He informed a number of his colleagues that he had concluded that explicit logrolling was inherently immoral, but that implicit logrolling of the sort used to build the "interstates" was quite different and moral. He was willing to concede that the end-result was about the same, but thought the means were more important.

Many people, when they finally are willing to concede the existence of logrolling, seem to take the view that explicit logrolling is somehow morally much inferior to implicit logrolling. I have never been able to understand this view, but perhaps the reader will find it congenial. At any rate, this is how implicit logrolling works.

Instead of voting on each segment of the system, it would be possible to vote on the system as a whole. In essence, a network of highways consisting of many segments, together with their supporting taxes, was proposed in Congress. However, the individual voter and taxpayer, instead of having to make up an explicit bargain with other people in which he voted for high-

31. J. M. Buchanan and Gordon Tullock, *The Calculus of Consent*, University of Michigan Press, Ann Arbor, 1962 (2nd Edn., 1965).

ways in other states in return for getting them in his own state, could look at the whole collection and decide whether he favoured it or not.

This procedure does not eliminate the logrolling but simply makes it less public. It makes the logrolling implicit. The details of the nationwide highway system and the tax to be used to pay for it must be so designed as to produce a majority of votes. Since it is still true that the citizens of Pennsylvania gain from highways there and, to a lesser extent, from highways in the vicinity, but lose on highways on the other side of the continent, the person who makes up this highway bill, which is a package of individual proposals for construction of highways, must analyse the preferences and the relative intensity of preferences of the citizens of the various states.

The Harvard professor had spent several years in this arduous activity, and finally he and his colleagues had produced a highway construction bill which could get through. He had gone through a negotiation process very similar to that which would have occurred had we used the explicit logrolling process; but the implicit logrolling was quieter, and more centralised.

It is possibly, though not certainly, more efficient to do it this way because it centralises negotiations in a small group of specialised people.

In any event, the outcome is apt to be similar, except that with implicit logrolling it is possible for a group, which could be almost 50 per cent of the population, to be left out of the bargain. In a way, implicit logrolling moves us back to the median voter situation in a special form (pp. 14–22).

LOGROLLING AND THE MEDIAN VOTER

What is the relationship between logrolling and the median voter analysis? The answer is simple if put in geometric terms.[32] In plain English, the difference is that there are some issues upon which people feel much more strongly than on others. It is these issues which lead to logrolling. Individuals are not motivated to make trades (exchanges) between two issues if they all feel equally strongly about both because there is no profit to be made by a bargain. It is only when the two parties feel more intensely about certain issues, and the issues are different, that a bargain can be made. If A is very much interested in having Liverpool harbour dredged at the government's expense and would, on the whole, prefer not to be taxed to pay his share of

32. The indifference curves around the optima in the median voter theorem were circles. In logrolling they are ovals.

the dredging of Southampton harbour, he may nevertheless be able to make a bargain with B, a resident of Southampton with the opposite preferences, under which both harbours are dredged. This kind of bargain cannot be presented by simple geometry because it requires more than two dimensions and algebraic tools.

IMPLICIT LOGROLLING IN BRITAIN: PARTY MANIFESTOES AND COALITIONS

The most obvious single case of implicit logrolling is the position taken by a party going into a general election. The manifestoes of the major parties in Britain (or the platforms in the United States) show that they involve implicit logrolling. Measures clearly unpopular with many voters are included because they are highly popular with a minority, which can be expected to accept other planks in the platform unpopular with it. Opinion polls seem to indicate that trade unions in Britain are disfavoured by a majority. Nevertheless, the Labour Party supports them and the Conservative Party has refrained from urging very radical acts against them. The reason is obvious. The strong partisans of the trade unions are likely to vote for the Labour Party because of its support, even if some of the other parts of its policy are contrary to their desires. And other members of the Labour coalition, although they are more critical of unions, are willing to accept a general programme which includes support for the unions because other parts of the manifesto promise policies they favour.

In a sense, almost every bill that passes through a legislative body represents this kind of implicit logrolling. The people who have drawn up the bill have consulted many other members of the legislature and have made changes to please minorities who can be brought to support the bill if given something in return. No doubt the supporters of the bill have also engaged in explicit logrolling in that they have promised to vote in favour of other issues in return for that support.

REFERENDA

In a way, the clearest example of implicit logrolling will be found in some referenda on local improvements in the United States. Sometimes these referenda involve a large project. The voters in my county in Virginia recently voted against a proposal for a new courthouse. Often the referendum proposal is a collection of unrelated projects except that if grouped together it is thought a majority will favour them, whereas it would oppose any individual one. Since this kind of referendum is frequently used in school financing, textbooks used to teach administrators of public education in US schools of education frequently contain instructions on how to make up this kind of bargain.[33]

We should not be unhappy about these very common democratic practices, although normal discussion of them is condemnatory. There is no reason why minorities should not be served by democracies. The problem is acute only if the advantage to the minority is less than the gain to the majority.

LOGROLLING IN BRITAIN: COMPROMISES IN THE CABINET

The description I am about to give is to a considerable extent hypothetical rather than based on direct personal knowledge. In the first place, I am a foreigner. Secondly, British politics is carried on in a highly secretive manner. It is not very obvious exactly who determines the policies that the parties adopt. It is clear that the party in power will, because of the party discipline that normally dominates the British Parliament, be able to get its will enacted. The question is: how does it determine what it "wills"? There are two possible and different procedures, but fortunately they lead to much the same conclusion.

For the first, let us assume that the basic decisions are made by the government itself, or in practice the cabinet, which is composed of a group of people who (*a*) are leaders of the party, i.e. represent various points of view within it, and (*b*) are the heads of branches of the executive government. In both of these capacities, they have ideas on what policy should be carried through. It is only possible, however, for, say, Mrs Shirley Williams to get something she favours if she can win the support of the bulk of the cabinet. As a consequence, an implicit, extremely tactful process of negotiation goes on in the cabinet, and a series of policies are adopted, mainly in the form of bills to be presented for passage by Parliament. If Mr Callaghan wishes to

33. This is, in my opinion, not to be criticised morally. But another aspect of these textbooks should be severely criticised: they also explain how to time the election so that people who favour the collection of expenditures are more likely to vote than people who do not.

remain Prime Minister and the members of the cabinet wish to remain members of the cabinet, this combination of bills must be such that at least a majority of the party will back it and the members of the cabinet are very good representatives of the politically active part of the party. Thus, a compromise set of bills worked out in the cabinet is apt to be one which the party as a whole will regard as acceptable. One minister accepts a Bill which benefits another, but which he would prefer not to pass, in return for the contrary favour to him.

The second procedure by which the same outcome is likely comes through the party apparatus. In the Conservative Party this is a set of committees of MPs who must maintain the support both of their local party apparatus and of the voters. These committees on various subjects do not in the true sense control the cabinet or the shadow cabinet (if the party is in opposition), but their expression of opinion has strong influence: the members of the cabinet or shadow cabinet hold their positions in essence because they have the support of at least one-half and preferably much more of their MPs.

The procedure is as described earlier (p. 41). Individual members of the committees have personal preferences. They make bargains with one another (no doubt in a most tactful way) under which they swap support. In consequence, the "position" (policy) papers adopted by these committees have general voting support, even though the proposition, if taken by itself, would often attract only a small minority of the party.

All of this is strongly reminiscent of the American system, except that it is concealed rather better. The American system is also rather concealed, and frequently congressmen will deny what they are doing. Indeed, a number of political scientists have succeeded in writing books about Congress without noticing the phenomenon of logrolling. This probably reflects their essentially moralistic approach more than their inability to see what is going on before their eyes.

BENEFITS OF LOGROLLING

But if logrolling can clearly create benefits, it can also cause harm. Consider a simple society of nine voters who confront a large collection of measures, each of which will be paid for by a tax of £2 on each of the nine, and each of which will confer benefits exclusively upon one of them. Policy A will cost a total of £9 in the form of a £1 tax on each voter, but will confer upon voter A a benefit worth £15. Clearly we would, on the whole, prefer that projects like this go through, although for any individual bill of this sort we might object to its effects on the distribution of income. Normally we would anticipate that the voters, if confronted only with this bill, would vote 8 to 1 against it; but with logrolling, assuming there were similar projects for other voters, it would get through while conferring similar benefits on other voters. The end-product would clearly be an improvement in the state of society.

But consider another project which similarly imposes a cost of £1 on each of the nine citizens and confers upon voter A a benefit of only £2. Here there is a clear cost of £7 to society as a whole. We would not want this bill to pass. And it would not get through under logrolling because the voter could not afford to vote for four other bills each of which would cost him £1 apiece, in return for four other people voting for his bill. This would lead to a loss for him of a net of £3, and hence he would not attempt to logroll the measure.

DEFECTS OF LOGROLLING

So far logrolling has worked efficiently; unfortunately, there is an intermediate class of issues where it does not. Suppose the return to voter A of a bill (which, once again, costs £1 apiece to every one of the nine taxpayers) is £7. He would be willing to trade a favourable vote on four other issues, costing him a total of £4, for four votes on his issue which would net him £2 on the entire deal. Society as a whole, however, would have been paying £9 for something worth only £7. We clearly do not want the government to undertake this kind of action. Is there something we can do to ensure that only those bills with benefit to society get through by logrolling? Unfortunately, the answer is "No," but we can do better than the present system. I regret to say that the necessary change, however, is one the average person will consider extremely radical.

Before indicating my radical prescription, let us begin with a theoretical analysis. Assume we have very many voters. Let us also consider various possible voting rules other than majority rule. On Figure 7 I have drawn the horizontal line as the possible voting rules that might be adopted: from requiring only one voter at the left, to requiring unanimity or all of the voters at the right.

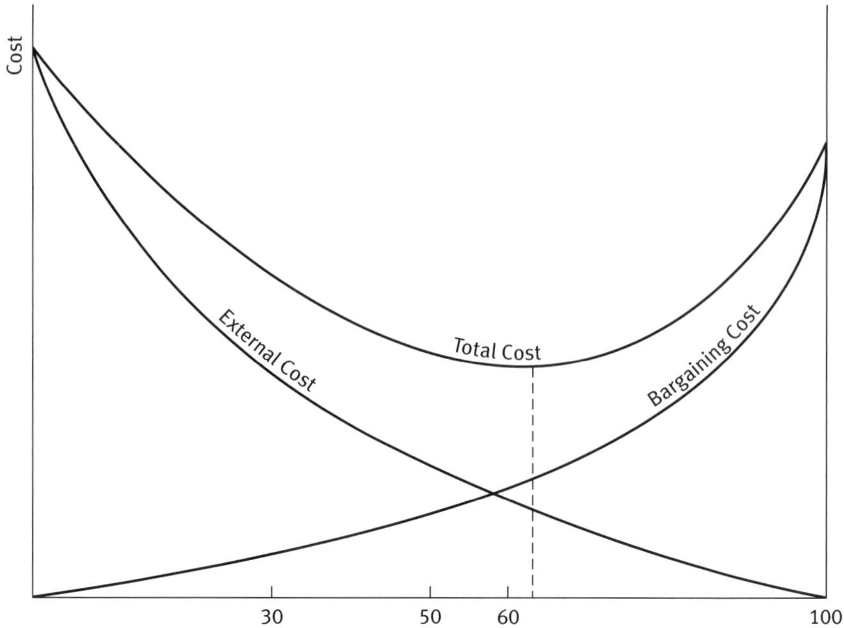

FIGURE 7
The costs of democratic decision

When I first present this diagram to students, I almost always encounter the view that a rule of less than majority is impossible. In the modern world, in which it is very common for candidates or even governments to be elected by less than the majority, as now in Britain, I find it hard to understand this position. Yet it is true that, although less than majority institutions are commonly used for electing *candidates* to office, they are rarely used for selecting *policies* or passing *laws*.

President Nixon was elected by 43 per cent of the popular vote in 1968. The last two governments of Britain have had much less than a majority of votes; indeed, none since 1945 has had a majority.[34]

In both countries, the voters vote for someone other than the ultimate government—MPs in Britain, electors in the United States. Yet these representatives are frequently elected by less than a majority. MPs have been

34. The American figures are not quite as extreme, but also not drastically different. Since 1870, only two-thirds of all American presidents have had a majority of the popular vote.

elected by as little as 36 per cent of the vote in their constituency, and electors in the United States can have even smaller percentages.[35]

We can use for policies the same procedure we use for selecting candidates. It is true that we will have to abandon Speaker's casting vote, invented to make a simple majority voting process work. It fits in nicely with majority rule and does not fit in with any other voting method. If we are going to consider other voting methods, we must assume that we use the same procedure used in selecting MPs in England, which is that anyone who wishes to be an MP puts his name up (and a deposit) and the one with the most votes is elected. For issues, anyone could present any proposal for voting and, in a series of periodic rounds of votes, the one with the most votes would be passed.[36]

Another complication is necessary for my diagram, though not for real-world voting. Many real-life voting systems have a minimum number of votes necessary for election. The Peruvian military government originated in a complicated dispute about whether a person elected to the Peruvian presidency did or did not have the 40 per cent of the popular vote the constitution required. The horizontal line on Figure 7, then, represents *all* such rules: from that which says the minimum number of votes necessary for an issue to pass is one to the rule which requires 100 per cent. The points indicate the percentage of votes necessary for passage: 50 is, of course, approximately the point normally used in majority rule.

On the extreme left end, the one-person rule would mean that any proposition favoured by any individual in society would be enacted. The £1 tax on all the nine members of our little society required to confer a benefit of £2 on one of them would be accepted under this rule. The "external cost" line indicates the cost of this procedure. The individual facing any voting system

35. The all-time record in this respect involves the 1960 election in the state of Alabama. Six of the 11 electors from that state were reported by Richard Scammon (Richard M. Scammon, *America at the Polls: A Handbook of American Presidential Election Statistics, 1920–1964*, University of Pittsburgh Press, Pittsburgh, Pa., 1965) as having been elected by 1.4 per cent of the voters. This is a mistake. The electoral situation in Alabama was extremely complicated and Scammon chose to resolve the difficulty in a way that had this result, and led to Kennedy having more popular votes in the national election than Nixon. If he had selected almost any other way of resolving the difficulty, it would have given Nixon more popular votes than Kennedy.

36. As is true with the election of MPs, some arrangement to prevent instantaneous reversal by the next vote would have to be included.

except unanimity will find that some bills are passed which, on balance, injure him. This clearly inflicts a cost on him and is an "externality" in the same way as the injury inflicted upon him by a smoking chimney.

As the number of votes required to pass a bill rises, the individual must select only those policies for which the cost to him of acquiring support is less than the benefit. The 30 per cent rule, for example, would eliminate our £2 benefit at the cost of the £9 bill, but not the £7 benefit bill. As the number of votes required to pass is increased, the likelihood of the individual being caught by a bill which injures him goes down; hence the external cost curve falls. At unanimity, it is at zero, although there are other reasons for not using unanimity.

If we deal with the kind of bill that does not concentrate its benefit on a few people but spreads it over a number, increasing the number of votes required for passage does not affect it until the number exceeds the number with net benefits. Then they must begin logrolling and, if the total benefit to society exceeds the total cost, they should be able to pass it even if the rule is unanimity. In other words, the external cost line is a genuine statement of the cost inflicted upon people by the passage of bills which, on balance, injure them under the different types of voting rules.

What about bills not passed? Surely they are as important as the ones that are. If we assume that bargaining and logrolling are absolutely costless and instantaneous, no bills for which the total gain exceeds the total loss would ever fail. This assumption, of course, has nothing to do with the real world; it is frequently very useful for analytical purposes and we have used it for the last few paragraphs. Let us now abandon it.

RADICAL SOLUTION: A PROPOSAL FOR "REINFORCED MAJORITIES"

Another line is marked "bargaining cost" on Figure 7. If we are following the "any-person" rule, there is no bargaining cost. I simply specify what I want done and it is done. When we require more voters, however, I have to make bargains with them. In the first place, there are resources committed to the bargaining process. More important, however, as the number of voters increases and in particular as it approaches unanimity, we will find that desirable legislation will fail because the bargaining process is too tedious and expensive. Hence, the bargaining cost line is partially the investment of time and energy in bargaining; but, much more importantly, imposing this bargaining cost means that desirable bills fail.

The total cost inflicted upon society by various rules is calculated by simply summing these two cost lines, as in the total cost line. The low point on this line is the optimal voting rule for the society. Only by coincidence would it be the simple majority. For important matters, I think in general it would be well above the majority and, indeed, most formal constitutions require more than a majority for at least some matters. The British constitution in this respect is something of an exception, but even in Britain so-called constitutional changes are not attempted unless there is thought to be more than a simple majority of support for them, regardless of the technical possibility. Even if republicans like Mr William Hamilton, MP, some day found themselves with 51 per cent of the MPs, it is extremely doubtful whether they would regard themselves as authorised to dethrone the Queen and confiscate her property.

Majority voting is thus generally not optimal. For important matters we would require something more. This conclusion is in general accord with constitutional processes throughout the world. But my opinion is that "reinforced majorities," say two-thirds majority, should be used much more widely than they now are. Indeed, I have on occasion recommended that the President of the United States always veto all bills in order to compel a two-thirds vote for everything in both houses of Congress. Startling though this proposal is, the analysis which leads to it is in the process of becoming the orthodox doctrine in public finance texts in the United States and, indeed, is now spreading to Britain.[37]

VI. Envoi

When I began this *Paper*, it seemed to me that instead of surveying the contributions of the new economic approach to politics, it would be better to present a few simple, but fundamental, examples. The reader can get an idea of the type of reasoning applied and some of the conclusions drawn from it. Even at this early stage, the conclusions are by no means uncontroversial; but I think they withstand scientific criticism. I hope I have aroused the reader's curiosity and that he or she will continue studies in this development of economics to government and politics. New knowledge is more valuable if

37. [Professor Tullock is, with Professor J. M. Buchanan, the originator of this analysis. —ED.]

used than if it moulders in a library. (To assist in further investigations, I append suggestions for further reading, p. 57.)

Today, in both Britain and the United States, there is a widespread feeling that the old solutions have failed. This is a time when a careful rethinking of our position is necessary. I hope the new economic approach to politics will provide the foundations for such a reconsideration.

A Note on Further Reading

For the British reader interested in learning more about the new economic approach to politics, a brief introduction to the literature may be helpful. On the theory that the reader of introductory *Papers* does not want to jump immediately into the most difficult and advanced work, I begin with more general books rather than highly specialised texts and journal articles.

On the subject of Chapter II, there are two general books, *The Logic of Collective Action* (Harvard University Press, 1965) by Professor Mancur Olson, and my book, *Private Wants, Public Means* (Basic Books, New York, 1970). Olson's was the pioneering work; my book, an undergraduate text, may be better as an introduction, even though it contains little original thought. On Chapter III, Professor Duncan Black's *The Theory of Committees and Elections* (Cambridge University Press, 1958) is the pioneering work. Professor Anthony Downs's *Economic Theory of Democracy* (Harper and Row, New York, 1957) and Professor James M. Buchanan's *Demand and Supply of Public Goods* (Rand McNally, 1968) are also essential.

A discussion of the voting paradox and an introduction to a large collection of other problems raised by voting is in *An Introduction to Positive Political Theory* (Prentice Hall, Revised edn., 1973) by Professors William H. Riker and Peter C. Ordeshook. This is a difficult book, but I know of nothing simpler. *The Calculus of Consent* (University of Michigan Press, Ann Arbor, 1962) by James M. Buchanan and me discusses the design of optimal voting rules and other problems of producing a constitution. Although easier than Riker and Ordeshook, it is more difficult than most of the other books I suggest below. Finally, on Chapter IV, my book, *The Politics of Bureaucracy* (Public Affairs Press, Washington D.C., 1965), and William A. Niskanen's *Bureaucracy and Representative Government* (Aldine-Atherton, New York, 1971), will set the reader well on his way.

The reader may then wish to turn to the more specialised literature. Dennis C. Mueller's comprehensive review article and bibliography of public choice is in the *Journal of Economic Literature*. It contains a comprehensive bibliography and surveys a good deal of work I thought too advanced for this *Paper*. As another fairly readily available source, the journal *Public Choice* carries about a third of the articles published in this new subject. Looking through issues of the journal in a library or, better still (from the standpoint of the editor), subscribing to it will provide an up-to-date view of the most recent work in the economic approach to politics (above, p. 3, text and footnote 1).

PART 4

RATIONAL IGNORANCE AND ITS IMPLICATIONS

POLITICAL IGNORANCE

Having discussed the provision of information by the media, we will, in this chapter, cross the street and deal with the individual "consumers" of information. Primarily our concern will be with information costs and their effect on political decisions. Any discussion of this subject must necessarily owe a considerable debt to Anthony Downs's *An Economic Theory of Democracy*.[1] Although I will follow along the general route he pioneered, the technical details will generally be different from the Downs model.

We may well start our consideration of information and politics by taking seriously a well-known joke. Mr. Smith, upon being asked who made the decisions in his family replied, "We have a division of labor. My wife makes decisions on minor matters and I make them on major problems. For example, my wife decides where we should go for vacations, the children's education, etc. I decide our attitude toward the recognition of China." It is always a mistake to analyze a joke, but let us, at least, inquire what is funny about this one. Most people would agree that relations with China are, indeed, more important than where the Smith family spends its vacation. However, most people would also feel that, in fact, the wife runs this family. This apparent paradox is easily explained. The decision of the Smith family on where they will spend their vacation will be the controlling decision on that matter, but although in a democracy their decision on relations with China has some influence on the country's relations with China, it is clearly only a tiny amount. If we evaluate the importance of the minor influence which the attitude of the Smith family has on our relations with China, then we will see that the Smith family decision on China is, indeed, much less important—as regards effects—than their decision as to where they will spend their vacation.

Public problems are normally more important than private problems, but the decision by any individual on a private problem is likely to be more important than his decision on a public problem, simply because most people are not so situated that their decision on public matters makes very much difference. It is rational, therefore, for the average family to put a great deal

Reprinted, with permission, from *Toward a Mathematics of Politics* (Ann Arbor: University of Michigan Press, 1967), 100–114. Copyright by The University of Michigan 1967.

1. Harpers (New York, 1958). In general I will not provide footnotes for each point where my analysis duplicates that of Downs, since there are a great many such places.

more thought and investigation into a decision such as what car to buy than into a decision on voting for President. As far as we can tell, families, in fact, act quite rationally in this matter, and the average family devotes almost no time to becoming informed on political matters, but will carefully consider the alternatives if they are buying a car.

The immediate reaction of the reader may be that this description of the behavior of the voting and buying public is not that which he observes among his friends and acquaintances. He may, of course, be correct in his observations, but they are made in a nonrandom sample. The reader is probably much better informed and more interested in political matters than the average. Since like appeals to like, it is probable that his friends are also much interested in political matters. Thus, he can hardly judge the average man on the basis of his friends and acquaintances. Not enough research has been done on the amount of effort put into political study by the common man, but it is reasonably certain that the figure would be small.

The individual may, of course, get a good deal of entertainment out of observing politics. He is apt to root for one team, just as he would if he were a baseball fan, and be interested in obtaining information about his heroes. As anyone who has had any contact with baseball fans knows, they do tend to acquire quite a bit of information about the team they favor and also about its potential opponents. This information, however, seldom causes them to shift their support from one team to another. The purpose of the information is to permit them to carry on the enjoyable occupation of conversing about their team, not as a basis for decision as to what team they will favor this year. Similarly, most people acquire political information so that they can participate in the conversation at parties, not in order to decide how to vote. Since strong partisanship is an asset in such conversations, a relatively objective interest in the facts is not likely to be prominent.

Both baseball fans and people interested in politics as a hobby find it easy to get a good deal of information on these subjects because the news media give them good coverage. It would be interesting to find out how many people read each sort of news in the average newspaper, but surely almost everyone, at least, sees the principal headlines and thus comes to know various things about both politics and baseball. The difference between the intent hobbyist and everyone else is simply that the intent hobbyist reads the whole article in areas of his interest instead of merely glancing at the headlines. Even the intent hobbyist, however, will normally depend solely upon news media for his information about politics. The widely sold books of statistics of baseball have no counterpart in the political world (although the revival of political pamphleteering, which was a feature of the 1964 campaign, may change this). Given the low importance of the decision on how to vote, it is rational to depend upon information which comes in automatically through some regularly available source rather than engaging in serious research. Clearly, most voters have always acted this way in spite of the horror of political scientists before Downs.

But if the rational voter is ill-informed, it still is true that voters, at least some of them, change their political position from election to election. It is these voters who do change their position who are most important to the political parties, not those who stick to one party regardless. Further, at some elections these shifts can be very large. Lastly, the United States has the primary system, and every man running for office must first win the nomination in a little election confined to the voters of his own party. Clearly, in these primary elections the firm commitment which most voters have to a single party is not relevant. In the primaries not only are the voters not guided by partisanship, they also have even less information than in the regular elections. The newspapers and other opinion media give much less attention to the candidates for nomination, since there are more of them. This means that the amount of information readily available is very small. Thus, it is highly probable that the primary voter is even more ill-informed than the voter in the regular election.[2] The ultimate outcome of our reasoning is that the basic decisions as to who shall hold public office are made by rather poorly informed voters.[3]

In order to discuss the matter with greater rigor, I would like to make use of several rather simple models. The first of these, the "rational-ignorance" model, assumes that the individual, in considering any political issue, makes a sort of estimate of the likely effect upon him of the ultimate governmental

2. Since the voters in a primary are normally much less numerous than in the regular elections, they may be a select group, and better informed than the average voter. This may partially counterbalance the effect of the poorer information available.

3. Again, this is only true as a general rule. Voting decisions may be made as the result of careful consideration of the issues. The switch of Iowa from firmly Republican to Democratic in the 1964 election fairly clearly resulted from the attitude of Barry Goldwater and the Republican congressional delegation on the continuation and expansion of farm subsidies. A good many firmly Republican farmers were forced to make a choice between their principles and their pocketbooks. They chose their pocketbooks, but clearly this involved a good deal of thought for most of them.

decision and of the likely cost of getting enough information on the problem so that he can understand it and take appropriate action.[4] If the estimated effect is less than the cost of becoming informed, then he will not bother with the matter. Suppose, for example, the individual feels that the likely effect on him of the Kennedy round of tariff cuts will be less than $500.00, but that the investment in time and effort necessary to really understand the economic issues involved would be greater than $1,000.00.[5] Clearly, he would be sensible not to bother with it.

It might be objected that the individual cannot make estimates of this sort without carrying out an extensive investigation. In practice, I think that people do use some sort of rough procedure like this in deciding about what they will worry, but the reader need not agree with me. In the next chapter we will shift to the "casual-information" model, which avoids this problem. Meanwhile, let us work out the implications of rational ignorance. The first thing to note is that the politician, in making up programs to appeal to rationally ignorant voters, would be attracted by fairly complex programs which have a concentrated beneficial effect on a small group of voters and a highly dispersed injurious effect on a large group of voters.

Note that at least some complexity is necessary. A proposal to tax everybody one dollar in order to give 1 per cent of the population a gift of $100.00 apiece would not work since the cost to the 99 per cent of the population in understanding the purposes and effect on them of the legislation would be less than $1.00 in such a simple situation.[6] If, however, the politician can work out a complex arrangement for doing the same thing in a less clear way, he may have a winning issue. Suppose, for example, a program is proposed to strengthen the national defense by keeping the glove-making industry in existence, it being alleged that the glove-making factories are read-

4. The action could be writing his congressman, or simply keeping the congressman's vote in mind until the next election.

5. Note that the cost would be largely in the form of leisure time devoted to study. Thus, the individual's relative appreciation for different ways of spending his leisure determines the cost of becoming informed. Here, again, the reader with both intellectual tastes and a good background must guard against assuming that the costs incurred by the average man would be as small as the cost to himself.

6. Log-rolling might lead to such a bill, passing as part of a much more complex chain of legislation. This is not strictly relevant to our present line of reasoning, but it should be noted that one of the by-products of log-rolling is a degree of complexity in the governmental process, which makes it considerably harder for the voter to evaluate any given proposal.

ily convertible into factories for producing some special type of military equipment. If it would take the average voter the equivalent of $10.00 to find out whether or not there will be a significant benefit to the national defense, and, if the likely effect on him, cost or benefit, is less than $1.00, clearly he would be rational in ignoring the issue. The small minority of glove-makers, on the other hand, would be completely irrational if they did not invest the $10.00 in obtaining the necessary information. Thus, the simple fact that the program has the "right" degree of complexity means that the politician proposing it can feel fairly safe in assuming that the people who will gain by the program will know about it and, thus, have their vote affected by it, while those who will be injured will not.

It may, of course, be possible to introduce a completely artificial degree of complexity. Farm subsidies are a clear and obvious example of an income transfer from the majority to a minority. The advocates of the program, however, have succeeded in so muddying the water that the average voter would have to undertake quite a program of study to appreciate its simplicity. Almost any readily available source of information on the farm program will present, in addition to the true picture, a set of rather complex rationalizations of the program. This makes what is basically a simple matter quite complex to the average voter. This artificially introduced complexity no doubt is one of the major reasons for the fact that this fairly straightforward transfer of income has not only been adopted but has grown in magnitude as the number of farms shrank.

One of the major themes of the "Chicago School" of economics has been the desirability of relatively simple and straightforward policies for such problems as cycle control and income equalization. It may well be that their simplicity is one of the reasons they have not been adopted. The people who would be injured by the change from the status quo can easily figure this fact out. Frequently, also, these Chicago School programs will inflict a sizable injury on some small group which is now receiving some sort of special treatment while giving a small benefit to a large group of people. If our present assumptions were to be accepted, it would normally be the case that the small group would take the trouble to understand the issue, while the majority, if there were any significant degree of complexity, would not. Hence the proposal would fail to attract votes.

It is unfortunate, also, but some political issues seem to be such that the information problem is exactly the reverse of what might be hoped. A program like TVA may appear quite complex to the many voters scattered throughout the United States who are injured by it. Since their individual injury is small, they are wise not to make any effort to understand the issue. The people living in the TVA area, on the other hand, are not only the recipients of sizable benefits but appreciation of these benefits is a very simple matter. It is easy to see that the electricity bill is smaller. Thus, in this case a program which imposes a small cost on a large number of people is quite complex from their standpoint while the benefits are simple and easy to understand from the standpoint of residents in the Tennessee Valley.

The fact that most government expenditures are not attached directly to tax measures further complicates the matter. Suppose, for example, that some project is proposed which would benefit a small minority of the population to the extent of $11.00 apiece at the cost of an increase in the government's expenditure of $9.00 per capita. The necessary tax will be quite a separate matter from the benefit. If we were to retain our assumption that individuals become informed only about matters which will probably affect them by the amount of $10.00 or more, then the prospective beneficiaries of this project would learn about the benefits, but not about the costs. If we were to assume that the minority to be benefited is 1 per cent of the population, then the cost-benefit ratio of this project would be 900 to 1, yet the project would probably pass through an elected legislature since it would be favored by a significant group and opposed by no one.

We can go even further; suppose that a project which will benefit a group is very simple in its direct effects, but the costs that it imposes are quite complex. If the cost of becoming informed about the benefits were, say, $2.00, while the cost of becoming informed about the indirect injuries that it would inflict were $20.00, then it might well be accepted by the voters even though the cost was greater than the benefit. If, for example, the benefit directly conferred was $5.00 per head, while the cost imposed in a devious and complex manner was $15.00, then a voter for whom the likely net effect of the measure would be a loss of $10.00 would vote for it. Paradoxically, his vote would be completely rational. The cost of becoming fully informed on the issue, which would lead to a negative vote, would be $22.00, so the rational man, in this case, would vote against his interest because he would be investing in information in a purely rational manner.

As coauthor of *The Calculus of Consent*,[7] in which log-rolling is stressed,

7. By James M. Buchanan and Gordon Tullock (Ann Arbor: University of Michigan Press, 1962).

I am naturally interested in the likely effect of these information considerations on log-rolling. In that book perfect information models are used throughout. It is assumed that each individual properly calculated the costs and benefits which he would receive from each measure. With this information, he engaged in vote trading and achieved a result which led to too much special-interest legislation. Our present model taking information cost into account points in the same direction, but the effect is much stronger. If we were to combine the two models, the net would be a still stronger bias toward special-interest legislation, particularly since the principal restraint on such legislation in the perfect information models is the cost of log-rolling. Since this is always highly complex, the individual would normally not invest enough resources in becoming informed to understand it. Thus, log-rolling could be expected to be carried to extremes because the voters did not really understand the cost part of the cost-benefit calculation.

It might be thought that these considerations invalidate the perfect information models of *The Calculus of Consent*. This is not so. Most of the models are simple, direct democratic systems, in which the tax cost of each measure is weighted against the benefit. Clearly, such situations do exist in the real world, particularly at the local level. Since it is very easy to understand the tax cost in such situations, and the benefit of each proposed measure is also easily understood by its beneficiaries, the perfect information model is not a violent distortion of the real world. Information costs come into such situations only as there are indirect secondary consequences which may not be easily understood. We could predict that the voters would behave as the perfect information models show them behaving for the simple direct effects of the benefits and the tax cost. Only if the proposal had additional effects which were hard to understand, would the information cost models be relevant. Such secondary costs and benefits probably do exist, the effect in discouraging industry of local property taxes may be taken as an example, and our present model would indicate that they would not be properly taken into account. On the local level, however, it seems unlikely that these secondary effects are terribly important. The perfect information model would thus be a reasonably close fit.

For representative democracy, the problem is more complicated. There are two sets of people who have to be considered, the voters and their representatives in the decision-making bodies. The representatives are normally much better informed than are the voters, in fact better informed than the voters could ever be expected to be. Moreover, in the case of the representatives, the cost of becoming better informed on one subject is normally a sacrifice of information on another. If we consider a congressman as a typical representative, he devotes full time to his job, and normally the limitation on the time he devotes to becoming informed about the substance of the legislation upon which he votes, is the time he devotes to becoming informed on the wishes of the voters. We thus have a rather well-informed agent trying to carry out the wishes of ill-informed principals.

Without going into this problem too deeply, there is a simple model which fits the situation fairly well. The voter will be well informed and deeply interested in any special benefits he receives or thinks he might receive from the government. He will also be well informed on any special injury, such as an "indirect tax"[8] which falls on him. In addition, he is aware of any general tax, such as income tax, which he pays. All of these things are either so easy to learn or so important to the individual voter that the rationally ignorant person can be expected to have this information. Certain general benefits provided by the government, such as police, schools, defense, etc., are such that at least some information on them is also easily obtained. In these cases the voter is more likely to know of some scandalous deficiency than of anything else, but at any rate, some knowledge on such matters as the need for repairing the streets, school conditions, number of unsolved crimes, etc., is apt to be held by the rationally ignorant voter.

We can group these factors into two general classes about which the voter will be informed and have preferences. The general taxes and special taxes which an individual pays will both be objectionable to him. He will oppose their being raised and favor their being lowered. With respect to any special benefits he may receive and the general benefits produced by the government, he has an equally simple preference function; he wants more and he certainly does not want them reduced. To these relatively realistic assumptions about the information and desires of the voter, let us add that he knows whether the budget is balanced and that he strongly favors balance. This last would have been descriptive thirty years ago, but may not be so now.

This set of preferences and this degree of knowledge on the part of the voters would lead the representatives in Congress to engage in vigorous log-

8. Although indirect taxes are normally thought of as concealed, this is only from the general public. In general, indirect taxes are very, very conspicuous to those individual members of the public who actually pay them. A manufacturer's tax on steel may be invisible to the average voter, but the steel manufacturer knows about it.

rolling with the objective of giving to a majority of the constituents in each of their districts as close a fit to their desires as is possible. The full log-rolling model, thus, can be utilized to analyze the situation. The lack of information on the part of the voters is only relevant in that they may not understand the general benefit portions of the governmental system and they may be overlooking longer range effects.[9] The voter is also basically affected by changes in the level of taxes or benefits; he does not have any clear idea of whether he is getting a good bargain in total. He cannot tell whether or not more efficient government would give him the same benefits with fewer taxes.

If the voter can hardly hope to have enough information to have any effect on the efficiency of the government, this might be assumed to merely put him in the position he is in normally in the market. He surely also does not know enough about automotive engineering to know whether the car he buys is produced as efficiently and priced as low as possible. In the market, however, there is competition, which can be relied upon to keep the producers efficient. If there were another government offering the same line of services for less, then the ignorant voter would have no difficulty in obtaining governmental efficiency.[10] The congressmen, of course, do have motives for improving efficiency since this would enable them to improve the satisfaction of their voters. Unfortunately, improvements in efficiency normally mean the discharge of government employees. Since such employees are also voters and this is a direct reduction in the benefits they are receiving from the government, there are other motives leading congressmen to oppose efficiency. What the outcome will be in any given case cannot be predicted, but the present American Congress shows little or no interest in efficiency.[11]

A basic assumption which we have been using in our discussion is that the voter objects to an unbalanced budget. Clearly, this was true not so long ago; equally clearly, it is becoming less true now. In a way, the principal effect of the "Keynesian" revolution has been to reduce the force of this objection. If this, basically irrational, preference changes, then the congressmen can solve their problems by simply spending more than the government takes in. The

9. In the casual-information model, which will be discussed in the next chapter, further effects of voter ignorance will be developed. These additional effects are ruled out by our present set of assumptions.

10. Something rather like this does happen with local government units.

11. See Aaron Wildavsky, *The Politics of the Budgetary Process* (Boston: Little, Brown and Company, 1964), for a discussion of the actual methods now used.

inflationary effect of such continual deficits is probably too complex to be understood by rationally ignorant voters. For people like myself who feel that any one of a number of methods of eliminating depressions by manipulating the quantity of money is desirable, this poses a most difficult problem. If we cannot expect the average voter to understand these systems and enforce compliance on his congressman, then the balanced budget, with all of its crudities, or continual inflation would appear to be the only alternatives.

Our model so far has been relatively crude. In order to develop a more rigorous model, let us consider a problem to which Downs devotes a great deal of attention: What is the payoff to the individual from voting? Assume that you are in possession of some information and from that information you have decided that you favor the Democratic party or, if it is a primary, some particular candidates. The payoff could be computed from the following expression:

$$BDA - C_v = P$$

B = Benefit expected to be derived from success of your party or candidate
D = Likelihood that your vote will make a difference
A = Your estimate of the accuracy of your judgment ($-1 < A < +1$)
C_v = Cost of voting
P = Payoff

Certain aspects of this expression deserve a little further discussion.[12] The B refers, of course, not to the absolute advantage of having one party or candidate in office, but to the difference between that candidate and his opponent. In Downs's presentation it is called the "party differential" to indicate that it is a difference, rather than an absolute measure. A good many of the intellectuals who voted for Johnson disliked him and would have opposed him for President if he had been opposed by his running mate Hubert Humphrey. In spite of their negative evaluation of Johnson, however, they would have shown quite a high "B" value because of the strength of their detestation of Goldwater. Choosing between two evils, they nevertheless

12. This equation was somewhat further developed and subjected to empirical tests in "A Theory of the Calculus of Voting," by William H. Riker and Peter C. Ordeshook (unpublished manuscript). The Riker-Ordeshook study which was, in part, the result of a reading of this book in draft, on the whole supports the purely theoretical conclusions drawn here.

thought the choice was a most important one because they thought the two evils were of vastly different magnitude.

The factor labeled A, the estimate of the accuracy of the voter's judgment, is normally left out of discussions of this kind. It is included here because we are preparing to consider variations on the amount of information held by the individual, and the principal effect of being better informed is that your judgment is more likely to be correct. Note that it is put in the subjective form because that is the only way that a judgment can be formed, but an objective figure could be substituted without any real change in the formula. The factor labeled A can take any value from minus one which represents a certainty that the judgments will be wrong,[13] to plus one, which indicates that the voter is sure he is right. The choice of this rather unusual way of presenting what is really a probability figure is due solely to its use in this particular equation, not to any desire to change the usual probability notational scheme. For the equation to give the right answer, it is necessary that A have a value of zero when the individual thinks that he has a fifty-fifty chance of being right.

The factor labeled D is the likelihood that an individual's vote will make a difference in the election; that is, the probability that the result if he were to vote would be different than it would be if he were not to vote. For an American presidential election, this is less than one in ten million. C_v is the cost, in money and convenience of voting. For some people, of course, it may be negative. They may get pleasure, or at least the negative benefit of relief of social pressure from voting. If we view voting as an instrumental act, however, something we do, not because it gives us pleasure directly, but because we expect it to lead to some desirable goal, then our decision to vote or not will depend upon weighing the costs and benefits. For most people, the cost of voting is probably somewhere between \$1.00 and \$5.00.

Let us put a few figures into our expression. Suppose I feel that the election of the "right" candidate as President is worth \$10,000 to me. I think I am apt to be right three times out of four, so the value of A will be .5, D will be figured as .000,000,1. Assuming that my cost of voting is \$1.00, the expression gives (\$10,000 × .5 × .000,000,1) −\$1.00 = −.9995. It follows from this that I should not trouble to vote. This result has shocked a lot of

13. There is a sort of concealed assumption that all votes are simple choices between two alternatives. This is realistic if we are talking about American elections and is also much simpler than choosing one among a number of alternatives.

people since Dr. Downs first presented it.[14] Since our concern is not with whether you should vote, but with information, we will not devote much time to the issue. A number of arguments have been advanced by various scholars as to why an individual should vote, but we need not go into them.

It will, however, be worthwhile to consider a few variations on the expression. In the first place, it is frequently argued that this line of reasoning would lead to no one voting. This is not true. If people began making these computations and then refraining from voting, this would raise the value of D, since the fewer the voters, the more likely that any given vote will affect the outcome. As more and more people stopped voting, D would continue to rise until the left-hand side of the expression equaled the right. At this equilibrium there would be no reason for nonvoters to begin to vote or for voters to stop. Presumably the people voting would be those among the population who were most interested in politics, since D would have the same value for everyone but $(B \times A)$ would approximate a positive function of political interest.

The equation, if it is thought to be in any way descriptive of the real world, would imply that people would be more likely to vote in close elections, and that they would be more likely to vote in local elections than in national ones since D would be larger in those cases. The first hypothesis was tested by Riker and Ordeshook[15] and found to be correct. The second would appear to be easily falsifiable. The problem is that A and B in the equation vary greatly between national and local elections. In local elections the party differential for the voter is apt to be small and the difficulty of getting information may be great, with the result that A approaches zero. As a result, a decline in voting would be expected as the political unit gets smaller, until it becomes so small that each individual knows the candidates. Here A would be large, and the probability of voting correspondingly increased.

It should also be noted that the equation is not strictly suitable for members of pressure groups. For them, the number of votes cast may well be important even if it does not change the result of the election. Insofar as the politicians are able to figure out how many votes were cast on the "farm issue," for example, they will take this bloc into account in their planning for the next election. Thus, in a sense, D is always unity. In another sense, how-

14. Dr. Anthony Downs must be listed among the people who are shocked. In fact he continues to vote regularly.

15. *Op. cit.*

ever, D is just as small for the pressure group voter as for the man trying to elect a President on broader criteria. In each case, your own vote is only a tiny fraction of the whole. The major difference here is that the pressure group need not be anywhere near a majority of the population to be effective. Thus, instead of contributing one vote to a national majority of something in excess of 35,000,000, the member of a pressure group may be one vote in a voting block of 1,000,000. Obviously, his influence is greater in the latter case.

Our voting expression requires another elaboration to bring out its full meaning. An individual, in deciding how to vote, may take into account both direct benefits he receives and a sort of charitable benefit he receives from helping others. Thus, the B of the expression could be replaced by $(B_p + B_c)$, with B_p representing the direct benefits that the voter expects to receive and B_c representing the benefit he will receive because he gains some satisfaction from other people being benefited. To use an example that one of my students used as part of a vigorous attack upon my general position, suppose an Iowa farmer estimated the value of retaining his farm subsidies if Johnson won, at $5,000, while he felt that the benefit to the United States, as a whole, from a Goldwater victory would be $10,000,000,000. (The fact that the farmer would receive his aliquot share of the $10,000,000,000 may be ignored.) If the farmer had the normal impulses for charitable activity, he would put at least some value on the benefit to the rest of the nation and, given the immense value of the benefit in this case, the value he put on it would certainly far outweigh the $5,000.

This logically raises two questions: whether the farmer would put enough value on the charitable benefit to get a positive payoff from voting, and whether he would put enough value on it so that he would vote against his direct interest in the farm subsidy. Starting with the first, we may use the values used above, to figure out the value that the farmer would have had to put on the $10,000,000,000 benefit to the nation to be willing to vote for Goldwater. The answer turns out to be $20,000,000. This is the minimum size of the benefit the farmer would have had to estimate that he would receive if his investment of $1.00 in casting a ballot, which has a one-in-ten million chance of being decisive, was to have a positive payoff. This is equivalent to saying that he would have had to be willing to pay $20,000,000 if such a payment would insure a Goldwater victory. Obviously, the farmer would not have been willing to make such a payment; in fact, he didn't have the money. But the St. Petersburg paradox is involved here, as is the fact that individuals do not necessarily act in perfect accord with the computed odds. I imagine that most people, if asked whether they would be willing (if they had the money) to pay $20,000,000 to confer a benefit of $10,000,000,000 on the nation as a whole, would reply "yes." I also suspect that few of them would, in fact, be willing to do so if their fortune were not very much larger than $20,000,000.

If the farmer had decided to vote for some such reason as duty or habit, however, he might still have put the public good above his private interest without giving it an evaluation of $20,000,000. Indeed, if he felt that the benefit he would receive from feeling that the rest of the country is well off exceeded $5,000, clearly he should have voted for Goldwater if he voted. In practice, of course, he was unlikely to face such a clear problem. Decisions as to which party will do the most for the "public good" are difficult to make. Both parties will be claiming that they will make more of a contribution than the opposition. The private benefits, on the other hand, are relatively easy to work out. The farmer is likely to have figured out which side would have given him the most personally and then permitted himself to be convinced that this side was also the best for the country.

We can, however, conceive of an experiment to determine how much voters weigh benefits to other persons. There is currently much concern in the rest of the United States with the politics of Mississippi. Suppose the state of Mississippi agreed to sell a vote to anyone who was not a resident of the state, not engaged in business in the state or selling things to the state government, and was not going to move to Mississippi for five years.[16] It would thus be possible for the people who are concerned with Mississippi's state of affairs to change it by obtaining control of the state government. With the restrictions we have imposed, the only motive they would have would be charitable—the desire to benefit other people. Thus, by changing the price of the votes, we could get a measure of the strength of the desires for the "public good" of a number of people. I would guess that a lot of votes would be sold at $10.00, rather few at $100.00, and almost none at $1,000.00.

We can vary our Gendanken experiment to produce somewhat different "results." Suppose that the state of Mississippi, instead of selling votes itself, permitted its *voting* citizens to sell their votes to persons from outside the state who had the qualifications listed above. This would not give a simple measure of the relative value that voters put upon their selfish and altruistic

16. In addition to these restrictions which are necessary to prevent corruption, it would be necessary to make sure that the purchaser of the vote used his own money. If the Ford Foundation, for example, were to provide subsidies, the whole experiment would be severely biased.

values, but it would permit comparison of the value that some voters (the Mississippians) put upon political decisions which are close to them and directly affect them and the valuation put upon more distant considerations by other voters. To make a guess, I would imagine that the result of this experiment would be an equilibrium price between $25.00 and $50.00, but with very few votes sold. If my guess is right, most Mississippians would feel their interest in retaining the status quo to be more than $50.00, while most outsiders would feel that their interest in changing it would be worth less. But this represents an excursion into possible methods of measuring intensity of feelings.

Returning to our problem of the effect of ignorance, let us once again complicate our model. An additional factor, C_i, the cost of obtaining information, has been included in equation (1).

$$BDA - C_v - C_i = P$$

This is, of course, the cost of obtaining additional information, since the voter will have at least some information on the issues as a result of his contact with the mass media. Of course, A is a function of information ($A = f(I)$),[17] and, hence, each increase in information held will increase A and, thus, raise both the benefits and the costs. The problem for the rational individual contemplating whether or not he should vote, would be whether there are any values of C_i which would lead to a positive value payoff.

Suppose, for example, that the investment of $100.00 (mostly in the form of leisure foregone) in obtaining more information would raise the value of A from .5 to .8. Using the same amounts for the other values as we used previously, $P = -100.992$. Clearly, this is even worse than the original outcome. Furthermore, these figures are realistic. The cost of obtaining enough information to significantly improve your vote is apt to very much outweigh the effect of the improvement. This is particularly true for the average voter who does not have much experience or skill in research and who would put a particularly high negative evaluation on the time spent in this way.

A further implication of our reasoning must be pointed out.[18] There may be social pressures that make it wise for the individual to make the rather

17. Subjectively, B is also possibly a function of information. Learning more might increase or decrease the voter's estimate of the importance of "his" side winning. Objectively, of course, the real benefit does not change.

18. This point was first made, I believe, by Dr. Roland McKean at the Faulker House Conference in October 1963.

small investment necessary for voting. In terms of our equation, C_v may be negative. In these cases, voting would always be rational. Becoming adequately informed, however, is much more expensive. Further, it is not as easy for your neighbors (or your conscience) to see whether you have or have not put enough thought into your choice. Thus, it would almost never be rational to engage in much study in order to cast a "well-informed" vote. For certain people, and presumably most readers of this book will fall within this category, A may already be quite high. For intellectuals interested in politics, the amount of information acquired about the different issues for reasons having nothing to do with voting may be quite great. Further, for this group of people, the value put upon the well being of others *may* be higher than in the rest of the population. It may be, then, that these people would get a positive payoff from voting even though the average citizen would get negative returns from taking the same action. Thus, for many of the readers of this book, voting may be rational. I have my doubts, however. The value put upon the well being of others must be extremely great. Further, my own observation of intellectuals interested in politics would not confirm that A is high for them. They may have a great deal of information, but this seems to have been collected to confirm their basic position, not to change it.

THE POLITICS OF PERSUASION

In the last chapter we made a type of cost-benefit analysis of the individual decision to acquire information. This analysis was confined to information acquired for essentially political reasons. Information acquired because a person enjoys acquiring information, or as a sort of by-product of other activities was ignored. People do, however, have curiosity, and enjoy, to some extent, acquiring information. It is this fact which largely accounts for the existence of the media discussed in Chapter VI. It is now possible to turn to discussion of the information individuals have even if they do not engage in any special effort to be well informed on political matters.

For the purposes of our model we shall drastically simplify the variations in the amount of information that individuals may have. Instead of a continuous variation, we shall assume that for each possible political issue, the voter is either: ignorant, casually informed, or well informed. In order to distinguish between these three states of knowledge it is necessary to devote a little attention to the mass media through which most voters obtain what information they have on politics. Most of the mass media which carry any political information at all, combine it with a great deal of other material. The newspapers, for example, carry some stories of political relevance, but they normally devote less space to them than to sports and sensational crime stories. There will also be a good deal of space devoted to society news and local and national happenings, which are of no particular importance to the voter qua voter.

It must be assumed that the people who operate these mass media have a good idea of their customers' tastes. Furthermore, it seems likely that most consumers of mass media do not simply go through from one end to the other. The typical newspaper reader[1] reads only the sections that interest him, possibly scanning the rest. For a great many readers, then, only occasional political pieces will be read. Moreover, the voter does not necessarily remember for any period of time what he does read. Last, but not least, it is

Reprinted, with permission, from *Toward a Mathematics of Politics* (Ann Arbor: University of Michigan Press, 1967), 115–32. Copyright by The University of Michigan 1967.

1. It should not be forgotten that many voters do not even read newspapers. In the course of interviewing an applicant for a teaching appointment who had a recent Ph.D. in economics, I discovered that his only source of news on the course of politics was radio newscasts.

unlikely that he gives much, if any, thought to most of the political information he does remember.

As a first distinction, then, the voter may, at the time he votes, be in complete ignorance on many issues. This is either because he actually never heard of them or because, although he did come across them in the course of his contact with some exemplar of the mass media, he was not impressed enough to remember them. In contrast, he may be aware of the issue and have some amount of factual information about it as the result of essentially casual receipt of information together with an evaluation of that information which made him remember it. We shall call this state "casually informed," and it will be our principal concern for the next few pages. Remember that it involves both the receipt of information and the intellectual effort involved in remembering it.

Remembering the models of the last chapter, it seems likely that for most voters, knowledge on most issues never goes beyond the casually informed stage. Thus, we must assume that most voters have not thought very much about most political issues when they enter the voting booth. Also they normally will have only a little information on most of these issues. This casual receipt of information, however, does give the voter some preliminary information on quite a number of issues. If there is some reason for him to become better informed on one of them, he can do so. Again, we shall simplify and draw an arbitrary line. If the voter is sufficiently interested in some particular issue so that he devotes as much thought to it as he would to the purchase of a new car, we will say that he is well informed on the issue—we would not expect to find many such voters. Note that our standard of "information" is actually measured by the amount of thought which the voter has devoted to the subject. Since it is unlikely that he would think seriously about the subject without at least some positive efforts to increase his information, however, this is not a serious objection. Normally, people with a significant interest in a given subject do at least some investigating in order to increase the amount of information they hold on that subject.

We have not assumed that the well-informed voter is capable of making accurate judgments in the field in which he is well informed, only that he has thought seriously about it. This may mean very little for many voters. People buy things in the market which are quite badly suited to their needs,[2] and it

2. Recent research indicates that the poor owe a good deal of their low standard of living, not to their low incomes, but to their inefficiency in purchasing. They buy shoddy merchan-

must be assumed that they are at least as inefficient in making political decisions. Still, well-informed voters at least know more than the casually informed or the ignorant. Note, however, that our definition implies only that the voter is well informed on some single issue. A voter might, of course, be well informed on several issues or even on all significant issues, but this is not required. The voters are either ignorant, casually informed, or well informed on each issue, and this state of information is what affects their voting. The well-informed voter on one issue may well be ignorant on others.

We might now inquire why people are at some given stage of information on various issues. Everyone starts out ignorant on everything, and given the variety of subjects which we could study and the amount of information available, everyone remains ignorant on very many subjects throughout his life. The average voter, however, is exposed through the mass media to a good deal of information on political matters. Some of this information will catch his eye so that he notices it and appear important enough to him so that he remembers. In part this is obviously a simple random process; in part, however, it is more. The casual reader is more likely to have his eye caught by an item which is nearer to his interests than other items. An Irish citizen of Boston who is employed in a bank and engages in a good deal of hunting on weekends is more likely to notice and remember items on these general subjects than on others. Thus, he may normally know the names of all Irishmen who are candidates for office, will be likely to have heard of any major expenditure of federal funds in the Boston area, be interested in any possible changes in banking regulations, and keep an eye on changes in the hunting and conservation laws.

It may be fairly assumed, then, that our Irish voter will notice articles on these subjects which appear in the newspaper, and remember, in general, what they say. He will also, no doubt, notice and remember a random sample of articles on other subjects. Will he, however, feel moved to improve his knowledge on any of these subjects so that he becomes well informed? Looked at in strictly rational terms, this is unlikely. As we have shown, the likely payoff which the voter will obtain through casting a more informed vote is very small, normally much smaller than the cost of becoming well informed. In most cases a voter will be well informed only if he has some reason for gathering the information, other than the possible effect on his vote.

---

dise at prices higher than they would need for better quality. D. Caplovitz, *The Poor Pay More* (Glencoe, Ill.: The Free Press, 1963).

Our voter might, for example, be well informed on the banking laws and regulations as a necessary part of his business and would naturally apply this knowledge in his political activities. At the very least, he would know enough about banking and the sources of information on banking laws so that becoming well informed on this matter would be very easy.

Similarly, the voter might live in a society where Irish politicians were very prominent both socially and as subjects of conversation, in which case he would automatically be well informed on this subject. He might also consider politics a sort of hobby, and devote a good deal of time to its study for the pleasure he gets out of it, or he may feel that it is the duty of a citizen to be well informed politically, and, thus, studies politics for a feeling of ethical justification. These last two motives, although perhaps widely applicable, apparently do not lead to much effect on the balloting. Most people who are well informed for these motives are quite firmly committed to one political position and do not shift.[3]

It might be argued that the members of pressure groups would find it rational to be particularly well informed. The argument would turn on the fact that pressure groups are normally much smaller than the total of voters, hence that each vote would be a larger share of the amount needed to get the boodle. Further, it is generally true that the absolute number of votes that can be mustered is important for a pressure group. In fact these matters are of little importance in deciding whether or not it is rational for the voter to seek out more information. Usually the potential member of a pressure group does not need much information to discover which side his bread is buttered on. The knowledge that Johnson was firmly committed to keeping farm prices up and that Goldwater proposed to adopt a gradual program of removing price supports was all that was needed for the average Iowa farmer in 1964.

It may, indeed, be better for the pressure group voter not to know much about the particular issue. Surely, the more the Iowa farmer had learned about the farm program, the more likely he would have been to have felt that there was a potential conflict between his ideas of right and wrong and his material interests. By not thinking much about the issue, he was able to follow his self-interest with a clear conscience. Similarly, the goldmining interests who were so shocked by the prominent role of Milton Friedman in the

3. Among intellectuals, a formal bow is normally made to impartiality by voting for a couple of minor candidates in the "other" party at each election.

Goldwater camp could have a simple clear identity between their devotion to their material interests and their devotion to the gold standard only so long as they did not learn enough economics to understand Friedman's criticism of that system. Even with a good knowledge of economics they might have remained believers in the gold standard, but they would have at least realized that their opponents had a case.

Further, the man who is well informed, in our rather restricted definition, on any given subject may, in fact, be very badly qualified to judge it. Bankers, for example, would be well informed about banking matters because they have given them serious thought. As every economist knows, however, they are almost impossibly bad judges of economic policy in this area. This is simply because the very large amount of information they have on the operation of their businesses normally leads them to make invalid inferences about the system as a whole. It is unfortunately true that many simple and correct principles for the management of individual banks are almost directly opposite to the correct principles for the management of the banking system. The well-informed banker knows the basic rules for operating his own business and, not unreasonably, assumes that the same rules apply to the system as a whole. This leads him into extremely foolish policy positions.

The voters who are well informed will frequently have a great deal of information which is not relevant to the specific political choice, but not necessarily much relevant information. This is because they have accumulated this information for reasons having nothing to do with the choice itself. They have acquired it in the course of their business, as a hobby, or because they enjoy politics. None of these reasons for "learning" would lead automatically to the particular set of information which would be of the most use in deciding on some particular political issue. Thus, the votes of the well informed may not be much more accurately calculated than those of the casually informed.

The model now gives us a simple idea of the information flows. (This model is essentially the same as that in Chapter VI except that it looks at the phenomena from the standpoint of the consumer instead of the supplier.) The mass media carry various items, mainly because they think that they will sell. In this connection it should be remembered that some "mass media" are actually rather specialized in their appeal. *Vogue* will do for an example. The individual voter is (at least to some extent) exposed to these mass media and, therefore, picks up at least some information on some subjects of political interest. To this point we can regard him as being ignorant on a number of political subjects, and being casually informed on others. Presumably there is a random component in the subjects which he remembers, but, in part, this also represents the result of some rational selection. He is more likely to look at and then remember items which appear close to his interests. Among the subjects upon which he thus becomes casually informed, there may be one or more which appear to him as worth further study. Upon these he will become "well informed."

The voter who is well informed on one or more subjects is likely to cast his vote very largely in terms of these particular issues. The reason he has become well informed is his greater interest in these fields, and this greater interest is likely to carry over into the voting booth. If it does not, he will differ little in his effect upon the election from a casually informed voter. Since the only areas where an individual will be inspired by rational considerations to become well informed are the areas where he has some special interest, the well-informed voter is the pressure group voter par excellence. Looked at from the standpoint of the congressional representative seeking reelection, the well-informed voter is probably a rare phenomenon, but he is at least easily predictable. There may be a few well-informed voters, but it is fairly simple to predict how the vote of any given one of them will be affected by a given piece of legislation.

The more normal voter, who has only casual information, is less predictable. Presumably he is casting his vote largely because he thinks it is his duty, because he gets enjoyment out of it, because it is something he was taught to do, or because there is considerable social pressure to do so. In any event, he surely does not think it very likely that his vote will make much difference, and hence does not regard his decision as being worth a lot of thought and study. Under the circumstances, he presumably inspects the information he has in his memory, and casts his vote in view of these various "facts." Let us, for the time being, assume that on each issue upon which the voter has any information, he knows, among other things, the stand taken by each candidate. Thus, he simply adds up the stands taken by the candidates on various issues in terms of his own opinion and the weights he gives to each policy problem, and decides how to vote. This means that the politician must take into account, for each issue, the likelihood that voters will be even casually informed about it, the policies which the voters will favor, and the relative weight they will put upon it in making up their mind in the polling booth.

In part, the information held by any voter is random and the politician can only assume that this information is evenly distributed through the population. (Some information held by the individual, because it affects his interests, may appear random to the politician, and he is unlikely to know much about who has what hobbies.) In part, however, the casual information of any individual reflects his relative concern with different problems, and here the politician will have a somewhat better idea of what he will know. The Irish will know if Irishmen have recently been put in high office and the bankers will know about new banking legislation, even if neither has more than a small amount of information on these points. It is fairly easy to guess what they will think about certain types of problems too. Those inhabitants of Richmond who know about the project to dredge the James River probably all favor it. This may, of course, be a mistake on their part. Surely some citizens of Richmond will gain markedly from this project, but it is by no means obvious that the gain made by an average citizen will exceed the tax cost to him, even if the tax is assumed to be distributed over the entire country. The individual benefits for most of the residents of Richmond, who are not directly connected with the project, will be small and indirect. Being casually informed about the existence of the project, but never having given the matter any serious thought, the individual is likely to have a vague idea of the benefits to be expected, but no idea of the cost. Thus, he may count it as desirable even if it would, in net, injure him.

The voter, in weighing the various issues, is likely to give the greatest weight to those closest to him, just as he is most likely to know about them. Thus, it seems likely, again, that the casual voter will act like a "pressure group" voter. He will differ from the classical idea of a pressure group voter only in that he may either be ignorant on any given subject or badly informed. These defects in the voter's information add a stochastic element to the equation. The congressman can never be sure when he will get an especially bad distribution of information among the voters, with all the things which will count against him known and all that would count for him unknown, but this merely makes his profession a dangerous one. In addition to increasing the risk, however, the existence of large numbers of ignorant and casually informed voters changes the parameters of the problem for the politician. He is, in the first place, less interested in the likely effects of a governmental action on the voter than in the view taken of the matter by the voter. The ignorant voter will take no view at all, so he can be ignored. The casual voter may be completely incorrect in his assessment of the problem, so the vote maximizing action may be directly contrary to his interest.

The pattern of behavior which this picture of the information held by the voters dictates for the politician is essentially that described by log-rolling. If there are any political problems on which there are widely and strongly held opinions, then he should try to follow those opinions. In addition, he should try to find opportunities to do things which will confer a simple, easily perceived benefit on small groups, but whose cost is dispersed and hard to understand. But he may be able to do better by manipulating the information held by the voters. Since this information is casually acquired, it may be possible to make it likely for the voter to casually acquire information favorable to the politician. The political campaign, the making of speeches and appearances, all have this effect. The dependence upon the real lack of voter interest in the issues, which characterizes most politicians, can, perhaps, best be illustrated by the fact that many politicians will not reply to charges made against them because they feel that this would give the charges a wider currency than they would otherwise receive.

In addition to these methods, advertising in the more conventional sense may be a big help to the politician, and most politicians engage in a good deal of it. They may also be able to influence the content of the mass media. In general, the editors of these sources of news are interested in obtaining the largest possible revenue with the smallest possible outlay. Under the circumstances, they are apt to be aiming at reducing the cost of their editorial matter, and the politician may be able to take advantage of this by providing suitable editorial matter at little or no cost. Furthermore, by regularly providing favors to the mass media, he may get them to give his "side" prominence and suppress information which might cause him political injury.

It must not be forgotten, however, that the politician is not the only one trying to influence the information held by the average voter. He will have an opponent who is trying to counter his strategies. This limitation means that the politician is unwise if he does anything which will seriously injure any important group of voters. If the injury is great enough so that it would pay his opponent to bring it to the voters' attention, he probably will. Thus, again, the politician should aim at policies which confer easily seen benefits and dispersed and hard to understand costs.[4]

So far we have been assuming that the voters know what the stands of the various candidates are on the issues. There is no particular reason why the ca-

4. As a limitation on this principle, there may be some voters who, for one reason or another, cannot affect the outcome of the election. Severe injury can safely be inflicted upon them.

sually informed voter should have any better information on this matter than on any other. The old lady in Vermont, who, because she was convinced that Barry Goldwater was opposed to TV, changed a lifelong habit of voting Republican, is merely an extreme example of the ignorance we may find in this area. This is, of course, one of the reasons for backing a party instead of individual candidates. It is easier to know what a party stands for than to know what each of a long list of candidates stands for. The casually informed voter may quite frequently be misinformed on this point, but he no doubt does have a better idea of what the party position on a given matter is than of what the individual candidates advocate.

In primaries, the voter does not have this crutch. He must make up his mind among candidates who receive little attention in the mass media, and who all appear to accept the positions of a given party. Under the circumstances, it is not very likely that he will have very good information on the stand of the candidates on those issues upon which he has made up his mind. Surely there must be an extremely large amount of ill-informed voting here. In fact, the democratic process may well have a basically stochastic effect at this level. It is also an area where public relations skill is of overwhelming importance.

Still, the expected pattern of behavior we would deduce for a politician would involve a great dependence upon log-rolling. The principal change which our limited information models make in the full information models of *The Calculus of Consent* and *Entrepreneurial Politics*[5] is to introduce an element of improper calculation. Further, since the limitations on information do not have an entirely symmetrical effect, the misallocation of resources to be expected under log-rolling is magnified. In justice, however, it should be pointed out that the principal advantage of log-rolling, the protection of minorities against exploitation, is also magnified by the ignorance present in these models.

On the basis of this relatively realistic view of the political information held by the individual voter, we can now discuss some problems of political persuasion. This discussion will, naturally, have some similarity to the media discussion in Chapter VI, but basically it will be concerned with individuals and will use variants of the equations developed in Chapter VII.

There is, however, another way to affect our government. Instead of wor-

5. By Gordon Tullock (Thomas Jefferson Center, Monograph No. 5, University of Virginia, 1962).

rying about our own vote, we may attempt to influence others. In equation (2), C_p is the cost of effort invested in persuasion, and D_p the likely effect on the outcome of the persuasion.

$$BD_pA - C_i - C_p = P$$

It is by no means certain that efforts to persuade will have a negative payoff even if voting does. In the first place, the number of people trying to persuade is a very small fraction of the number of voters. Since the average voter doesn't do a great deal of personal thinking about politics, and picks up his ideas from the mass media, it is reasonably certain that D_p in equation (2) for the average "persuader" must be very much larger than D in equation (1). Putting the same thing another way, advocacy is more likely to affect the outcome of the election than is voting. Needless to say, this is only for the average persuader. There will be very great variation in D_p from person to person. In some cases it may even be negative.

Another difference between equation (2) and equation (1) is that C_p is very small for some people. Persons engaged professionally in providing material for the mass media may be able to put a considerable "persuasive" effect into it with almost no cost. In some cases, indeed, it may have a negative cost. Consider a news broadcaster who must fill a half hour and who feels strongly that it is his duty to show the "truth." If "truth" for him means the position taken by one side, then he will obtain positive pleasure out of inserting it in his newscast. Similarly, the author of a TV series script may get a feeling of moral justification out of selecting his topics and treatment so that they "improve" the political ideas of the viewers.

The management of the mass media will put some limits on this process, of course, since it might reduce sales. In general, however, they do not care very much about the political position of their output.[6] As long as the writers do not offend too many potential customers, they will be left alone. In addition, the managers may feel the controversy is likely to sell, and actively encourage the taking of strong stands without much concern for what these stands are. Given that the average man gets almost all of his political information from the mass media, it is clearly true that individuals employed to produce material can have a very great influence with very little cost. Thus, for this small portion of the public, at any rate, the P in equation (2) would normally be positive.

6. In a great many American cities a morning and an evening paper are jointly owned. It is perfectly normal for these two papers to take different editorial positions.

This phenomenon is not limited to the producers of material for the mass media, however. At the lowest level, strong support of some political activity of the sort that involves membership in committees, local party leadership, or the signing of political manifestos is normally undertaken largely as a hobby. The individual gets a positive enjoyment both from the activity itself and from a feeling that he is "doing his duty." In any event, such activity is not irrational. It should be noted that it is not necessary to devote much in the way of resources to obtaining information. Most political activists, in fact, have more information than the average man, but not necessarily very much more.[7]

There are a great many people who are able to work political advocacy into their normal work without any cost or with small cost. In addition to the mass media, we have "class" media. The writer for the *New Yorker* or the *New York Review of Books* can put a good deal of political content into his output without annoying his editors. They may, indeed, require that he do so. Some journals, such as the *New Republic* and the *National Review*, exist solely for the purpose of political advocacy. Teachers also are in a good position to push their political views with little or no cost. This is particularly true of college teachers in literature or the social sciences who can hope not only to influence their students but also to influence other people through their students. The political science major is likely to be an opinion former in later life and thus spread his professor's ideas to a number of other voters.

Whether this sort of advocacy will, or will not, have costs will depend to a considerable extent upon both the status of the teacher and his positions. Advocating the position which is held by the overwhelming majority of his departmental seniors and members of the profession at other schools is likely to help rather than hinder the advance of an assistant professor. If he happens to hold views which are regarded simply as wrong by his immediate superiors, he is unlikely to be retained. Thus, the cost to an individual who happened to favor Senator McCarthy and was an instructor in an Ivy League School in the early 1950's would have been very heavy.[8] Even with tenure positions, a

7. In the academic community, those members who are taking an active role in politics are apt to be quite well informed. They are, of course, a small and biased sample. A fairly short conversation with the people who exert low-level political leadership in nonacademic environments is enough to indicate that for them, C_i is low.

8. These costs are largely imposed by members of his own department. Occasionally, however, the central administration will get upset about what is being taught in some course and attempt disciplinary action. Normally the "victim" of this process will find numerous and vig-

sufficiently great deviation can be costly. But, in any case, giving his opinion to his students will not involve any extra work to the teacher and is thus, in this sense, costless.

Those teachers who teach potential teachers have even greater leverage. Their ideas may, after a number of years, be spread to thousands of voters. The time lag, however, must be kept in mind. It is probable that only the people who work in the mass media can have any significant effect on an upcoming election. The writers for the intellectual journals and the university professors will have sizable effects only after a considerable delay. Since there will necessarily be this delay, it may be that they will be less interested in strict partisan politics than in trying to spread certain ideas or philosophies. As has been discussed in earlier chapters, the political parties adjust themselves to the spectrum of preferences in the society, and changing this spectrum may be a more effective way of influencing developments than developing party loyalties. The situation can be shown by equation (3):

$$A \times S - C_i - C_p = P$$

"S" is the amount of shift in "opinion" on some given issue, which is the result of the persuasion measured in terms of the "utils" obtained by the potential persuader.

Clearly, for people who have relatively low C_p's, this type of action can have a high payoff. Speaking personally, I am interested in improving the rationality of the political system under which I live, which is a complex of ideas. By writing on the subject and by teaching my views, I clearly have at least some effect in that direction.[9] Since I am paid to teach and write, and there is really little restriction on my choice of subject, the cost of my activities is substantially zero. Under the circumstances, P is almost certain to be positive if I give any sizable value to S and do not evaluate A at a low figure.

Diagrammatically, we can show the situation by Figure 1. On some issue the population is distributed as shown. The two parties, near the center of the

---

orous allies and will suffer no net costs. The situation is quite different if the junior member of the faculty differs with the members of his own department. Fortunately, many departments are quite tolerant of such deviations.

9. Needless to say, this effect may show up in a retardation of movement in an undesired direction rather than in actual movement in the desired direction. Any one individual will be only a tiny fraction of the influences in action at any time.

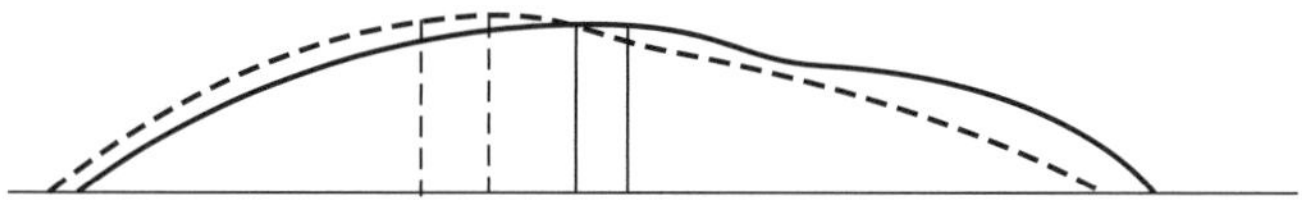

FIGURE 1

distribution, are at R and D. The persuader changes the distribution of the population to that shown by the dotted line. The two parties, conforming to the now existing distribution of public opinion, move to R′ and D′. Since one or the other party will be in power, the government's policy has been moved to the left. The persuader can feel that he has had a very real effect on "politics" even though his work may have had no effect upon which party is in power.

Needless to say, the mass media also can devote their attention to shifting public opinion rather than helping one party or another win. The television story writer, for example, who shows almost all businessmen as grasping and self-centered, while almost all of his politicians and civil servants are self-sacrificing and only interested in the public good, will surely have an effect on the "climate of opinion." Similarly, the writer of light fiction for the women's magazines who occasionally introduces farmers who are vacationing in Florida on the money they receive from the taxpayer for not farming, will probably have an effect on the public attitude toward the farm program. In a sense, the whole purpose of "public relations" is to exert this sort of influence through the mass media.

So far, in discussing the problem of persuasion, I have more or less ignored the costs of obtaining additional information for this purpose. It had been rational to engage in persuasion because the costs of doing so are zero or near zero to the individuals I have discussed. The costs of improving one's information in order to increase the accuracy of the decision as to what to advocate is not likely to be either zero or near zero. Thus, it is perfectly possible for an individual to be in a position where it is rational for him to try to persuade others of the correctness of his views, but not to engage in any research to find out whether those views are accurate. General experience would indicate that many people have drawn this conclusion. A great many people engage in rather vigorous advocacy of their positions without much effort to improve their information on them. Furthermore, as a bit of casual empiricism, most of the "information gathering" done by people who are engaged in persuasion seems to be aimed at improving their efficiency as persuaders, not at obtaining information which might lead them to advocate some other position. Such magazines as the *Nation* and the *National Review* serve the function, mainly, of a sort of "Agitator's Notebook" for their faithful readers. The liberals who read the *National Review* or the conservatives who read the *Nation,* are few. Neither group really wants information which might lead it to change its mind.

This relative unconcern for information by "persuaders" theoretically should be pretty general, and, to my mind, the theory fits the real world. In writing to persuade, inaccuracy in your information is only important if the person whom you are trying to persuade knows or is likely to find out that you are in error. Thus, you need only avoid factual misstatements which will be detected by your relatively ill-informed audience or which will be of use to the people trying to persuade in the other direction. There may not be anyone on the other side, and public ignorance may be deep and pervasive. A dictatorship will normally make public ignorance one of its main objectives. Even in a free society it may be possible to drown opposition in a sea of words. Milton Friedman has pointed out that 98 percent of all published work on the Federal Reserve System emanates from the Federal Reserve System itself. Under the circumstances, it is not surprising that its public image is a strong one.

So far we have been discussing the costs and benefits for anyone interested in attempting to change the world by political methods. There is, however, a strategic decision which also must be made. An individual can vote, try to influence voters directly, try to influence voters indirectly by influencing people who will influence other people, or he can (directly or indirectly) try to change the climate of opinion with the objective of shifting the point upon the spectrum at which the parties will locate. Depending upon his situation, any, all, or none of these actions may be rational.

In order to consider the advantages and disadvantages of direct or indirect persuasion, let us consider an abstract model of the transmission of ideas through society. In Figure 2 we have a society of ten individuals, each of whom holds a separate idea in Period 1. The ideas are denominated by the first ten letters of the alphabet. Each of the individuals tries to convince the others of the truth of his idea, and the result in Period 2 shows that ideas A, G, and I have been eliminated.[10] In Period 3, B and H drop out and in

10. For simplicity I assume the same ten persons throughout. The same process may take place more slowly with different generations being involved. The usual book in intellectual his-

	1	2	3	4	5	6	7	8	9	10
Period 1	A	B	C	D	E	F	G	H	I	J
Period 2	B	C	C	D	E	F	F	H	J	J
Period 3	C	C	D	E	E	E	F	F	J	J
Period 4	C	C	C	E	E	E	E	F	F	J
Period 5	C	E	E	E	E	E	E	F	J	J

FIGURE 2

Period 4 ideas C and E assume dominant positions. It would be fairly easy in Period 4 to predict that the eventual outcome would be the adoption of either C or E by the majority of the population. In Period 5, E has obtained a majority and if it involves a political policy, it is reasonable to assume that it will be adopted.[11]

What has all of this to do with the choice between direct and indirect persuasion? At any given time there are groups of ideas which are similar to the group held in Period 4. That is, most members of society hold one of a few positions and it is fairly certain that one of these few positions will be adopted shortly. The person interested in affecting the immediate outcome is more or less compelled to adopt one of the "popular" positions and argue directly to the voters for it. There will be other groups of ideas, however, which are each held by relatively few persons.[12] At any time, then, there are ideas which can be said to be in any one of the periods of Figure 2. For those ideas which are currently dominant, or which appear to be very close to achieving dominance, direct persuasion in the mass media is the most suitable procedure.

---

tory will take the form of an account of how some such idea as "E" gradually spread through a society over a considerable period of time.

Our diagram can be regarded as simply a geometric representation of this sort of growth, although I have included some ideas that did not spread.

11. Strictly speaking, this involves the additional assumption that the holders of the other ideas do not have strong enough feelings to log-roll E down. During the 1964 election, 88 percent of the population favored permitting prayer in the schools. That clever politician Lyndon Johnson, however, realized that the minority which was opposed felt much more strongly on the issue, and hence that there were more votes to be gained by supporting the Supreme Court than by supporting prayer.

12. In Figure 2 these "unpopular" ideas predominate in Period 1, but there are two of them, C and F, still in existence in Period 5. Ex ante it is no less likely in Period 5 that F will be the dominant idea in Period 9 than it was in Period 1 that E would be the dominant idea in Period 5.

For the ideas which are held by few persons, however, an indirect strategy is necessary. These ideas can become dominant only if people now plan to persuade others who will persuade others, etc. If you choose an unpopular idea you must plan not for immediate success, but for long-range influence.

There are several reasons why you might choose an unpopular idea to back rather than one which is now held by enough people so that it seems likely that it could be converted into a dominant idea in the next period. In the first place, since there are a great many unpopular ideas and only a few, ex-definition, which are held by large numbers of people, it is more likely that the idea which most appeals to you will be unpopular rather than popular. (This assumes, of course, that your preferences are not closely correlated with those of the average man.) Thus, unless you happen, by coincidence, to find that your first preference idea is one which is on the verge of becoming dominant, you will be confronted with a choice between an idea which you much prefer but which is unlikely to be widely adopted for some time and an idea which you like less but which may be adopted very soon. As an example, consider person 10 in Period 4 of Figure 2. He finds that J is the idea which he likes best, but he feels that J will surely not be adopted until Period 8 at the soonest. It is obvious, however, that either C or E will be dominant in Period 5; and we can assume he prefers C of those two. Thus, his decision as to whether to push C or J (he may be able to push both) is largely a choice between working for his maximum preference, obtainable some time in the distant future, or seeking to make a less significant improvement in the immediate future.

Obviously there can be no general solution to this problem. It depends, in part, upon the strength of the individual's preferences and, in part, on his estimate of the likely future developments. We can, however, consider the factors which must be taken into account. It is sometimes said that only the decision to push an idea such as C is "practical." Partly this view is based on simple blindness about possible long-run effects, but partly it reflects the fact that the odds are against any given idea now held by a tiny minority.[13] There are a great many such ideas and the odds against any one of them achieving dominance are correspondingly large. Thus, in Period 1 the odds against E achieving dominance at any time were about ten to one, while in Period 4 the odds against C were not much more than fifty-fifty.

13. Any new idea is, naturally, held by a tiny minority (originally a minority of one). In the natural sciences such ideas rapidly are tested by the majority of the profession. We need, but are unlikely to obtain, a similar mechanism for the social sciences.

There are two possible answers to this argument. In the first place, persuasion in favor of some given idea may not result in that idea being adopted, even in the distant future, but it may lead to the idea ultimately adopted being closer to the one originally favored than it otherwise would be. In Figure 2, the people who originally argued for D did not get their desires, but it is possible that if they had not taken this position, argument F would have won out instead of E. Second, and more important, the individual should be interested not in advocating a winning idea, but in maximizing the effect of his persuasion. It is by no means obvious that the man who argues for an idea held by a large group of people and who then sees it adopted is doing more to move society toward his goals than is the man who argues for a position held only by a tiny minority and, after a similar period, sees that the minority is less tiny. In both cases, the problem is "What difference would it make had the individual not exercised his persuasive powers?" and it is more likely that the widely held idea would have been adopted than that the tiny minority would have grown.[14]

But, again, the answer to the problem depends upon the particular circumstances of the case. Liddel-Hart once said that attacks on the enemy's lines of communication had more rapid effects if they occurred close to his battle line, but that the eventual effect was greater if they occurred far to the rear. It is possible that this is also true in politics. In any event, I myself have chosen to advocate ideas which are now held by few people, in the hopes that I will be able to convince people who will then convince others, etc.

There is another strategic variable, however. It may be that political changes in normal times (emergencies may provide an exception) must always be made in a series of small steps with the voters concerned mainly with each step, not with the ultimate objective. If this is so, then it is useless to recommend a major change unless a small step in the same direction was also desirable. In order to clarify the point on Figure 3, the vertical axis shows the "desirability" of various measures according to some evaluation system. Along the horizontal axis, possible states of some social variable are shown. The status quo is A, and it is assumed that society can only make changes by steps of one-fourth inch as shown on either side of A. Under the circumstances, it would be possible for society to reach the suboptimum B by a series of small steps each of which was an improvement, but it could reach the optimum optimorum only by taking a big step or a series of small steps

14. See "'Realism' in Policy Espousal," Clarence E. Philbrook, *American Economic Review* (December 1953), p. 846.

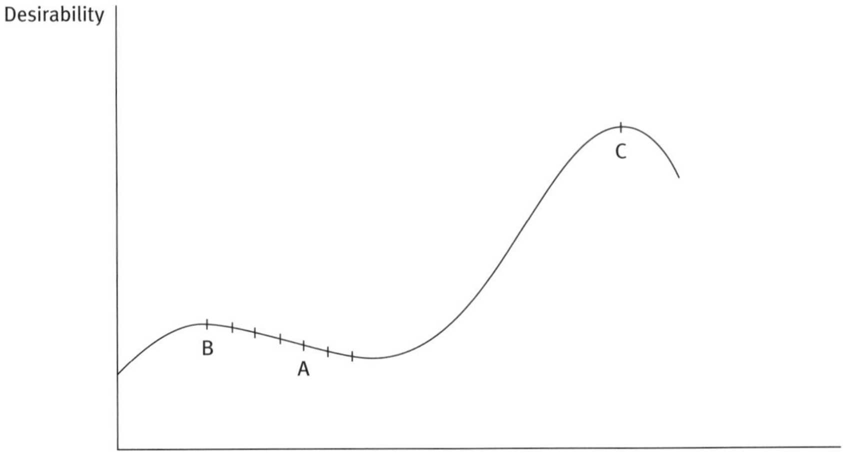

FIGURE 3

which, at first, would each make things worse. Given our assumptions about the type of actions which are possible, it would be sensible to argue for movements to the left, with the objective of making some improvement by reaching B rather than wasting time on the impossible task of arguing for movement to C.

But why should we make these assumptions about the type of political change which is possible? The answer is that if the reasons are not deducible from what has already been said about voter information, they require only a few additions. Let us suppose, reasonably, that the complexity and length of the arguments necessary to convince a man of the necessity of some social change are roughly proportional to the size of that change. From our previous work it seems likely that few voters would be willing to concentrate on an argument for some change for very long. In consequence, it would not be possible to convince them that moves to either B or C were desirable, but they might be talked into a single step up the hill toward B.[15] Accepting this argument, then, the types of social improvement which can be advocated with reasonable chance of success are restricted. Society could only move up to the nearest peak, and could not cross a valley in order to climb a higher mountain.

15. This argument can, without much difficulty, be made stochastic, with different people having different "attention spans."

THE ECONOMICS OF LYING

So far we have discussed the provision and consumption of information with only occasional attention to the fact that much of the content of political persuasion is deliberately deceptive. This chapter is intended to remedy the deficiency by discussing the use of lies and deception. It will be shorter than most of the preceding chapters, but this will not be because the subject is relatively unimportant, but because I have been unable to develop the analysis above the elementary level.

Let us begin by considering a political propagandist, a man or organization which aims to change public opinion in order to obtain some political objective. Some of the results of our analysis will be superficially paradoxical, but most of them will be in good accord with the actual behavior of the lobbyists and the public relations counsels who play such a major role in our political life. As one example, books on rhetoric normally urge placing great emphasis on the strong points of your argument while skimming over the weak. The pressure group may be well advised to do just the opposite if the weak argument will appeal to large numbers of people who are only vaguely interested in the subject, while the strong argument will appeal to a small but highly motivated group. Thus, in arguing for the farm program, its alleged benefits for the public in general, for the poor, and for national defense, etc., are much stressed. These benefits are all vague, weak, or frankly fraudulent. The benefits for the farmer, which are direct and strong, are not played up in the propaganda. The reason for this pattern is clear. The average voter does not have very much interest in becoming well informed about the program, but may well pick up an argument for it from the large volume of "general interest" propaganda. He is unlikely to be impressed favorably by the fact that the program will benefit the farmer, but if this fact is not stressed, it will probably escape his notice. The farmer, on the other hand, is motivated to find out about the program for material reasons, and is, thus, likely to look into it enough so that the material benefit for himself becomes clear.

Suppose, for example, that the average voter will, in the course of a year, see ten pages of material put out by the farm interests, and the average farmer will see about one hundred. If 98 percent of the output of the propaganda

Reprinted, with permission, from *Toward a Mathematics of Politics* (Ann Arbor: University of Michigan Press, 1967), 133–43.

mill is devoted to "public interest" arguments for the farm program, and 2 percent to pointing out its sectional importance for the farmers, then few of the nonfarm voters will see the 2 percent, but substantially all of the farmers will. Furthermore, the farmers are likely to devote much more attention to the 2 percent dealing with direct benefits to them than to the remaining 98 percent of the output, while those nonfarmers who happen to chance upon this 2 percent in the course of their reading, will normally not give it any more attention than the other material which argues for the program on broader grounds. Thus, even the minority of the nonfarm voters who chance upon the special interest arguments will probably think of the program as mainly aimed at public rather than private goals.[1]

This principle has wide application; in fact, it permits a sort of honest deception. A politician can (and most of them do) underplay his promises to specific groups and heavily emphasize his appeals to "the public interest." It is also possible to make statements which are interpreted by each of two conflicting interest groups as supporting themselves. The dangers of this process, of course, are also obvious. In a campaign, the politician has an opponent, and the opponent has a strong incentive to bring the first politician's statements strongly to the attention of the groups they are most likely to alienate. Pressure groups are normally free of this check upon their activities. As a general rule, we do not have a set of directly opposed pressure groups. The glove manufacturers want an increase in the tariff on gloves, but there is no specific group which finds it worthwhile to organize a counterlobby.[2]

Let us, however, not confine ourselves solely to politics. Lies are found in all spheres of life. Adam Smith thought that businessmen would seldom take advantage of their customers because of the discipline of continuous dealings. In modern times, the contrary impression, that businessmen will cheat if not forcibly prevented, is, perhaps, more widely held. If we look at the real world rather than the literature, we find the widest possible variation in hon-

1. This will be particularly likely if the parts of the propaganda which mention the material gain to the farmer present this gain as a method of obtaining a more general good. Thus, statements that agricultural prosperity is essential to the national prosperity not only provide the farmers with a rationalization for the program but also make it likely that the nonfarmer who happens to read about the program will not interpret it as simply aimed at getting money for farmers.

2. For a general discussion of the whole problem of the organization of pressure groups, see Mancur Olson, Jr., *The Logic of Collective Action* (Cambridge: Harvard University Press, 1965).

esty of businessmen. The stock market works almost entirely by oral communication, with only the most casual written records. Yet, fraud is almost unknown. At the other extreme, certain businesses, like the provision of patent medicines, are almost purely fraudulent. The same diversity of both reputation and actual performance can be seen in politics. Politicians are simultaneously thought to be dishonest and to be people upon whose word you can rely.

Scientists are a particularly interesting group because they produce a large volume of literature of remarkable accuracy although they are not particularly noted for honesty or accuracy when they get involved in nonscientific matters. The company which used to make Carter's Little Liver Pills (now called Carter's Little Pills as a result of a rather belated awakening of the FTC to the fact that the pills have nothing to do with the liver) fell into the hands of an aggressive businessman who sharply stepped up their more or less fraudulent advertising—which led to the difficulties with the FTC. He also decided to improve his business in other ways, however, and to this end established a laboratory. Needless to say, the reputation of the company was not such as to attract leading scientists. As a result, he ended up with personnel of very little reputation. This rather ill-omened research laboratory made the principal medical advance of the 1950's—the discovery of the tranquilizers.[3] The result was that the same organization was simultaneously selling a quack nostrum by quite dishonest TV commercials and a drug that was a major medical advance, by rigorously accurate reports in the scientific journals.

Obviously, there must be some reason why people seem to be strictly honest in some situations and not so in others. It would be rational to lie if the anticipated benefits exceeded anticipated costs. The general relationship can be shown in the following fourth equation:

$$B_1 - C_1 = P_1$$

B_1 = Anticipated benefits from lying
C_1 = Anticipated costs of lying
P_1 = Payoff

Although the equation, as it stands, will not help us much, it can be developed into a more meaningful form. Before adding to the equation, however,

3. No Nobel prizes have been awarded, presumably partly because of the reputation of the scientists involved and partly because accident seems to have played a larger role in the discovery than it usually does.

let us exclude certain factors. There are many reasons why one might lie, ranging from the polite lies of normal society to sheer lunacy. For the rest of this discussion, let us confine ourselves to lies told by individuals within their professions. This is not because such lies are more important or more interesting than other lies, nor because other lies would not fit our equation, but simply to make the scope of the discussion manageable. Thus, only lies told to assist in making a living will be covered by the remainder of this essay.

As a further restriction, only a deliberately untrue statement will count as a lie. This may seem to be laboring the obvious, since this is what the word means in ordinary speech, but we do not normally know for certain that when an individual makes an untrue statement, he knows it to be untrue. Further, the effect of a given statement is, presumably, not affected by the belief or lack of belief of the person who utters it.[4] There is a whole spectrum of mental states which a man making an untrue statement may have. He may be honestly mistaken; he may be mistaken, but his mistakes may always be such as to advantage himself; or he may be incapable of distinguishing between what is true and what is to his advantage. In restricting ourselves solely to the situation in which the false communication is made as the result of deliberate calculation, we are ignoring much economically relevant behavior. Once again, the only defense I can offer of this exclusion is that it keeps the scope of the investigation small enough to be manageable. Fortunately, the curious reader will find it fairly easy to extend the analysis to the cases we have excluded.

Returning to our equation, let us try to give the basic concepts more meaning. The anonymous author of *A Practical Guide for the Ambitious Politician*,[5] discussing one class of deliberate lies, said, "In calumny, two things are to be observed: The first is, is it sufficient. . . . The Second, is it probable?" This neatly lists the two problems involved in lying, which we may summarize as the likelihood that the lie will be believed and the probability that it will persuade the hearer to take the desired action. The lie will always be part

4. Unless his belief is somehow communicated to the hearer, perhaps by tone of voice. If this occurs, however, the person attempting to lie has failed, since he has conveyed the truth to the listener although he did not intend to. An untrue statement expressed in such a way that the hearer realizes it is untrue may be a lie in the strict use of English, but it is an abortive, nonfunctional lie. For our purposes, we shall ignore this class of statements.

5. Edited by Gordon Tullock (Columbia: University of South Carolina Press, 1961), p. 96.

of an effort to persuade some person or persons to take some action or to refrain from some action. It is a persuasive effort, and its benefit will come from the success of the persuasion. This being so, we can expand equation (4) to equation (5) by substituting these three factors for B_1.

$$BLP - C_l = P_l \qquad 0 < L < 1 \qquad 0 < P < 1$$

B = Benefit expected to be derived from the action being urged
L = Likelihood that the lie will be believed
P = Persuasive effect of lie; probability that the lie, if believed, will bring about the desired action

Since the lie may be addressed to more than one person—in politics it may be addressed to millions—we should have a set of B's, L's, and P's for each of them. For simplicity, however, I will develop the equation solely in terms of one person although I will frequently discuss situations in which deception of more than one person is desired. Equations which dealt with many people would be much more elaborate in appearance than the ones I intend to use, but in principle they are merely summations of a set of individual equations. It seems unnecessary to confuse the issue by complicating the equations in this way.

The costs also can be presented in a more detailed form, as equation (6) below.

$$BLP - C_c - (1 - L)(C_pL_p + C_rL_r) = P$$

C_c = Conscience, internal cost of lying
C_p = Costs of punishment
L_p = Likelihood of punishment if lie is not believed
C_r = Injury to reputation through other's knowledge that an individual has lied
L_r = Likelihood that injury to reputation will occur if lie is not believed

Some of these costs require a little discussion. C_c is the "pain" of doing something which you think you should not do. It, presumably, results from indoctrination in various socially approved ethical principles, primarily in childhood. Assuming, as I think we can, that the existence of lying is a factor reducing efficiency of the social apparatus, it is rational to try to strengthen this indoctrination. Thus, it would be sensible to devote resources to "moral education" for children and to try to reinforce this indoctrination among adults. On the other hand, for each individual the conscience has a negative survival value. The man for whom C_c is infinite will never be able to lie no matter how much could be gained thereby. This means that he should, in the long run, do less well in obtaining worldly goods than those for whom C_c is a distinctly minor item. Thus, if you want your child to do well in the world, you should advocate generalized moral instruction against lying while privately telling the child that lying is alright, provided only that the liar is not caught.

The conscience pain will be felt simply as a result of lying; the other two costs will be felt only if the lie is unsuccessful, i.e., if it is not believed.[6] In consequence, I have multiplied the individual costs and their individual probabilities by the probability of the lie failing. Society sometimes provides formal punishments for lies, particularly in the case of what the law terms fraud. Other examples include the honor system at West Point, impeachment, etc. If the particular lie is such that it might be covered by such a punishment system, then there will be some probability that the liar will be punished if he is caught, and C_pL_p is the product of that probability and the cost of the punishment. Since the punishment and the probability that it will be imposed are socially determined, we have here another mechanism by which lying can be reduced. If $(1 - L)C_pL_p$ is made greater than BLP by either making C_p very great and/or investing large resources in "police" activities so that L approaches zero, then no rational man would lie.[7]

C_rL_r measures a more informal cost which may be inflicted on the liar whose lies become known. If it is known that he has told a lie in this case, then he may be suspected of telling lies on other occasions, and this may impose substantial costs on him. Note that this suspicion of his work might affect the particular transaction in which he is lying. If a man is trying to sell something and feels that five "factual" statements will help in making the sale but only four of these statements would be true, then he must make a rather involved calculation about whether he should or should not lie about the fifth. If he tells the lie, and it is believed, this improves his chance of making the sale. If he tells the lie and it is not believed, then the information about

6. It might be believed long enough so that the desired action was taken, and then be discovered to be untrue with the result that the liar suffers some sort of punishment, as in the case of prosecutions for fraud. This would require a somewhat more complicated set of probabilities than the ones I have specified.

7. The possibility of miscarriages of justice should be taken into account if this line of reasoning is further extended. Since I am working on a book on the general subject of the law, I will put the matter aside in this essay.

that particular factor held by the potential buyer is the same as it would have been if he had not lied. The buyer also now knows, however, that the seller is willing to lie if there is a prospect of profit, and hence may disbelieve his other statements, which may make the sale less likely. All of these factors affect only this particular sale. But the potential seller may have to deal with the same customer again, and he should be interested in what the customer thinks of his honesty in these future transactions. Finally, the fact that he tells lies in his sales talks may become generally known, which will also affect his future sales. Note that this particular damage to reputation is quite different from the formal punishment. Potential buyers are refraining from buying, not in order to injure the liar, but simply because they doubt whether they will get a good bargain.

Considering only the $C_rL_r(1 - L)$ part of the equation will give us some information about the areas where lying is or is not likely to be a normal part of the professional activity of individuals. First, and most obviously, the more expert the customer, the less likely that a lie will be believed, hence lies will be less common when dealing with experts. The importance of the transaction will also be significant since the more important, the more likely that the potential victim of the lie will make an independent investigation and hence find out that the lie is a lie. Also, the more important the transaction, the more likely that the potential victim will inquire about the reputation of the potential liar, and hence the more important that reputation is. Most important of all, however, is Adam Smith's suggestion, repetitive dealings. It would be very stupid indeed to cheat a man once if the total profit you can make is small compared to the business you may do with him in the future.

From all of this we can deduce in a general way the likelihood of lying in various professions. Consider the salesman of some industrial product such as steel. He will be dealing with rather expert purchasers who buy in fairly large lots so that it is sensible for them to give careful consideration to each transaction. Moreover, even if they are deceived at the time of purchase, they are almost certain to find out about the deception shortly when they put the steel to use. Not only will the salesman be calling on the same customers in the future, the users of steel know each other and engage in a lot of trade gossip, so any successful cheating of one customer is almost certain to become known to others. Under the circumstances, the salesman would be most unlikely to lie to his customer. It is quite possible that the incentives for honesty may be so strong that the customer may depend upon the salesman as one of his major sources of technological information.

At the other extreme, consider a door to door salesman of some trivial gadget which does not cost enough so that the housewife will devote much thought to her decision to buy or not to buy. If the salesman does not intend to return to the same neighborhood, all of the terms in $C_rL_r(1 - L)$ may have substantially zero values. Thus, any reluctance to lie on his part would have to be based on his conscience or upon the likelihood of punishment. Most commercial dealings probably lie somewhere between these extremes. The man who confines his dealings to merchants of reputation, who therefore have a reputation to lose, and deals repeatedly with the same store probably has little chance of being lied to. In "one shot" transactions or in dealing with people whose reputation is not established, on the other hand, it would be wise to take precautions. Note that this does not apply only to direct salesmanship. The considerations involved in deciding whether to run a dishonest advertisement would be much the same as those in deciding whether to lie orally. The only major difference would be the fact that an ad leaves fairly certain evidence of the lie, while an oral statement can always be denied.

Turning from general business to specialized trades, journalism is an interesting case because a false statement can readily be given much wider currency than the truth. If a newspaper chooses to lie about some subject and refuses to publish a correction, then for the average reader of that newspaper the L is high and the $(1 - L)C_rL_r$ low. For some readers, specifically those libeled, L is very low and good social policy would suggest that they be permitted to make C_p high. The law of libel and slander, of course, is an expression of this line of reasoning. Interestingly, Brazil takes a completely different tack. Newspapers cannot be sued for libel, but they must print a reply from anyone they have attacked. This totally eliminates the C_p but makes the value of $(1 - L)C_rL_r$ rather high. It would be an interesting research project to find out which of these techniques puts the most pressure for accuracy on the press.

Probably the most "honest" field, in terms of accuracy of publication, is science. The reason for this accuracy is fairly simple. "B" is small for minor scientific discoveries, but high for major ones. A false announcement of a cancer cure, if believed, would surely get me a Nobel prize. But this variation in B is countered by an opposite variation in L. I could probably get away with a false "discovery" on some highly obscure subject, but this would bring little reward. My false cancer cure, on the other hand, would be known to be false almost immediately. The fact that scientists repeat experiments, and naturally are most likely to repeat important ones, and the fact that new discoveries are promptly applied by other scientists, which will normally turn up any falsification, means that the likelihood of getting away with a lie of importance in this field is substantially nil. Since the benefit from a lie of no importance is also substantially nil, lying doesn't pay.[8] It should be noted, however, that there are certain areas where a scientist might find lies helpful. The senior scientist who claims credit for a discovery actually made by a junior man in his laboratory might well get away with it. In conversation with scientists you will not infrequently hear gossip about this form of dishonesty, although I cannot say how accurate the charges are.

When we have a dispute of some sort, we may refer it to an "impartial" person for decision. "Impartial" in this case normally means simply that B is zero. The person or persons chosen to decide are supposed to be so removed from the issue that he or they will derive no personal gains of any sort from their decision. The problem of conflict of interest is important only in this context. Judges, juries, and many government officials are supposed to be free of any connection with the matters they decide. With B as zero, they would incur costs but no benefits from lies. The problems which this technique raises are largely ones of motivation. The judge will normally not be directly motivated to bring in a false decision, but he may also not be motivated to give the matter enough consideration so that his decision is very accurate. The method reduces lies, but increases random error. It may also not really get rid of the motive to lie. B may be very small but not zero, but the costs may be even smaller. This is particularly true if the "impartial" person is given the contempt powers of judges to punish persons who circulate stories of his dishonesty. Still, the method has been very widely used, and there is no reason to doubt that it is valuable in many situations.

The politician, in the sense of the elected official, presents a more difficult problem. The extremely weak motives for accumulating information on the part of the voter means that he is unlikely to detect any inaccuracy in the politician's public statements on general matters. (Statements on some matter of special concern to the voter who is a member of a pressure group will be discussed below.) In an opposed election, however, there will be someone who is motivated to check statements and publicly attack the politician for lying if those statements are wrong. One solution which has been widely used is to imply things without actually saying them. If this technique is skillfully used, and most politicians have had much practice, the voters may think

8. Gordon Tullock, *The Organization of Inquiry* (Durham, N.C.: Duke University Press, 1967).

that a definite statement on some subject has been made but the politician's opponent may not be able to find the statement in such specific form that he can charge dishonesty. This is, of course, only one of the reasons why the politician's public utterances are normally so definite in claims that he will be a better choice than his opponent and indefinite in the reasons why this should be so.

Still, straightforward lying may be very helpful to a politician. With the voters largely inattentive, they normally only learn things about the campaign that the candidates force on them by public relations techniques. With most of the voter's information coming from the output of the candidates, and with most of the voters and sources of opinion already committed before the campaign starts, a repetition of a false charge may be very effective. The decision of whether or not to lie will depend largely on an estimate of the efficiency of the public relations organizations of the two candidates. If I can be confident that the lie will be more widely spread than the fact that it is a lie, I should lie [$BLP > (1 - L)C_rL_r$]. Another useful technique is to have the false charge spread by someone else. You cannot be accused of lying, but some of the mud will stick. One can go on in this vein almost forever, and politicians have, in fact, developed an almost infinite set of practices of this sort. The basic point, of course, is the extremely poor information of the average voter and his lack of motives for improving that information.

The pressure group voter, however, has somewhat stronger motives for being at least moderately informed (explained in the last chapter). Furthermore, he is apt to have more casual information on the specific subject of "pressure" and will find it relatively easy to get more. Thus, although the member of a pressure group is unlikely to be really well informed, he is much more informed, and much more interested in getting more information, than is the average voter. Thus, the likelihood of his detecting a false statement is greater and the dangers of lying more severe. The sensible politician will actually support most pressure groups rather than simply saying that he is doing so.

This analysis could be extended, without much difficulty, to the question of the rationality of keeping a promise if it looks as though that might be inconvenient. In general, the problem would be that violating a promise will make it harder to get people to depend upon your word in the future. In areas like the black market, gambling, or the politician's promise in a log-rolling "deal" where legal enforcement is impossible, the reputation of the individual for strict performance is particularly important. The basic equation could also be complicated to permit consideration of other factors.

The fact that lies are being propagated also affects the behavior of consumers of information. It means that it is harder to improve the accuracy of their judgment, the "A" in the equations in the last chapter, because some of the "information" they examine may have been designed to mislead. In essence, the cost in research of a unit increase in "A" is now higher, and normal economic principles would indicate that the consumer of information, if he is deliberately trying to improve some decision he is to take, will now choose to "purchase" less accuracy. Whether the existence of lies in the body of available "information" will lead him to put more or less time into research, will depend upon the elasticity of his demand for "A." The situation is exactly analogous to the increase in the price of an economic good.

Most consumers of political information, however, are not engaged in a rational process of trying to improve the accuracy of their voting decision, but simply picking up the information because they get satisfaction out of it. If the invented information was, somehow, more to their taste than the truth, they would be motivated to increase their consumption of it. Since it may be easier to tailor lies to the taste of the consuming public than it is to perform the same task with the truth, the introduction of entertaining but untrue stories about politics into the media may actually increase their circulation. In general, people are more strongly motivated to obtain correct information about items they are contemplating purchasing in the market, with the result that intriguing lies would have less attraction there. The existence of special services providing information for consumers of economic goods, while there is no *Consumers Digest* selling information to the voters on individual candidates, would be explicable on the basis of this consideration. The fact that we have rather stringent laws against fraudulent claims in the economic marketplace, while lies are not legally penalized in politics, might also be explained in this way. In the latter case, of course, there are many other possible explanations for the difference.

SOME FURTHER THOUGHTS ON VOTING

Public choice scholars continue to be perplexed by the paradox of voting, as Frans van Winden's recent article clearly indicates.[1] The purpose of this short note is to offer my most recent thoughts on why many individuals vote despite the very small probability that their individual votes will have any effect on the outcome of an election.

In my view, complex explanations of this phenomenon, relying on such notions as minimax regret theory, are quite unnecessary. The real explanation ignored by the large majority of public choice scholars is that the cost of voting for most individuals is really very low. In such circumstances, it is not sensible for the individual citizen to expend energy and time thinking about whether he should or should not vote.

He will have been indoctrinated by the education process and by media hype into believing that it is important to vote in order to preserve democracy. At election time, he is bombarded with an immense amount of propaganda put out by interested parties urging that he should vote in favor of their respective candidates. He confronts no counter-active propaganda in favor of not voting. In such circumstances, a decision not to vote requires independent thought.

Roland McKean used to argue orally at the University of Virginia that individuals were indoctrinated not only to vote, but also to cast well-informed votes. Most individuals accept this as good advice. But, as McKean then would point out, whereas it is very difficult for an individual to deceive himself about whether he has voted, it is very easy for that same individual to deceive himself about whether or not he is well informed. Thus we should expect the great masses to go to the polls and to cast ill-informed votes.

From this perspective, the explanation why people cast their votes is much the same why they cheer in support of their favored sports team. Surely no one consciously thinks that his own cheers affect the outcome of the game. Nevertheless people talk about getting out to support the team. In both

1. Frans van Winden, "On the Economic Theory of Interest Groups: Towards a Group Frame of Reference in Political Economics," *Public Choice* 100 (1999): 1–29.

cases, there is no reason to give much thought to the issue. Granted a strong public sentiment in favor of the action, why bother to think about the question? Thus, the low-cost of voting offsets, not the low expected benefit from so doing, but rather the fact that discovering the low expected benefit takes more intellectual energy than the act of voting.

PART 5

VOTING PARADOXES

A MEASURE OF THE IMPORTANCE OF CYCLICAL MAJORITIES

Colin D. Campbell and Gordon Tullock

The problem of the cyclical majority was first raised by Duncan Black in his classic article "On the Rationale of Group Decision-making" almost seventeen years ago.[1] In its simplest form this is the case in which the results of voting are as follows: motion B beats motion A; motion C beats motion B; but motion A, which lost to B, beats motion C. No one motion can beat both of the others. It is cyclical because the winning motions repeat themselves over and over again. The cyclical majority problem discussed by Black—and the tests reported in this study—assume that the different individuals considering the various motions have independent preferences.

Since the publication of Black's article, Arrow's *Social Choice and Individual Values* has brought the problem of the cyclical majority squarely into the field of welfare economics.[2] Arrow presented a reasonable set of minimum conditions for the aggregation of the preferences of a number of individuals into a group choice. The particular group choice to which he addressed himself was the selection of a social-welfare function, but the proof is equally applicable to any social problem. He then demonstrated that no method of aggregation existed which would always meet his basic conditions if individual preferences are taken to be independent. His method, although put in very general form, depends upon the fact that the individual preferences might be

Reprinted by permission of Blackwell Publishing Ltd. from *Economic Journal* 75 (December 1965): 853–75.

1. D. Black, "On the Rationale of Group Decision-making," *Journal of Political Economy* 56 (1948): 23–34. Although Black was not the first to discover this phenomenon, his work is the foundation of all subsequent research on the problem. The investigations in this field of his principal predecessors, Condorcet and Lewis Carroll, had made no impact on the intellectual community of their day and had been completely forgotten. Their work is known today only because Black, after discovering the phenomenon himself, discovered his predecessors. See D. Black, *The Theory of Committees and Elections* (Cambridge University Press, 1958), 156–238.

2. K. Arrow, *Social Choice and Individual Values*, 2d ed. (Wiley, 1963). The book was first published in 1951, but the 1963 edition is much to be preferred. In addition to a reprinting of the original text, it contains a valuable discussion by Arrow of further research stimulated by the original publication.

so ordered as to lead to a cyclical majority.[3] In any given case, however, the individual preferences may happen to be so ordered that there is no cycle, then for that particular group of people it is not difficult to produce a method of aggregating their preferences which satisfies Arrow's conditions.

This naturally raises the problem of the frequency of cyclical majorities. Black regarded this question as so important that in *The Theory of Committees and Elections* he included a table on the proportion of cyclical majorities that could be expected. Almost all of the cells in his table are blank, and Black remarks: ". . . we have been unable to derive the general series which would enable us to make the calculations for the table and have entered only a few figures in the cells."[4]

The importance of this question is obvious. If human preferences would give rise to a cyclical majority only once in ten billion decision situations, then Arrow's proof might remain perfectly true, but it would be of little importance. Methods of aggregating preferences which would be totally rational could not be constructed, but the appearance of irrationality on such rare occasions would cause little concern. The importance of Arrow's proof to welfare economics, and Black's work to political theory, is based on the widely held view that such cycles would be quite common. The problem of giving some quantitative measure of the frequency of such cycles has remained an open one. It is the purpose of this article to provide a first step in the solution of this problem.

Like Black and others, we have been unable to derive a general function, but have turned to a method suggested by Black in his first article. He wrote:

> By writing down groups of schedules in which 6 or 7 motions are arranged in various ways and by constructing the group matrices, the reader can quickly satisfy himself that such cases—in which no motion exists which can get a simple majority over each of the others—are by no means exceptional. The greater the number of motions put forward in a committee of any given size, the greater will be the percentage of the total number of possible cases in which there exists no motion which is able to get a simple majority over each of the others.[5]

3. Ibid., 56–59. See J. M. Buchanan and G. Tullock, *The Calculus of Consent: Logical Foundations of Constitutional Democracy* (University of Michigan Press, 1962), 331–34, for a discussion of Arrow's proof and its relation to cyclical majorities. For Arrow's comments on this discussion, see Arrow, *Social Choice*, 109.

4. Black, *Theory of Committees*, 50–51.

5. Black, "Group Decision-making," 33.

TABLE I ***Committee Members***

MOTIONS.	#1.	#2.	#3.	#4.	#5.
A	1	4	3	5	2
B	3	2	5	3	5
C	5	1	4	2	3
D	4	3	2	4	1
E	2	5	1	1	4

Our procedure is to have a computer "write down groups of schedules" and then test them for cyclical majorities.[6]

The Monte Carlo method for determining the outcome of a probabilistic problem for which it is not possible to develop an equation was originally developed by the physicists, but it is well suited to this problem. Consider a committee of five members choosing among five alternative motions as illustrated in Table I. The numbers in each cell represent the preferences of the committee members, with the motion designated by the highest number most preferred. Thus, member #1 would select motion C as his first choice, but would vote for D as against B if that were the choice offered.

If motion A is put against motion B we find that B is preferred by three members and A by two, hence B will win the vote. Similarly, B can defeat C, but is beaten by D. Motion D can beat motion E, and would be the winner if there were no cyclical majority. In order to determine whether there is a cyclical majority, D must be tested against each motion it has not already met, *i.e.*, A and B. When we put motion D against motion A, A wins, and hence there is no motion that can get a majority against all of the others. The set of voter preferences shown in Table I produces a cyclical majority.

A computer can rapidly duplicate the process just described. A random-number-generating programme was used to place numbers from 1 to 99 in a matrix like Table I. In order to avoid the problems raised by the possible indifference of a member towards the choices offered, the same number was not allowed to appear twice in the preference series of one member.[7] No precautions were taken to prevent two voters from having the same preference schedule. Once the matrix was filled with numbers showing the members'

6. 205,000 groups, to be exact.

7. Indifference could result in tie votes, which raises a series of complex but unimportant mathematical problems.

preferences, the machine duplicated the routine described in the last paragraph and determined whether there was a cyclical majority. It then made note of the result, put a new set of random numbers in the matrix and repeated the operation. When it had run the routine 1,000 times it printed the number of cyclical majorities it had found.[8]

The results for the combinations of numbers of members and motions we tested are shown in Table II. In general, we ran more than one sample of 1,000 with the most heavily sampled numbers mainly being the ones which took up the least time on the machine. The percentages in Table II are averages of these samples. Detailed lists showing the results of all of the samples of 1,000 tested can be obtained from the authors.

With independent preferences, the cyclical majority is clearly an important phenomenon, and hence Arrow's proof is not a trivial one. Although this will not surprise many people, it is useful to have definite evidence on the point. The general shape of the table also is more or less as expected, although the rate of increase in the percentage of cyclical situations is faster than we had anticipated. Since the "best estimate" available before we made these computations was little more than a guess, however, this also is not surprising. The dips at 13, 19 and 29 voters, on the other hand, were completely unexpected. The standard tests of significance do not fit this problem very well, but it would appear that the dips at 13 and 19 are significant and the one at 29 may well be. We are at loss to account for the phenomenon. With the shape of the function known to a reasonable degree of accuracy from our Monte Carlo run, it may be possible to work out a general equation.

Although the possibility of error exists, Table II in general exhibits a good deal of internal cohesion, which is evidence that it is reasonably accurate. It adds significantly to the previous knowledge of the importance of cyclical majorities. Prior to these calculations, the only combination of members and

8. The programme was first written in Fortran for use on Dartmouth's GE-225. After 47 runs of 1,000 each it was mechanically translated into Algol for the Virginia Bu 5000. The random number generator used on the GE-225 had to be replaced by one suitable for the Bu 5000, and a few minor changes made to permit more efficient use of the input and output hardware of the Virginia machine. A repetition of the same 47 runs with the Algol programme showed good agreement with the Fortran programme. We will be glad to provide an Algol or a Fortran deck to anyone interested. The present programme can deal with any number of motions or voters up to 29. Expanding it to deal with more than 29 voters and/or more than 29 motions would be simple, requiring replacement of only one card, but the programme becomes extremely time consuming as these numbers are increased.

TABLE II

	3	5	7	9	11	13	15	17	19	21	23	25	27	29
3	5.7	7.8	8.4	8.9	8.5	7.3	7.4	8.4	8.0	8.9	9.1	9.7	11.1	11.1
4	10.7	14.6	15.9	15.6	15.1	14.7	15.5	17.3	16.9	17.2	16.4	18.0	18.6	17.4
5	15.4	18.3	21.5	23.0	25.1	22.4	25.3	23.7	23.9	24.8	25.4	24.3	24.0	21.1
6	20.1	25.5	25.8	28.4	29.4	28.1	29.8							
7	23.9	29.9	30.5	34.2	34.3	34.1	35.9							
8	27.7	32.5	36.7	37.8	38.6									
9	30.2	36.7	39.5	41.8	42.1									
10	32.4	40.8												
11	35.2			46.4			49.7							47.5
12														
13														
14														
15														
16														
17	46.4								62.6					
18														

The vertical axis shows the number of issues, the horizontal axis the number of voters. The numbers in each cell show the average percentage of the numbers of cycles found in 1,000 cases.

motions for which the proportion of cycles was known was three members and three motions.[9] Professor Black had calculated this as 12/216.[10] The development of a general function would be an improvement over the Monte Carlo procedure, but until such a function is discovered, the technique used here is the best available. The knowledge of the structure of the problem that is contained in Table II may be a valuable aid in the development of such a function.

9. While we were making our computer runs Professor William Riker worked out the number of cycles to be expected for three issues with 5 and 7 voters by a different method. His results are in good agreement with ours. W. H. Riker, "Voting and the Summation of Preferences: An Interpretive Bibliographical Review of Selected Developments during the Last Decade," *American Political Science Review* 55 (1961): 900–911.

10. Black, *Theory of Committees*, 50.

THE PARADOX OF VOTING— A POSSIBLE METHOD OF CALCULATION

To the Editor:

In "A Computer Simulation of the Paradox of Voting,"[1] Klahr measured the frequency of cyclical majorities by the Monte Carlo method. The use of computer simulation is justified for problems in probability only when it is not possible (or extremely tedious) to derive a general equation for the distribution. Although the use of the Monte Carlo technique by Klahr and by ourselves was the result of the inability to find such a general equation, an equation by a French mathematician, Georges T. Guilbaud, has since been brought to our attention.[2] In our opinion this equation raises more problems than it solves, but the problem is such a difficult one that any purported solution deserves careful attention. This is particularly so when such a distinguished mathematician as Guilbaud proposes it. Our purpose in this note is to bring Guilbaud's equation to the attention of those students in the field (presumably the overwhelming majority) who have not heard of it and to discuss the problems that it raises. We hope that other researchers may be able to solve them.

Guilbaud begins by giving the percentage of paradoxical results to be expected with three, five, and nine voters choosing among three alternatives.[3] His explanation of how he got these figures is that they were "easily (calculated) by the usual method of combinatorial analysis." No one else has found the problem "easy," and the values for five and nine voters have never been calculated by anyone except Guilbaud. Further, there is evidence that his calculations are incorrect. In Table 1, Guilbaud's figures are compared with

Reprinted with the permission of Cambridge University Press from *American Political Science Review* 60 (September 1966): 684–85.

1. This *Review*, 60 (1966), pp. 384–90. See also Colin D. Campbell and Gordon Tullock, "A Measure of the Importance of Cyclical Majorities," *Economic Journal*, 75 (1965), 853–57 for a basically similar approach.

2. See "Les Théories de L'Interêt Général et La Problème Logique de L'Agregation," *Economie Appliquée*, 5 (1952), 501–84. Our attention was called to it by a brief comment on our paper in N. Lawson, "Spectator's Notebook," *Spectator*, Jan. 14, 1966, p. 38.

3. *Op. cit.*, 519.

TABLE 1 ***Percentage of Cycles Choosing among Three Issues***

NUMBER OF VOTERS	GUILBAUD	CAMPBELL AND TULLOCK	KLAHR
3	5.6%	5.7%	5.5%
5	7.0	7.8	7.0
9	7.8	8.9	—

those obtained by Klahr and by ourselves. The difference between Guilbaud's results and the ones we have obtained is clear. Since the results in the Campbell and Tullock and in the Klahr columns are the result of sampling procedures, there is a possibility of sampling error. The result obtained by Klahr for five voters, however, was derived by the method of exhaustive enumeration and should be exact.

Having presented these values, Guilbaud then gives the following equation for the limit of the series as the number of voters grows:

$$1 - 3/\pi \text{ arc } (\cos 1/\sqrt{3}) = 0.0877$$

If this equation is correct, it is clearly an important discovery. Unfortunately, Guilbaud does not tell us how he got it, and we have been unable to derive it for ourselves. It is, of course, an equation for only three alternatives, but if we understood its derivation we might be able to use the same method to work out similar equations for larger numbers of alternatives. It is this possibility, in fact, that led us to write this note. We have been unable to derive the equation, but perhaps someone else can; and if so, it would be a significant improvement in our knowledge in this field.

Here again, however, the possibility that Guilbaud is wrong must be faced. In Table 2, a portion of the results we obtained by our simulation run are reproduced. This portion consists of our samples for 21, 23, 25, 27, and 29 voters choosing among three alternatives. Our method was essentially the same as Klahr's, but we drew our sample 1,000 at a time. Although the numbers do seem to be approaching a limit, this limit appears to be substantially higher than 8.7 per cent. Because our method raises possibilities of sampling error, we cannot say for certain that Guilbaud is wrong. Still the average value for all of the samples (13,000 runs) shown in Table 2 is 9.7 per cent, which seems to represent an extreme sampling error if Guilbaud is correct.

TABLE 2 ***Percentage of Cycles Found in Samples of 1,000 Cases, Choosing among Three Issues***

	NUMBER OF VOTERS				
	21	23	25	27	29
Percentage of Cycles	9.3%	9.6%	8.8%	13.4%	14.0%
	9.6	8.6	10.5	8.8	8.1
	8.7	9.0			
	7.9				
Average	8.9	9.1	9.7	11.1	11.1

The net result of our investigation, then, must remain inconclusive. Guilbaud may have opened an important new channel of investigation, or he may have made a mistake. The problem is important enough, however, so that further research in the field is called for.

COMPUTER SIMULATION OF A SMALL VOTING SYSTEM

Gordon Tullock and Colin D. Campbell

From the publication of Arrow's *Social Choice and Individual Values* until very recently the social sciences have been in the paradoxical situation that there appeared to be a good proof that all social decisions must be dictatorial or essentially random. Recently, it has been demonstrated that although Arrow's proof is mathematically correct, its practical application is less important than was previously thought. Criticisms of Arrow have taken two lines. Coleman demonstrated that in the presence of logrolling it is possible for groups to obtain a suitable outcome through a trading process. The outcome is not a perfect match of the Arrow conditions, but is relatively close. In addition, Tullock and Professors Davis and Hinich have "argued convincingly that if the distribution of opinions on social issues is fairly uniform and if the dimensionality of the space of social issues is much less than the number of individuals, then majority voting on a sincere basis will be transitive."[1]

The general thrust of these two attacks on the Arrow problem has (we think) been generally accepted by the economics profession. Nevertheless, it has been argued by Taylor and by Mackenzie that the Arrow proof is still relevant in dealing with smaller voting bodies. If we examine a functioning democracy we find that small voting bodies—city councils, county boards of commissioners and the committees of the legislature—are much more common than voting bodies which have a large number of members. If Macken-

Reprinted by permission of Blackwell Publishing Ltd. from *Economic Journal* 80 (March 1970): 97–104.

1. K. Arrow, *Social Choice and Individual Values* (Wiley, 1951); J. S. Coleman, "Individual Interests and Collective Action," *Papers on Non-Market Decision Making* (1966): 49–62. The quotation is from a paper by Kenneth Arrow read at the National Bureau of Economic Research Conference on Economics of Public Output, April 26–27, 1968, in Princeton, New Jersey, to be published in the proceedings of the conference edited by Julius Margolis. The two articles referred to are G. Tullock, "The General Irrelevance of the General Impossibility Theorem," *Quarterly Journal of Economics* 81 (1967): 256–70, and O. A. Davis and M. J. Hinich, "A Mathematical Model of Policy Formation in a Democratic Society," in *Mathematical Applications in Political Science*, vol. 2, ed. J. L. Bernd (Southern Methodist University Press, 1966), 175–208.

zie and Taylor are correct it would have to be concluded that the Arrow proof is of considerable practical significance.[2]

The basic objections of Mackenzie and Taylor can be split into their objection to the logrolling defence of majority voting and their attack on the applicability of the spatial model of voting systems used by Davis, Hinich and Tullock. They believe that logrolling is not common in local government units. Our own observations would indicate the opposite. Small voting groups composed of friends, amateurs and persons who have had considerable experience in dealing with each other would be in a position to engage in almost continuous and fairly elaborate implicit logrolling. These opinions, however, rely solely on impressions, and until some empirical research is done on this problem the answer must be uncertain. In this article we will assume that logrolling does not occur. Thus, we are making the least favourable assumption for democracy. The purpose of this study is to deal with the other of their two objections—the objection to the conclusions presented in "The General Irrelevance of the General Impossibility Theorem" being applied to small voting bodies. The argument in that article was that where the number of voters is much larger than the number of issues, cycles are likely to be trivial, although they do occur. The critics, essentially, are pointing out that in small committees the condition in which the number of voters greatly exceeds the number of issues is not met and hence that cycles are to be expected.

The background for the use of spatial models of voting systems is found in the work of Duncan Black.[3] Black dealt not only with the possibility that individual preferences were ordinal and totally independent but also developed an issue space which both linked and partially cardinalised the preferences of different individuals. The first published effort to determine the probability of intransitivity assuming the complete independence of preference functions was a note in this journal by the authors of this article.[4] Since then a considerable amount of further work has been done, some using Monte Carlo routines similar to those used by us and some using complex

2. M. J. Taylor, "Graph Theoretical Approaches to the Theory of Social Choice," *Public Choice* (Spring 1968): 35–48; W. J. M. Mackenzie, personal communication (see also *Politics and Social Science* [Pelican, 1967], 144–51).

3. D. Black, *The Theory of Committees and Elections* (Cambridge University Press, 1958); D. Black and R. A. Newing, *Committee Decisions with Complementary Valuation* (Wm. Hodge & Co., 1951); C. D. Campbell and G. Tullock, "A Measure of the Importance of Cyclical Majorities," *Economic Journal* (December 1965): 853–57.

4. Campbell and Tullock, "Cyclical Majorities."

commensal procedures. These studies may be summarised by saying that it was found to be difficult to produce accurate measures of the frequency of cycles, but that the approximations that have been obtained indicate that intransitivity in the ordinal case may be quite common, making up as much as 70% of the total examples if the number of alternatives to be chosen among is sizeable.

Black's spatial model is based on the fact that many issues voted on in legislative bodies, whether large or small, involve what may be called continuous issues. An appropriation of funds is an obvious example, because the amount appropriated may vary all the way from a very small sum to a relatively large sum. For many other government activities it is also not a choice between radically different alternatives but between more or less of something. In these circumstances most economists would anticipate that the average individual would have some point on the continuum which he prefers to all others and that his satisfaction with other alternatives would fall off as he moves away from his optimum.

In addition to being continuous, most issues involve a number of different continuous variables. An example of an issue with three variables might be a defence budget with three component parts—the appropriations for the army, navy and air force. Fortunately, in these more complicated cases, choice among the various proposals may be analysed by arranging the variables on several continua in a multi-dimensional space. The first use of this technique was in Black and Newing's *Committee Decisions with Complementary Valuation.* A similar model is to be used in the remainder of this article.

Figure 1 shows a two-dimensional issue space with the appropriation for the air force on the vertical axis and the appropriation for the navy on the horizontal axis. In this figure three voters, A, B and C, each has an optimum point as indicated, and two proposals, X and Y, are before them. If it is assumed that each of the individuals prefers points that are closer to his optimum over points that are farther away it can be determined whether X would beat Y. By introducing an additional simplifying assumption that all indifference curves are perfect circles around the individual's point of optima,[5] with the use of the Pythagorean theorem we can deduce ordinal numbers measur-

5. This simplifying assumption was used in Tullock, "General Irrelevance," and G. Tullock, *Toward a Mathematics of Politics* (University of Michigan Press, 1967). It is contrary to the real-world situation, where we would anticipate only a general convexity. Nevertheless, it probably does not make any difference. It would just as likely eliminate intransitivities that would otherwise occur as create them.

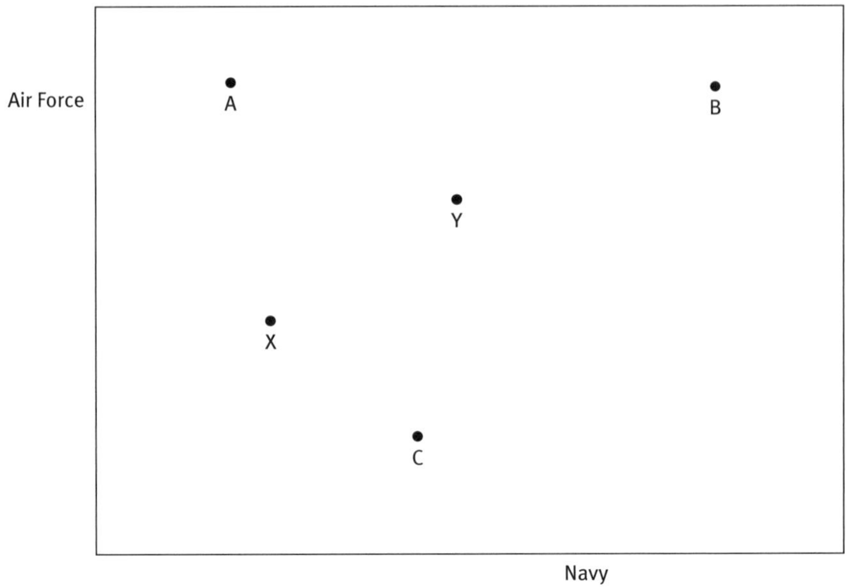

FIGURE 1

ing the preferences of the individual voters, and hence which way each of them would vote.

The estimates of the frequency of cycles in this study are based on the conditions shown in Figure 1 and thus assume that each motion has more than one variable or dimension. Because most issues in the real world probably have more than one dimension, the resulting tests should give a more realistic measure of the importance of cycles in small voting bodies than has been made thus far. A computer programme with a random number generator was used to place in the issue space the optima of a varying number of voters in random locations.[6] A set of such locations for members in a three-dimensional issue space is shown in Matrix 1 of Figure 2. Then the issues or motions are similarly located, as shown in Matrix 2. The computer then finds, using the Pythagorean theorem, the square of the distance from each individual to each motion to produce Matrix 3, thus calculating what amounts to the ordinal utility of the motion for each individual. A voting routine similar to that used in "A Measure of the Importance of Cyclical Ma-

6. The authors would be glad to provide copies of the computer programmes used to anyone interested.

Matrix 1

DIMENSIONS	COMMITTEE MEMBERS #1	#2	#3
x	45	38	96
y	87	19	40
z	98	51	72

Matrix 2

DIMENSIONS	COMMITTEE MEMBERS *A*	*B*	*C*	*D*	*E*
x	11	85	54	46	1
y	27	46	84	86	40
z	51	15	29	56	84

Matrix 3

MOTIONS	COMMITTEE MEMBERS #1	#2	#3
A	6,965	793	7,835
B	10,170	4,234	3,406
C	4,851	4,965	5,549
D	1,766	4,578	4,872
E	4,341	2,899	9,169

FIGURE 2
Example of the determination of the preferences of committee members assuming a committee of three members voting on five motions with each motion having three dimensions

jorities" is used to determine whether or not there is a cycle. In Figure 2 there is.[7] The computer, after determining whether there is a cycle, erases all of the random numbers, puts new ones in and begins all over again. When it finishes

7. For example, the preference of committee member #1 for motion A is equal to the sum of the squares of the difference between the quantity of *x* that he prefers and the amount of *x* proposed in motion A, the quantity of *y* that he prefers and the amount of *y* in motion A, and the quantity of *z* that he prefers and the amount of *z* in motion A. This is calculated to be 6,965. If there were no difference between the amount preferred of each of the dimensions and the amount proposed the preference of the committee member for the motion would be measured as zero. Thus, the smaller this total, the greater the preference of the committee member for the motion. For example, committee member #1 prefers motion A to motion B because 6,965 is less than 10,170.

If motion A in Matrix 3 is put against motion B, A wins, since A is preferred by two of the three committee members. If motion A is then put against motion C, A again wins. But when motion A is put against motion D, D wins, and D also wins over motion E. Now motion D must be tested against both B and C, and it will be seen that motion D loses to motion B.

1,000 trials it records the number of cycles discovered. For 3 × 5 tables like the one shown in Matrix 3 of Figure 2 it turns out that 7.5% of the trials lead to cycles.

In determining how common cycles would be in the real world we must first develop some way of specifying what motions would be put before the committee, city council, etc. We have chosen two procedures. In one the members each put forward their first preference as a motion. In the second the motions placed before the legislature are randomly selected. It is our feeling that most real-world situations which might lead to cycles will fall somewhere between these two extremes. Hence one can anticipate that the number of cycles also would fall somewhere between the numbers shown by these two methods. Note that these two methods of selecting motions assume that the members have very little knowledge of each other's preference schedules.

Presumably, if individual members did have such knowledge they might attempt to guess what particular motion would go over best. Choice of motions for strategic reasons by an individual who is better informed than his fellows may lead to advantages for him, but is not likely to lead to cycles.[8] There are so many tactical devices available to the most intelligent and best-informed member of small groups which do not involve the cycle that there is probably little point in concentrating attention on intransitivity when considering situations of this type.

Another possibility is that there may be several committee members who know the preference structure of the members of the committee. But under these conditions there is usually no difficulty in avoiding the cycle. All that is required is that certain members vote contrary to their preferences on certain individual votes in order to obtain their true preference in the final outcome. This type of conduct is quite common in both legislatures and committees. We are thus led to assume that individual committee members do not know much about the preferences of the others as being the only situation likely to generate cycles.

The first of the two situations which we have tested in which the members do not know each others' preferences is one in which motions are made at

8. The possibility that one member of a small group of voters may deliberately contrive a cycle in order to divert the vote has been discussed by Taylor, "Graph Theoretical Approaches."

random. A number of cases using two dimensions, numbers of motions up to six and committee members up to twenty-five are shown in the top section of Table 1. A similar experiment using three dimensions is shown in the middle section of this table, and a much smaller experiment with five dimensions is shown at the bottom. The most interesting feature of these results is that the difference made by adding more dimensions is small. It also appears from Table 1 that the percentage of cycles declines as the number of committee members increases. This may be the result of the considerable statistical variation in these estimates.

How reliable are these individual estimates? Since they are drawn from samples of only 1,000, the variance expected for each estimate is sizeable. Given the cost of this routine in computer time, larger samples would probably not be justified. For an individual estimate in Table 1 the 0.05 confidence limit is between 1½ and 4%, depending on which estimate you choose. Thus, the confidence limits are large relative to the estimates of the proportion of cases that are cyclical. In addition, with 84 estimates in Table 1 there must be some where the true proportion of cyclical majorities is outside the confidence limits. It should also be remembered that different random numbers were used in calculating each of the estimates in the table. In general, the reader should recognise that each of the estimates in Table 1 is an approximation, but the overall structure of the table is no doubt correct.

A remaining problem is the reason for restricting the number of motions to six. As the number of motions increases, the likelihood of cycles increases. Nevertheless, in the case of small voting bodies six motions are probably more than adequate. The reason is that although many more motions sometimes occur, there are seldom more than two or three basic positions represented by the various motions. The additional motions normally are efforts to obtain compromises between the small number of basic positions, and hence are likely to reduce the likelihood of cycles.

Our second basic case assumes that each committee member offers as a motion his own personal optima. To test the outcome in situations of this type, the computer was programmed to assume that the motions offered were the optima of each of the committee members. In this case the figures in the columns of Matrix 2 of Figure 2 would be identical with the figures in Matrix 1. The results are shown in Table 2. In these circumstances it is not possible for the number of motions to exceed the number of voters. In those cases where there are more voters than there are motions the preferences of a

TABLE 1 ***Percentage of Cyclical Majorities Found in 1,000 Cases with Randomly Selected Motions***

TWO DIMENSIONS

MOTIONS	NUMBER OF COMMITTEE MEMBERS											
	3	5	7	9	11	13	15	17	19	21	23	25
3	1.9	1.8	2.3	1.5	1.6	2.1	2.1	1.6	1.9	1.4	1.5	1.1
4	3.3	4.6	5.1	4.1	3.8	4.0	3.9	2.6	2.5	3.0	1.9	2.0
5	5.2	6.4	6.3	5.9	5.9	4.5	5.0	5.5	4.6	3.1	3.7	2.9
6	7.0	8.7	9.0	7.4	7.1	6.6	5.5	7.8	5.4	3.5	4.9	5.8

THREE DIMENSIONS

MOTIONS	NUMBER OF COMMITTEE MEMBERS											
	3	5	7	9	11	13	15	17	19	21	23	25
3	2.5	2.3	2.5	2.9	2.4	3.3	2.2	2.8	2.2	1.8	1.2	2.3
4	4.1	5.0	5.4	5.9	5.2	4.3	3.6	4.0	3.6	2.6	3.2	3.1
5	7.5	8.1	8.2	7.1	6.6	7.1	6.2	5.1	5.3	5.5	5.3	5.4
6	10.0	10.4	11.9	10.2	9.1	9.2	8.2	8.7	6.3	6.6	6.6	6.0

FIVE DIMENSIONS

MOTIONS	NUMBER OF COMMITTEE MEMBERS			
	3	5	7	9
3	3.3	4.2	3.1	3.7
4	4.9	6.1	7.0	5.0
5	9.3	9.6	10.7	9.2

TABLE 2 ***Percentage of Cyclical Majorities Found in 1,000 Cases Assuming the Selection Is from the Preferences of the Committee Members***

TWO DIMENSIONS			
	NUMBER OF COMMITTEE MEMBERS		
MOTIONS	5	7	9
3	2.4	1.5	2.1
4	4.7	4.7	3.0
5	7.8	6.6	6.6
6		9.3	7.8

random selection of the individual voters was used. As long as the number of motions is restricted to six, the results in Table 2 are approximately the same as those for two dimensions in Table 1. The differences are within the limits of the statistical variation anticipated with samples of this size.[9]

It is interesting that in the circumstances assumed in Table 2 there can be no cycles with three voters. Although this is obvious when analysed, it was at first unexpected. If individuals present their own optima as the motion which they urge it is mathematically impossible to have a cycle if there are only three voters.

The most obvious conclusion of this study is that the number of cycles using the special type of issue space developed by Black and Newing is considerably less than the number estimated in our previous article which assumed complete independence of the votes of each individual. This is shown in Table 3, which compares a selected sample of cases.[10] The likelihood of cycles appears to be much lower even with small groups. Nevertheless, the number of cycles is not zero.

In a way, the outcome of this study is the most disappointing of all the

9. A few values with more than six voters and more than six motions were computed, mainly for reasons of curiosity. Since we do not think they represent the real world, they are not included in Table 2, but any reader who wishes to have them, possibly for further research, is welcome.

10. The estimated percentage of cycles in the first row of the last two columns of Table 3 are from Table 1 and not from Table 2. If they were from Table 2 the first two numbers in these columns would be zero. The estimated percentage of cycles for ordinal and independent preferences are from Campbell and Tullock, "Cyclical Majorities," 855.

TABLE 3 ***Comparison of Percentage of Cyclical Majorities Out of 1,000 Trials for Motions with One, Two and Three Dimensions***

THREE DIMENSIONS

MOTIONS	NUMBER OF COMMITTEE MEMBERS	ORDINAL, %	TWO DIMENSIONS, %	THREE DIMENSIONS, %
3	3	5.7	1.9	2.5
3	25	9.7	1.1	2.3
6	3	20.1	7.0	10.0
6	7	25.8	9.0	11.9

possibilities. It has not been demonstrated that cycles in small committees are trivial, nor has it been shown that they are important. There is an intermediate number of cycles which, depending on the assumptions made and one's ideas of efficiency, is either encouraging or discouraging. Nevertheless, if cycles are only as common as these estimates indicate, small committees can be expected to operate with reasonable efficiency. The possibility of an additional error term of 7–10% which is what the estimates here indicate as an outside limit, would not greatly reduce the efficiency of small voting groups. Thus, the Arrow theorem is relevant to these small committees, but this study indicates that such groups are not much less efficient than they would be even if the Arrow theorem were false.

THE PARADOX OF NOT VOTING FOR ONESELF

In most states it is permitted to write in the names on the ballot, and these write-in candidates can win if they assemble enough votes. Thus, in all elections in which I might conceivably participate, there are at least three candidates: the Republicans, the Democrats, and my own favorite candidate for president—Gordon Tullock. Indeed, using the notation of the Ferejohn and Fiorina article, assuming that we are talking about 1972, I would find k having a value of about .001. Under the circumstances, if I understand the article correctly, I should always vote, and the vote should always take the form of writing in my own name. Further, as far as I can see, this advice can be generalized. Everyone who would really like to be president should vote and write in his own name, because the minimum regret that they produce for three-candidate elections is also correct for the elections in which there are 30 million candidates. The only problem here is that it would, of course, amount to participating in a lottery, and my possible gain from writing in my own name might turn out to be less than the cost of writing it in. Granted that people are willing to buy lottery tickets, even when the various states offering them take very substantial rakeoffs, I do not imagine this would be much of a disadvantage.

This same conclusion could have been deduced from the Casstevens article, which Ferejohn and Fiorina quite properly criticize as being mathematically incorrect.[1] There is, of course, nothing wrong with the Ferejohn and Fiorina mathematics. Nevertheless, the conclusion is such as to raise considerable doubts about whether they have chosen the right assumptions. Like them, I have always felt that the *ad hoc* procedure of putting in a "D" is undesirable.[2] I would like a better solution. It does not seem to me, however, that their solution is really better.

It is possible to sketch out at least a partial solution to this problem. Clearly the cost of voting is very slight. Under the circumstances, individuals

Reprinted with the permission of Cambridge University Press from *American Political Science Review* 69 (September 1975): 1295–97.

1. Thomas Casstevens, "A Theorem About Voting," *APSR*, 62 (March, 1968), 205–7.

2. The assumption that C_p takes a minus value is made in Gordon Tullock, *Toward a Mathematics of Politics* (Ann Arbor: University of Michigan Press, 1967), p. 110.

would not be well-advised to invest large resources in determining whether the conventional wisdom (which they picked up in school) about the duty and value of voting is correct. Further, in the present state of the literature, it must be admitted that finding out that voting is not a paying proposition would be quite expensive. Under the circumstances, people making decisions about whether or not to expend resources on *investigating* whether or not they should stop voting might, quite rationally, decide not to make the *investigation*. This explanation for widespread voting is, of course, in addition to the usual social pressure arguments for voting, and the other conventional argument that many people have been indoctrinated in such a way that they get a positive pleasure from voting.

AVOIDING THE VOTER'S PARADOX DEMOCRATICALLY: COMMENT*

Although I agree with Michael Davis that Arrow's *Social Choice and Individual Values* did not disprove the desirability of agreeing upon a decision process, his view that the "filling-in-the-blanks" procedure avoids the Arrow paradox is false. Consider voters who have the preferences he specifies on page 305 in explaining the Arrow paradox. I have presented them below in the usual matrix form.

49	2	50
A	*B*	*C*
B	*C*	*A*
C	*A*	*B*

The chairman presents the alternatives as first *A*, then *B*, then *C*; *A* will be beaten on the first motion and *B* will get two-thirds of the vote on the second. If, on the other hand, they are presented *B*, *C*, *A*, *B* will be beaten on the first vote and *C* will win on the second, etc.

If the chairman is well-informed about the preferences of the voters, then in essence he is a dictator; and, if he is badly informed, the outcome will be random. Among the advantages to his procedure that Davis lists are "(b) every member of the body will get a decision he prefers to doing nothing" (p. 307). Normally, doing nothing is considered as one of the alternatives, let us say, *C*, and this can easily lose. Another of his points is "(c) no alternative actually voted on will have had more support than that chosen" (p. 307). Suppose that the number of voters were shown at the top of the matrix; *B* can easily win under either the regular *Robert's Rules of Order* procedure or the filling-in-the-blanks method.

In all of the above, I have assumed that the individuals vote "sincerely," i.e., they simply vote for their first preference unless it has already been elim-

Reprinted, with kind permission of Kluwer Academic Publishers, from *Theory and Decision* 6 (November 1975): 485–86. Copyright 1975.

*Michael Davis, "Avoiding the Voter's Paradox Democratically," *Theory and Decision* 5 (October 1974), 295–311.

inated from consideration; at that point, they vote for their first preference among the remaining possibilities. Any other assumption as to how they vote would lead to the same ultimate result, although the examples, of course, would be different.

AN APPROACH TO EMPIRICAL MEASURES OF VOTING PARADOXES

John L. Dobra and Gordon Tullock

There is very little in the literature on the frequency with which voting paradoxes could be expected in the real world. The point of this note is to add a little, unfortunately very little, to this scant information and to suggest a method of getting more. One of the authors was on a search committee set up to select a new chairman for the Political Science Department at V.P.I. The Political Science Department established an elaborate voting procedure under which each of the candidates was to be evaluated by each of the six committee members on six specific dimensions, such as scholarly ability, administrative skill, etc., and also given an overall evaluation. The evaluation was on a scale of 1 to 10, but this could easily be converted into a simple ordinal scale with, of course, some ties. There were 37 candidates to be graded.

Unfortunately, a number of the members of the committee shirked and did not fill out all the schedules, with the result that only the overall rating and the rating on scholarly competence were suitable for a test of cycles. Further, on the overall evaluation, one member of the committee rated almost all candidates in the group of 10 finalists identically and another member of the committee did not rate any of the candidates. The result is that effectively we have a committee of four rating on overall ability and a committee of six on scholarly ability. The result was fairly clearcut, but unfortunately of no great importance, because of the extreme small size of the sample. There was a Condorcet winner (No. 6) on scholarly ability, and on the general rating, there was one candidate (No. 32) who could not be beaten by anyone else, but who tied with candidates 7, 9 and 13. The tie was only possible, of course, because of expressions of indifference by one member of the committee in each case. Candidates 7, 9 and 13 all participate in cycles in which they can be beaten by other candidates, who were beaten by 32, so this is an example of tie intransitivity. The table below may help to explain the result. This shows the paired voting outcomes for the 10 candidates who we judged stood at the top of the 37.

Reprinted, with kind permission of Kluwer Academic Publishers, from *Public Choice* 36 (1981): 193–94.

We also looked for the lack of independence of irrelevant alternatives, using the Borda method for the candidates and then inquiring as to the results of removing low-ranking candidates. We tried a number of different methods for removal of low-ranking candidates, some of them quite radical. In one case, for example, only the top five were retained. In all of these cases the winners remained stable and were the Condorcet choices of the pairwise voting method. If the procedure had been used to select the committee, however, it would have been extremely unstable indeed. The second and third choices, to say nothing about the fourth and fifth, changed radically.

The result of this little empirical test is not very impressive, but worth publishing, simply because there is so little other information on the subject.

The Public Choice Society has now a very considerable number of members and in the average year it seems likely that 30 or 40 of them will have the opportunity to participate in at least one election in which the ranking of the candidates by the electors can be deduced. No such individual election is of much statistical importance, but if each member would transmit them to the editor, either in the form of a brief comment or just as a set of election results, we might over a period of three or four years get empirically useful results.

The first column lists the number of a candidate *i*, the second column lists the numbers of candidates who can defeat candidate *i*, and the third column lists candidates who tie *i*.

CANDIDATE *i*	CANDIDATES WHO DEFEAT *i*	CANDIDATES WHO TIE *i*
6	7, 9, 10, 13, 14, 15, 32	11, 23
7	11	9, 13, 15, 32
9	15	7, 10, 11, 13, 14, 23, 32
10	7, 11, 13, 14, 15, 32	9
11	13, 32	6, 14
13	14	7, 9, 32
14	7, 15, 32	9, 11
15	11, 13, 32	7
23	7, 10, 11, 13, 14, 15, 32	6, 9
32		7, 9, 13

PART 6

THE MEDIAN VOTER THEOREM

DUNCAN BLACK: THE FOUNDING FATHER

23 MAY 1908–14 JANUARY 1991

The main purpose of this paper is to discuss Duncan Black's work and his role in founding public choice. Nevertheless, I'd like to start by making a few personal remarks. Duncan Black was a wonderful person. All who knew him liked and admired him. His very important work, and as the rest of this paper will indicate his work was important, came from selecting an important problem which no one had previously dealt with and concentrating on it. No Nobel prize winners can actually claim to have had more effect on a discipline than he had on his newly invented field of study.

Turning to his actual work, he quite literally is the founder of public choice. The first six articles which can be regarded as public choice were all written by him. Further, Kenneth Arrow, then a very young member of the economics profession, was given one of his papers to referee by *Econometrica* and this may well have attracted his attention to the problems which made him famous. He gives considerable credit to Black in that book. Anthony Downs was a student of Arrow who wrote his pioneering book as a doctoral dissertation under Arrow. We have here a fairly clearcut chain of influence.

Black, like other pioneers in science, did have precursors, but they were all obscure. Indeed, we wouldn't even know about most of them had Black not himself dug them out and discussed them in *The Theory of Committees and Elections*.

I don't read French, but I've read a translation of Condorcet's work which Black was apparently the first person to fully understand. Having read it, I have doubts as to whether Condorcet really understood what he was saying. I have extraordinary admiration for Black for having penetrated through the language to the heart of the problem.

Another important predecessor was of course Lewis Carroll and work in this field had been literally completely lost until Black dug up parts of it. This had the intriguing result that, when Black was a visiting professor at the University of Virginia, members of the English Department would appear to listen to lectures by an economist.

Reprinted, with kind permission of Kluwer Academic Publishers, from *Public Choice* 71 (September 1991): 125–28.

It should be emphasized here that these predecessors are not important in the history of thought for the simple reason that nobody knew they existed. They had no influence, they were forgotten. In the case of Condorcet, nobody understood what he was saying; in the case of Lewis Carroll his papers were mainly lost. Indeed, it seems likely that the ones that Black was able to dredge up are only a part of the total product. Thus, Black was a true originator who not only solved important problems but discovered that the problems existed. He drew nothing from his predecessors in public choice because effectively, at the time he wrote, there weren't any. It is true he later found some, but they had no prior influence on him or on anyone else.

Black as a mathematical economist had undoubtedly read Hotelling's "Stability in Competition."[1] At the end of this article there is a remark that it would apply to politics. Not very long ago, there were several articles pointing out that it did not actually work in the particular economic situation that Hotelling used. In private conversation with Arrow, he said that he had known this for a very long time, but as a student of Hotelling he didn't want to criticize him on the matter.

As an interesting further sideline having to do with public choice, I remarked that I had not noticed the error, but probably partly because it did work for politics. His response indicated both that he agreed and that this particular idea had not previously occurred to him. Downs, of course, specifically gives credit to Hotelling.

Another possible intellectual predecessor was Schumpeter, who had a good deal of influence on me. But apparently not on most of the other people in public choice. Although his work is not in any sense formal and would not conceivably have founded public choice, it nevertheless set me in what you might call the proper frame of mind. Skepticism about motives of government was already in my mind but I didn't realize that this was more than generalized skepticism. It was Schumpeter who first convinced me that this kind of thing was intellectually respectable.

It's interesting that this particular train of thought is almost entirely missing from Black's work. I don't think he had any immense admiration for politicians, but very little in his work implies that kind of attitude towards them which is now held by so many public choice scholars. In this I think

1. *Economic Journal* 39: 41–57.

he was a rather typical graduate of the English system and, like Keynes, really thought of the government as a gentlemanly occupation.

To go on to his work in general. He apparently on his own reinvented the cyclical majority, although he did not produce any general proof. He simply convinced himself by running a number of examples that it must be fairly common.

His great achievement, however, was the realization that there is one simple situation in which a cyclical majority was not likely. This was the single peak preference theorem. This theorem these days is rarely credited to Black because it has been so built into our minds. It's also very, very simple and straightforward and most people seem to think that it's almost part of nature. The fact is that no one before Black had ever thought of it.

Such simple ideas are generally rather hard to discover, but once discovered they look so simple that people cannot believe that their discovery was intellectually trying. Watt's realization that a separate condenser in a steam engine would make it possible to immensely save fuel by permitting keeping the cylinder heated instead of having to cool it off and then reheat it for every stroke, as was true with the Newcomen engine, is simple minded today. A great many very intelligent people didn't figure it out, however, until Watt came along.

The same can be said of Black's single peak preference curve. It could be said that a priori this looks as if it would only have rather limited application. Indeed, Black himself in both *Committees and Elections* and his book with Newing pointed out the theoretical limits on its application.

In practice, it seems to have considerable application. In many, many places, the political parties and political contests seem to array themselves along a single dimension. If you look at their programs in detail it always turns out that it's much more complicated than that. But it would appear that in the minds of the voters they are literally frequently arranged on a single continuum which, as a result of the organization of the French chamber of deputies, is usually referred to as a left/right.

This means that the single peak preference structure has considerable relevance at this simple level. The work essentially of Hinich and various collaborators has demonstrated that in a much more elaborate and complicated multidimensional manifold of many issues, the fact that the voters are not perfectly informed permits the use of stochastic tools. These stochastic tools and the two-party system lead to a conclusion which is clearly a generalization of Black's median preference theorem.

I, myself, in a paper which became obscure and is now being revived as a result of mathematical progress,[2] reached a somewhat similar result for the outcome of legislative process. In other words, the very narrow restrictions which appear to apply to the median preference theorem have to a considerable extent broadened.

Although his great achievement was the median preference theorem, in order to be an achievement, it, of course, required that he first discover the problem of the cyclical majority. He did. Thus, in a way he had two achievements but by the time he began publishing he emphasized the median preference theorem rather than the cycle itself. If he had first written several articles on the cycle, and then partially solved the problem, he would no doubt have a greater reputation today.

It's not true, however, that this is by any means all of his work. He did a large number of other things in connection with the voting model and of course, as I have mentioned, he engaged in historical research and dredged up Lewis Carroll, etc. Indeed, by reputation in any event, he wrote a considerable number of manuscripts which as a perfectionist he did not want to release but which we may hope are still in existence.

I titled this essay "The Founding Father" and there's no doubt that he indeed was the founding father of public choice. Having done his most important work more than 40 years ago and having been in retirement in recent years, a great many of the younger public choice people do not even know his name. This is depressing. We all make use of his results but a student entering public choice now regards these things as elementary. Indeed they are. So is Euclid.

I'd like to close by repeating something I said in my salute to Black in the Festschrift for him.[3] The Chinese at a dinner will drink a toast to the host calling him "the father of all of us." Black indeed was the father of all of us.

2. "The General Irrelevance of the General Impossibility Theorem," *Quarterly Journal of Economics* 81 (May 1967): 256–70. Reprinted in Gordon Tullock, *Wealth, Poverty, and Politics*, pp. 55–67 (Cambridge: Blackwell, 1988).

3. *Toward a Science of Politics*, Gordon Tullock, ed. (Blacksburg, Va.: Center for Study of Public Choice, 1981).

HOTELLING AND DOWNS IN TWO DIMENSIONS

Harold Hotelling, in his early work on monopolistic competition, proposed a model in which two drug stores were seeking optimal locations in a community which lay along a single road. He suggested that this model might, with suitable modifications, be applied to politics. Anthony Downs, in his book *An Economic Theory of Democracy*, made this application and derived from it a number of very realistic conclusions.[1] This model, however, can be subjected to several criticisms. In the first place, although it gives very good predictions for two parties, Downs's model does not seem to fit very well the situation involving more than two parties or candidates. Second, clearly most political choice situations are not one dimensional, as the Hotelling-Downs model assumes. Finally, the model does not easily deal with the log-rolling situation, or, indeed, any situation in which the voters fall naturally into small, special interest groups. It is the purpose of this chapter to broaden the model to two dimensions. It will be demonstrated that this two-dimensional model gives the same conclusions as Downs's one-dimensional continuum in the special case of two parties or candidates; and that it gives different and more helpful results if there are more than two parties. Only special cases of log-rolling and differential intensity may be shown on two dimensions, but analogical, higher-dimensional models may use any number of issue dimensions, and log-rolling may be analyzed with these higher-dimensional models.

Turning to our first objective, Downs's basic assumptions do not exactly fit our present purposes, but they require only very slight alteration. We may assume the following conditions:[2]

1. A single party or candidate is chosen by vote to carry out some set of activities.
2. Elections are held periodically.

Reprinted, with permission, from *Toward a Mathematics of Politics* (Ann Arbor: University of Michigan Press, 1967), 50–61. Copyright by The University of Michigan 1967.

1. Harper, 1957. Downs's contribution was not, of course, limited to application of Hotelling's model.

2. For Downs's conditions see *An Economic Theory of Democracy*, pp. 23–24.

3. The number of people eligible to vote is fairly sizable.
4. Each voter casts only one vote. (Analogical models with differential voting can be easily constructed.)
5. The party or candidate who receives the most votes will be given control over the relevant activities.
6. Normally there will be more than one candidate or party in each election.

Given this political system, we can assume voters with some given set of preferences, and examine the outcome. Let us use first the assumption that they are evenly distributed over a two-dimensional issue space, and that their indifference curves are perfect circles about their optima. As in the last chapter, these assumptions are convenient, but not really necessary. As a further condition, I shall assume that all voters always vote for the alternative which stands highest on their preference schedule.[3]

Under these circumstances the geometry developed in the last two chapters can be readily applied. Suppose that a party or candidate, knowing that there will be one and only one opposition party or individual, is contemplating a platform taking some position on Figure 1. If they can get to the exact center, then they have won, since there is no other point which can get a majority over the center. Errors occur in politics as in other sectors of human life, however, and they may miss. If the first party chooses a point which is not in the exact center, such as A on Figure 1, then the second party has a chance of winning. Probably the information on voter preferences available by the time the second party or candidate makes a choice, will be better than when the first choice was made. The optimal strategy for the second party is easily determined. It should draw a line from point A through the true center of the surface, and then take a position on that line which is on the same side of A as the center and as close to A as is possible without merging into A's position in the view of the voters. B is such a point. The vote for the two parties may be obtained by simply erecting a perpendicular bisector on the line connecting A and B and observing which side has the largest area and, hence, the most votes. In Figure 1, A has chosen well, and there is little difference between the two points in terms of the number of votes they can draw.

3. This assumption differs from that used by Downs, but permits somewhat simpler reasoning. See Gordon Tullock, *The Politics of Bureaucracy* (Public Affairs Press, 1965), pp. 88–96. The strict Downs model will be generalized later.

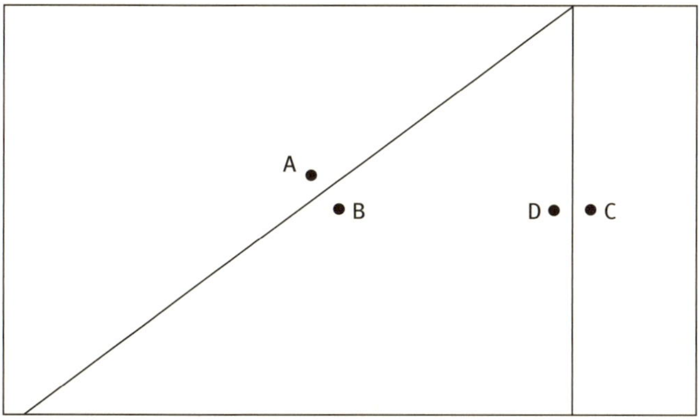

FIGURE 1

Suppose, however, the first choice of position is badly wrong, like C in Figure 1. In this case the same rule applies. The vote-maximizing position, D, is not near the center, but very close to C and on a line connecting C with the center. Thus, an extremist candidate can pull a vote-maximizing opponent far off toward the extremist's desires. These conclusions are exactly those drawn in the *Politics of Bureaucracy*[4] from a two-dimensional model. The reason is simple. If we extend the line connecting the two points chosen, we have a one-dimensional continuum. The votes for each position can be projected upon this continuum, and the conclusions we have drawn will follow from this simplified model.[5]

The model here developed, however, is a vote-maximization model. Dr. William Riker in his *The Theory of Political Coalitions*[6] argues that the rational political party would, instead, aim for the minimum winning coalition because the gains per capita are greatest with such a coalition.[7] This situation is shown on Figure 2. If one party makes a mistake and takes position A, then

4. *Ibid.*

5. In *The Politics of Bureaucracy*, the voters are distributed, for simplicity, evenly along the line. If they are projected from the space onto the line, they would only, by coincidence, be so distributed. Fortunately, all of the conclusions drawn from the linear model are true regardless of the distribution.

6. Yale, 1962.

7. John Moore, who read the manuscript of this book, suggested that the problem here is closely similar to the difference between a "sales maximizing" and a "profit maximizing" model of the firm in economics.

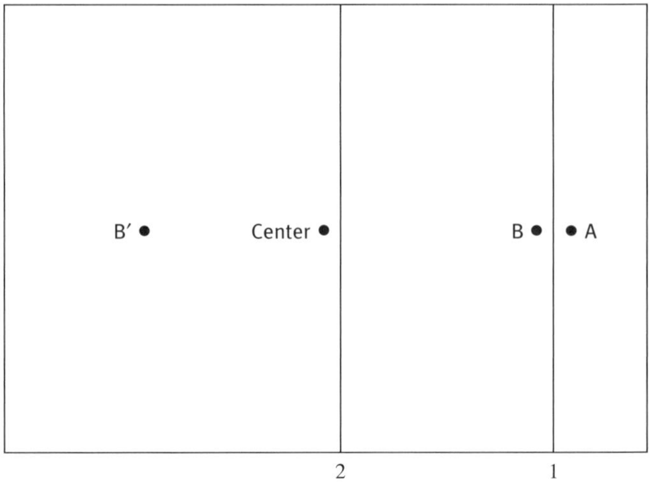

FIGURE 2

the vote-maximizing reply is position B. All of the voters whose optima lie to the left of line 1, will then vote for the second party.

For those voters at the left end of the issue space, however, this is a fairly small gain. B is still a long way from their optimum. If the second party takes position B′, it can still gain a majority of the voters, all those to the left of line 2. Further, by almost any definition of "members of the party," much more than a majority of party members would prefer B′. If, for example, we assume that all those who would have voted for the party if it had taken position B are members, then B′ would get almost two-thirds of the votes in an intraparty ballot. The switch from B to B′ is, in essence, a change from a position which gains a little for a large group of people to a position which insures a larger gain for a smaller group.[8] One might hypothesize that a party with a well-established organization of professional politicians in power might choose the B strategy, while a group of young rebels, trying to take over the party, would espouse policy B′. Intraparty revolutions would normally consist of throwing the B clique out. After the B′ clique was firmly established, it would probably drift gradually in the direction of B, and then have trouble with a new group of "Young Turks."

8. This conclusion is, of course, Riker's. This whole section is a translation of Riker's reasoning into our geometrical model.

It would probably be possible with little trouble to convert our simple election model into an intraparty contest for control and subsequent election. But it will not be attempted here. One word of warning is perhaps in order. I have placed B′ as far to the left as it can be and still win over A. It could be reasonably assumed that the party or candidate who had originally taken position A would shift leftward if their opponents took a position to the left of B, and, hence, B′ as I have drawn it would probably not win. Before deciding on a position for the second party it would be necessary to make some calculations of the likely response of the first, and this would surely lead to a position closer to the center than B′. Models of this sort would be easily developed, but many different sets of assumptions seem about equally descriptive of the real world, so none will be presented here.

If the two parties have gradually drifted into a position like A and B, then the party with a majority may have an intraparty revolution which will shift the controversy nearer the center of the issue space. Although the details are radically different, something similar might happen within the minority party too. In Figure 3 we assume that the two parties have gotten themselves into positions A and B. Obviously, the minority party hasn't much chance. In a strategy carried out by Bryan and Goldwater, a rebel group within the party might propose a drastic reorientation of party strategy. If they can seize control of the party, they might seek to shift to a position such as C which appeals to a different combination of voters than does A. If the strategy is a winning one, only part of the party, defined as those who would have voted

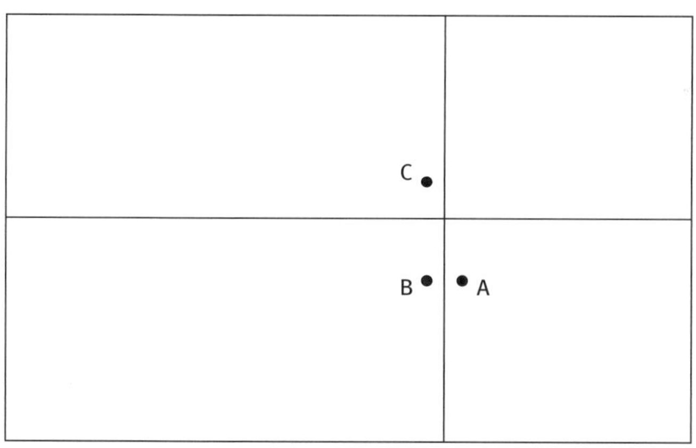

FIGURE 3

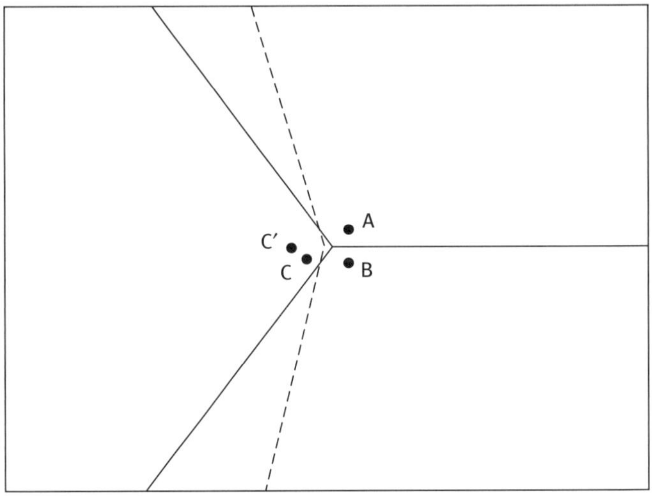

FIGURE 4

for A, will benefit. Again, part of the party is sacrificed, this time in a search for new allies rather than a simple quest for improved returns. Note that the new position of the two parties is not very close to the center, but with this arrangement, movements to the left by either party are likely to be highly profitable. Hence, it can be assumed that they will occur and the eventual location of the parties will be near the center of the issue space. Note also that the space between A and C is greater than that between A and B. This is based on the assumption that the voters will be able to make finer distinctions along the lines of division they have grown used to than upon a new set of issues.

So far, however, we have been using our geometric tool simply to duplicate results already obtained by other methods. When we turn to more than two parties or candidates, it shows a clear superiority over the previous models. In Figure 4 a three-party system is considered. Suppose that A and B have adopted positions and a third party C is considering what position it could adopt. Further, suppose that whichever party gets the most votes will be elected. In any effort to deal with this problem in general terms, the corners of the rectangle make problems, and hence it is better to adopt a circular issue space, but for our present purposes we can get by with a rectangular issue space.

If the third party chooses a point which is close to A and B (C, for example), then it will surely lose, as shown by the solid lines which divide the area into the segments closest to each of the three. If, on the other hand, the party chooses a point somewhat further out, C′, then it will win, as the dotted lines show. Of course, it is possible to lose by moving too far out, but, at any rate, the optimum location is not as close as possible to the location of the other two parties. This result, of course, applies also to A and B. If more than two parties or candidates are expected, then the vote-maximizing position is not close to your opponents, but well away from them.[9] In the real world, multiple party systems always involve significant differences among the parties, so our result is realistic.

Previous discussions of multiparty systems have usually been based on a single-dimension, left–right continuum. The assumption that the parties differed along only one axis hardly seems justified. To name but one problem, almost all countries with multiparty systems have some sort of farmer's party which doesn't fit into the left–right structure. Our system, which can be generalized to any number of issue dimensions, has no difficulty in dealing with such interest-oriented groups. Nor would it be difficult to fit in a set of parties organized from left to right, if such a structure were found. It seems likely, however, that the customary left–right system reflects the analytical tools available, not reality. The rules first adopted to seat the members of the French legislature are surely not universal natural laws. It seems likely that all parties in multiparty systems should be thought of as occupying portions of a multidimensional issue space, which are differentiated by their direction from the center, not by their location upon one particular dimension.

So far I have used my own version of the Hotelling-Downs model to demonstrate that it can be generalized to two or more dimensions. Downs's version is somewhat more complicated than mine, but it also can be generalized in the same way. The principal differences between the models are two. My model assumes that the voter always votes for the alternative which is closest to his optimum; Downs's, that he does so only if the nearest alternative is closer than some crucial distance to his optimum. If it is farther away,

9. An example using a circular issue space may be more helpful to some. Suppose the circle is 1000 inches in radius and we start with three parties at the points of an equilateral triangle, one inch on a side, and centered on the exact middle of the circle. The perpendicular bisectors of the three sides of the triangle will divide the circle into three 120 degree pie-shaped sections. Suppose one of the parties moves directly outward .52 inches. This changes the triangle to a 40 degree, 70 degree, 70 degree shape and gives the party which had moved a segment of 160 degrees. This segment will have its apex .45 inches away from the center, but this loss will be much less than the gain from the widening of the angle.

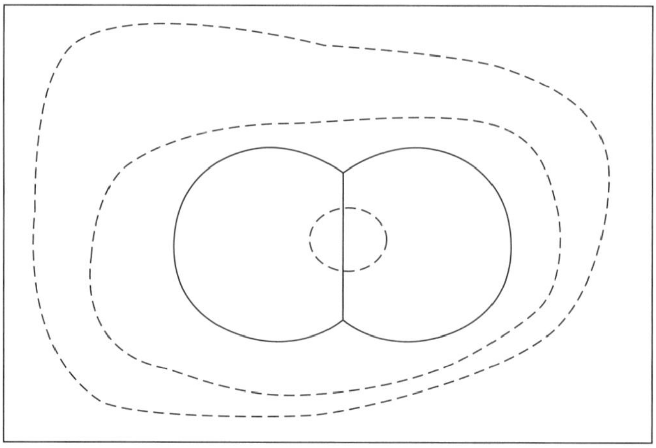

FIGURE 5

he does not vote. With this model the distribution of the voters becomes crucial, and Downs must therefore make realistic assumptions about this distribution, while I can get away with very simplified distributions. There is no particular difficulty, however, in specifying such distributions on our two-dimensional model, and the next few pages will be devoted to duplicating Downs's reasoning, using such models.

In Figure 5 a roughly bell-shaped distribution of the voters, comparable to that in Downs's Figure 2 (p. 118), is shown. The voters are assumed to vote for the nearest alternative as long as that is no more than three-fourths of an inch away. Vote maximization on the part of the two parties leads to positions much like those shown, with the voters within the compass-drawn circles voting for each party. Downs's Figure 3 (p. 119) shows that, with his assumptions, a two-party system can lead to parties which are far apart, if the voters' preferences are arranged properly. Figure 6 duplicates his model in two dimensions. Neither party can gain votes by moving closer to the other, yet they are very far apart. With such a distribution it would be mere coincidence if the hills upon which the two parties sat were of equal size. Downs's Figure 4 (p. 121) shows the situation in which they are not, which is presented in a two-dimensional model in Figure 7. The party in the upper left-hand corner could hardly expect to win any elections.

Finally, Downs shows in Figure 5 (p. 122) a distribution of voters which he feels will lead to a multiparty system. This distribution could be displayed

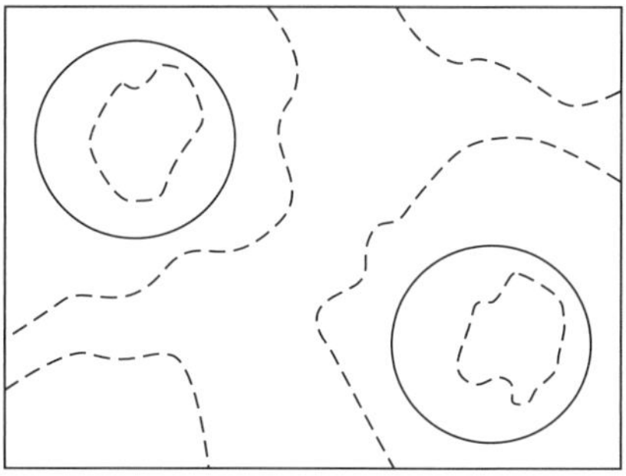

FIGURE 6

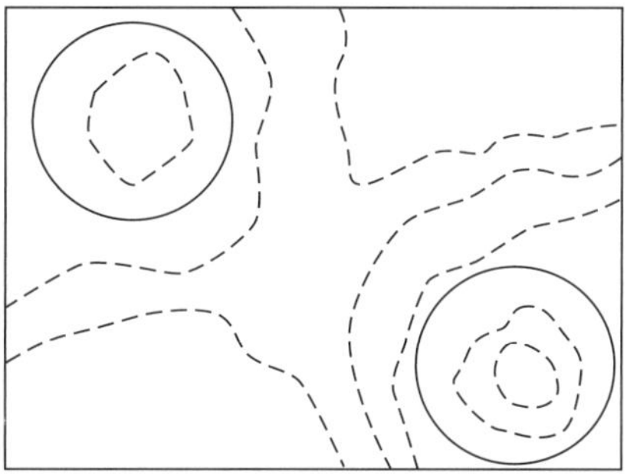

FIGURE 7

in two dimensions in a variety of ways, but Figure 8 shows the simplest distribution. Needless to say, the choice of which assumptions are the more useful is, in the present state of knowledge, necessarily a matter of subjective judgment. It should not, however, be impossible to test which set is more in accord with the real world. The issue distribution of the nonvoters would be quite different in different models, and this could be investigated quite easily. There are, also, numerous more complicated models which could easily be developed. For the time being, however, these models have considerable explanatory and predictive value. Walter Lippmann ran a number of columns explaining that Goldwater would be drawn to the left by more or less similar forces, and the sharp shift to the right by Johnson after Goldwater's nomination is a further demonstration of their power.

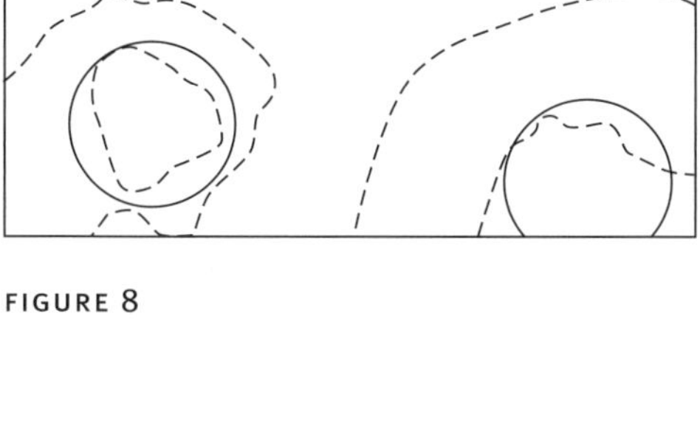

FIGURE 8

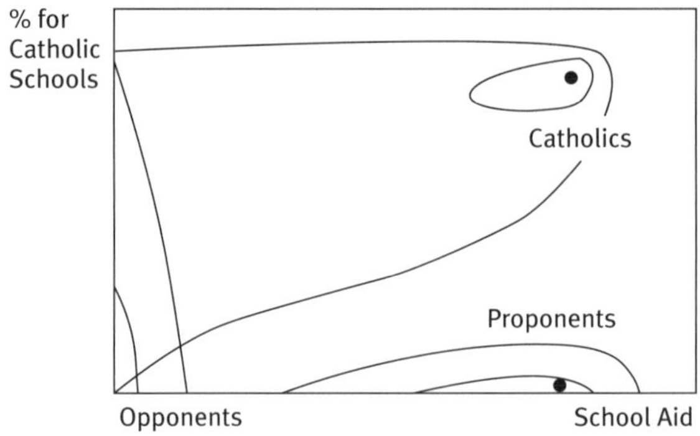

FIGURE 9

Turning now to the problem of log-rolling, only peculiar and special cases can be shown on a two-dimensional issue space. Even for these cases we will have to represent the preferences of interest groups, not individuals. Interest groups, of course, are built up out of individuals, and normally do not represent a group of people with identical preferences, but people who feel strongly on one issue and less strongly on others. Their individual optima, both on the dimension in which they feel strongly and on the others, may vary, but the ultimate effect is an approximation of the interest group preferences, which we will use in our analysis. Figure 9 shows such a set of group preferences arranged to "explain" the lengthy delay in providing federal funds for local schools. It is assumed that the population fell in three rough groups. The optima of the Catholics who favored school aid but who were against such aid if they were excluded is shown near the upper right-hand corner. The opponents of the aid program generally wished to include the Catholics if there was to be such a program. Their optimum was at the origin. The proponents of the program, on the other hand, were normally strongly opposed to any aid to Catholic schools. Their optimum is far out on the horizontal axis. The result, the defeat of the proposal, can be thought of as the result of a deal between the Catholics and the opponents, and thus as representing log-rolling, but this is straining the concept somewhat. Similarly, if we have three persons on a two-dimensional issue space, an agreement among two of them to vote in some point along the contract locus connecting their optima, might be thought of as log-rolling.

Log-rolling, essentially, involves one group of voters or representatives making a trade with one or more other groups under which, say, group A,

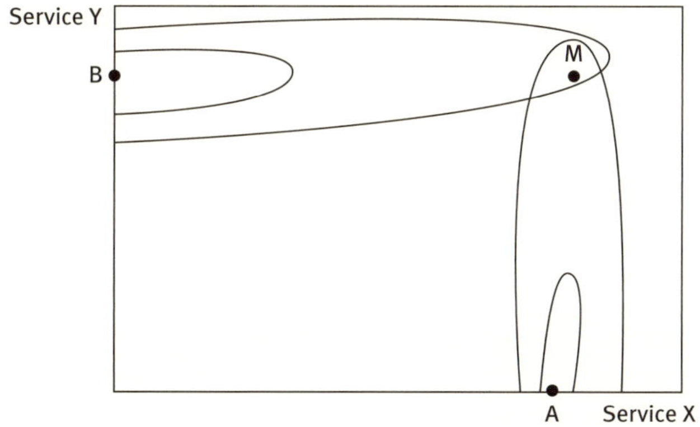

FIGURE 10

which favors measure X and opposes measure Y, agrees with group B, which favors Y and opposes X, to vote for Y in return for group B's vote for X. They agree to vote against their own preferences in return for compensation, and this, obviously, is only possible if their desires are of different intensity. Simple log-rolling involves such trades over a sequence of votes. Thus, X would be voted upon and then Y. Implicit log-rolling occurs when the various issues are made up into a large, combined project, usually called a political platform. Thus, a party will run for office on a program calling for both X and Y, and both groups A and B will support it.

The reasons for our inability to present this situation directly on a two-dimensional graph will become clear from an examination of Figure 10. A and B are shown with their optima and indifference curves. The shape of the indifference curves, of course, indicates their much greater interest in X and Y, respectively, than in Y and X.[10] Assuming that these two groups are the total electorate, then there is no need for a bargain unless A and B happen to have exactly the same number of voters. If either were to have even one more vote than the other, then the larger group could simply impose its desires by majority voting and ignore the wishes of the other. Only if the two groups were of identical size, would a compromise on point M be sensible. If, however, there are other voters, say a set C who favors measure Z but is opposed to X and Y (and if the A and B voters also oppose Z), would we ex-

10. In practical politics this degree of difference in intensity would not be likely unless there were a great number of other groups each interested in its own small issue.

pect such a result? If neither A nor B has a majority, but if the two of them make up such a majority, then agreement on point M becomes sensible. A party offering M, combined with strenuous opposition to Z, would get the votes of groups A and B and win.

This situation, however, cannot be fully represented in two dimensions. Z should be placed along a third axis sticking vertically out from the paper. At best, Figure 10 can be thought of as a cross section of the three-dimensional figure at the point where Z is zero. If we think of the matter in this way, then the indifference curves of group C would roughly be segments of circles centering on the origin. Our diagram, then, is not determinant. It helps us to understand, but it does not show the entire situation because the possibility of agreements between groups A and C, or B and C, does not appear on this cross section. Obviously, the real-life situation with many issue dimensions cannot be put on the two-dimensional continuum.

How, then, do we explain the apparent close fit between such two-dimensional models and the complex multidimensional world in which log-rolling is the norm? Clearly the answer lies in the fact that the two types of space are identical to the political candidate or party. If we choose a position in our two-dimensional space, movement in any direction will result in some voters being pleased and others disappointed. If there is another candidate or party, the problem is to choose a position which is preferred by a majority of the voters. If there is more than one party, a position which will maximize votes must still be chosen. We can think of the party as moving through the issue space in search of its optimum locations. In its motion it will continually pick up voters and lose others. The exact shape of the indifference curves of the individual voters is of little interest to it. Since the principal difference between log-rolling and voting for other motives lies in the shape of the indifference curves, with the individual feeling very intensely about some subjects in log-rolling, the log-rolling and non-log-rolling models are more or less indistinguishable from the standpoint of our hypothetical model party. The conclusions drawn from two-dimensional space without log-rolling are, thus, fully transferrable to a multidimensional Hilbert space which depends largely upon log-rolling. Although the two models are greatly different, the difference is not relevant to the party seeking an optimal position. It follows the same rules of action and ends up in equivalent positions in both situations.

PART 7

VOTE TRADING AND LOGROLLING AS MECHANISMS OF POLITICAL EXCHANGE

A SIMPLE ALGEBRAIC LOGROLLING MODEL

In the rapidly developing literature in which essentially economic tools are applied to political problems, there have been two major models of voting performance. One of the models, by all odds the most widely used, is essentially spatial. In it, individuals are assumed to have a preference mountain and to prefer the points which are closer to their optimum to points which are farther away. This model, which started as a very simple one-dimensional continuum in the work of Harold Hotelling, Duncan Black, and Anthony Downs, has developed into a more complex, many-dimensional model in the later work of Black, Otto Davis and M. J. Hinich, and Gordon Tullock. The many-dimensional version of this model must be represented, of course, by some variant on the Cartesian algebra since it is not easy to represent graphically more than two dimensions on a piece of paper. In general, these models have been used mainly to demonstrate that in a two-party system, the two parties will normally have platforms that are very similar and that these will represent median preferences. The other model deals with the phenomenon of logrolling and has normally been represented by other tools; see James Buchanan and Tullock. The interrelation between these two models has been discussed in general by Davis and Hinich and Tullock, but no very rigorous joint model exists. It is the purpose of this article to demonstrate that the two approaches are not inconsistent by presenting a spatial model which will also cover logrolling.[1]

Reprinted, with permission, from *American Economic Review* 60 (June 1970): 419–26.

1. H. Hotelling, "Stability in Competition," *Economic Journal* 39 (March 1929): 41–57; D. Black, "On the Rationale of Group Decision-making," *Journal of Political Economy* 56 (February 1948): 23–34; A. Downs, *An Economic Theory of Democracy* (New York, 1957); D. Black, *The Theory of Committees and Elections* (Cambridge, 1958); O. A. Davis and M. J. Hinich, "A Mathematical Model of Policy Formation in a Democratic Society," in *Mathematical Applications in Political Science*, vol. 2, ed. J. Bernd (Dallas, 1966); Davis and Hinich, "Some Results Related to a Mathematical Model of Policy Formation in a Democratic Society," in *Mathematical Applications in Political Science*, vol. 3, ed. J. Bernd (Charlottesville, 1967); Davis and Hinich, "On the Power and Importance of the Mean Preference in a Mathematical Model of Democratic Choice," in *Public Choice* 5 (Fall 1968): 59–72; G. Tullock, *Toward a Mathematics of Politics* (Ann Arbor, 1966); J. M. Buchanan and G. Tullock, *The Calculus of Consent: Logical Foundations of Constitutional Democracy* (Ann Arbor, 1962); Davis and Hinich, "Power and Importance," 68; Tullock, *Toward a Mathematics of Politics*, 57–61.

I. Three-Person Model

Suppose that an individual must choose government policies with respect to three different issues which we shall designate *A*, *B*, and *C*, and that each of these issues represents a continuum, such as the appropriation for the army or the appropriation for the welfare program. This situation can be represented by a three-dimensional issue space with each of the issues representing one dimension and an individual having some point which is for him optimal, let us say [10, 10, 10]. Presumably his level of satisfaction will fall off as the actual social choice moves away from his optimum. If we assume that this fall-off is uniform in every direction, we may express his loss from not achieving his optimum by the equation:

$$L_A^2 = [A - 10]^2 + [B - 10]^2 + [C - 10]^2 \qquad (1)$$

If we had a number of people with varying optima in the issue space, we would be able to deduce from the resulting set of equations similar to equation (1) how they would vote on each proposition that was put before them.[2] As has been demonstrated by the spatial models so far published, except with very special distributions of optima, the outcome under simple majority voting would be some point which is approximately at the median of the entire distribution. This conclusion is readily generalizable up to any number of issues, since the Cartesian system can be applied to an issue space of any number of dimensions.

The use of perfectly spherical indifference surfaces in this model does not appear to restrict its utility very much. In the real world, we would not anticipate such perfection, but the deviations from it would be essentially random and the law of large numbers should lead, where there are many voters, to much the same outcome as if we used our spheres. For a demonstration, see Kenneth Arrow.[3] Systematic deviations from the spherical model, together with appropriately structured locations of the individual optima, could lead to voting cycles, and the conclusion that the median preference dominates would be undermined. It is the purpose of this article to consider an important case in which we would anticipate that the individual indiffer-

2. See C. Campbell and G. Tullock, "Computer Simulation of a Small Voting System," *Economic Journal*, forthcoming, and Tullock, *Toward a Mathematics of Politics*, for an application of this process.

3. K. Arrow, "Tullock and an Existence Theorem," *Public Choice* 6 (Spring 1969): 105–11.

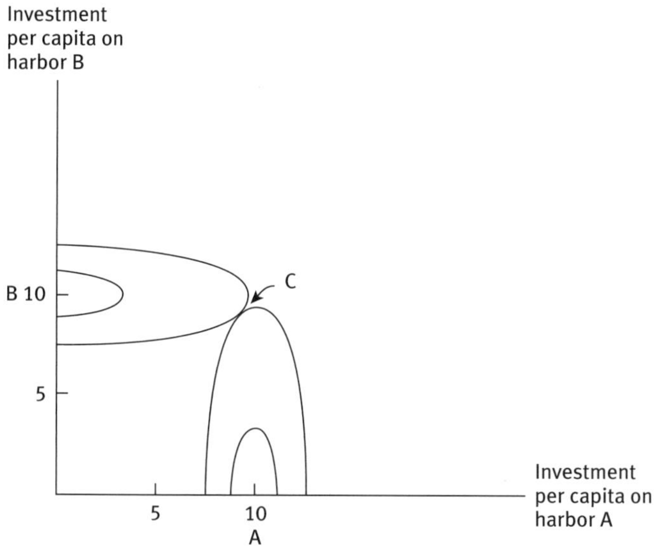

FIGURE 1

ence curves would systematically vary from the spherical in a particular way, and in which we would anticipate that individual preferences would have a structure such that the combination of these two effects leads to quite different results than have customarily been dealt with by the spatial models.

If we consider those situations in the real world in which we observe logrolling and compare them with those situations where logrolling appears to be relatively unimportant, we observe immediate differences in the structure of the individual preferences. In logrolling, we observe a number of people who are highly interested in one particular project, let us say, the dredging of the James River so that Richmond becomes a deep-water port, and only mildly interested in other projects which, generally speaking, they oppose. The rivers and harbors area is the *locus classicus* of logrolling, but similar phenomena will be found throughout a very large part of modern governments.

The indifference curves of the individuals engaging in logrolling are somewhat similar to those shown on Figure 1. Mr. A wants his harbor dredged at the expense of the general taxpayer and feels quite strongly about it, but he would rather not pay for dredging Mr. B's harbor. Since he is only one of many taxpayers, however, his feeling about the dredging of Mr. B's harbor is much feebler than his feeling about his own. Mr. B's feelings are the converse. If we assume that all of the citizens of the town in which Mr. A lives

TABLE 1

$$L_A^2 = 5(A - 10)^2 + B^2 + C^2$$
$$L_B^2 = A^2 + 5(B - 10)^2 + C^2$$
$$L_C^2 = A^2 + B^2 + 5(C - 10)^2$$

feel much the same as Mr. A[4] and the other citizens of the town in which Mr. B lives feel much the same as Mr. B, then logrolling becomes rational. Point C is better than the origin for both A and B. It is not, however, possible to represent a many-dimensional logrolling process in two dimensions and, if we consider such a piece of legislation as the rivers and harbors bill, it is clear that several thousand dimensions would be necessary.

We can begin with a simple three-dimensional model using the ordinary Cartesian algebra. This model for logrolling will differ from the usual spatial model only in that the individuals are assumed to have intense preferences on certain subjects. If we assume a three-person society where harbor dredging is paid for by equal per capita taxes, and that there are three harbor dredging operations contemplated (A, B, and C), then Mr. A's preferences can be represented by the first equation in Table 1. Mr. A is assumed to have his personal optimum at the point [10, 0, 0]. L_A is the "loss" he suffers if the government chooses some other point. As in the real world, he is much more interested in the dredging of his own harbor than in preventing the dredging of the other two harbors, although he doesn't like paying taxes to benefit other people. Note that Mr. A's optima include his own per capita share in terms of tax payments for his own harbor. For simplicity we will continue to assume throughout that all expenditures on logrolled projects are paid for by a tax which is evenly divided among the taxpayers and the per capita cost is our metric on each issue dimension.

II. Logrolling Results

Taken on the two dimensions represented by axes A and B and holding C equal to zero, the indifference curves generated by the equations of A and B in the positive quadrant will approximate those shown in Figure 1. In three

4. This does not mean that their optima or intensities are the same as Mr. A's, but simply that all of their indifference curves would have the same general shape as Mr. A's.

dimensions, *A*'s indifference surfaces in the positive part of the issue space would form a quarter of a disk with its center at the point [10, 0, 0]. The other three individuals in our current simple model would have similar disks attached to the other three axes. If the voting rule is simple majority voting, and each individual votes for his preference on each of the three harbor proposals, then there will be two votes against each proposal and all will fail. L_A would equal 22.4. The individuals, however, should notice the possibility for gains from trade. If two of them could get together and vote for each other's harbor dredging project, then they can make a quite considerable gain. Bargaining difficulties in this case are apt to be minimal since each party to the bargain has the alternative of turning to the third party and hence in essence they are operating in a market-type situation.[5] Thus, if we assume that there is some agreement between Mr. A and Mr. B and that they choose an equal amount of harbor dredging in each of their harbors, it's fairly easy to determine the point in the issue space which would result.[6] It is [8⅓, 8⅓, 0]. L_A and L_B will be 9.1, very much better than the situation without the agreement.[7] L_C, on the other hand, is now 27.2, much worse than the situation before the agreement was made. The reason, of course, is simple. Mr. C's harbor is not being dredged and he is paying taxes to dredge the other two.

This may be taken as a very simple example of the type of bargain which occurs in logrolling. In practice, things are more complicated. There are basically two types of logrolling. The first is explicit logrolling, most often observed in Congress although it does occur in other situations. It involves in-

5. A modern theory of bargaining can be said to have been initiated by J. von Neumann and O. Morgenstern, *Theory of Games an Economic Behavior* (Princeton, 1944). For a summary of developments since publication of *Theory of Games and Economic Behavior* and some interesting experimental results in a three-person situation, see William Riker, "Bargaining in a Three-Person Game," *American Political Science Review* 61 (September 1967): 642–56.

6. The assumption of equal division is not strictly necessary for the general conclusions reached below. The equations would also be solvable for other assumptions as to the division of the spoils between the members of the logrolling bargain.

7. The derivation of these results is simple but not obvious. Since *A* is equal to *B*, and *C* is equal to 0, the first equation in Table 1 reduces to: $L_A^2 = 6A^2 - 100A + 500$. Differentiating [the variable L_A^2 with respect to *A*] and setting the differential equal to 0 produces a value of *A* equal to 8.33 which minimizes both L_A^2 and L_A. Substitution of this value into the equations of Table 1 gives the numbers shown. Similar methods are used for all further computations in this article. The computations were carried out on a slide rule, which is rather unusual in these days of computers, and hence there is a possibility of error in the final decimal.

dividuals who trade their votes on many individual issues to many others for votes on other issues. Under these circumstances, there is no reason why any particular person would be left out. Everyone may trade with anyone else and the result amounts to a peculiar market solution. Since in making the trades, each individual is only attempting to make up a majority coalition, the cost calculations are similar to those informing the agreement we just discussed. Nevertheless, the fact that everyone may get their project means the outcome is different.[8] With just three voters this result would not occur, but with more voters the outcome of this process might well be that all of the harbors would be dredged at a level equivalent to 8⅓.[9] The individual is in marginal adjustment on those logrolling deals in which he has participated and loses on those in which he has not. L_A, assuming that all three harbors are dredged to the level of expenditure of 8⅓, is 12.3. This is worse than Mr. A obtains from his simple agreement with Mr. B, but it is certainly much better than he would obtain if no agreements were made at all.

The other type of logrolling is called implicit logrolling and involves political parties or candidates who present "platforms." These platforms, in essence, are complex mixes of different measures. A proposal to dredge two of three harbors would be an example of such a platform. Assuming that this type of logrolling is adopted, then the individual *ex ante* has two chances out of three of being a member of the coalition and having his harbor dredged, and one chance in three of having to pay taxes for the dredging of two other harbors. Discounting this out in a simple manner, L_A *ex ante* would be 15.1. Once again, it is much better than a no-logrolling solution. Unfortunately, this type of solution is not mathematically stable, but we will defer discussion of the matter, closely related to Arrow's general impossibility theorem, until the latter part of this article.

8. See J. S. Coleman, "The Possibility of a Social Welfare Function," *American Economic Review* 56 (December 1966): 1105–22, for a discussion of this point. His article led to comments by R. E. Park and D. C. Mueller which, together with a reply from Coleman, are printed in the December 1967 issue of this *Review*, pp. 1300–1361.

9. The simplest way of understanding this problem is to assume that an individual purchases other people's votes with his own. There is no obvious reason, if there are more than three voters, why the votes purchased by Mr. A should be the same votes as those purchased by, say, Mr. C, although Mr. A's collection of purchases includes Mr. C's vote and Mr. C's collection of purchases includes Mr. A's vote. Mr. A could, for example, make up his majority in a 5-man voting system out of A, B, and C, and Mr. C make up his out of C, D, and E. Mr. E, similarly, might have a majority which consists of C and B as well as himself.

So far, we have said nothing about Pareto optimality. If we require unanimity, clearly the bargaining costs would be high, but the economists would normally anticipate that the ultimate outcome, if we disregard the bargaining costs, would be better than the outcomes obtained by partial agreement. The Pareto optimal area is, of course, quite a complex surface running across the three-dimensional space. We can, however, fairly easily compute the value of one particular point on that surface. With our highly symmetric model, side payments would lead to a decision to dredge all three harbors equally at $7\frac{1}{7}$ each and the loss function of that point to Mr. A would be 11.8. *Ex ante* the side payments would cancel out and this is better than any of the other possibilities we have discussed. Needless to say, for an individual who can feel sure that he will be one of a pair of voters who have only their harbors dredged, that outcome would be better than the Pareto optimal outcome.

III. Five Voters

The method of calculation we have been describing can readily be applied to any number of dimensions. For example, assume that there are five harbors and five voters (groups and voters) whose loss functions are as shown in Table 2. Once again, if all of the projects for dredging harbors are put up individually and all the individuals vote on them strictly in accordance with their preference on each issue, in each case there will be four votes against and one in favor. The resulting outcome will be the origin of the five-dimensional Cartesian axis system and L_A will be again 22.4. If we assume that three groups of voters, those on harbors A, B, and C, get together to form a majority, they would agree to vote for $[7\frac{1}{7}, 7\frac{1}{7}, 7\frac{1}{7}, 0, 0]$. This gives L_A equal to 12.0, much better than would be obtained without bargaining. Messrs. D and E, not members of the winning coalition in this case, however, find that the payoff of 25.6 is worse than would have been obtained had logrolling not existed.

TABLE 2

$$L_A^2 = 5(A - 10)^2 + B^2 + C^2 + D^2 + E^2$$
$$L_B^2 = A^2 + 5(B - 10)^2 + C^2 + D^2 + E^2$$
$$L_C^2 = A^2 + B^2 + 5(C - 10)^2 + D^2 + E^2$$
$$L_D^2 = A^2 + B^2 + C^2 + 5(D - 10)^2 + E^2$$
$$L_E^2 = A^2 + B^2 + C^2 + D^2 + 5(E - 10)^2$$

TABLE 3

MINIMUM COALITION SIZE	PLATFORM	PAYOFF TO MEMBER OF WINNING COALITION	PAYOFF TO NON-MEMBER	*EX ANTE* PAYOFF
2	$8\frac{1}{3}$, $8\frac{1}{3}$, 0, 0, 0	9.1	27.2	19.9
3	$7\frac{1}{7}$, $7\frac{1}{7}$, $7\frac{1}{7}$, 0, 0	12.0	25.6	17.4
4	$6\frac{1}{4}$, $6\frac{1}{4}$, $6\frac{1}{4}$, $6\frac{1}{4}$, 0	13.7	25.6	16.1
5	$5\frac{5}{9}$, $5\frac{5}{9}$, $5\frac{5}{9}$, $5\frac{5}{9}$, $5\frac{5}{9}$	15.0	—	15.0
No logrolling	0, 0, 0, 0, 0			22.2

Using our group of five, however, we can consider a variety of voting rules. Table 3 shows on the left the minimum size of the coalition which is required by various voting rules. The outcome in terms of the amount of dredging in each harbor is shown in the second vertical column, the third column shows the payoff to a member of the winning coalition, and the fourth, the payoff to a man who is left out. In the final column, we show the *ex ante* value of the arrangement for some person who does not know whether he will be a winner or a loser but who assumes his probability of being in the winning coalition is proportional to the number of people required. For comparison purposes, we have put the no-logrolling outcome at the bottom of the table.

The reader may be surprised at the existence of a voting rule permitting a coalition of two to obtain the dredging of their harbors. It is not, however, an unrealistic situation. Most modern democracies use a representative assembly. Under these circumstances, a majority of the voters in a majority of the constituencies may be able to control the outcome. Thus, less than a majority of the voters is necessary. Our two-voter coalition is an example.[10]

It will be noted that the numerical outcomes we have obtained from our simple calculation procedure are in exactly the form which would have been predicted from the nonnumerical discussion in Buchanan and Tullock. The costs of coalition formation, of course, must be offset against the numbers in

10. The proportional representation system used so much on the continent of Europe generally speaking makes it impossible for less than the majority of the voters to have the influence shown. In Anglo-Saxon countries, however, the possibility does exist for the minority of voters obtaining the type of profits shown here.

Table 3 to find the optimal voting rule. The point of this model has not been to advance the line of reasoning started in Buchanan and Tullock. Instead it provides a basis for future research by demonstrating that it is possible to obtain their conclusions through a model which differs from the widely used spatial models only by a minor change in parameters.

The outstanding characteristic of the type of issue that normally involves logrolling as opposed to the type of issue that normally does not, is simply that there are groups of voters who feel much more strongly about one particular issue than about others, and that these different groups of voters are arranged roughly in the symmetrical way that we have shown. Needless to say, the perfect symmetry which I have given the model is an aid to calculation, not an effort to describe the real world.

IV. Other Models

In order to move from the model we have here to the type of model that was used in Davis and Hinich and Tullock, we may begin by assuming that the individuals favor all of the goods provided to some extent. Suppose, for example, that individual A's preference for the dredging of harbor B is not simply an aversion to taxation for this purpose but that he actually does think it would be nice to have it dredged. Under these circumstances, the center of the disk which now describes his loss function would be moved away from the *A*-axis a short distance and corresponding computations would indicate that there would be somewhat more dredging of harbor B. This could also lead to the ellipse being shorter and fatter. In the limit, if we continue such operations, we would end with a circle with its center somewhere near the middle of the issue space.

However, we do not have to change our loss functions from disks to spheres in order to obtain approximately the results obtained by the analysis which shows the central policy is dominant. All that is necessary is to relax our extremely strict restrictions upon the shape of individual preferences. We have grouped the individuals in clusters along the axes very strongly favoring certain projects which benefit them and being opposed, mainly because of the tax cost, to individual projects of the same nature in other areas. This is, indeed, a very tight restriction. Unfortunately, it would appear that it is very commonly met in the real world. If we assume that this type of clustering does not occur, then we are back in the world of Davis and Hinich, and Tullock. Thus, we have obtained logrolling essentially out of the spatial model simply by assuming that there are people with the type of preference that we observe in logrolling situations.

So far, however, we have assumed that our function is stable. In actual fact, what we have referred to as explicit logrolling is indeed a stable situation, but what we have called implicit is not. For example, if we return to the set of equations in Table 1, the platform [10, 10, 0] can be beaten by the platform [10, 0, 0] which can be beaten by [0, 0, 0] which in turn can be beaten by [10, 10, 0]. Further, [10, 10, 0], [0, 10, 10], [10, 0, 10] are all possible winning outcomes. In my *Toward a Mathematics of Politics*, I argued that the instability (implied by the Arrow theorem) in respect to voting was of little real importance. My demonstration, however, depended on the assumption that the number of voters was very much in excess of the number of issue dimensions. When the voters are clustered well out on each of the issue dimensions as they are in our logrolling model, the proof that I offer ceases to be relevant. In essence, each cluster of voters acts as one voter and the number of such clusters is the same as the number of issue dimensions.

V. Applications

In the real world, voting would appear to cover many issues in which the preferences of the individual voters do not have the high degree of structure required for logrolling issues. The classical solution for such a problem for a party wishing to maximize votes would be to seek the middle position on the nonlogrolling issues, and on the logrolling issues, attempt to seize a position which is superior to whatever his opponent has offered. This would lead to sharp changes of policy and great differences between the two parties. We do not observe either of these things in the real world.

It should be noted that a good deal of the logrolling actually done in Congress is on an explicit basis rather than by the parties on an implicit basis. Both the Republican and Democratic congressional candidates from Richmond will be in favor of dredging the harbor. Both will also be against (although not very strongly) dredging other harbors. When they get into the House, the explicit bargaining scheme which is stable will explain their behavior. Unfortunately, there are many types of logrolling which take place at the platform level and hence, the instability problem still remains.

Why do we not see this kind of change in the real world? One possible solution is simply that without the high degree of symmetry which I have imposed upon my model there may be genuinely superior coalitions. Riker discussed one particular set of conditions under which certain coalitions are "better" than others. There may be many other similar situations.[11]

This solution, however, obviously has its drawbacks and I think we can construct another solution which is both simpler and closer to the real world. In his recent article, Arrow pointed out that "Since the effect of any individual vote is so very small, it does not pay a voter to acquire information unless his stake in the issue is enormously greater than the cost of the information." These theoretical considerations which indicate that people should not bother to become informed about politics can be matched with empirical data which seem to indicate that they do not, in fact, know much about politics. If we assume that individuals will only make an effort to find out about policies when the effect on them is greater than a certain amount, then the individual would normally know, at least, something about what we might call public interest issues, such as police and national defense and also something about those logrolling issues which particularly concern him, i.e., those upon which his feelings are intense. However, he would not know anything about those logrolling issues which did not greatly affect him.

All the inhabitants of Richmond would know about the James River dredging project but few of them would know about the dredging of the river to Tulsa, Oklahoma. Under these circumstances, a political party making up its platform would assume that different voters have somewhat different information positions. In the extreme, the voter in Richmond would respond to a political world in which he saw general issues and the dredging of the James. In this area of his information there will be no possibility of strict logrolling and hence both political parties would choose approximately the center of this issue space. With our assumptions of voter ignorance of other issues, this would involve dredging the James to the level of 10. With many voters in Richmond, the point chosen would be the median of *their* preferences. The party also assumes similar positions with respect to other electorates which have different fields of knowledge and preferences. The outcome would involve logrolling in a sense that the individual groups would be given special treatment but would depend upon the ignorance of the voter

11. W. Riker, *The Theory of Political Coalitions* (New Haven, 1962).

with respect to the logrolling "payments" to other parties. Whether voters actually *are* this ignorant is something which can be questioned. Certainly they are opposed to taxes in general, and are aware of the fact that other people's projects, in one way or another, contribute to the tax load. The empirical investigations which do show appalling voter ignorance have never been addressed to this specific problem. Further empirical research would appear to be called for.

MORE COMPLICATED LOG-ROLLING

So far in talking about votes and log-rolling, we have used very simple bargains. As a matter of fact as you will note if you go back to look at the examples in Chapter 3, the real legislative bargains are frequently complicated. It is sensible to discuss these complicated types of log-rolling bargains before we turn to the question of election of legislators themselves. Although the intention of this chapter is to deal with complicated log-rolling bargains, I am going to try to use reasonably simple models, not the models we have used before, but still not too complicated.

In general log-rolling can take either one of two forms. There is what I call explicit log-rolling in which I agree to vote for something that you want in return for you agreeing at some later date to vote for something I want. The other type is implicit log-rolling where we stick the two items into the same bill.

Mathematically and theoretically I see little difference, but a number of people have seen a very great moral difference. Duncan Black, for example, thought that the first type was viciously immoral, but the second type was all right. His argument was that in the first type the person agreed to vote for something that he did not actually approve of, hence his vote was lying. In the second type, although he would naturally have preferred not to have to vote for part of the act, he favored the whole bill, and hence was not lying.

I feel that this was a little naive since the bill had to be put together somehow, and putting it together would involve the same kind of "lying" as actually voting against your preferences in the legislature, rather than in the committee. Although there are people who regard this as important, I do not, and the distinction will be slid over in my examples.

As is customary in dealing with these things I will start with a very simple model. We will, for a start, assume that there are only three legislators. These legislators would, in fact, be motivated by a desire to win the next election and hence represent individual citizens. Later we will discuss in a general way more than three.

The use of three is for reasons of simplicity, but as a matter of fact, very small groups of the sort that I am talking about here, if we turn to the real

Reprinted, with permission, from *On Voting: A Public Choice Approach* (Cheltenham, U.K., and Brookfield, Vt.: Edward Elgar, 1998), 105–24.

TABLE 1 ***Strength of Preferences***

ALTERNATIVES	1	2	3
A	7	−1	−2
B	−1	5	−4
C	−4	0	6

world, would begin to show signs of small group social interaction, and the type of bargaining that I am talking about would be replaced by something more complicated. I am going to ignore these small group effects and assume that the meeting is impersonal even if the number of people meeting each other is small enough so that this does not seem very reasonable.

Let us now consider a three-person legislature as shown in Table 1 where Mr. 1, Mr. 2, and Mr. 3 are choosing among three alternatives, *A*, *B*, and *C*. In each case, a majority vote of no on each alternative means the status quo remains in that particular field. As a concrete example, assume that each of them is a proposal to build a school in a different part of the city. Note that these numbers are not just the tax or expenditure, but the strength of the preferences or aversions of these people.

As you can see, in this case these numbers make bargaining possible. Various coalitions are possible as shown in Table 2.

Indeed, if all three of them were passed, in other words, a unanimity requirement, the outcome would be Pareto optimal, but Mr. 3 would neither gain nor lose; the other two would gain.

But any pair can do better in a two-man coalition. In each of these coalitions, as can be seen from Table 2, the third man, the one who is left out, not only gains nothing but actually loses. This illustrates the occurrence of external costs in governmental actions. The reader may notice that there is a cycle

TABLE 2 ***Payoff to Coalitions***

	1	2	3
1,2 (*A*,*B*)	6	4	−6
2,3 (*B*,*C*)	−5	5	2
1,3 (*C*,*A*)	3	−1	4
1,2,3 (*A*,*B*,*C*)	2	4	0

among these three coalitions. In this case the cycle is accidental, but with larger numbers of voters and alternatives, it is almost inevitable.

Note that the existence of the cycle does not necessarily lead to any difficulties. In the procedure normally used to put matters up for a vote any of the coalitions could carry their proposals. This is true whether the matters are put up as a group of two or possibly three for a single vote or whether there are successive votes with the trade being honored. Assuming the members kept their bargains there would be no cycle. This, although the numbers in this table are accidental, is an illustration of the point that with standard methods of voting, when previously defeated proposals are reintroduced to be voted upon, cycles are not produced even if the raw preferences are cyclicalsome.

Note, however, that if there were other things which would be exchanged, or you could simply make cash payments, another bargain could be made. A bargain between any two of these could not be replaced by a bargain by another pair, because that would damage the credit of persons who entered into the first bargain and then switched. If you are to continue playing you cannot ruin your credit.

In the real world straight cash payments are generally barred, but there are a very large number of other bills, clauses, and so forth. Also payoff by one of them is always available. Presumably, these different clauses are worth different amounts. As we have discussed before, there is some particular bargain which has a higher total value than any of the others. In other words, it is rather like a market situation in which one assumes that victory will go to the highest bidding group.

Nevertheless, granted the secrecy which people maintain for their own preferences, it is possible that we would never find that particular combination which had the highest group payoff. It is also possible that we would, but we can say that the bargain would always improve the outcome unless there were serious mistakes.

In any event, the bargaining is likely to end with something being put up to a vote, and being either accepted or turned down. If it is accepted, it is unlikely under most rules of procedure that contrary bargains would be permitted on the floor in that particular session of a legislative body.

In a way the cycle is stopped by two things, one of which is the bargaining process, and the second is the fact that many votes on the issue are temporarily restricted. In practice, as we have pointed out before, it is likely that everybody will get something at either one or the other of these bargains, and there is no strong pressure to repeal any single one of them.

Looking at our simple little group it is fairly obvious that 2 has less to gain from coalitions as opposed to the Pareto optimum than the others, but that does not mean that he will not gain. Voters 1 and 3 have very strong motives for entering into some coalition, but unfortunately their preferences are almost diametrically opposed. The coalitions as I have drawn them are not by any means the only possible coalitions if other matters are to be voted on.

In this example the problem does not arise, but in many cases somebody might be motivated to vote in favor of something that will actually injure him in order to avoid greater injury. We can design another matrix with that characteristic, but since it is obvious I do not think that it is worthwhile.

In this case the only way of getting a majority is getting a two-thirds majority. Still, unanimity would be arguably desirable. If we just drew lots and let each one of them, one after another, choose an alternative, interestingly enough they would end up with the Pareto solution also. I would not like to argue that this is a general phenomenon; it happens to be true in this particular matrix.

Logically, we should now go on to a larger matrix of voters. Unfortunately, this becomes too complicated to handle on the pages of a book. For example, if there are five voters choosing among five alternatives there are ten possible coalitions with a simple majority vote, and five if there is an 80 percent majority required. Adding in a unanimity requirement means that there would be sixteen horizontal lines in our tables. Having had a great deal of difficulty avoiding arithmetic errors on the three by three table, I would suspect that some would creep in on this larger one. If we move to realistic numbers, even if not 435, the problem would become completely unmanageable. We might compete with Archimedes' sand reckoner.

If we assume as we did in a prior chapter that there is a good deal of symmetry in the problem, specifically that each of them wants a particular expenditure and does not like paying taxes for any of the others, clearly we will get the kind of situation described in the road model. Reading Stockman's discussion of the Federal soup kitchen, you get the impression that this is what is going on there, but it is not true that all of the projects were worth the same amounts, or that the tax cost falling on other people was always the same. Thus, this would be much more complex.

To repeat, we are dealing here with professional legislators who have lots of time and money, and professional assistants. They are organized in committees, small coalitions, and parties. All of these can act as intermediaries within the legislature. Of course, the fact that in the American legislature there are two houses, and the bargain that will get you through one does not necessarily get you through the other, makes it more complex.

The general structure of what goes on is fairly obvious. An individual or small group thinks of putting forward some issue. It might be a formal committee or a subcommittee of Congress, a group of people with similar views who have in the past voted together, or one of the parties.[1] It is much like the situation I was talking about earlier in which a few citizens decided they would like to have a Green Belt along the Iowa River. They are trying to maximize their own preferences, but they know they must get it through the legislature, or the popular vote, as the case may be. Thus, they try to get the most that they can for themselves, but remember, they are a coalition with different interests to some extent, while still making it something that has a good chance of getting through the whole legislature.

When you have a two-house legislature, like the United States, you have the problem of getting it through two houses, and the personnel in the two houses, elected by different ways, may have different preferences. In the individual states, since the Supreme Court decided that the Federal Constitution required that the two houses in a state both be elected on a per capita basis, these problems are easier because what gets a winning coalition in one house is apt to have it in the other.

There are sometimes cases in which the two houses disagree on details but agree on the main point. The standard rule is if there are differences between the two houses in a bill which is generally similar, it is referred to a conference committee drawn from both houses. The result of this conference committee is a report which "merges" the two and is put to a vote with no amendments permitted.

There was a period of time in which people in both houses of Congress were attempting to get restrictions on appropriations for the Institute for Humanities prohibiting it from funding pornographic material. When put to vote in the form of an amendment, it won overwhelmingly in both houses. The conference committee always deleted it. The apparent reason was that a majority in at least one house did not like the provision, but wanted to conceal their dislike from the voters.

1. It should be remembered that in the United States, party discipline is weak, and when we speak of the party we should more accurately speak of a considerable part of the party.

There are a number of things that come out of this simple straightforward model, which are also characteristic of the more complicated world. Let us now turn to discussing these.

The "*A,B*" coalition has the highest point payoff for its members and is higher than the total Pareto payoff. On the other hand, taking all three into account, the "*A,B,C*" coalition has the same total payoff as the "*A,B*" coalition. "*A*" loses, "*B*" stays the same, and "*C*" gains, but the losses and gains more or less cancel.

This particular log-rolling game differs from the earlier one on roads. The coalition of the whole does not actually have a higher payoff for the whole group than some sub-coalitions but the distribution is different. This is simply an accidental result of particular numbers here, and since I got the numbers by writing some down at random, and making a few revisions to get the example to work, there is no evidence that this is the way things are in the real world.

Before we turn to more complex arrangements, let us consider some of the problems. The numbers I have put down are preference weights of the individuals, and we never have any real information about this. The individual himself can cardinalize his preferences over a set of three alternatives, or a set of coalitions, but the outsider cannot. Further, the other members of the potential coalitions do not know the value of a given alternative to any particular party.

In this particular case with only three people voting and choosing among three alternatives, it is not improbable, following the argument of David Hume's meadow,[2] that the parties could make pretty good guesses as to the other parties' value of the various alternatives. They would be guesses, of course, and there is no reason to believe that they would turn out to be correct in all cases.

When we turn to larger numbers of people choosing among more alternatives, this lack of information is very important. All of this indicates that in bargaining in actual legislature that kind of talent that helps a man win at poker is of great value. In poker there is no need to try and convince other people that you personally are honest and sincere. Log-rolling is different.

Lyndon Johnson, or for that matter our recent Republican presidential candidate, Robert Dole, was extremely good at this kind of bargaining; mak-

2. Hume said that two owners of a meadow could easily reach agreement on draining a meadow. With many owners this would be very difficult.

ing up coalitions among other people in which they must weigh the relative preferences they have for various combinations of bills. To say that they are extremely good does not mean that they are even close to perfect. A lot of errors are to be expected.

Further it should be noted that strictly speaking none of these coalitions dominate any of the others except that all of the two-party coalitions from the standpoint of those two parties dominate the Paretian outcome. Once again referring back to earlier work, that was also true in the log-rolling road model.

At this point I would like to switch to a larger model rather similar to that shown in Tables 1 and 2, but with more voters and more alternatives. Unfortunately, as I pointed out before, this in essence is impractical. Under the circumstances I am forced to use verbal, rather general terms to discuss the situation. I believe that what I am about to say is as rigorous as a numerical set running over a small library even if it is not quite so impressive in appearance.

Think of a considerable number of people who are using simple majority voting, and have a considerable number of alternatives which they can consider. Note that any one of these people can add another alternative or so to the pot, if he thinks that he can gain from it, so in essence the number of alternatives which are available at least theoretically is much in excess of the number of the representatives.

We continue with the realistic assumption that although each individual is capable of cardinalizing his own preference order over all of these real and potential alternatives, he does not actually know what the cardinal values are of the other members of the group. He can make guesses, but they are only guesses. Is the representative from a farming district in Iowa really more interested in the farm program than he is in getting a new post office in his largest city? If he is so interested, by how much?

Obviously the answers to these questions are important in setting up a coalition and equally obviously the representative from Iowa has a fairly strong motive, like a poker player, to prevent the other people from making exact estimates. Perhaps he can get both. If he succeeds in convincing them that although he is indeed in favor of the post office, his preference is relatively weak, he may get two post offices.

What I have said so far does not require any differentiation between the two different kinds of log-rolling described before. Johnson was good at both of them. In general that is characteristic of the legislature except that modern legislatures pass so many bills that a good many provisions like the ones discussed by Stockman actually go in without many people having seen them. Thus there is no direct trade but there is some kind of quota arrangement that keeps too many of these things from going in.

A good deal of log-rolling legislation depends on getting public support. Government activity can and frequently does create externalities, as well as in many cases dealing with a private market externality. In the present agricultural program, the citizens who pay more for their food are the victims of the externality. The externality that is eliminated by this program is that the farmers would be injured if the price were lower as a result of there being no government program.

It is usual in economics to refer to this kind of externality as a "mere pecuniary externality." Why we use that term I do not know. In any event, most economists, including myself, feel that this kind of externality should not be the source of government action, but most of us know that it is. That government action may create both pecuniary and the classical kind of externality is unfortunate, but the world is in many ways an unsatisfactory place.

We can take the farm program as a very simple case. In the first place it is likely that individual farm representatives and for that matter individual groups of farmers are more interested in some crops than in others. There are a good many aspects of the farm program which substantially every farmer and substantially every congressman from an agricultural district favors. In this case it is a question of making up a package of units in which this collection of things is matched with things in other fields with the result that people on the whole are in favor of it or do not know that it exists.

You must keep in mind that the congressman must be reelected. To repeat a very old aphorism, "In order to be a great senator one must first of all be a senator." An act attracting support through log-rolling almost of a necessity takes the form of a long bill with a large number of special provisions in it.

This is being written right after a presidential election. I do not think that anybody paid a great deal of attention to the formal platforms of the parties. Indeed both presidential candidates said publicly that they have not read them. Still, the candidates produced in their speeches a bundle of political proposals on which they hoped that they would gain. These are examples of complex log-rolling bargaining in which an appeal is made to millions of people with each and every provision, but they are not the same million as you move from one to another.

I realize that there is a great deal of simple personality involved in this kind of campaigning. Clinton claimed that Dole was irresponsible in offering to balance the budget and cut taxes. Dole did not specifically call Clinton a crook, but a number of public opinion polls indicate that although a majority of the populace of the United States favored Clinton over Dole, a somewhat larger majority of Americans thought that Clinton was a crook.

The voters have to weigh judgments of personal integrity, intelligence, and so on, against specific promises that politicians make. The voter realizes that he does not know all the specific promises and does know that a good many of them will probably not be carried out. The last is not a statement that they are deliberately making false promises, but that the situation as it develops may make it impossible for the winner to carry out things that they have promised.

The situation here is complicated and as a matter of fact, empirical research has not been very helpful. It has been possible to demonstrate that there is some connection between special interest pressure and the passage of bills. These tests are difficult because if somebody from a farm state is observed to vote against some provision that will in fact benefit his state, you do not know if he has been paid off for this vote elsewhere. Thus the empirical tests look at only part of the results of these bargains and hence have a very large error component.

It does appear true that congressmen usually vote in accordance with the issues favored by their constituents and where they do not, they have a tendency to be beaten. It is true that congressmen like the rest of us are sometimes willing to take sacrifices for the public good or to help the poor, and sometimes will vote against the interest of their constituents even if they are aware of the fact this may lead to their losing an election. It is even possible that the constituents will reward them for doing something which injures the constituents but looks morally justified.

Thus we can see that the log-rolling problem is extremely complex, requires difficult calculations, which difficult as they are by no means are obviously correct and may lead to unintentional consequences.

The original civil liberties act was opposed by Judge Smith, the head of the House Rules Committee, and as a sort of joke he stuck women in as another group that would be protected. It seems likely that he thought this would be easily voted out of the legislation or, preferably, it would kill the whole bill. As it turned out this joke of Judge Smith was the most important part of the bill. Far more people were affected by it than by the remainder of the bill. This was a completely unconscious bit of log-rolling by a man who was an extremely competent and experienced performer in the area.

It is obviously impossible for say 435 congressmen, or the 600 plus members of the Vermont legislature to make complex individual bargains with each other. It is necessary to some extent to centralize the bargaining procedure. Some time ago there was a book written which alleged that in the early part of the 18th century the organization of bargaining procedure was essentially by way of the particular boarding houses that congressmen stayed in when they went to Washington. This was disproved by further research.[3] Still, it was not improbable.

The easiest place to study the matter is the British House of Commons. In most of this century there was a very strict and firm party discipline. Presumably the reason for this party discipline was the party control of almost all resources that could be used in campaigning. In a mild way this control has been breaking down recently mainly because the balance between the parties is so extremely close that the Conservative prime minister did not dare to throw people out for violating orders.

In this case there is no doubt that the bargaining that goes on is actually performed in the cabinet. It is true that the individual ministers, and to some extent the civil servants that work with them, bargain among themselves.[4] In practice, however, civil servants do not have the power and deviousness of Sir Humphrey Appleby, and the cabinet ministers are not bunglers like the Honorable James Hacker.

It is clear that much the same kind of thing comes out of the Houses of Parliament as comes out of our legislature. Further, the concern for the next election with careful examination of pressure groups and the like is equivalent. The only difference is that in their case there is a far more efficient method of making the bargains. Further, in their case because the party has such control over the individual members of Parliament, bargains are simpler and normally point to things that are expected to affect the entire next election. In the United States they very frequently turn on matters which will not affect the election as a whole, but will affect somebody from the Third Dis-

3. I am not giving the name of the young political scientist that made the original error or attacking him. It was an honest mistake and an easy one to make.

4. *The Complete Yes, Minister* and *The Complete Yes, Prime Minister* are delightful books, and the television programs were equally delightful. Further, there is an element of truth in them.

trict of Illinois. The vast collection of very narrow special provisions described by Stockman is much less characteristic of the House of Commons.

It should be kept in mind that this is only an approximately correct description of the House of Commons. The cabinet not only has to worry about whether it is getting help at the next election, it has to worry about whether it can get it through the House of Lords. The House of Lords is the mere shadow of what it used to be, and further, it is no longer overwhelmingly hereditary. There are a lot of people who have been appointed to it by the Prime Minister of the day, and remain members until such time as they die.[5] It does not have a complete veto. But it can impose considerable delays and inconvenience on the government of the day if a majority of the Lords object to some bill.

Further, "majority" of the Lords is in itself a work of art. The number of Lords is very large, and only a fairly small minority of them actually turn up for its deliberations. Something that excites "country members" so that they come up could cause great difficulties. Thus the bargain made up must contain not just the members of the Commons, but at least something for the Lords.

The second place that we will look at is more complicated than the English House of Commons, but not anywhere near as complicated as the American House of Representatives. This is in countries where what is called proportional representation in Europe is applied.[6] This is practiced in its pure form in Israel and The Netherlands. Since Israel gets a good deal more attention in the American press than The Netherlands, let us talk about that.

Once again the party discipline there is very strict, although it is possible for an individual to simply leave his party if he wishes. The voting method is one in which a party puts up a list, and people then vote for the party and the party gets, let us say, 20 percent of the seats in the legislature if it has 20 percent of the vote. These seats are awarded by starting at the top of the list submitted by the party and running down until they reach 20 percent of the Knesset.

The party organization determines where the name of the candidate will be on the list, and troublemakers will be put far enough down so that they never get elected. It is possible to quit and start your own party and people

5. Australia and Canada have a sort of copy of this in which there is no hereditary component.

6. This will be much more fully described later.

do from time to time. Since the method permits tiny parties to continue to exist, this is not as hopeless as you might expect.[7]

The result of this is that there are a number of small parties, and particularly religious parties. The Arabs are so badly organized politically that they do not mean much. There are also occasional small parties formed by members of the major parties who have moved out. As a general rule, all of these parties have policies which are made up within the party not by the kind of log-rolling I have described above, but by the organization at the top which decides who will occupy the seats.

They will then have to form a coalition government with the other parties. Normally the coalition consists of one of the two major parties, Labor or Likud, together with a number of religious orthodox parties. The orthodox parties seem mainly to be interested in straightforward political pork, in the way of payments for religious schools, etc., but they have feelings about religious matters; the rules that say that you cannot drive in certain areas on Saturday, that you must wear a hat when you enter certain areas, etc.

This system means that individuals attempting to exert personal influence must first go to their party leadership, which is quite different from the system in the United States. Occasionally there are votes in which people are told to vote their conscience, but this is an unusual phenomenon. Log-rolling negotiation then takes place among the parties, and the religious parties, by threatening to change over to the other large party from the one that they are currently in coalition with, have very great leverage.

Of course, the party leadership are members of the cabinet, so this is somewhat like the situation in England. In any event, you can put your fingers on who organizes substantially all coalitions. Both of these systems are simple compared with that which we observe in the United States, particularly in the House of Representatives, or in the various American state legislatures. Sometimes with cabinet government it can be much more complex. France until de Gaulle's reforms and Italy for a very long time had almost rotating cabinets. In this case the log-rolling negotiations were still carried out by the parties, but the current cabinet ministers do not have any clear ideas whether they will be in the same position tomorrow. Even so, the actual log-rolling bargains were made in a rather centralized manner because of the compara-

7. Some time ago a man who was under indictment for various crimes started his own party, campaigned vigorously, and was elected to the Knesset with enough votes so if he had only put his wife in as a candidate she would have been elected too. This made him immune to arrest.

tive strength of the parties. Extreme decentralization as in the American system is unusual. In our case it comes from the weak party discipline which in turn comes from the fact that the party has few tools to punish deviant members.

People frequently regard descriptions of this kind of thing as actually an attack on the system. I am not wildly enthusiastic about it, but it is not something that we need to worry about terribly. In public finance theory you get the impression that the point of government is the internalization of externalities. We have something like, let us say, the weather bureau, which benefits the whole United States, but where no one would, by and of themselves, be willing to pay for it. We therefore turn to the government and in this case the national government.[8] Of course the government weather bureau also generates negative externalities for those who do not want to pay taxes for such a purpose.

Many things which have externalities, however, have strictly limited short-range externalities. I mentioned post offices and traditionally, although not today so much, that was one of the major sources of political pork. Clearly putting it somewhere benefits people only in its immediate vicinity and injures everyone else that has to pay taxes, except insofar as the location might possibly improve the efficiency with which mail is delivered.

It probably would be most efficient if we could somehow or other provide a set of narrow voting constituencies concerning only those people who benefit and lose from a given act. This would require literally thousands and thousands of separate jurisdictions and is too complicated. Our present system involves trades, sometimes in the state or local government.

Through log-rolling something with a rather restricted area of influence is provided by a larger government in return for putting something of similar restricted interest elsewhere. This cannot be objected to, although it is not entirely optimal. It does greatly simplify the voters' problem. They only have to vote on a relatively few officials.[9]

The basic problem here is, if we go back to the road model and assume that it is not perfectly symmetrical as it is there, that with simple majority voting you get a considerable amount of investment in these local public

8. Since similar activity is carried out in Europe with a lot of countries, many of which are smaller than our states, it is not clear that it has to be national, but that is the domain for the current discussion.

9. See my *The New Federalist* (Vancouver: Frazer Institute, 1994), for further discussion of this point.

projects. If the people who vote on them are representatives who are themselves elected by simple majority vote, you may have as little as one-quarter actually benefitting and therefore have something like four times as much of whatever is provided as would be optimal. This is inefficient and both Professor Buchanan and I and a number of other people think that the voting majority should be increased. Note that this inefficiency does not come from log-rolling, it comes from the voting rule. Further, our actual procedures require more than a majority, although not enough.

Without log-rolling either these things would not be provided at all, or in any event, only those which directly advantaged one-quarter of the populace would be put through and could inflict injury on the remaining 75 percent. Increasing the required majority is one remedy.

It should be repeated here that we in the United States are not accustomed to simple majority voting as I pointed out several times before. A bill requires a majority in the House, but 60 percent of the actual members of the Senate if it is thought to be important. It also needs the president's approval. If the president does not approve it requires two-thirds in both houses. This is undoubtedly much more efficient than the simple majority vote that we see in places like Israel.

Personally, I favor one house elected by proportional representation, and the other by the English first-past-the-post system that we use. The argument is that this would be equivalent to having two radically different legislatures, and a majority in both would be equivalent to considerably more than a majority in a single-house legislature.

There is the fact that the minorities would get at least one representative in the house that is proportionally elected, and the geographical areas would continue to be represented as they are now. It would probably be wise to elect the president by another method than either of those. The one we now use is inefficient, but there is a wide choice of these and I shall not select one here.

All of this does not eliminate log-rolling, but it simply requires that the coalitions to get something would be both larger and more diverse than in our present legislature. This should make it harder to get things passed which are supported by a bare majority of voters in a bare majority of the constituencies.

It should reduce the number of log-rolling coalitions that are put through, but the ones that would be cut are the ones where the total benefit is markedly less than the total cost. Going back to our road model, if we required a 75 percent majority, then people deciding to repair roads, and setting up coalitions for that purpose, would have to take into account 75 percent of the costs. This would mean that many log-rolling coalitions to repair roads would be eliminated, but these would be the ones where the cost is less than 75 percent of the actual social costs.

This may seem a modest goal. What we would like is to get governments to do things that are Pareto optimal and nothing else. As a matter of fact we cannot do this and if one thinks carefully about the market he will quickly realize that we do not have that in the market either. The reason that we do not have it in the market is quite simply that the combination of the imperfections of the property institutions together with transactions costs means that not everything is taken into account.

What we should do is select those institutions which, over the long run, and granting many different transactions, accepting that we will sometimes be on one side and sometimes on the other, give us the highest present discounted value. This means that any of these transactions, voting or in the market, looked at just by itself without the general pattern will turn out to be non–Pareto optimal.

The original decision to adopt a general set of institutions with this characteristic may, however, be Pareto optimal. It may literally be the best thing for everyone even though the individual transactions that are taking place after that agreement could be improved upon if we were not concerned with transaction costs and if everyone concerned had a veto power over the agreement. In the real world we will be compelled to use log-rolling and not to require unanimity because the costs of unanimity are just too great. We consciously accept the probability of having difficulties from time to time on individual transactions because we feel that the entire collection of such transactions gives us a better deal than would be the case with another set of institutions.

This does not of course indicate that the present set of institutions is ideal. Indeed as the reader probably knows I am a fairly radical reformer. Reform however should not aim at Pareto optimality in each transaction. It should simply aim at a set of institutions which over the long run and over many transactions will give people as good a return as is possible.

EFFICIENCY IN LOG-ROLLING

The very meaning of "efficiency" when we deal with log-rolling requires some explanation. It is clear that government actions are rarely Pareto optimal. Some people are injured and receive no direct compensation for that injury. An obvious case of this is the victim of a war, but there are many less dramatic examples. At the moment in Tucson we are having a radio telephone arrangement using very short wavelengths installed and this requires that the transmitters and receivers be at considerable height above the ground. They are putting up towers, which, personally, I think are inoffensive, but certainly are not beautiful. A number of people are complaining. Nothing will be done about these complaints except that they may get a visit from some plausible representative of the telephone company who will try to soothe them.

There are many other examples such as the farm program and the Washington Metro system, which is heavily subsidized by people who never use it. An example which got a great deal of publicity was the federal government subsidization of certain "art" objects created by Mapplethorp. This is particularly interesting because no subsidy was necessary. He is a moderately wealthy man as a result of selling various of his productions. He surely could have sold these objects, or if he felt in the mood made a contribution. The government sponsorship irritated an awful lot of people who were not compensated.

What we actually mean when we talk about government efficiency is efficiency over the long run; that is, we want the government on the whole to give people the best bargain that is possible granted the existence of transaction costs and the impossibility of getting everyone's agreement to all projects. I have at various times referred to this as Pareto optimality in the large. This would mean that there is no arrangement which would give everyone a better deal.

Most people who talk about government being efficient or, more commonly, inefficient, do not define what they mean. The question of whether log-rolling is or is not efficient is even more difficult. This makes claims made by some scholars that log-rolling is not efficient hard to evaluate.

Reprinted, with permission, from *On Voting: A Public Choice Approach* (Cheltenham, U.K., and Brookfield, Vt.: Edward Elgar, 1998), 125–41.

People who make such claims are mainly proponents of democracy and democracy everywhere functions by way of log-rolling. Nor is there any way to get rid of it. I should say also that something very similar to log-rolling appears in non-democratic governments, so in a way it is simply a characteristic of governments *per se*.

Some governments consciously inflict injury on some people in order to benefit others. In some cases the group that benefited is the majority; in others, the immediate family of the House of Medici. We should not, however, assume that governments are often motivated by a positive desire to injure people; indeed frequently governmental officials are consciously trying to help. Nevertheless, they must know that some people are injured and there is no way of helping *A*, *B*, and *C* without injuring *D*.

There has been some debate in the literature about whether log-rolling is or is not a contribution to efficiency. In *The Calculus of Consent*[1] Buchanan and I said that it was, but there are various people who have objected. There was an actual debate, not of great length, in the *American Political Science Review* in which William Riker and W. E. Brams argued that it was inefficient, giving an example in which log-rolling apparently led to an outcome that was for all parties inferior.

I responded rather weakly.[2] The reason for the weakness in my response was that Peter Ordeshook orally told me that Riker and Brams had simply chosen the wrong log-rolling bargain. There was another coalition that had paid off very well. I confirmed this but did not mention it in my response because I thought it belonged to Peter Ordeshook. Later I heard that he, a student of Riker, did not want to use it and had hoped that I would. Under the circumstances, the Riker and Brams paper has not been demolished as it should be.

As far as I know this is the only real argument that log-rolling is inefficient, but we have not done very much to indicate that it is efficient. I would like to take up this issue here.

To begin with let us consider the efficiency of ordinary bargaining. I bought a house not very long ago, and this was the third time that I had done so. The housing market is normally referred to as a well-organized market,

1. Gordon Tullock and James M. Buchanan, *The Calculus of Consent: Logical Foundations of Constitutional Democracy* (Ann Arbor: University of Michigan Press, 1962).

2. "Letter to the Editor" ("Paradox Lost" comment on Riker-Brams article), *American Political Science Review* 68 (December 1974): 22–23.

although there are certain cartel aspects to it. What happened was that a real estate lady and I looked at a number of houses, discussed the price, made an offer (traditionally) 15 percent under the asking price, had difficulty with the seller, and eventually got it.

There are two possible inefficiencies, one of which is the need to use a real estate lady, but I was going to a totally strange city, and I must say she was remarkably good at figuring out my preferences on just a brief acquaintance. Still, it seems likely there were other houses available in Tucson which both in price and in amenities would have suited me better. I stopped my search without having exhausted the market, which is what every shopper does.

We do not normally regard this as inefficient, but it does mean that the distribution of resources and other things in the society is not really perfect as seen from God's eye. We all spend limited time in search, and the bargaining process is not perfect, etc. Nevertheless, no one will regard this as an inefficient market even though it is not one that is divinely perfect.

My reason for bringing this up is that it will turn out to be true in log-rolling also. But there is another problem with the private market. If having bought my house I proceeded to paint it purple, because I like purple, I would have been inflicting a cost on my neighbors. Perhaps a significant cost, if they were hoping to sell their own house at a good price.

This is one of the straightforward externalities that we are not at all surprised by when we find them in the private market. When I buy a house I take into account what I might need and what the man who is selling it to me considers his needs.[3] We do not directly worry about what other people might be affected by the transactions. As the reader no doubt knows, there are various rules about housing, zoning, structure, etc., which are intended to deal with those, but these are all government activities, not part of the private market.[4]

The outcome of the market process in the real world, even a very well-functioning marketing process, is one in which there is not a perfect match in the sense that each buyer gets the ideal product for his price, and each seller sells it to the best buyer, nor that the transaction covers all of the effects of the transaction. As we shall see log-rolling has the same negative characteristics.

3. Also what the real estate lady needs is taken into account.

4. As it happens in my case the house that I bought was in a homeowners' association which had been set up originally by a private firm, but even that depended upon courts to enforce its rules.

Suppose I want some change in the law. First, just wanting the change does not do me any good. Let us assume there are other people who will agree with me that this change is desirable, but by ourselves we are not numerous enough to get it through. In other words there are people who do not want the change.

If there is no log-rolling, we would simply count the heads, and if there is a majority on one side that would get it. Note, firstly, it is not obvious that the level of intensity of the wants on either side is the same, and secondly, it may well be that the people who will be injured by the law being passed are in favor of something else and could be readily compensated by an agreement.

If we were trying to maximize the well-being of the world we would like a system in which externalities, injuries inflicted on people who are not included in the agreement, are taken care of. If my neighbor wants to paint his house purple, it does indeed lower the value of my block. The fact he got a number of his friends to agree that his house could be painted purple (preferably friends who live some distance away) would not mean I do not suffer an externality. I would be injured even if a vote put through by the relevant constituency said he could do so.

The fact that government actions can create externalities, just as well as eliminating them, is almost unknown to most economists. Why this is so is very difficult to say. It is obvious when you think about the matter. It is indeed possible for a government to inflict great externalities. There were a number of citizens in Baghdad, a short time ago, who suddenly discovered that they were suffering from fairly severe externalities from the actions of a democratic government.

We do not have to look internationally for this kind of thing. There are many laws enacted by legislatures which are strongly opposed by some of their own citizens. I can be as much, or more, injured if a majority of my neighbors vote on something I object to as I would be by offensive private action. Both impose externalities.

Let me go back to the case used by Douglas Rae to criticize the supermajority requirement.[5] The reader will recall this concerned a railroad car back in the days when smoking was perfectly legal in such places, and some of the passengers wanted to smoke, and others did not want them to smoke.

5. Gordon Tullock, "Comment on Rae's 'The Limits of Consensual Decision,'" *American Political Science Review* 69 (December 1975): 1295–97.

Rae argued under this circumstance the simple majority vote is ideal. Of course, this assumes as I mentioned before that the intensity of the preference of the two groups is the same, which is not obviously so.

Suppose we put in the equivalent of log-rolling. We say that you can make trades on other issues; then even if it turned out that only a small minority wanted smoking discontinued, they could simply offer a joint motion, that (i) smoking shall be discontinued and (ii) they will buy a "free beer" for all the other people. This is a clear-cut log-rolling transaction and would no doubt get through if the trip was going to be fairly short. If it was going to be long, you might need several beers.

Turning from the Rae example, generally speaking things that are suggested for vote fall into two categories. Firstly, they are things that will benefit or possibly prevent injury to a fairly small group, and this is a fairly large benefit of injury, and will cost the rest a small amount of money per head. As you will recall on Table 1, I had a set of preferences for 3 voters, and explained that we would think of them as preferences for 3 schools, in 3 distinct parts of the city.

Presumably, on a completely uncompensated vote for each of the schools, they would not be built because in each case the people who had to pay the taxes would be more numerous than the people who would benefit from the school. On the other hand, it is fairly obvious that compensation in that case, other schools, in other parts of the city, could get it through.

What we would like is a system that does two things: firstly, it prevents things which actually inflict more injury than gain from going through. As we will see this consideration is not strictly speaking possible, but we can limit the maximum loss inflicted.

Secondly, we would like everybody to be treated well. For example, I would regard providing the mug of "free beer" to people who are prevented from smoking, although they would like to do so, as a better arrangement than just preventing them from smoking. In this case the decision for smoking or non-smoking is a general one, and does not provide specialized benefits, or prevent specialized injury to a small minority, but still I would argue that it is sensible to compensate, if we can. In cases where the beneficiaries of the bill or the particular project are a small minority, but where the benefit to them is greater than the total cost we would like to have, and other than a possible charitable motive on the part of the majority, compensation is the only way. We can put together a bundle of such proposals so that a majority will benefit from the entire bundle. Or we can vote on them one at a time with people agreeing to vote for a friend's position, if he votes for them. As far as I can see there is no significant difference between them.

It is fairly clear log-rolling can generate a benefit. As a matter of fact people who are engaged in the legislative process know this, and engage in log-rolling. They seem to do it in a somewhat bad conscience, however. Those who object to log-rolling are simply objecting to it because they have not thought about the matter very much. The examples they use against log-rolling are like the one Douglas Rae used in which there is a simple majority and nobody is much injured. It should be noted that even in that case the minority, if it feels strongly, may be able by compensation to get its preference.

Long ago when Buchanan and I were working on *The Calculus of Consent* we discussed the situation of the Jews in Germany. If there had been a well-functioning democratic legislature, it seems fairly certain that the Jews, by trading their votes for a number of other projects, could have prevented severe discrimination against themselves even if the majority of those in Germany favored it because they would not favor it enough so that they would not accept compensation.

To look back to an American example, Booker T. Washington was a man who did a great deal for his race, although it is not popular right now to say so. The Tuskegee Institute, which he founded, depended very heavily on the payments that he received from a white-dominated state legislature. It seems fairly certain that this was the result of a trade in which he used what political power he had to support that group on some things, and they responded by supporting the Institute. Once again the trade was not only good for Booker T. Washington, but no doubt good for his race.

There are two arguments for compensating the minority for its loss. The first of these is sort of an equity argument, although I believe there are many people whose moral code does not support it. Nevertheless, it is clear that people can be badly injured by government action, and compensating them is at least nice, if not morally required.

The second argument is one of efficiency. To repeat what we have said before, there are many government activities which benefit only a minority, but where the cost is spread over a larger group. There are also cases where the opposite happens, where the action removes an injury to the minority once again at a minor cost to a larger group. With pure majority voting with everybody simply voting for their preference on each issue these could not get through, and most people would agree that it is desirable they do so.

I should say here that there is another way for dealing with these matters.

We could set up specialized small constituencies for each of these issues and put the tax entirely upon that small constituency. Unfortunately, as a general solution, this is impractical although clearly in some cases it can be done. It would be nice to try it when we could.

Returning to the main theme; getting through these many minor projects by grouping them together with other projects either in the form of one bill, as in the bond issue I have continuously referred to in Tucson, or by making trades on several bills clearly permits them to be passed when it would not be possible otherwise.

Is this actually efficient? If it is efficient, is the simple majority rule the best bet? There are other possibilities. We could permit any small minority to have one project of its own, with every minority being included. I doubt many of my readers will favor that approach.

The standard procedure which is to hold a vote on it does raise immediately the question of what kind of vote. If we look at the American Constitution there are many cases in which the answer to that is something more than a majority. Getting a bill through both houses of Congress, with the two houses being elected differently, and then having the President sign it into legislation, or sending it back and having it win by a two-thirds majority in both houses is clearly something more than a simple majority.

A number of states, including Arizona, have recently been passing constitutional amendments which require more than a simple majority for various matters, mainly tax increases. Finland actually requires an 80 percent majority for a tax increase. Some time ago, Jack Goode and I[6] suggested requiring a two-thirds majority in the Supreme Court to establish a precedent.[7] Whether you agree with this or not it is clearly a possibility. Juries, after all, vote unanimously. Is this more or less efficient? If we have a single issue upon which some people are in favor of a particular action, and some oppose it, and we have good reason to believe that the intensity of their preferences is about the same, one can make an argument for simple majority voting. Note those conditions. It has to be a simple yes or no choice, and the preferences for people on both sides have to be roughly the same, and in particular, we are not interested in compensating the people who are injured for their injuries. These are very strict conditions and probably seldom met.

6. Suggested that the Supreme Court cases should only be regarded as precedence if at least two-thirds of the Justices agreed with the decision.

7. A simple majority would decide the instant case, but not set a precedent.

If we are going to engage in log-rolling, and to repeat, it is something that everyone knows is the basic way in which modern democratic governments operate, then the arguments for using more than a simple majority in order to pass bills are strong. Suppose we can, by making up a log-rolling bargain, get a majority of the vote while injuring 49 percent of the population. It is essential for this to work through that the total benefit which is generated by this bill be at least 51 percent of its total costs and preferably more. If we go up to requiring a two-thirds majority, the benefit necessary to log-roll the bill through is at least 66.66 percent of the cost. The reader will recall that this was demonstrated in the simplified road model given earlier.

So far we have not talked about voting to prevent something from going through. Suppose that Hitler had acquired power in Germany, but not dictatorial power. In other words he had to get things passed through the legislature.[8] Then suppose that a majority of the population were anti-Semitic, although whether they wanted to kill was another matter. (Perhaps their attitude was not much stronger than in my hometown of Rockford, Illinois, in the 1930s. There was minor social discrimination against the Jews, but nothing serious.) Under these circumstances, the Jews by making a significant log-rolling offer could no doubt get a bill weakened or even stopped.

This is an extreme example, but in general log-rolling works both ways. A promise to some group to give them a special bill in return for their vote for something I want can be countered by someone on the other side promising a gift in return for a vote against my bill.

As a result of this, in general, it will normally not be possible for a log-rolling coalition to inflict serious injury upon sizeable minorities. If we did not have log-rolling that could be perfectly possible, and fairly easy to find many examples other than the Jewish one which I gave above.

For a long time now the tobacco interests have been able to follow this technique to prevent what is clearly the majority from bringing in anti-tobacco legislation. It is a slow and desperate guerilla war, and they are slowly losing, but they have been able to hold it off for a considerable time.

My readers may think that this is unfortunate, but it is true in this case that legislation which would badly injure a minority has been bought off by log-rolling agreements mainly entered into by the representatives from the tobacco states. The same kind of thing can be said with respect to the various efforts to get rid of the agricultural farm-subsidy program. The final act

8. In fact that is how he started, but he converted to dictatorship with great speed.

which was passed by Gingrich and his friends arranged that it would be gradually eliminated, and here again we have a set of bills in which an overwhelming majority would benefit, but which would remove a considerable subsidy to a minority.[9]

These have been simple examples. Let us think about the matter more generally. Suppose that in society there are possible various changes in the status quo to benefit some people, and in general they would injure some other people. There is an ideal way to deal with this problem which is unfortunately impossible. We could assess the gain and loss to everyone. If the gain is greater than the loss, take the action and assess the winners to compensate the losers. Contrarywise, if the loss was greater than the gain, the change would not be made.

There might be some who would suggest under these circumstances the winners from the inaction be assessed in order to compensate those who should benefit from the change. Granted the number of possible changes in the status quo, even in the impractical universe where the first proposal was feasible I doubt that this would be.

We do like people who lose from any given transaction to be compensated, but more important we want to make sure that on the whole the gains from various transactions are greater than the losses. This is obviously true in my effort to buy a house. We have been reading about the situation in Bosnia in which people got houses without paying for them, and I take it that we all think that is a bad idea.

Much of economics has been devoted to discussions of the way in which private transactions can be structured so that the gains will normally more than balance the losses, and in general we hope that nobody will be injured very much. We should do the same in politics.

We do not require in the private market that everybody who is affected by the transaction be compensated. We do not give all of them the right to veto transactions, unless they are so compensated. We should also not give a complete veto to anybody injured in politics. The reason is the same in both cases. In both cases this would provide an unfortunately strong bargaining position for many small groups. I could maintain that the sale of one of the houses in my homeowners' association[10] injured me and demand

9. I should say that I am in favor of inflicting this injury on this particular minority because the cost to the average citizen is very much larger than the benefit.

10. Or for that matter the sale of a house in Washington, D.C.

compensation. Essentially I could attempt to obtain the whole of the benefit of the bargain for myself.

The fact that people who do have a veto right may do just this is the reason that land assembly for large projects is so difficult. The holdouts gain more than the people who are cooperative and everyone is motivated to hold out. The same would be true in politics.

Let us temporarily ignore these problems and assume that we have an infinite amount of time to make any political change. To repeat, it is not a reasonable condition but it makes it easier to talk about the matter. In these circumstances everybody would have to be compensated, and the end product would in fact not injure anyone, and the gains would be distributed among the interested parties. The problem, of course, is the infinite time which, in the real world, would be extremely costly. In fact, it is an impossible system.

Note here that compensation for everything except the transaction cost would be complete. Leaving aside the (tremendous) transaction cost, projects in which the gain is greater than the loss could be got through and the society as a whole would gain from these projects but so would each individual, or at least none of them would be injured. The moment we go down from requiring unanimity these two conditions cease to be true. On the other hand, the transaction cost shrinks.

Once again this is true in the private market. If we permitted anyone who felt they were in any way injured by any given transaction to veto it, this would provide that no one was injured, and the externalities are eliminated, but all agree that the cost of introducing this type of bargaining is greater than the gain.

In the private market what we try to do is to see to it that the people who might be injured in a major way by a given change in ownership are compensated. The major person injured if I move into my present house without paying for it would be the previous owner, as so many Bosnians have discovered, but our laws will see to it that he is compensated. People who suffer less are normally not compensated.

In politics, oddly enough, we would not do this if there were no log-rolling. Log-rolling does move in the general direction of compensating the losers, and moves in that general direction more strongly if the requirement for the vote is greater than a simple majority.

Let us consider how log-rolling does work. The first thing to be said is that, in general, the provisions that are brought up for discussion will be those in which it is thought that the gains from those who win is great enough so that they can compensate at least some of the losers. The number of the losers who must be compensated is a product of the voting rule.

In the market it is possible that there are transactions when the purchase of something may actually be socially negative because the people who are not permitted to veto it are injured more than the buyer and seller gain, but that is presumably rare. In politics if we use simple majority voting it is not at all obvious that this would be rare.

We can easily put our finger on projects like the farm program mentioned above, protective tariffs, the Washington Metro system,[11] which violate this condition. With a higher majority, the cost would be closer to the benefit. Still, all three examples I gave above were enacted by our present national system which implicitly is fairly close to a two-thirds majority.

The fact that these bills can be got through is evidence that our present system is not perfect, but nobody thinks it is. Once again I refer to the analogy of the real estate market. The outcome there is not perfect either but granted the cost imposed by putting additional requirements on it, it is better than we could expect if we did not have such transactions.

Let me make a suggestion of a change in the real estate market which is not intended seriously but which has something to do with the proposal that the majorities be more than simple majority. Suppose that each lot which is to be sold can be sold only if the owners of all the other lots which adjoin it give their consent.[12] I take it that the readers would all agree that the cost of such a system would exceed the benefit, although it would guarantee that certain externalities, e.g., the cost to a neighbor by the sale of a house to somebody that he detests, would be eliminated.

This is a case in many ways like the voting case we have given. In both cases some kind of arrangement is made under which we balance the reduction of externalities by requiring larger numbers of people to consent against the transaction cost which that would generate. In both cases the outcome cannot be made perfectly efficient, but we can hope for reasonable efficiency.

It is not normally noted but in addition to the people who are setting up the log-rolling bargain for a given bill there are people who will be injured by

11. It is not widely known, but the fares on the Metro pay only a small part of its costs. They do not even pay its operating costs, let alone the capital cost.

12. If the owner proposes a use of the lot which would violate the zoning code, then a variance must be obtained. This normally requires consent of 80 percent of the people in the immediate vicinity.

it and are not going to be compensated and they will be attempting to set up another coalition either to simply eliminate this from consideration in favor of another basic proposal, or at least beat it. Thus, as in the real estate market, you have bargaining with two parties involved, and there are more than two parties.

The outcome is presumably reasonably but not perfectly efficient. In this case when we say that it is reasonably efficient in the political arena we are conceding that there may be some people in the minority who are very badly injured. Nevertheless, it is efficient in the sense that there is no other coalition put together which can beat it.

This is one of the basic reasons that we do not see cycling in the real world. I earlier remarked when talking about the paradox of voting that one of the reasons it does not seem to have remained in the center of thought in politics is it is very hard to find any examples of it actually occurring. The fact that these bargains are not dominated explains this. In our example before we had *A*, *B*, and *C* in a cycle. If it is *A*, plus two post offices, then it is likely that *A* will be voted in and will turn out to be stable.

This is not proof that it is desirable because the people who wanted *C*, may in fact be opposed to *A* very strongly, but not in any need of post offices. Under the circumstances, they will be left in the uncompensated minority.

The net result of this is that the final bargain that comes through is as we have said quite stable. It is not terribly well known but it is true that the higher the required majority the less likely there will be cycling. That does not mean it is impossible with any majority you care to name, but it requires fairly stringent restrictions on the shape of the different curves, etc. as the majority requirement goes up.

The end product is that log-rolling which is dominant in all democratic societies[13] leads to outcomes that are efficient in the same sense that market outcomes are efficient. This is efficiency within the constraints of the system. It is easier to restrict externalities in the market than it is in politics.

This is probably true because the existing literature on democratic government rather assumes that we have majority voting and we normally do have voting which is not wildly different from majority. The example that I gave above of an 80 percent majority for tax increases in Finland is rare. Normally you will have something like the British Houses of Commons and Lords, which is almost pure majority voting, or like the American com-

13. As a matter of fact, it is dominant in dictatorial societies, but takes a different form.

plex system[14] which is equivalent to somewhere around a 60 to 66 percent majority in a single house.

Both of these permit significant negative externalities to be inflicted on numbers of people and are less efficient in that sense than in a regular market in which we have better transaction laws. To say that they are less efficient than the market is not to say that they are basically inefficient. It is that we could do much better.

We terminate here the main text of this book. We have a system that works but not, until fairly recently, subject to any kind of scientific analysis. It certainly could be improved upon. Indeed, for myself, I would like to have somebody invent a totally new form of government, although I am not positive that this could be done. Nevertheless, we have a system which we should attempt to improve, and for which improvements are possible. This book has attempted to lay the foundations for such improvements.

14. We have in the United States the most Byzantine way of passing laws of any modern democracy.

PART 8

MORE ON DEMAND REVEALING

SOME LIMITATIONS OF DEMAND-REVEALING PROCESSES: COMMENT

T. Nicolaus Tideman and Gordon Tullock

In their five warnings about demand-revealing processes, Groves and Ledyard do not mention the limitation that we regard as most serious, namely, that, like all other methods of making collective decisions, it undermotivates participants to obtain relevant information, or even to ascertain their own preferences. Thus, a great deal of random grit may be thrown into the process. But this is true not only of other methods of making collective decisions, but also of markets for private goods.[1] The suggestion by Green and Laffont in this volume might ameliorate the problem, and there may be corresponding adjustments that could be made in other collective decision procedures and in markets, but such improvements would clearly leave us, at best, in a situation inferior to what we could imagine in the absence of transactions costs. However, in evaluating any proposal, the relevant standard is not a count of the number of defects it possesses in comparison to an unattainable ideal, but rather a judgment of the seriousness of those defects, and a comparison with available alternatives. In that spirit, we turn to the specific warnings of Groves and Ledyard.

Their first point, that the demand-revealing process may lead to a waste of resources compared to the results of majority rule, is obviously true. And dictatorship may lead to allocations that are more efficient than those of majority rule, but that is not relevant. Expected waste is the relevant criterion. Majority rule requires a distribution of marginal net benefits with a mean equal to its median to achieve efficiency in decisions about continuous parameters. Since such a coincidence would generally happen with "probability zero," majority rule is generally somewhat inefficient. If one believed that the

Reprinted, with kind permission of Kluwer Academic Publishers, from *Public Choice* 29 (Spring 1977): 125–28.

1. Sanford J. Grossman and Joseph E. Stiglitz, "Information and Competitive Systems," *American Economic Review* 66 (May 1976): 246–53.

distribution over potential decisions of discrepancies between mean and median marginal net benefits was highly concentrated at zero, that might be a reason for preferring majority rule to the demand-revealing process. However, there are good reasons for believing that marginal net benefits of public activities will be distributed asymmetrically, and will therefore be highly unlikely to have equal or nearly equal means and medians. Two important determinants of benefits are distance from the location of a public project and income. Since both of these characteristics are distributed asymmetrically, any discrepancy between benefits and assigned tax shares tends to lead to an asymmetric distribution of net benefits.

An important virtue of the demand-revealing process is that it is not hampered by such asymmetries. Discrepancies between tax shares and benefit shares do generate waste in the demand-revealing process. But unlike majority rule, the relative waste tends to approach zero as the number of participants increases. The reason for this is that the component of each person's taxes that is wasted may be viewed as a triangle with height equal to the discrepancy between his tax share and his benefit share, and slope equal to the slope of the vertical sum of all other schedules of willingness to pay for public expenditure. As the number of participants increases, the sum of the heights of all triangles tends to remain constant because the *share* represented by each discrepancy tends to fall in proportion to the number of participants. On the other hand, a doubling of the number of participants tends to double the slopes of the triangles, reducing their total area by one-half. This is the reason that the waste relative to the expenditure becomes insignificant as the number of participants increases, and why we do not regard the lack of Pareto-optimality as a serious limitation.

The objection that the demand-revealing process may result in bankruptcy for some participants may be, in part, an objection to the possibility of implementing the process without constitutional limitations. Most methods of making collective decisions, including majority rule, have the potential of driving some persons into bankruptcy or even having them killed. Not only is it possible, but historically it has happened from time to time. Constitutional limitations on what governments can do are usually thought desirable, but every constitutional limitation carries with it a cost in eliminating some possible alternatives. In this respect, the demand-revealing process is no different from majority rule, dictatorship, random sampling, or any other method of making collective decisions.

There are two different sources of potential bankruptcy for individuals in the demand-revealing process that should be distinguished. One is excessive cost shares. If a person with an income of $10,000 is told that he must pay 1% of the cost of the community's schools, and if the community decides to spend more than $1,000,000 on schools, then the individual's taxes will be greater than his income and he will be bankrupt. Any system that assigns cost shares to individuals that are different from their income shares has such a potential for bankrupting individuals.

However, this is not the source of the bankruptcy in the Groves-Ledyard example. There the tax shares of the three participants are equal to their income shares. But two of the participants have such strong demands for the public good that they want to spend all their income on it, given their tax shares. And substantial payments are required to compensate them for accepting a public sector that absorbs less than all of their income. The income that the third participant has left after paying his share of the resource costs of the public good is insufficient to compensate the others for their loss of utility from the less than all-absorbing public sector, and so the third person is bankrupt. This is akin to the possibility of taking your television to a repair shop, and then finding yourself bankrupt because the repair bill exceeds your resources. It can happen, but the possibility does not keep people from having their televisions fixed.

There are two reasons why bankruptcy is quite unlikely to occur in applications of the demand-revealing process, particularly if tax shares equal income shares. The first reason is that the "Clarke tax" or compensation component of taxes, which can conceivably cause bankruptcy, is generally so extremely small. As mentioned earlier, the Clarke tax on each participant is a triangle with a height equal to the discrepancy between his tax share and his share of benefits, and a slope equal to the slope of the vertical sum of all other schedules of willingness to pay for public expenditure. It is unlikely that the discrepancy would often exceed $1/N$, where N is the number of participants. The slope of each participant's willingness to pay may be expressed as $\eta E/\alpha$, where η is his elasticity of demand, E is the level of expenditure, and α is his tax share. Ignoring the fact that elasticities will vary among individuals and that shares will not all equal $1/N$, one can say that the sum of slopes for all N persons will be roughly ηE, and the area of the triangle corresponding to the Clarke tax for one person, which can be calculated as half the height squared times the slope, will be roughly equal to $\eta E/2N^2$. The typical resource cost to a participant is E/N, so the Clarke tax comes to roughly $\eta/2N$ times the resource cost. Unless the typical value of η is astronomical, this will be a very small proportion of resource cost when the number of participants is large. And that is why the Groves-Ledyard example that generates bankruptcy seems to us not particularly relevant. A surcharge on taxes on the order of 1/N is not going to put many people in bankruptcy court. Furthermore, anyone whose tax share departs substantially from his benefits and who is concerned about the magnitude of his Clarke tax can easily estimate the Clarke tax from an estimate of the typical elasticity of demand for the good in question. These payments will not be estimated to be zero by sensible participants.

The very small size of the Clarke taxes also leads us to be unconcerned about warning 3, that income effects could lead to instability. It is true that a change in one person's reported schedule will generally change everyone else's income (very slightly) and therefore change their demand schedules (unless income elasticities are zero), but these effects are so small that we strongly doubt that an example of explosive cycles could be constructed in a "realistic" setting, say more than 100 participants, less than ⅓ of income to be spent on the public good, and income and price elasticities smaller than 5. Furthermore, cycling does not in itself undermine the operation of the system. In each period people can respond based on their beliefs about the taxes they will pay, and the indicated level of public expenditure can be made in that period. If a slightly different level occurs in the next period, it is of no great moment. The cycling possibilities are certainly less significant than those of majority rule.

The fourth warning, that income effects could lead to manipulability, is similarly valid but quantitatively unimportant. If, by varying my stated benefits I can change the taxes of another person by a small fraction of 1/N, the resulting income effect on his demand is generally not going to be detectable. I would do as well to try to lower the price of tomatoes by buying more shoes, which would raise the price of shoes, lower my neighbors' real incomes, and therefore lower their demands for tomatoes. It is with good reason that we generally ignore such possibilities.

The last Groves-Ledyard warning is that if coalitions form, they can be expected to move the outcome away from Pareto-optimality, by misrepresenting their preferences. As it happens, the power of coalitions to distort outcomes to their own advantage is a characteristic of all group processes of which we are aware, including markets and majority rule. The fact that the demand-revealing process possesses this characteristic is not evidence of its inferiority to any other process. It is possible that in an application of the demand-revealing process some precautions and sanctions against coalition activity would be desirable, just as anti-trust laws seek to prevent coalitions in markets.

All told, we do not find anything in the Groves-Ledyard warnings that would discourage us from applying the demand-revealing process. We recognize that there is an innate conservatism in people that leads them not to trust new ideas, and for this reason we do not expect the demand-revealing process to catch on quickly. But we persist in our view that the demand-revealing process is superior to the alternative mechanisms for collective decisions that have been suggested so far.

COALITIONS UNDER DEMAND REVEALING

T. Nicolaus Tideman and Gordon Tullock

Riker's criticism of the demand revealing process essentially involves pointing out a number of opportunities for coalitions that are raised by the process. He apparently uses the word coalition a little differently than we do, and the first two cases that he mentions, on pages 878–81, are not regarded as coalitions by Riker although we would have so regarded them. This is merely a matter of language, and we see no point in debating language.[1]

In a way Riker's comment is more properly considered as a comment on Tullock's article "Demand-Revealing Process, Coalitions, and Public Goods" rather than the article in the *Journal of Political Economy*. In our *JPE* article, 2nd paragraph, we said ". . . all existing social choice processes are subject to exploitation by suitably designed coalitions. This process is no exception." Further, on pages 1157 and 1158 we discussed in some detail a general method of producing coalitions in a rather more complex setting than Riker has used.[2]

Thus, in demonstrating that coalitions are possible, Riker is pushing on an open door. Coalitions are also possible in all other voting procedures and our claim for superiority of the demand revealing process did not involve alleging that coalitions were not possible. At the time we wrote that article, we thought that demand revealing shared with other voting methods the problem of coalitions and was superior on certain other dimensions.

It is true that since we wrote this article Tullock published, in a special issue of *Public Choice* edited by Tideman, an article in which it was argued that in the politically relevant cases, where there are many voters and many pos-

Reprinted, with kind permission of Kluwer Academic Publishers, from *Public Choice* 36 (1981), 323–28. Copyright Martinus Nijhoff.

1. William H. Riker, "Is 'a New and Superior Process' Really New?" *Journal of Political Economy* 87 (1979): 785–890. The Riker article was published without having been sent to us for a reply, and when this reply was sent to the *Journal of Political Economy* it was rejected. Riker has been invited to continue the debate in *Public Choice*.

2. Gordon Tullock, "Demand-Revealing Process, Coalitions, and Public Goods," *Public Choice* 29 Suppl. (Spring 1977): 103–5; T. Nicolaus Tideman and Gordon Tullock, "A New and Superior Process for Making Social Choices," *Journal of Political Economy* 84, no. 6 (1976): 1145–59.

sible outcomes, public goods considerations would normally make coalitions impossible. Only one of Riker's examples, however, turns on the large number case and hence we could confine our attention to that one case and accept the rest of his article. We feel, however, that the general subject of coalitions under public choice deserves further airing and we have certain objections to the specific coalition analysis presented by Riker, for example, the case given by Riker on pages 884–85 will lead, he feels, to one of four outcomes which he lists. Each one of these outcomes is dominated not only by a particular other member of that set but by a very large number of others outside the set. Like all contests for distributional gains, there are cycles,[3] and there is no strong reason that we can see to believe that any particular outcome would occur.

Further in all his cases if the person left out of the coalition wishes to, he can inflict very severe costs on the coalition participants by suitable false bidding. But arguing about special cases when cycles are present seems to us pointless. A general discussion of the opportunities for coalitions is more productive.

Riker (pp. 887–88) gives three conditions for "manipulation." There is a fourth which he doesn't mention which is that bribery and blackmail not be illegal. We nowhere suggest that the law against these two crimes be repealed, although as a matter of fact we do think that they would be less important under the demand revealing process than under current methods. Why we feel this way will be discussed below.

The laws against bribery and blackmail in voting which now exist are not perfectly enforced and we presume they would not be perfectly enforced under the demand revealing process. They would, however, eliminate certain types of bribery such as the last coalition mentioned by Riker in which there is the telephone blitz to get a hundred people to each pledge $50,000 to bribe another ten for $500,000. We will point out below why this particular coalition would not work anyway, but the mere fact that the contract to make the payments would not be legally enforceable would undermine this particular scheme. Further, at least one of the hundred and ten people necessarily involved would presumably leak it.

Turning to the other necessary conditions, they are "one that bidding not be secret." Riker apparently feels that this is required by the demand reveal-

3. Gordon Tullock and James M. Buchanan, *The Calculus of Consent: Logical Foundations of Constitutional Democracy* (Ann Arbor: University of Michigan Press, 1962).

ing process but as a matter of fact, it is not. In the extreme there is no reason why the bid needs to be known by anybody except the voter and a computer. In less extreme forms the bid made could presumably be kept at least as secret as current income tax forms. As a specific proposal, suppose that there are the usual present voting booths, which individuals must enter alone to present their bid.[4]

If people had to make payments, their bills would be a little harder to keep secret. Surely, however, although a little harder, it is not by any means impossible. Any voter who wished, for example, could receive in addition to the genuine bill another one for some higher amount which he specified. He could exhibit the second as proof of the size of his bill. Alternatively, bills could be collected from funds already on deposit, with no physical image of the bill ever created.

Thus, the first of his conditions need not be met. The second is that voters be able to communicate after initial or pre-election surveys. Apparently what Riker has in mind here is something like current public opinion surveys. The problem is that if people are going to behave in a way which Riker assumes, that is, put together coalitions on the basis of this preliminary information, then persons surveyed would no longer lack a significant motive to lie to a survey taker, as they do in the present situation. As Riker says "since the process with honest initial bid is vulnerable to strategic manipulation one wonders if honest bids can even be expected initially if voters also stimulate manipulation." The same point was discussed at greater length in Tullock (103–5). Granted that part of the bargaining process would involve making false pre-election statements or false preliminary bids, coalitions would indeed be hard to negotiate.

Riker's condition three seems to be a repetition of two, since it merely provides that the voter who has answered one way on a public opinion poll is not required to answer the same way when he actually votes. Thus the conditions which he gives for the success of manipulation in general would not be met by the demand revealing process. It should be said that they are not met by the present voting process either, and that does not seem to prevent the existence of coalitions. We would not like to argue that the absence of these particular conditions means that no coalitions will exist under demand revealing.

4. The modifications which would permit the use of telephone bidding but maintain secrecy are a little complicated and we won't discuss them here.

Coalitions among large numbers of voters, however, are very likely to be impossible because of public goods considerations. Consider, for example, the last case given by Riker, in which there is in excess of three million voters, with a coalition of one hundred and ten of these discussed by Riker; we should like to demonstrate that this coalition could not succeed. For this purpose we reproduce here his Table 9. The coalition suggested is that all members of groups 3B and 3C tax themselves $50,000 apiece in order to bribe members of 1C and 1D[5] $500,000 apiece provided that all ten members of groups 1C and 1D put down, as their valuation for X, $10 million and lower their valuation for Y to zero. This will lead to X winning.

It is clear that this act if carried out would lead to X winning, which is greatly to the advantage of 3B and 3C, who will do better than they otherwise would as will members of 1C and 1D. It seems very dubious, however, that this particularly large coalition could be organized if there were even the most minimal enforcement of current law, but let us waive the point. We also waive the point that the actual valuations held by individuals would probably be rather obscure, because all individuals have motives to pretend they have different valuations than they actually have if there is any prospect at all that negotiation of this sort is to be undertaken. Just look at what would happen if the members of 3B and 3C did indeed put up the money and signed a legally binding contract to pay 1C and 1D if X were adopted. We will assume that the actual bids made by the members of 1C and 1D will be secret, although whether or not X wins will of course be known publicly.

Consider the situation of one person in group 1D, who has received a binding promise that if X wins he will receive $500,000 from 3B and 3C and a request that in order to accomplish the adoption of X he bid $10 million. Firstly, the value to him of X has now risen from $100,000 to $600,000. Note that this type of effect will not raise the total votes for X because the value for each member of 3B and 3C has now gone down by $50,000 so instead of putting in $200,000 they will each rationally put in $150,000. But what should 1D do? Let us confine ourselves to two possible strategies, $600,000 and $10 million. He does not know what the other people will do for certain, but there are four possibilities. The first of these is that issue X will not pass even if our member of 1D puts in $10 million. Obviously, in this case he is indifferent between the $600,000 and the $10 million bids. The

5. It is not clear to us what the difference is between groups 3B and 3C, or what the difference is between groups 1C and 1D. There seems to be some unnecessary printing here.

TABLE 9*

A

CLASS OF VOTERS	NUMBER IN CLASS	INDIVIDUAL VALUATIONS			SUM OF VALUATIONS		
		X	*Y*	*Z*	*X*	*Y*	*Z*
1*a*	1,000,000	$10	$20	$0	$10,000,000	$20,000,000	$0
1*b*	100	10,000	20,000	0	1,000,000	2,000,000	0
1*c*	9	100,000	200,000	0	900,000	1,800,000	0
1*d*	1	100,000	200,000	0	100,000	200,000	0
2*a*	1,999,999	0	20	10	0	39,999,980	19,999,990
2*b*	1	0	20	10	0	20	10
3*a*	500,000	20	0	10	10,000,000	0	5,000,000
3*b*	99	200,000	0	100,000	19,800,000	0	9,900,000
3*c*	1	200,000	0	100,000	200,000	0	100,000
Total					$42,000,000	$64,000,000	$35,000,000

B

VOTER	SUM OF VALUATIONS WITHOUT *i*'S VALUATION			TAX ON *i*
	X	*Y*	*Z*	
$i = 1d$	$41,900,000	$63,800,000	$35,000,000	0
$i = 2b$	42,000,000	63,999,980	34,999,990	0
$i = 3c$	41,800,000	64,000,000	34,900,000	0

*Reproduced from Riker, "New and Superior Process," 888.

second is that X would pass with no actual payments made by any of the bidders for it, even if he puts in $600,000. Once again he is indifferent between the $600,000 and $10 million bids. The remaining two cases, however, are cases in which he is by no means indifferent. The first of these is one in which issue X will pass if our member of 1D puts in $10 million, but will fail if he puts in $600,000. Note that in this case the bill that he is charged will necessarily be in excess of $600,000. In other words, he loses in this case from having put in $10 million. The fourth case is where the bill will pass whether X puts in $600,000 or $10 million, but that in both cases he will receive a bill, let us say for $300,000. Once again, he would be indifferent between the two bids.

Thus, it is clear that if our member of 1D calculates and follows his self-interest carefully in making his choice between $600,000 and $10 million, he will choose to make a bid of $600,000 and tell the other members of the coalition that he has put in $10 million, free-riding on the coalition. If all ten of the people who are receiving bribes make these calculations and act accordingly, X will not pass. If only a few do so, then these few will make at least as much money as the others, and they will avoid some large risks.

As a general rule in large groups, free-riding behavior is apt to dominate coalitions. This is not necessarily true with a small group. Riker points out that under present circumstances within legislatures there are normally only a fairly small number of special cliques. He then assumes that this will continue if the demand revealing process were adopted in the legislature. Why he says this is hard to know, because he also says "but we know from experience (with, e.g., proportional representation) that new methods of voting profoundly change voters' behavior." In fact, it seems likely that manipulation and coalition formation will be less common under the demand revealing process. It should first be noted that the coalition formation which Riker refers to in legislatures today involves two steps: first, the formation of a few cliques, which are quite large, and second, negotiations between these. The motives for this behavior are numerous, but surely among the most important are making it possible to express relative intensity of preferences for different issues before the legislature and, particularly, trying to find reasonable compromises among people with different intensities of preferences for different objectives. This is quite unnecessary with the demand revealing process. The individuals can express their relative intensities in the voting process itself and need not make trades with other people. This does not, of course, prove that there will be no such cliques, merely that the motives for forming them are much weaker than they are under standard voting procedures. Thus, one would anticipate that there would be less manipulation, logrolling, and formation of what Madison called "factions" with demand revealing than with ordinary voting.

But all of this is merely the beginning of what should, and we hope will, be a continuing discussion of the way the demand revealing proceess would work in practice. Riker agrees with us that coalitions are possible in the demand revealing process, but apparently he does not agree with us that they are much less likely than in ordinary voting. It can be said, however, that he has not demonstrated that they would be more likely than they are with ordinary voting, only that they can exist.

MORE THOUGHT ABOUT DEMAND REVEALING

In a number of conversations between myself and Howard Margolis it has always been clear to me that he did not understand my point of view. He apparently thinks that I do not understand his, and I must concede that this is possible. This puts me in some difficulty in the joint role of author and editor because if I understand him properly, once again, I am not sure that I do, he is making an elementary mistake and therefore I should not have published his paper. If, on the other hand, I do not understand him properly, then this reply is misguided and should not have been published. In view of the importance of the subject, however, and the fact that we do seem to continually misunderstand each other, I thought that bringing the debate out in the open would be worthwhile. Perhaps some of the readers of this journal can either decide who is misunderstanding whom or perhaps explain both of us to the other.

To begin with the elementary mistake, the demand curve that economists draw is literally the demand curve, i.e. what the person demands with no attention whatsoever to why he demands it. Thus, if some individual has two different motives for demanding something or other, we simply look at the sum of these two motives when we draw the demand curve. We may, of course, and indeed it is not particularly uncommon among economists, decide that we would like to disentangle the two component parts of his demand and in doing so we might draw in two partial demand curves. In Margolis's case, there are two component demand curves, one by the individual for himself, and as a second his interest in having other people get the right amount of the public good. The demand curve referred to in "The Demand Revealing Process," however, is simply the total demand that the person has for the public good.

It is indeed true that most economists having observed the functioning of the market and government for some time tend to think that most people, most of the time, have a demand curve, the overwhelmingly largest component of which is their own selfish desires. None of us, as far as I know, think

Reprinted, with kind permission of Kluwer Academic Publishers, from *Public Choice* 38 (1982): 167–70. Copyright Martinus Nijhoff.

that is the only component but we do think it is a large enough component, let us say 95%, so that we sometimes talk as if it was the only component we were thinking of. Still, proponents of the demand revealing process assume that in drawing in their demand curve people will indeed draw in their total demand curves regardless of the motives which lead them to demand various amounts, not sub-sections of them, which deal only with their selfish demand.

Thus, as a first approximation the Margolis discussion misunderstands the demand revealing process. Those colleagues of his who, being asked how much they would pay to move the outcome a short distance, said they would contribute a penny would note that the contribution had already been made and the movement he discusses had already occurred if they had drawn their demand curves appropriately. It may be, of course, that having given the demand curve and noted the outcome, on second thought they decide they have a higher demand. People frequently change their minds when more information is provided, particularly if it is on a subject for which there is normally not much motive for thinking hard. But, if they have drawn their demand curve in appropriately, the desire on their part to increase the public consumption would already be incorporated in the curve.

The actual shape of the joint curve, that is the individual's personal desire to consume the public good, together with his feeling that other people should consume the good at what he regards as a desirable quantity, is something of a problem. I have on a number of occasions urged Howard to show me what the curve looks like and he finally drew it like Figure 1. This curve is, to me, odd. If we assume that the elasticity of demand for the product for one's own use has the ordinary shape and subtract that, we get the resulting

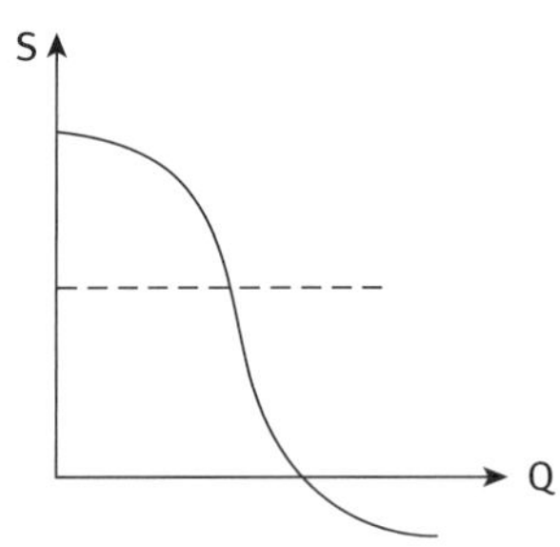

FIGURE 1

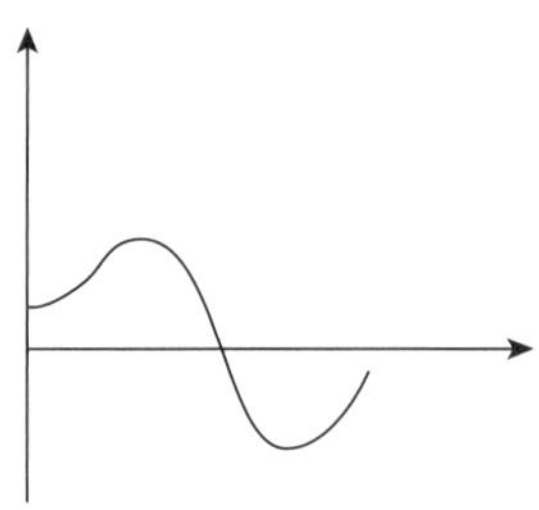

FIGURE 2

feeling that the individual might have for the benefit of others. The resulting portion of his demand which represents his regard for others looks like Figure 2. This seems unlikely, although of course the fact that it is unlikely does not prove that it is not correct. Further, note that the individual actually has a sharp negative demand for quantities in excess of the amount which he regards as optimal. He personally values every single unit of the demand positively, but his aversion to having other people give more than the optimal quantity means that his total demand curve is negative.

I don't want to argue that this demand curve is impossible. Further, it may not in fact represent what Margolis has in mind. I had to push him very hard to get him to draw it and it was clear he had not given it great thought. In any event, it is my purpose here not to argue that his views of the demand curve are wrong, but to argue that granted his views of the shape of the demand curve, his conclusions do not follow.

Let us for this purpose turn to his Table 1 and I will confine myself to one number simply because it is easier, specifically the cost to the voter of 10¢ in order to change the outcome by $20,000. I should begin by noting this is the total outcome, not per capita outcome. The intuitive argument that Margolis offers is a good deal weaker if you assume the voter is paying 10¢ in order to increase per capita consumption of whatever public good it is, by something less than 1/100th of a cent. Still, let us grant his proposition that people would be willing to make that investment. The problem here is that he is assuming there is only one voter willing to do so. If all of the voters have demand curves which are inelastic enough so that they would be willing to "pay the penny" then the effect on the outcome of one of them doing so would be immensely smaller than here shown. Indeed, it would to all intents and purposes be infinitesimal.

If the individuals have demand curves which are, to all intents and purposes, very close to vertical near the point where they intersect the individuals' cost and fairly close to horizontal, but extremal, either positive or negative, at all other points, then the cost of making even a small change in the sum by changing your own line is extremely high. Thus, those who would be willing to spend the penny would find that they made very little change in the outcome from that investment. Indeed, I would imagine that in most cases if all people had demand curves steep enough so that they would be willing to pay 10¢ to change the outcome by $20,000, then the actual effect of paying the 10¢ would change the outcome something in the order of one cent. Only if we are talking about one voter who has an extremely inelastic demand and all the others have the more or less elastic demands does the Margolis result follow.

But there remains one not insignificant objection to the demand revealing process which Margolis has offered to me privately, although it is not very obvious in his note, and that is that the Clarke tax would be much higher than Tideman and I calculated it if Margolis's view of people's behavior is correct. If we confine ourselves simply to arithmetic, it is not certain Margolis is correct. Even if he is, however, it is not obviously a criticism of the system. If people, however, feel deeply on the exact amount which is to be spent because they are much concerned not only with their own well being but with the well being of others, and they define that well being in terms of consuming the exact amount of public good which the individual thinks is the optimum, then the total importance of the expenditure becomes much greater than Tideman and I estimated it should be.

Using Margolis's example in which an expenditure of approximately a billion dollars is to be made, the total social importance of this expenditure might be several hundred billion dollars. That is, the utility of individuals in the range right around the billion dollars might be changed so greatly by small changes in it that they would have the kind of demand curve shown in Figure 1 and if we summed the effective demand over all people in that range, we might well find numbers massively greater than the physical cost of the good. If this is so, and I have not concealed my skepticism, then the matter is vastly more important than Tideman and I thought it was and it is, in my opinion, no criticism of the system that it treats it as more important, i.e. that it collects a much larger Clarke tax.[1] The Clarke tax would still be very small compared to the importance of the issue in the view of the voters.

It should also be said that if this is true, the argument for the demand revealing process, as opposed to ordinary voting, becomes almost overwhelmingly great. Ordinary voting surely would never choose the point where full demand curves, positive and negative, sum to exactly the cost of the object. That is the point, however, which minimizes the total social cost. If the social cost of deviating away from that point is very great, and that is indeed the conclusion one draws from Margolis's argument, then it is particularly important that we choose a system which leads to achieving the optimum.

1. It is not obvious it would. With individual demand curves much steeper, the Clarke tax might be smaller.

I should like to end this paper as I began it by saying that I am not really sure that I have fully understood Margolis's argument. I may be simply wasting the reader's time. If I have understood it, however, then he is either wrong in his estimate of how people would behave or if he is right his position indicates that the demand revealing process is even more desirable than I had originally thought it to be. I must leave it to the reader to judge the outcome of this debate.

PART 9

VOTING METHODS AND POLITICAL MARKET BEHAVIOR

PROPORTIONAL REPRESENTATION

Democratic voting systems in use today may, in general, be divided into two major categories, the single-member district system used in most English-speaking countries and a few other countries, and a system in which more than one member is elected from each district, with the seats in parliament being divided roughly in proportion to the number of votes each party receives. The Anglo-Saxon system is much the older; in fact the "proportional representation" (PR) system was invented in the late nineteenth century to eliminate some of its defects. The advantages of this newer method of representation are so obvious that most countries which have given serious attention to a choice between the two methods have chosen it. Nevertheless, the traditional methods of voting are so firmly established in the public mind in Anglo-Saxon countries that few citizens of these countries have even heard of this recent advance.

The original inventors of PR were concerned with the fact that the single-member district left a good many voters, those who had voted against the incumbent, unrepresented in the legislative assembly. In discussing this point with American political scientists, I have found that they use the word "represent" in a different way than did the European scholars who invented PR. To the American student of these matters, "represent" means little more than "elected from the district." Thus, they will say that a left-wing Democratic member of the House of Representatives "represents" a right-wing Republican who hates him and will never, under any circumstances, vote for him. In the European usage, "representation" is closer to an agency. A man only represents me in the legislature if, to some extent, he is dependent upon my support and/or has my approval. Presumably the left-wing Democrat would seldom, if ever, take the opinion of the right-wing Republican into account in pursuing his legislative duties. (He might even dislike the right-wing Republican enough to take a positive pleasure in doing things which will annoy him.) The Europeans wanted to make sure that minorities, even quite small minorities, were properly represented in the legislature by people of their choice, not of the majority's choice. That the legislature should more or less mirror the population was their proclaimed goal.

Reprinted, with permission, from *Toward a Mathematics of Politics* (Ann Arbor: University of Michigan Press, 1967), 144–57.

Before discussing the advantages of the system further, however, let us examine the possible institutional arrangements which have been tried or of which use could be made. First, I would like to discuss a system which I have invented myself, and which has never been used or, so far as I know, even been suggested. Indeed, until the development of the computer, the system would have been impracticable, which is probably the reason it has not heretofore been proposed. Let us assume that each representative in Congress simply be authorized to cast as many votes as the voters have cast for him. The total would be added by computers and the differential weighing of the various members of the representative assembly would represent their relative standing with the voters. No one would be unrepresented (with certain minor exceptions to be noted below) or "represented" by a man he detests. The voting on each individual measure would come as close to a national referendum as any representative body can achieve.

Note that this procedure would probably be more convenient if we combined our present districts into large areas, equal to five or more of the present districts.[1] This would permit popular members to acquire large numbers of votes, which would more accurately represent the popular will than artificially restricting them by geographical boundaries. In the extreme, the entire nation could be one voting district, with people running for Congress being free to pitch their sales appeal either to geographical areas or to groups of voters united by some nongeographical tie. It might be wise to make sure the result was not an elected dictator, however, by providing enough "constituencies" so that the most votes any representative could have would be some small fraction of the whole, say, 10 percent. Probably, however, this would be unnecessary. It is likely that the voters would spread their votes widely in order to get representation of their own particular political interests.

This system provides for electing representatives. It does not necessarily provide for defeating any candidate. With modern electronics there is no necessity for all representatives to meet in the same hall; consequently there is no maximum on the number of representatives. Voting could easily be done by wire, and the proceedings could be broadcast. In the extreme case, there

1. The size of the districts used by countries following European types of PR varies a good deal. In the case of Israel, it is the entire country. Most of the others use varying sizes running from five to thirty. One of the minor advantages of the system is that it makes redistricting, to take care of shifts of population, relatively easy. A seat can be added or subtracted if changing boundaries is inconvenient.

seems no reason why people who wish should not vote for themselves and then fill their days by casting their single vote for and against the various proposals. Probably many elderly people and invalids would take advantage of this opportunity to obtain a feeling of importance and achievement. The pay of representatives, of course, would vary with the number of voters who had voted for them, and this would tend to lead candidates who had received few votes to decide not to spend their time on such an unremunerative occupation.[2] If it were desired, of course, a minimum number of votes necessary to be "elected" could be provided. This would keep the number of representatives down to some specified maximum if that is thought sensible.

So far I have not said anything about how this highly representative body would debate. I would like to defer any discussion of this problem until later since my suggestions are for fairly general rules which would fit many types of assembly. For the nonce, let us assume that only those representatives who receive more than some specified portion of the vote will be permitted to speak and sit on committees, with the remainder merely listening to the proceedings and casting their votes. Thus, the assembly would be perfectly representative of its constituents in its votes, but not in its debates, although the difference might not be much.

Real-world PR systems are normally much less radical than the one I have outlined above, but they can be taken as efforts to approximate the same results without the benefits of computers. If each representative in the assembly has exactly the same vote as any other, then there will necessarily be a less perfect fit to the voter's desires, but the defect may be slight. The simplest system was proposed by Lewis Carroll. He suggested that if a candidate received more popular votes than the minimum necessary to elect him, he be permitted to give them to some other candidate. This would, over time, mean that popular candidates would have their effective vote in the legislature increased by the use of stooges. Interestingly, the system in use in the Netherlands is in legal theory very similar to Carroll's proposal.

If we are interested in representing the people in an assembly, however, there is no obvious reason why we should insist that this be done by individuals rather than corporate groups. Most democratic systems do develop such corporate groups in the form of political parties, and the voters fairly fre-

2. Charging a fee for being hooked up to the electronic voting network and for the broadcast of the proceedings of the assembly might further reduce the number of people who choose to vote on measures in spite of very small popular support.

quently are more interested in which of these parties "wins" than in the individual politicians who sit in the legislature. It is, of course, relatively easy to divide the votes in a legislature between several corporate bodies so that each has about the same proportion of the legislature as it does of the popular vote. In the simplest scheme, used in Israel, Sweden, the Netherlands, Austria, etc., the party decides who will occupy the seats assigned to it (normally by use of a priority list which is put on each ballot) so that the legislative representative is entirely dependent on the party machine for his seat. In a recent instance, a rather high official of the Mapai party of Israel went to the United States on government business and discovered, upon his return to Israel, that he had been moved far down the list so that he had no chance of being reelected to parliament. This power of the party machine over its representatives in the assembly is frequently regarded as a defect of the system. It is, if the members of the assembly are supposed to make up their own minds, but if we think of the voters as simply favoring one corporate body over the others, there is no reason to object to the corporate body casting its votes as an entity. In any event, as will be explained below, this is not an inevitable result of proportional representation. Voters can both select their party and the particular people who will represent it in the assembly.

Before discussing this possibility, however, let us turn to certain other methods which produce a legislature which is something like "a mirror of the voters." The first of these systems is used, so far as I know, only to elect a portion of the upper house in Japan. There are one hundred seats available in the "national constituency," a vast number of people run, and each voter casts one vote for his favorite. The one hundred who have the largest numbers are elected. Needless to say, this does not result in each voter being represented by a member of the legislature for whom he voted, and does not result in each member being elected by the same number of votes, but it probably comes closer to at least the first of these objectives than the Anglo-Saxon system of one-member districts. It also provides representations for "interests" in a particularly direct way. In this respect it should appeal to those who rather approve of functional representation à la the corporate state.

A second way of approximating proportional representation has been used, off and on by France since 1870. Under this system, individual constituencies send single members to the parliament. It differs from the Anglo-Saxon system simply in that if no candidate gets a majority in the first balloting, a runoff is held in a few weeks in which only a plurality is necessary for election. These simple rules, together with the French talent for intrigue, have led to a functioning proportional representation system. A fairly large number of parties put up candidates in each constituency. Usually no single candidate gets a majority in the first round, and the period before the runoff is occupied by elaborate bargaining in which some candidates withdraw in favor of others. For example, the Socialist candidate will withdraw in one district and the radical in another, thus assuring the radicals of the first seat and the Socialists of the other. The system puts a high premium on ability in intrigue, and does not guarantee proportional representation, but on the whole has produced something very much like it.

There are two other systems which have been discussed theoretically but only rarely applied. In one of these, the voter has as many votes as there are seats to be filled in a multimember constituency, and can cast them in any way he wishes, all for one man, for example. My home state of Illinois uses this procedure for electing the lower house of the state legislature. A second system is the "single transferable vote" method which is what is described in most American textbooks as proportional representation. The system is complicated, little used, and already well described, so I shall waste no space on it here. Perhaps I should warn the reader, however, that I personally dislike this system, which seems to have the disintegration of parties as almost its only special effect. My decision not to discuss it at length, thus, may be an expression of prejudice.

I must now redeem my promise and explain how proportional representation of corporate bodies may be combined with selection of the actual persons who sit in parliament for the parties. In a sense this means combining the function of an American primary with that of an election. The simplest system is that in use in Italy. If you vote for the Communist party, you also are permitted to mark up to five individual Communists. After the total number of votes has been counted and it has been determined how many Communists will be sent to parliament, the votes cast for individual members will be used to determine who will occupy the seats. A somewhat more elegant system is in use in Switzerland. Although the following description is greatly simplified, it is not, however, oversimplified. The voter may simply cast his vote for, say, the Socialists, and if so, he will help to determine how many seats the party will have in parliament. If he is concerned with who actually sits in parliament for the Socialists, however, he will strike the name of one or more of the Socialist candidates for office from his ballot and write in the name of some other candidate in their place. Since the man whose name he writes in is already on the ballot, this means he has voted twice for him and cast a sort of negative vote against the man he struck out. Only about 10 percent of the voters avail themselves of this privilege, and this minority of the voters determines who actually sits in the legislature. This procedure permits the election not only to sum the preferences of the voters but to give heavier weights to those voters who have more intense preferences.

Having rather sketchily surveyed the institutions available for proportional representation, let us now give somewhat more serious consideration to the reasons which may be urged for and against this form of representation. So far as I know, there are only three lines of reasoning used by proponents of the single-member constituency. Two of these, I am prepared to argue, are based on a misunderstanding of the nature of government. The reader should, of course, take warning, realize that I have an ax to grind and that it is therefore possible that I am being less than fair to the system which is traditional in the Anglo-Saxon world.

The first standard argument for the single-member constituency is that it leads to a two-party system and one-party governments. To this is often appended the subsidiary claim that it also results in a succession of governments with policies which differ little because they represent about the middle of the electorate's opinion. This last part of the argument must be admitted, both observationally and in theory, to be true. The coalitions which normally govern in systems which do not have only two parties, however, normally also follow approximately the policies favored by the median voter, and for exactly the same reason. It is, therefore, impossible to argue for (or against) the single-member system on this particular ground. As for the basic claim, that the single-member system leads to a two-party system, the tendency is much weaker than normally assumed. Canada, for example, has a single-member district method of electing members of her parliament, but has an extraordinarily diverse collection of parties. Some of these parties represent distinct geographical areas, the French and English provinces, but in other cases they are not to be explained by ethnic differences.

It is fairly easy to design a model where the single-member district will lead to a stable set of three, four, or five parties if there are geographical differences in the population. The Canadian system is an obvious example, the Parliament of Great Britain when Ireland was part of it is another, and the American Congress is a third, if one is willing to recognize the distinctive nature of the Southern representation in Congress. In each of these cases we have multiparty systems essentially because of geographical differences. Since some of these systems developed out of a two-party system, as in Canada, it is clear that there is no normal historical progress toward two parties. It even seems possible that, where there are strong geographical differences within a nation, the proportional representation system may lead to fewer parties than the single-member district.

But even where there is no particular geographical component in the preferences of the voters, the tendency of the single-member district to lead to a two-party system is far from established. England, for example, is perhaps the best example of this system, and has had at least three parties represented in Parliament for more than sixty years. At present, one of the parties is much weaker than the other two, but the weak party of 1900 is now the government, which would suggest that there is no reason to believe that the smallest party will necessarily disappear. Further, for almost forty of the last sixty years, England has been governed by coalitions of two parties rather than by one party. Since this situation developed after many years of a two-party system, we again have evidence that the single-member district does not necessarily lead to a two-party system. The development of a new third party in Australia would also argue against the stability of the two-party system in single-member districts. (Australia, of course, has a transferable vote, but there is no obvious reason why this should affect the matter.)

If we examine more recent applications of the single-member district, the results are equally hard to fit into the two-party theory. In India there are many parties, but one wins all of the elections. The single-member constituency simply means that for twenty years the Congress party held three-fourths of the legislature, with about 45 percent of the popular vote, because its opposition was so splintered. The Korean case, although more complicated, is equally hard to explain under the two-party rubric. Indeed, it appears that the United States is nearly a unique example of a two-party system, and in order to use even that, it is necessary to ignore the difference between the Democratic party in the South and the Democratic party in the rest of the country. Historically, the United States has tended to move from a two-party system to a single-party system, which is followed by a splitting of the single party into two. Whether this represents mere coincidence or is a natural consequence of the American electoral system, I do not know. In any event, the American electoral system is radically different from most others because of the direct election of the President and the primaries.

Even if, however, we agree that the single-member constituency leads to a two-party system, the reasons why this is an advantage are hard to discern. It is true that we are accustomed to this system, except in the South and New

York, but tradition is not, by itself, a major argument. Neither the South, with its traditional system of primary elections, nor New York City, with its more recent tradition of coalition governments, is an example of outstandingly efficient government, but they are not clearly inferior to the two-party systems by which they are surrounded. The normal argument for the two-party system is that it produces a single-party government which is "strong," as opposed to a coalition government. Granted that if you have a two-party system, one is likely to win the election, it is still true that the United States Constitution was built on the desire to keep the government divided. A majority of both houses of Congress and the President would all have to come from the same party (something which is almost unknown when the existence of the Southern bloc is taken into account) for such a "strong" government to exist. It has, in fact, been urged by prominent political scientists that the Democratic party which elects Congress is a different party from the Democratic party which elects the President.[3] Since we have gotten along for some time now with this system, it is hard to offer any practical evidence that it is a bad thing. It is possible to offer theoretical arguments for a unitary government, but I notice that people who make such arguments seem to aim at unitary government by the group which they think is closest to their own aims. They seldom argue for a strong unitary government when it seems likely that such a government would be run by their political opponents.[4] The system of checks and balances may not be the ideal government, but clearly it is not something which can be dismissed with a wave of the hand. People favoring a strong single-party government should explain why they really think they would be better off if the party which they least like had complete power in the way that the British cabinet has.

But in view of the difficulty of establishing that the single-member constituency leads to two parties, the matter can be left in abeyance. There is a third, much more subtle defense of the two-party system invented by Anthony Downs. He points out that a multiparty system will usually lead to government by coalitions of parties, and he points out that the voter can hardly know in advance what coalition will form, and what policies it will fol-

3. James M. Burns, *The Deadlock of Democracy* (Englewood Cliffs, N.J.: Prentice-Hall, Inc., 1963).

4. As an exception to this, some prominent political scientists who were basically partisans of the Democratic party suggested that Truman appoint a Republican Secretary of State and resign after the 1946 election.

low. Thus, if we accept this argument, the multiparty system suffers from the very serious defect that the voters do not know what they are voting on. Clearly, this could be a very serious defect. Perfect knowledge, the voters will never have, as many people who voted for Johnson are beginning to realize, but we do have some idea of the policies to be implemented by the party we choose if it wins.

Obviously, this is an argument which deserves careful consideration, and I will not be able to disprove it in any strict sense. I will, however, suggest that it puts the emphasis on the wrong point. We are interested in controlling the government, not strictly speaking in the knowledge we have when we cast a vote. The deficiency in knowledge pointed to by Dr. Downs seems to also be a deficiency in our possibility of control, but this has not been demonstrated. Suppose we contrast a system of five parties, generally representing five different political positions, with two parties. First, the information transmitted to the politicians by the votes in the five-party system is obviously much greater. This information differential does not result solely from the fact that the voter can cast his vote five ways instead of two, and hence can more closely approximate his opinion in his vote. It also results from the different conditions of the parties themselves. Downs proved that in a two-party system the parties will have very similar platforms, and our empirical evidence would seem to indicate that this is so. In earlier chapters, I have demonstrated that in multiparty systems the parties are well advised to keep some distance apart in their positions. Again, the empirical evidence seems to support theory. Thus, the votes transmit much more information under the multiparty system than under the two-party system. The shift of votes from one to another of a pair of virtually identical parties with virtually identical platforms shows little about the opinion of the voters. Shifts among a number of quite different parties are much more informative.

Dr. Downs's answer to this presumably would be that the voters would not be able to make sensible initial choices among the many parties because they would not know what the shape of the eventual coalition government would be. Thus, he would argue, very little information would be transmitted by the votes because the voters would cast them in ignorance. This, of course, assumes that the voters must vote for a government, not for a sort of agent who will negotiate to form a government. I may have no real idea what parties will make up the coalition government after the election, but still be very much interested in strengthening the bargaining power of a party which is urging further aid to agriculture. If I vote for the agricultural party, I can be no more confident that the party of my choice will eventually be part of the coalition government than the voter in the two-party system can be sure that the party he votes for will win. I can, however, strengthen my party, which will improve its negotiating position and hence improve the likelihood that the policies I favor will be a part of the government's policy.[5]

There, thus, does not appear to be any decisive solution to the problem raised by Dr. Downs. Still, if there is a reasonable argument for casting a vote for the party which most closely approximates your own opinion in a multiparty system, then it is likely that the voter will do so. The fact that some political scientists doubt that he can really make up his mind intelligently will not prevent him from trying, and if he tries, the information content of his vote will be the same as if he were fully informed about the outcome of the coalition negotiating process. Thus it is possible, although not certain, that the objection raised by Dr. Downs is largely irrelevant; that the individual does not need to know the policy which will be followed by the government coalition formed after the election to cast an informed vote. Even if this possibility were not present, however, the improved information content of the vote itself to the politicians should provide a counterbalance to the difficulty he has emphasized. Still, the issue is a difficult one, and I would not like to give the impression that I feel that Dr. Downs's objection to the multiparty system is entirely without merit. Clearly, this is a problem which will require further study.

So far I have talked about the arguments for the single-member district system, and found little merit in them. Now let us consider the positive arguments for the proportional representation system. Before turning to the major arguments, however, a minor point should be made. Proportional representation produces single-party majority governments. For many years Norway, Denmark, and Sweden were governed by powerful single parties that in each case held a majority of the seats in the legislature. If one party succeeds in convincing a majority of the population that it can best represent them, then it will be able to elect enough members to dominate the legislature (this is not necessarily true of single-member constituency systems). Thus, coalition governments are not inevitable under proportional representation. They occur only when the voters do not give majority support to one

5. This is not always so. In William Riker's *The Theory of Political Coalitions*, it is demonstrated that the power of a clique engaged in negotiation to form a majority coalition is not a smooth function of its size. In general, however, the larger the party, the more powerful.

party. Nevertheless, when the voters are given more than two choices, they quite frequently do not give any one party a majority, with the result that some sort of coalition is formed to govern the country. Since our own system normally leads to a coalition of the Southern Democrats and one or the other of the Northern parties dominating our legislature, this should not impress Americans as a bizarre phenomenon.

Turning now to the arguments for proportional representation, the original argument for it has been rehearsed above. It aimed at insuring voters of representation in the legislatures for whom they had voted. The inventors of the system in the nineteenth century thought the single-member constituency system, which was already old at that time, deprived the minority in each district of any real say in the legislative assembly. They were not content with believing them to be represented by the man against whom they had voted, and whom they might well distrust to a great degree. This seems to me a respectable motive, but I would like to refer people who wish to see it elaborated to the nineteenth-century literature on the subject, and devote the rest of my space to some newer arguments for the system.

The first of these newer arguments may seem much more economic than political. Economists regard a system of competition between two companies as better than a monopoly, but far from ideal. In general, it is too easy for the two competing corporations to find a common bond in exploiting the public, to become conservative and shun innovations. The more competitors, the more pressure on each one to behave in an efficient manner. The details of this argument can hardly be carried over to politics, but its general outline applies. In particular, the two-party system bars new parties from entering if the two existing parties get out of touch with the voters' desires. The multiparty system lets them in easily. Further, the party out of power in a two-party system is likely to have had at least some responsibility for the initiating of many policies now being implemented by their rivals. Under the circumstances they may have good reason not to engage in violent criticism when a third party would not be so inhibited. It is much harder to keep five parties, together with some small splinters that would like to be parties, quiet on a matter in which the government is in difficulties than it is to keep a single opposition party satisfied to leave the matter unmentioned. In this sense, the voter is apt to get much better information from a multiparty system. Sacred cows are much safer in an atmosphere in which there are only two parties, each trying to appeal to the middle range of voters, than if there are five, each appealing to a rather different audience.

More importantly, however, the proportional representation system has the advantage that it insures that a majority in the legislature represents a majority among the voters. The single-member constituency system permits a majority in a majority of the districts, in the limit, 25+ percent of the population to control the government. It seems likely that log-rolling normally goes on under roughly these conditions, although a two-house legislature can somewhat mitigate these problems. If this is so, then the results of voting must be highly nonoptimal.[6] The switch to proportional representation would result in the minimum coalition of voters which can get a measure through being raised to 50+ percent. This may not be optimal, but it is far better than 25+ percent.

The main purpose of this essay, however, is not to prove the superiority of proportional representation, but simply to acquaint the reader with the range of alternatives open. The first version, my own invention, seems to me the best in an age of computers, but the others approximate it to varying degrees of accuracy. It could be easily adjusted to permit corporate bodies (usually called parties) to be represented, and could also be made to permit the voter to not only select the corporate bodies but also decide who shall be on their boards of directors. It would even be quite simple to make the system follow the Swiss in giving the more intense voters greater weight. Instead of elaborating these rather tedious details, however, I would like to close with a brief examination of a problem of representation which is hardly ever seriously discussed: the allocation of time during the debates.

One of the most brilliant, and at the same time one of the most ignored, pieces in political theory was Bertrand de Jouvenel's "The Chairman's Problem"[7] in which it was demonstrated that most members of a legislative body (or public meeting) can play little part in the debates. His classically simple way of showing this was simply to divide the time to be devoted to a given subject by the number of members to get the average time available for each member if each could speak. The result is normally a period too short for effective presentation of a point of view. De Jouvenel then suggested that what actually happens is that the presiding officer selects a few persons who he thinks will more or less cover the spectrum of opinion, and lets them speak.

6. See James M. Buchanan and Gordon Tullock, *The Calculus of Consent* (Ann Arbor: The University of Michigan Press, 1962), and Gordon Tullock, *Entrepreneurial Politics* (Thomas Jefferson Center, University of Virginia, 1962).

7. *American Political Science Review* (June 1961), p. 368.

The number of speakers would not, if the theory is true, vary much with the size of the legislative body. This, of course, is in accord with empirical observation, although it is not at all certain that the selection of the speakers is always through the mechanism suggested by De Jouvenel.[8]

In practice, methods of managing debate vary tremendously. The English Parliament, for example, has a well-worked-out system under which most members are seen but not heard very much. They aren't even seen as much as might seem normal since the House does not have enough space for them all to sit down at once, with the result that some of them are necessarily always absent. The House of Representatives, by contrast, makes a conscientious effort to give every member a fair share of its "debating" time. As a result the normal situation in the House is an almost empty room[9] in which an obscure representative is droning on about some subject which interests him. Most representatives turn up for votes, and important debates will attract a sizable crowd. In the important debates, also, the average member has little chance of being recognized if he is so temerarious as to ask for the floor. The time is largely taken up with the leaders of the House, almost as if it were the British Parliament.

This general system of selecting people has worked reasonably well for thousands of years, and there would appear to be little reason to change it. Here again, however, the invention of the computer makes it possible to do better. Let us assume that we have a legislature of one hundred persons. Each one has a "right" to one one-hundredth of the time. The computer could easily keep track, crediting each person with a point for each moment of listening, and subtracting one hundred points for each moment of speech. The individual members would be permitted to either hoard their own points or to give (sell) them to others. Thus, each point of view would have an allotment of time strictly proportional to its strength among the voters.[10] The computer, in fact, could take over many of the more routine duties of the presid-

8. Teachers normally have a roughly similar problem in dealing with questions from the class. As a general rule, the number of questions asked by a class of thirty will not be markedly different from the number asked by a class of ten. Further, it may well be the case that in each case almost all of the questions come from two or three of the students.

9. Except for the spectators. Teachers of political science who bring their students to Washington to see how the nation is governed normally get quite disturbed by the sight.

10. It may be thought unwise to give strong points of view so much time. If so, the computer could be instructed to make the appropriate adjustments in the points allotted to the members of different points of view.

ing officer. It could, for example, choose the next speaker by simply noting how many points each applicant had and giving priority to the one with the most.[11] If a number of members wished to speak on a given subject, and they did not expect the computer to select them in the order they desired, they could make use of the present "yielding" system to order their arguments as they desired. The presiding officer could, being relieved of the necessity of deciding who was to speak, devote himself to the more complex parliamentary problems which periodically come up. Individual members would not be subject to control by the speaker, because any small group which felt oppressed could always arrange to pool their points and get a chance to put one of their members into any debate they wished.

It may appear that this is a wildly unconventional suggestion. It is. The view that the procedure we have become used to over the last 2000 years is necessarily the best, however, seems highly suspect. Only by considering new ideas can we hope to improve, and only by reconsidering even the best established institutions can we decide where improvements would be desirable. The whole point of the "new political science" is to raise questions about received doctrine, and to try to find the best answers to both the traditional problems of politics and the new ones. New ideas always seem radical and bizarre. I would not claim that the new ideas I have advanced in these essays are the best possible suggestions. I hope, however, that they will play at least some role in the search for a better and more scientific political structure.

11. It would be necessary to introduce some arbitrary rule to get the system started and to break ties. It might be wise to permit members to get priority so that they could speak out of turn if they agreed to "pay" twice the normal rate in points.

DEMOCRACY AS IT REALLY IS

The Least Imperfect System

Up until now we have simply assumed that the government will be democratic and have said relatively little about how democracy works. It is now time to repair the omission.

Democracy, like other human institutions, is not perfect. Indeed, it is decidedly imperfect. Winston Churchill once said that "Democracy is the worst of forms of government except, of course, for those others that have been tried from time to time." This chapter will tell you a number of things about democracy that may disillusion some enthusiasts. They should keep in mind that although democracy is far from perfect, the other forms of government are generally much worse.

A point to be kept in mind is that democracy at its best carries out the will of some of the people. The problem with this is that the people are generally not very well informed, have not thought very much about what is going on, and may be completely ignorant of what most intellectuals would think of as rather basic facts. Intellectuals frequently are quite annoyed by the decisions taken by democracies. Intellectuals tend to be attracted by powerful myths and the totalitarian systems that generate such things. The common man or woman tends to be more sceptical. That is not because they are better informed but simply because they are less easily influenced. They are as likely to be sceptical about a new and true idea as about a new and false idea.

The Role and Behaviour of Elected Officials

Let us begin by looking at the other end of the democratic government, the elected officials. The first thing to be said about this is that there is a very considerable difference between the elected officials of large central governments and the elected officials of small organizations like my Sunshine Mountain Homeowners' Association. The first group are obviously people

Reprinted, with permission, from *The New Federalist* (Vancouver: Fraser Institute, 1994), 53–60.

who are in the business of making a living by winning elections. The second group are made up of people who, in a way, are pursuing their hobbies.

Consequences of Vote Maximizing

The fact that the high or low official has to get elected or, in the case of civil service, has to deal with superiors who are elected, has distinct effects on their behaviour: to survive in office they will have to maximize votes.

The politician who has carefully studied the problem is more informed than the average voter. This informed politician might develop a platform which does not simply reflect the preferences of his or her constituents precisely because it *does* reflect their interests, which they do not fully understand. Such a platform does not maximize votes. And the politician who behaves contrary to the wishes of the voter might be an admirable person but he or she would not be carrying out the "will of the people." The fact that the average voter is not well informed, may have very narrow interests, has only average intelligence, etc. means that most of us frequently feel that the decisions produced by these "maximizing politicians" are depressing.

Vote Trading and Voter Ignorance

A politician, if he is a good politician, does not simply find out what a majority of his constituents want and then do it. He is aware of the fact that people not only have views on various issues but that these views vary in intensity from one person to another. A great many of the voters might not even find out how the politician voted on many issues or if they do find out, will forget about it by the time of the next election. This combination of ignorance and differing intensity of desire allows what is known as "vote trading" or "logrolling." An example can best be used to describe and understand this phenomenon.

Large amounts of money are spent subsidizing rather prosperous farmers. Further, food is made more expensive and the gain to the farmers is much less than the social costs. How do these things get through? After all, only a minority of all congressmen represent farm districts. The vast bulk of Congress represents people whose only concern with this matter is that they will end up paying higher taxes and food prices.

The answer is a combination of trades and voter ignorance. Let us begin with the trades. Agriculture is a particularly good example because we recently had an effort by Congressman Armey, a former professor of economics, at least to restrict the agricultural subsidy and price-raising conspiracy run by the federal government. He offered in the House an amendment to the agricultural program providing that no one whose income from non-farming activities exceeded $125,000 a year was to receive any subsidy.

One would think that Congressman Armey's amendment would have been bottled up in committee, but he is a clever congressman and succeeded in avoiding that trap. Once it had appeared on the floor, you would think that practically no congressman would be willing to vote openly against it. As a matter of fact, he was beaten by 2-1 on a recorded vote.

Armey's own comment about all of this was revealing: "There are no weak sisters on the agricultural committee—they do what committees do very well. They spend five years filling their silos with chits and then they call them in." What happened was simple. Individual members of the agricultural committee had cast votes for various things that benefitted other special interests. In return, when the farm issue came up, the congressmen for whom they had done these previous favours paid off by voting for the agricultural program.

A great many European governments, although they operate in just exactly the way I have described above, do so in a rather covert way so it is not obvious. Vote trading is also less obvious in Canada where very strong party discipline precludes Members of Parliament from voting against their party. However there are issues on which all parties vote together, and laws are often modified at the committee stage to reflect the concerns of opposition parties. The process of bargaining is simply less obvious in Canada than in the U.S.

Is vote trading undesirable? First, consider the simple argument in favour of vote trading: suppose that I want A and object to B, but my feelings with respect to A are much stronger than those with respect to B. I find someone else who wants B and objects to A, but whose feelings are much stronger with respect to B than to A. If we now agree to have both A and B, both of us would be better off than if we didn't have either A or B. Intensity of preference should be taken into account in voting as well as simple direction of preference.

This is so obvious that it is surprising it is not discussed more frequently. If one looks over the vast mass of legislation passed by Congress each session, it is fairly obvious that most of us would be indifferent to most of it. By this

I do not mean that we are indifferent to the whole Department of Defense budget but that we are indifferent with respect to such issues as which particular air base shall be opened or closed.

There are, however, two problems with this favourable view of vote trading, the first of which is that after all you only have to get a majority in order to get a bill through. This means that the bargain must benefit only a majority of constituencies and can injure the country as a whole. Suppose, for example, we have some collection of special interest measures which benefit 218 (a majority) congressmen's constituencies by $1,500 apiece, but which impose a tax of $1,000 on each of the 435 constituencies in the U.S. There is thus a tax of $435,000, and benefits of $327,000. The benefit is less than the cost.

Of course, such cases are marginal, but nevertheless they can occur even if everyone is perfectly informed. Granted that people are far from perfectly informed, however, this kind of thing can become much more serious. It is probably true that most citizens are reasonably well informed about measures that are directly aimed at their particular small special interest, but pretty much uninformed about other matters. This is not a criticism or even a statement that they are irrational. It costs time and energy to become well informed. Being better informed about things that directly concern you than about things that are only peripheral is a sensible economy.

The result of this, however, is that bills can be, and are, passed in which the cost is very, very much greater, spread thin across the country as a whole, than the benefit to the small special interest group that does benefit. The Central Arizona Project (CAP), at immense cost to the taxpayers of the United States, will provide water to certain parts of Arizona at a very, very heavily subsidized price. Although the total cost to the citizens of the United States is very great, the cost, if divided out citizen by citizen, is low. The benefit to people living in certain parts of Arizona, however, is highly concentrated and hence this was a politically paying activity. Canada is no stranger either to the perverse consequences of concentrated benefits and dissipated costs. Phone companies, textile mills, dairy farmers, and a host of other producers survive on government granted monopoly rights, at the expense of consumers. These consumers grumble, but the extra few cents they pay per quart of milk or for a phone call gives them little incentive to protest on Parliament Hill or lobby their representatives. The humble consumer sits on the sidelines as politicians balance the different intensities of special interest group feelings.

This is probably the reason that the average citizen is shown regularly in public opinion polls as disliking his legislature, which he realizes puts a heavy tax burden on him, but being very strongly in favour of his own representative who he realizes gets him various special privileges. It is presumably true that in a vague way the citizen knows that his representative is making these bargains and probably that the bargains on the whole are not to his advantage. He also knows, however, that if his representative, alone of all the representatives, refused to enter into these bargains, he would be much worse off than he is. He assumes that the representative is making a good thing out of a basically bad institutional structure. And as a matter of fact, in most cases he is quite right.

Small Government Limits Vote Trading

One of the advantages of decentralizing the government, or what we call "federalism," is that it does indeed make these bargains somewhat more restricted. The relatively restricted geographic scope of the bargains that can be made makes it more likely that the voters will know about those bargains which inconvenience them, even if only slightly, than they will in a massive government area.

Conclusion

All of us are members of the Great Society or the Just Society, but also the members of very many smaller groups. Getting the government to do things important to the Society's interests and in accord with those of the small groups is desirable. Unfortunately, these are sometimes in conflict and also it is very commonly true that the interests of one small group are in conflict with those of another. This chapter has tried to set out these conflicts and explain how they can be resolved, at least partially.

The federal system does not eliminate every clash, but it does reduce the total number. At the same time, it changes their nature somewhat. Problems between different branches of the government become more common and squabbles between bureaucracies in the same government or between different groups of citizens within a jurisdiction become less common. On the whole, there is a net gain from federalism.

Once again, the main theme of this book up to this point has been that democracy is better than other forms of government and that a federal democracy with a good deal of decentralization is better than a centralized democracy. I emphasize, however, that this does not mean that either of these forms of government is perfect. There are defects to all human institutions, including federal democracy.

Bibliography

Olson, Mancur. *The Logic of Collective Action: Public Goods and the Theory of Groups*. Cambridge: Harvard University Press, 1965, pp. 111–67. When written, this was a major contribution. Now it is the orthodox theory of pressure groups and a treatment of the dynamics of special interest groups.

Rowley, Charles K., Tollison, Robert D., and Tullock, Gordon, eds. *The Political Economy of Rent-Seeking*. Boston: Kluwer, 1988. A compendium of recent work on pressure groups.

A BOUQUET OF GOVERNMENTS

The purpose of this chapter is to describe simply and critique briefly the very wide diversity of different kinds of democratic institutions that have been used both in federal and non-federal states. Diversity is greater among federal countries than among non-federal, but it's quite significant among unitary states as well.

What Is "Necessary" Government Service?

The existing diversity among governments is great enough so that many things most people think are inevitable are by no means universal. To take one example, sewage disposal is usually regarded as an activity which requires a good deal of centralization because of the economies of scale. In other words, it's much cheaper for the city of Tucson and its suburbs to all have one sewage disposal plant than it would be to have a set of small ones.

Water is another example which is normally thought to require centralization. On one occasion I visited a rather posh suburb of Athens in Greece and discovered, to my surprise, that the water there was provided privately by tank trucks. Each house had a cistern and they bought water as they needed it from various private water companies.

This had one unusual convenience. Water was available in several different qualities and prices. If you were going to be away from your home and simply wanted to keep the lawn watered, you bought cheap water, but if you were going to be there and expected to drink it you bought the high quality.[1] Once again, I have no idea whether this is more or less efficient than providing water by a centralized pipe system, but certainly the people in the suburb did not seem to be annoyed by it.

These two examples have been given as an indication that many things which we tend to think of as necessary activities in government may not be.

Reprinted, with permission, from *The New Federalist* (Vancouver: Fraser Institute, 1994), 61–76.

1. Tucson has a rule which is rather similar. Golf courses are required to water their fairways with second-hand water from the sewage disposal plant. It sometimes smells.

In other words, careful thought should be given to each activity. Needless to say, it is easier to give thought to local problems if you have a federal state than if you have a unitary one.

What Is the "Best" Way to Run Government?

Now let us turn to actual governmental organizations. I should like to start discussing very small local governments such as the one that runs my Sunshine Mountain Ridge Homeowners' Association. The first thing to be said is that the members of the governing council are not paid. We have no judiciary, although the council or its members on occasion might perform functions which are somewhat like that of a judiciary. They may deal with a quarrel between two members of the association by listening to both of them and then making a decision. Our little government also has important diplomatic functions. Dealing with the higher level of governments and with neighbouring local governments is one of its more important activities. This description of the local government would fit very many small farming villages.

As we move to larger governments with greater responsibilities, the level of formal structure grows. One example is that usually the legislators and higher executives of national governments receive a salary. But although this is usual, it is not by any means universal. The Swiss legislature receives no pay, although there is a rather generous expense account.

This of course raises the questions of whether we want the legislators to be true professionals, i.e. people who make their living as legislators, or whether we want them to be amateurs, people whose primary role in life is something else and who are willing to devote part of their time to being a legislator. There are arguments for both of these positions.

The professional legislator would presumably be better informed about legislative business than the, let us say, lawyer who spends six weeks every two years (officially this is what is supposed to be done in Virginia) as a legislator. On the other hand, such a legislator is not as good a representative of the average person as one who is himself closer to the average.

There is another aspect to this, which is that amateur legislators are apt to spend very much less time legislating. In other words, the total number of laws passed is apt to be much smaller and their length is apt to be shorter.[2]

2. "No man's property is safe: the legislature is in session." Normally attributed to Mencken.

Of course under present circumstances, with national legislatures passing very long bills that no member has actually read in full, this characteristic may not be very important.

However, some form of voluntarism still exists at this higher level of government. Voluntary boards are to be found throughout democratic governments. Indeed, they are frequently found in dictatorships as well. They may be temporary, appointed to consider a given problem, or permanent, like the board of a university. In both cases they bring prominent citizens who are not formally members of the government into a decision-making role. In some cases they are brought in to avoid decisions. Politicians sometimes appoint a commission to investigate some problem for the sole specific purpose of delaying a decision. The British and more recently the Canadians have made an art of this procedure.

There is another example of individual citizens who make quite important decisions in Anglo-Saxon countries and some other democracies. These are the jurymen. This is a form of conscription, in which the average citizen is called upon occasionally (selected by lot) to serve on a small board to determine the outcome of criminal prosecutions and lawsuits. In the United States, more than in Canada or perhaps any other country, it is probable that this particular democratic institution makes more decisions in an average year than all of the other democratic institutions put together. Of course these are particular detailed decisions, but nevertheless they are quite important.[3]

It should be said with respect to all of these groups of private citizens that they are normally neither very well informed about the subject matter that they are dealing with nor deeply impressed with the existing law. Juries in particular are well known to follow their conscience rather than the law when the two are in conflict.[4] Whether this is an advantage or a disadvantage is not obvious.

Moving to larger governments—county, city, etc.—the first thing we note is that there is often a distinction between the legislature and the executive.

3. In order to be candid with the reader, I should say that I do not like the jury. See my *Trials on Trial*, Columbia University Press, New York, 1980.

4. According to the *New York Times*, May 5, 1991, page 11, a poor Hispanic immigrant had a sick three year old. He and his wife took her in their car to get some medicine. Since the child was feverish and crying, her mother held her, rather than strapping her into a safety seat as required by an enforced law. There was an accident and the child was killed. The father was charged with murder. The prospect that a jury would convict in such a case is so small that I suspect the prosecutor could stand psychiatric help. The judge, who retained his sanity, dismissed the case without bothering a jury.

One of the explanations for this is that as the government gets larger the number of total decisions made grows and there is much to be said for allocating a lot of the less important decisions to permanent, non-elected officials. Of course, in many cases there is a sort of mix. In Canada and in the cabinets of most European governments are elected members of the legislature and in many cities, like Tucson for example, the mayor is both the chief executive and a voting member of the city council. Indeed, he presides over the city council.

Large Government Must "Contract Out"

In larger governments, however, more formal arrangements for performing their various activities will normally be made. We begin by an extreme example, the Lakewood Plan.

Lakewood is a suburb of Los Angeles with a population of about 80,000 who decided some time ago that they really did not need to have many employees. Specifically, their government consisted of the city council, an engineer who negotiated contracts with suppliers of governmental services, and one secretary. They obtained all the other government services by contract, mainly with other government agencies in the immediate vicinity. For example, they got their police by contract with the Los Angeles County Sheriff's Department, the city of Los Angeles undertook to collect their taxes, the streets were cleaned by private contractors, and so on. The system was quite successful and a number of other cities in that area have copied it more or less. But Lakewood itself has recently switched to doing some of the activities itself.

All over the United States there are lots of experiments by local government in contracting things out instead of maintaining their own staff. I have mentioned before that if my house catches on fire the fire extinguishing will be done by Rural Metro, a private company. The local van service for the handicapped is contracted out by the city. The difference between contracting out and hiring your own personnel is not quite as severe as it might appear. In both cases, people are hired to do the job. The difference is whether they are hired in collective groups by way of a contract, let us say the Los Angeles Sheriff's Department, or individually.

In Canada there has been less experimenting with contracting out and this may be related to a trend away from local government responsibility. The provincial governments have in recent years come to exert a greater control over municipalities. The provinces have encouraged small local administrations to amalgamate, and many services that were once provided at the community level are now provided by regional administrative boards.

Job Security and Government Efficiency

The basic point of this discussion is that there are many different ways of running a government. There is, however, something to be said about the efficiency of the various ways. The first thing to be said is that employment security is undesirable if you want to get the work done. Waste collection in the area around Tucson is contracted out. Sometimes there are shifts from one contractor to another, which means that we get better prices and service than we would if we entered into a 30-year contract.

One of the reasons we get better service is that the companies we deal with do not have 30-year contracts with their employees. Most modern governments have adopted various civil service arrangements which involve more or less lifetime employment unless the employee voluntarily quits. This normally leads to much less efficient performance of the government's business than it would get if it had more normal employment relations with its employees.

The civil servants, then, are a powerful political group who become more powerful as their numbers increase and who push very heavily for their own interests. It is to all intents and purposes impossible to fire an American Federal Government civil servant unless he decides not to fight.[5]

5. The *New York Times*, Friday, May 3, 1991, pages 1–13, LA edition, carried a story about a serious problem in the New York City Civil Service. New York has a very large welfare program and as part of this program it maintains a large warehouse in which various supplies for the administrators of the program or things to be distributed to the poor are kept. For many years the staff of this warehouse have been engaged in systematic large-scale theft, sometimes driving things away by the truckload. Mr. Fourey, in the city's Department of Investigations, found out about this and began investigations and submitted a great many memos to his superiors demanding that some action be taken to stop it. The result was that during an economy drive he was fired. The *New York Times*, in a long story, shows great indignation about all of this, but notably does not suggest that the civil servants running the warehouse be fired. Indeed, it would probably be much easier to convict them of crimes and imprison them than it would be to discharge them.

In practice, I do not think it makes a great deal of difference whether you hire your employees in the executive branch individually or by groups through contracting. What does make a difference is ensuring that they not have permanent tenure. This, of course, is directly contrary to the conventional wisdom.[6] The present situation in many governments is that the elected officials and those higher ranking officials whom they are permitted to appoint at will cannot fire lower level officials if the lower level officials do not do as they are instructed.

On the other hand, the lower level officials, by way of carefully calculated leaks to the press or possibly in some cases deliberate disobedience to orders, can generate very bad publicity for their political superiors. This may well lead to the dismissal of the higher level, political, appointees. Under the circumstances, the higher officials are normally unwilling to grab the bull by the horns and attempt to force their permanent civil servants into efficiency. If they could fire them, or if the inferiors were employees of a corporation which could lose its contract, they would have much more control.

The problem is exacerbated by the fact that most civil servants' positions are either over- or under-paid. Civil service rates are determined by elaborate committees that allegedly set them at their private equivalents. Of course, it is not obvious what the private equivalent of any given government job is. We frequently observe long queues of people trying to take some government jobs. On the other hand, other government jobs are impossible to fill unless you are willing to accept very poor quality people. It would appear that these pay scales are badly out of equilibrium. There are far more people who want to work for the Post Office than are needed. They are also paid more than their much more efficient private enterprise equivalents in Federal Express, Purolator, etc. On the other hand I have observed two state-run universities in which the salaries for secretaries are low enough that qualified secretaries cannot be hired under that title.

The above remarks will be regarded by many as such a severe deviation from the norm as to be actually sinful. The view that we need civil service is very widely held. I would encourage governments who do not already have one to avoid falling into this trap. The civil servants will rapidly organize themselves into a pressure group and once they've done it, democratic government has very great difficulty in dealing with them. An indication of the

6. Conventional wisdom also frequently maintains that civil servants can be fired if they are inefficient. Most of the people who say this haven't tried.

power of this group comes from surveys which show that in Canada, a country with a vast and well-entrenched civil service, interest groups devote 40 percent of their lobbying efforts to bureaucrats. In the U.S. the figure is closer to 20 percent.

The Executive and Political Branches

The radical distinction between the executive and the political branch is frequently much less obvious in smaller government units. In the American system, the Chief Executive is normally directly elected. In Canada and in most European democracies that person is chosen by the lower house of the legislature. The result is that in the United States, the Chief Executive is frequently of opposite party from the majority of the legislature. As American Chief Executives have veto power over legislation, this means that in a way they serve as a third house of the legislature. Their veto can normally be overruled only by a reinforced majority of both houses.

This problem (or advantage, as the case may be) does not arise in Parliamentary systems where the Prime Minister depends throughout his tenure on maintaining support of a majority of the legislature. In two- or three-party systems this is fairly easy, but in multi-party systems keeping the coalition together may be quite complex. France is experimenting with a sort of combination.

Many American state governments have officials in the executive branch who are elected, not appointed, by the governor. One very common example is the chief fiscal officer, who is frequently separately elected. This seems to me a very sensible institution, since one of the purposes of the chief fiscal officer is to check on expenditures, and having an independent official there is sensible.

Most levels of U.S. governments have converged on the Canadian practice of appointing most executive positions. The state of Arizona has only a few executive officers, mainly holding not very important positions, who are directly elected. The holder of one of these minor and unimportant offices, the secretary of state, suddenly became the governor of the state about two years ago as a result of an impeachment of the elected governor. She served efficiently and well but apparently decided that she would do badly in the upcoming election and therefore did not run. She has been replaced by a directly elected governor.

The Veto

The American institution of the executive veto perhaps deserves some comment. It exists in three forms. The first of these is the one in which the original Constitution permits the President to veto any congressional bill as a whole. Congress has the right to overturn his veto by two-thirds majority of both houses.

The second form permits the governor of many states (the President now wants this power) to go through a bill and veto specific clauses in it. This is primarily thought of for budgetary provisions and is called the line item veto. Once again, it can be overturned by two-thirds majority in both houses, although the exact rule varies from state to state.

The third form permits the governor, and once again the President would like this power, to reduce a given appropriation item rather than abolishing it. He might make it only 90 percent of what the legislature has passed. Although it looks minor, it is actually the strongest form, because it is much harder to get a two-thirds majority, or even a simple majority, to overturn a small reduction in a budget item than to overturn the actual abolition of some particular expenditure.

Whether the veto is a good idea or not depends on a lot of general philosophical considerations. It is more or less useless if you have a cabinet form of government. If the Prime Minister is in fact selected by the legislature then this whole process would have no purpose. The veto for a separately elected executive, whether the President or governor or for that matter the mayor, is an excellent idea because an executive elected by the entire body of the voters is somewhat less subservient to local pressure groups than are the legislators who individually are elected by only a part of the electorate. A majority of the voters in a majority of the legislative constituencies can be only a little more than 25 percent of the voters. They might get something through the legislature, but it would be harder to avoid the presidential veto.

Relationships between Governments

Let us now consider the relationships between governments. The first thing to be said is that if you go to a Canadian, American, or Swiss city, you find a dense web of additional government organizations performing all sorts of functions. It may be park boards dealing with parks scattered through a number of different geographic institutions. Even if there are no unified boards it is likely that the various government units have some arrangement for cooperatively planning their parks. This is, indeed, the way it is done in Tucson.

As I mentioned above, there are frequently unified water and sewage facilities for quite large areas because it's cheaper that way. Mosquito abatement covers a fairly large area and you will find that there are large mosquito abatement organizations. Pollution control of all sorts frequently requires units that are larger than the individual city, but not as large as the state. In some cases units are larger than the state but not as large as the nation. There are also cases in which pollution control requires units that are larger than nations. In all of these cases some kind of agreed-upon organization is necessary.

In spite of the often unsightly appearance of the process of policy coordination, the outcome is usually quite good. Indeed, a very distinguished American political scientist, Vincent Ostrom, has devoted a large part of his life to looking at this kind of negotiation and arguing that it works well.[7]

Government Pressuring Government

Let us turn now to the other relations between these various government levels. First of all, they are fairly uniformly set up so that the higher levels have power over the lower levels. The second thing to be said is that the lower levels are extremely good in lobbying the higher levels to get what they want. The reason for the success of the lower level governments in dealing with the higher levels is simple and straightforward. The mayor of, say, New York City is in a very real sense speaking for the voters of New York and they vote in state elections too. He expects members of the state legislature who come from New York City to be on his side even if they happen to be political opponents of his in city politics. The governor also will need New York votes to get re-elected.[8]

This pattern persists throughout the whole of the government. The states

7. His work is dispersed in many articles in many journals. I can think of no "master" article to cite, but most of his articles are worthwhile.

8. If the governor would like to become President of the United States, he will need New York City votes for that, too.

have great influence in Washington and many of them, as well as many of the larger cities, maintain formal lobbies in Washington in addition, of course, to their representatives in the House and Senate. The same is true of certain regional blocks in Canada, namely, the Maritimes, Quebec, Ontario, and the West.

The effects of intergovernmental pressures are most clearly seen when it comes to the shift of funds between different parts of the government. There are reasons why one would want to shift funds from one area of the country to another. In the 19th century, for example, the United States had a series of forts along the coast. These were paid for by taxes collected not only from the coastal states but from inland states, too. No one particularly objected to the arrangement for obvious reasons. The forts are mainly gone now, although it's still true that naval support facilities are all on the coast and are supported by taxes collected from the country as a whole.

Today we are more likely to talk about transfers from one part of the country to another in terms of helping the poor. The average per capita income in Mississippi is lower than that in New York. Hence one could argue that funds should be transferred from New York to Mississippi. As a matter of fact, if you look at the way the U.S. Federal Government acts, it is not obvious that this kind of transfer does in fact occur on any great scale. It is true, however, that this kind of transfer is talked about a great deal. In Canada, on the other hand, regional transfers are an important item in the federal budget and have been the cause of much strife between the "have" and the "have-not" provinces.

Even if the actual equalizing transfers are relatively small, it is clear that to some extent expenditures from the higher level organizations should not be simply divided equally among all the states. In the U.S., the congressmen of the wealthier states, of course, disagree with this and make every effort to get it equally divided, and they're quite successful. The same phenomenon has recently been evident in Ontario, one of Canada's richest provinces, which argues that it deserves a net transfer from the rest of the country.

In general, it's obvious why local officials would prefer to have a federal government collect the taxes and then spend the money themselves. It's not obvious why the federal government officials are willing to collect taxes which will be spent by local governments. It is possible, however, that there is a sort of double counting here. Both the federal and the local official get credit for the expenditures and only the federal official is blamed for the tax. If the local officials support the federal official in return for the payment, there could be a mutual profit for political purposes.

In any event, it is clear that in recent years all over the world local governments have been able partially to transfer their tax problems to the central government. In the United States it isn't as far along as it is in, for example, England. This has been combined with considerable growth of the local government. This, in fact, probably explains it. Government expenditures that somebody else pays for are something that any official would like. The anguish officials feel when they are forced to pay the bill themselves is clearly illustrated in Canada. In Canada, the federal government shares in the cost of provincially administered education, health, and welfare. The provinces are now screaming because of a phenomenon known as federal "offloading." Having examined its finances and discovered them to be in disarray, the federal government has slowed its transfers to provincial governments. These governments had become used to the injection of federal money and were caught by surprise in the midst of ambitious social spending programs to which they expected the federal government to chip in its regular share.

Even if we temporarily put aside the problem of helping the poor, it seems likely that there will be very strong efforts to maximize central government expenditures which are beneficial to individual local governments. There is no end to the opportunities for political pressure that are generated by this kind of activity.

Conclusion

We have now finished our survey of government institutions. The reader has no doubt noticed that it's quick and, of necessity, somewhat oversimplified. Nonetheless, I think it's helpful to anyone thinking about designing a federal government to know what has been done in the past. The variety of existing governments is great. Selecting from among this large bouquet of governments is difficult. To do it, one must have some general idea of its composition.

Bibliograpy

Adie, Douglas K. *The Mail Monopoly: Analysing Canadian Postal Service.* Vancouver: The Fraser Institute, 1990.

Bish, Robert. "Federalism: A Market Economic Perspective," in *Cato Journal* V7, Fall 1987, pp. 377–97.

Bryan, Frank, and John McClaughry. *The Vermont Papers: Recreating Democracy on a Human Scale*. Chelsea, Vermont: Chelsea Green Publishing Co., 1989, pp. 308, 100–200. A model for structuring government units into smaller units. This model, the authors feel, would represent individual interests and allocate public goods more efficiently.

Dye, Thomas R. *American Federalism: Competition among Governments*. Lexington Books, 1990, pp. xvii, 219, 1–13. Definition of federalism, models and brief descriptions of federalism.

Hamilton, Alexander, John Jay, and James Madison. *The Federalist*. Edward Mead Earl (ed.). New York: Modern Library.

Kohr, Leopold. *The Breakdown of Nations*. New York: E. P. Dutton, 1978, pp. xxi, 250 (originally published in 1957), pp. 170–87.

THOUGHTS ABOUT REPRESENTATIVE GOVERNMENT

If we define democracy as government in which the government depends upon the vote of a large number of people, then it is a rather old form of government having possibly existed in Sumer. It certainly existed in Greece and Rome, and persisted in some city states throughout the Middle Ages. It was even used in such despotic places as China for local government.[1]

In general, after a period of development, ancient democracy tended to be replaced by despotism of one sort or another. That will not necessarily be our fate, particularly because the new forms of democracy differ from the earlier ones in that they are representative democracy rather than direct democracy.[2]

A further difference between modern democracy and democracy in the earlier periods is that essentially all adults are permitted to vote. This is a very recent development. In the United States almost all free adult males were permitted to vote from very early times, but women only achieved the vote around the turn of the century. In England, more conservative than we, it was not until almost the end of World War I that all adult males could vote, and women did not receive the full franchise until the 1930s. In a way, we are in an experiment with a new and radical form of government.

But my duty here is to talk about representative government and that is certainly characteristic of most modern democracies. Permitting almost every adult[3] to vote is also a modern feature. Indeed that is one of the reasons for the representative nature of modern democracy. If the number of people permitted to vote was quite restricted, the Roman Senate for example, representation would be unnecessary.

Reprinted from *European Journal of Political Economy* 10 (May 1994): 27–39, with permission from Elsevier.

1. Some democracies, including the one in which Bernholz lives, do a good deal of direct public voting on various issues. Use of random samples drawn from the population on the whole has also been characteristic of many democratic governments. Its commonest modern example is the jury.

2. In Greece and Rome there was something vaguely like representative democracy in that voting was by tribes. The particular members of the tribe who turned up at the forum cast votes for the whole tribe. The people who turned up were not selected.

3. Felons and lunatics are common exceptions.

Modern representative democracies fall in two general classes,[4] one of which is (roughly) copied after the English parliamentary system, and one of which is (even more roughly) copied after the American presidential system.[5] As a very rough rule of thumb presidential systems are found on the American continent, and parliamentary on the others.

Most modern democratic systems have two-house legislatures although there are exceptions to that rule. Almost all of the public choice work on representative government has dealt with governments where there are two chambers. Further, both of these chambers are normally elected, rather than having one semi-hereditary like at the House of Lords, or appointed like the traditional Canadian Upper House.

If one looks at the United States prototype, it really is a three-house legislature. The president, or in the American states, the governor, normally has veto power which can be overridden by the two houses casting a re-enforced vote of some sort. For the federal government a bill to pass must either achieve the majority in both houses and the assent of the president, or achieve a two-thirds majority in both houses.

If we think of the president as a third house, then it is likely that the two-thirds majority in two houses is not terribly different from a simple majority in both houses with the president also going along. They all represent the same voting body, i.e., citizens of the United States. Still, the method of selection and election is enough different so that a majority coalition represents somewhat different voters in each of the "chambers." It is often pointed out that the president, being elected by all of the voters is less interested in parochial issues than is the House of Representatives.[6]

It is an interesting fact that most of the research dealing with representative government has concerned itself with only one house. Indeed, it has tended to concentrate on a particular body, the House of Representatives of the United States. Even if we confine ourselves thus narrowly there are a great many problems and important matters to concern us. Further, it is likely that all representative bodies have a good deal of resemblance so things we find out about one are apt to be true of another.

4. Perhaps we should say three classes because Bernholz's country, Switzerland, doesn't fit into either category. Although I admire the Swiss constitution, nobody has copied it, so it remains outside the main streams of constitutional development.

5. Small local governments frequently follow other patterns.

6. It would be even more true if we did not have a House of Electors and cast direct votes for the president.

The individual houses, even if we ignore the interactions among them, can be quite complicated. Further, the European or parliamentary system in which one of the houses is either dominated by or dominates the executive branch is quite different from the American system in which the executive branch is separate but has the veto. Nevertheless, the problems which this article will mainly address seem to occur in all representative bodies and indeed for elected officials in general.

The next thing to ask is: "What are the members of the legislature trying to do," i.e., what motivates them? There are four major "theories." Listing them, the first is the legislators are people selected for outstanding virtue and knowledge who proceed to go to Washington or Berne for the purpose of providing good government. There are few public choice people who regard this as a totally correct model. Still I think there is no doubt that the voters to some extent think of their representatives in this way, and the representatives themselves to some extent are so motivated.

Secondly, the public choice approach is more or less that a politician is a man who makes a living by getting elected and he engages almost entirely in an effort to get re-elected once he has been elected. There is no doubt that there is a great deal of truth in this particular approach[7] but it is also true that it is not 100% correct. All human beings are at least to some extent interested in helping those less well off and in promoting the public good. Everybody is willing to give away something like 5% of their income to help people who are less well off than they are. This rule applies to politicians as well as to other people. In fact, it may well be that politicians are willing to sacrifice even more, perhaps 10%.

The third "theory," and this is in accord with the first, is that the politician in office simply tries to maximize his personal preference. By this I do not mean that he aims only for luxurious quarters and elaborately organized and catered trips to Paris.[8] Although that would be part of it, there are decisions on public policy in which individuals do have personal preferences.

The dispute in the American House of Representatives about whether we should or should not aid one or the other of the two sides in Nicaragua was almost entirely a question of the personal preferences of the various congressmen. There were more on the left than on the right and hence the group which we now know, as a result of the election, was backed by the majority

7. It is the one I usually use.

8. They do make these, of course.

of Nicaraguan people did not get much support from the United States. Still, minorities do have influence, and it got some.

Now all three of these may co-exist in the mind of the individual congressman. The fourth has that same characteristic. The congressman usually regards himself as a sort of ambassador for his district. His duty is to get things like the Central Arizona Project or the Tulsa Ship Canal to benefit people in his district. In the European systems where proportional representation is used, it may not be a geographic district but a particular segment of the population which is thought to vote for the party of the representative.

Congressman Udall of Arizona due to a hung election arrived in Washington as the most junior member of the House of Representatives. As a result he faced a very poor selection of committees, even though he was in the majority party. He ended up on the low ranking postal committee. He was told by a senior congressman: "Now you can put a new post office in every town in your District." Congressman Udall recounting this always added: "And I did."

To repeat, I think these are the four major theories of what congressmen do and I think that some aspects of them are present in the minds of every congressman. It is essential to add that most modern legislatures are confronted with so many legislative problems that they can hardly be more than very sketchily informed about each one. The consequence is that simple ignorance must be put down as a very major part of the factors which control the congressman's vote, even if it can hardly be listed as a "motive."[9] You can hardly blame the representatives for this ignorance. Still, it is likely that if we reduced the total legislature burden the reduction in the total number of bills would be much more than compensated by the increase in the average quality.

One of the results of this mass of proposals is a high level of specialization on the part of the members of the legislature. People who visit the American legislature whether it is national or state are frequently shocked to discover

9. I have a friend, a professor of public finance, who with a number of his friends and colleagues set up sort of a committee to advise a newly elected member of the Connecticut state legislature. Their idea was that each of them would read those items of proposed legislation which were within their specialty and assist the member of the legislature. They rapidly gave up. In the first place they discovered that even though they were each reading only about 10% of the total volume, it was a killing business. Secondly, they discovered that the member of the legislature paid little attention to them. Normally she was only interested in one specific aspect of each bill and she found out about that by talking to her colleagues, making trades with them, etc.

that there is practically no one on the floor. It is less true in most other countries, but is rapidly becoming the rule. Now that there is a lot of television coverage almost all legislatures have enacted a rule that the television cameramen must concentrate on whoever is speaking and not turn his camera to show the empty benches.

How do representatives legislate? The answer is that there is a web of committees and flow of contacts between the members and the representatives which permit them to cast a vote even if it is not obvious that this is an informed or intelligent vote.

In general, the bills themselves are written by the civil service, by congressional assistants, or, in many cases, by special interests who offer "advice" sometimes in the form of a completely worked out piece of legislation. All of this, which sounds like criticism, is not criticism of the individual legislators or even the way they are handling their problems, granted that they have this large number of bills.

If the government were a good deal more limited in its scope with the results that fewer issues came up with each session of the legislature, they could be more careful in their consideration of the individual items and there would be more debate. Several places such as Virginia and Switzerland have attempted to reach this objective by simply restricting the amount of time that the legislature can be in session. Whether this actually works or simply means that the legislature is even less informed about what it does is not obvious.

Any careful description such as this looks like criticism, but let us consider the situation if we had direct voting. Switzerland and California do directly vote on very many issues and the average voter is even less informed for the average issue than the average congressman would be.

There are advantages to direct voting. But consider the situation of, let's say, the Roman Republic. If they had left decisions as to where a road should be built or whether there should be cavalry reinforcements to the army, etc., up to direct vote there would never have been a Roman Empire.[10] Many decisions have to be delegated. Of course, the delegation does not have to go to the legislature, it could go to the president or to other high officials. Roman armies were in fact commanded by consuls who were elected for a one-year term. They can be regarded as representatives just as readily as can an American senator.

How then do modern bodies of representatives make decisions? Let us follow such of the public choice literature and start by considering only the

10. The Senate, of course, was not an elected body.

activities of one house. For this purpose we will ignore both the existence of a second house and of a president or other officials who make many of the decisions. We will also assume here that we have the American system and the house we are describing is not the House of Commons which in fact delegates most of its power to the cabinet.

Further, we will ignore the information problem, not by alleging that the representatives are well informed, but by saying that they know as much as they themselves feel is worthwhile, i.e., they are not willing to put more time and energy into becoming better informed. It should perhaps be said here that they are normally much better informed about whether their constituents like or do not like a given bill than they are with the details of the bill itself.

Among my possible motives, however, I can go a little further because there has been some empirical testing done. If the congressmen are merely simply trying to get re-elected then a congressman who is not going to be re-elected, because he lost the last election and is still holding on as a lame duck, or because he has decided to retire should behave somewhat differently than he had done before the loss of the election or decision to retire.

This is subject to empirical testing and there have been a considerable number of such tests.[11] It would be tedious to go through them all but the general conclusion is fairly simple and straightforward. Congressmen who know that they are not going to face another election do behave differently than they did when they were still potentially running for re-election, but the difference is not gigantic. It requires fairly careful statistical work to detect.

Whether this indicates that trying to get re-elected is not the major motive or something else is not clear. I think that over a period of time in Congress they have become so accustomed to a given pattern of behavior that once it no longer becomes necessary they in fact do not immediately make radical changes.

If we had congressmen who continued voting for years and years after they realized that they could not be re-elected you might detect major effects. If the present move to limit the term of a congressman becomes effective, they will behave rather like presidents in their second term. Many students have noticed the presidents in their second term do not behave as they do in the first term, but once again the difference is not gigantic.

It should be pointed out that a congressman may be motivated to follow

11. More often with the Senate than with the House.

somewhat the same policies even if he is not actually running for re-election. He is probably going back to his own district, keeping a lot of friends, and for that matter keeping contacts. I think habit is also important. If congressmen never faced re-election problems, for example, if they were elected for a single term, they might behave differently.[12] Unfortunately, the other possible motives are harder to test.

Let us proceed to other matters. That the American congressmen consider themselves as sort of superior lobbyists for their district is perfectly obvious to anyone who watches Congress at all. Some people refer to this as "pork" because a very large number of small specific projects are pushed by congressmen for their districts. The current issue of *The Public Interest* has a very strong article, "In Praise of Pork," by John W. Elwood and Eric M. Patashnik.[13] As the title suggests, it is a vigorous defense of such small special projects. No one who has read much about American congressmen can readily refute them, although most of us are not as enthusiastic.

They argue that congressmen confronted with a bill which is of general benefit, but might to some extent hurt some of their constituents have to be bought off. They are bought off by some special privilege for some other group of their constituents. In other words the whole thing is legal bribery. The congressman has not directly received any payment, but it does improve his likelihood of being re-elected.[14]

All of this is much more open and above board in the American legislature.[15] It is much quieter in other legislatures, but it is still there. To take but one example, the famous television program "Yes, Minister" has the politicians continuously worrying about "marginals," i.e., districts which are likely to change party in the next election. I do not regard this work of fiction as a final authority,[16] but it is notable that none of the many people who commented on it ever raised any questions about this aspect of it.

In other countries the same is true. I have been confidentially informed by

12. Periodically an amendment to the American Constitution in which the president instead of serving two possible four-year terms would have a single term of six years is suggested. Presumably those six-year presidents would, in fact, behave differently than current presidents do, at least during their first four years.

13. No. 110, Winter 1993, pp. 19–33.

14. See *The Triumph of Politics*, David Stockman, for a general denunciation of the process by a man who had much experience with it.

15. It is not completely open and above board as congressmen frequently deny they do this.

16. As a matter of fact it is a very good portrait.

high ranking members of a number of parliamentary-type democracies that the only difference from the American House of Representatives is simply that it is done in secret. In all cases this kind of trade takes place, in some places they are less secretive than the others.

With proportional representation the bargaining is frequently between the parties representing different interest groups which are not geographical rather than purely geographical constituencies. Still at the time when the Prime Minister of France was also Mayor of Paris, one can feel fairly confident that Paris was not left out in this bargaining process.

One of the major differences between most European representative assemblies and most American ones is the existence of fairly strong party discipline in Europe and an almost total lack of it in the United States. It is true that in the United States a Democrat is more likely to vote with the majority of other Democrats than with the majority of Republicans.[17] But there is a great deal of independence. The individual congressman represents his constituency and perhaps more accurately the Democrats or the Republicans in his constituency rather than the constituency as a whole, but still he is pretty independent.

The Europeans on the other hand for various reasons are generally speaking quite strongly disciplined by their parties and do not have all of the independence. It should be kept in mind that although they are disciplined by their parties, they also discipline the party. The party decisions are made by an internal mechanism in which its elected representatives play a role. In many cases there is simply a party caucus in which all of the representatives in the body can vote for what their particular party will do.

It is not exactly obvious how their differences developed. Certainly if you go back to the 19th century you find in England, and I believe in those other places where there was a representative assembly, a good deal of independence with parties not really having firm control. In various ways this firm party control has developed and has been steadily strengthened into the present form.

Take two examples. In Israel proportional representation is used and there is a party list with only the names at the top of the list having much chance of being elected. The central body can and on occasions does simply move a delegate down near the bottom of the list. In essence, somebody is given a blackball.

17. This is rather like Baumol's law: "The average driver in a two-lane road is in the more crowded lane."

England has a simpler procedure in which money and television time are allocated to the parties for campaigning, but the individual M.P.'s are put under very strict financial and other controls when they campaign. This is the reason for the otherwise apparently silly business of canvassing. It means that the individual M.P. knows that he is far more likely to be removed from office by the failure of his party than by his own dereliction if he keeps on good terms with the party. It is true, however, that British M.P.'s do a great deal of what is called constituency work in the United States.

The result of all this is that modern governments in addition to doing things which can be arguably stated to be in the public interest also do a great many things which are of value only to a very narrow collection of voters. It should be pointed out that this is not necessarily a criticism although if one looks at things like the Central Arizona Project or the Tulsa Ship Canal it's hard to feel neutral about them.

There are a good many things within any government affecting only some minority. If it were done privately you would have to get unanimous agreement among a fairly large group of people, but nevertheless far less than the total voting body. Having these done by the larger government is sensible.

Unfortunately, it is easy for government to get far beyond programs which confer a net benefit. The European farm programs, like the Japanese farm programs, is in fact much more extortionate than the one in the United States, even if it tends to be done in a more quiet and secretive way than the American one.

Thus the role of specialized lobbyist which the average congressman adopts in Washington or the average state representative in the state capital by no means is something we should condemn out of hand. Still, it is very hard to look at this activity without realizing that it leads to an appalling amount of waste. It should be emphasized that the waste that goes to non-geographically located special interests under proportional representation probably is greater.

Although it seems fairly certain that this role of ambassador for his district is important for a congressman,[18] empirical studies sometimes cast considerable doubt on it. For example, cross-section studies frequently show that congressmen on general issues like price control for gasoline, vote in accord with their ideological position rather than for the well-being of their district. This would be in accord with the "wise and virtuous" or the "follow own preference" models rather than the ambassadorial one.

18. Ambassador for special interest such as unions or the farmers in Europe.

On the other hand nobody who watches congressmen in action has much doubt of the ambassadorial role. To take a very local example which affects me, Arizona is a desert state and more than one-half of the population live in Phoenix or its immediate suburbs. The only other large city is Tucson, in which I live.

Certain taxes, especially the sales tax, are collected by the state, and then part of them are distributed to the local governments according to a prearranged formula. The Phoenix delegation has an absolute majority of both houses of legislature, and I suppose no one will be surprised to hear that they have arranged this formula in such a way that Phoenix gets a lot more per capita than Tucson. Small towns scattered around the rest of the State of Arizona, do even worse.

This is simply an example. How do we account for the empirical fact that congressmen from Texas who are politically on the left are less likely to vote against a price control on gasoline, by quite a large margin, than congressmen from Virginia who are politically on the right? The first thing that can be said is that although this is true, it is not as simple as all of that. The new administration has a Secretary of Treasury, former Senator Bentson. He is not specifically an oil millionaire, but he is a millionaire whose assets are mainly in Texas, and do depend to a considerable extent on the prosperity of the oil business. Further, he has for many years represented Texas in the Senate.

When the transition team was operating there was a great deal of discussion of either a straightforward tax on gasoline or tax on carbon as a way of raising income for the government, which is in deficit, and at the same time reducing air pollution. Since Bentson has been Secretary of the Treasury designate this tax has been pretty much abandoned for a general energy tax which would fall as well on such things as water power, nuclear power, etc. He is to some extent still acting as a senator from Texas.

Nevertheless, there are these studies which show considerable ideological coherence on the part of some congressmen even when it conflicts with the interests of their local district. There are two problems with the empirical studies, one of which is they only deal with a few very general projects and do not consider the innumerable local provisions built into the bills. It may well be that the individual congressman is in fact serving his constituency very well, having inserted several special provisions into this general bill that will benefit it in return for his vote.

This is by no means the only explanation. A congressman represents not all the voters and constituency, but only some of them, i.e., the ones who are likely to vote for him. He may have a constituency in which his supporters are let us say rather antagonistic to the wealthy oil man even though they indirectly benefit from the oil industry. Under these circumstances making a show of being opposed to the "fat cats" may be helpful. This is particularly likely if he can so arrange the rest of the bill in such a way that it does not injure the interest of his constituency. It is very difficult to straighten this kind of thing out in empirical research.

Most of the things I have said about the representatives can be taken as criticism or at least not as praise. This is correct, but one of the fundamental ideas of public choice is that to criticize an institution is not the same as saying it should be replaced by another. You must look carefully at the other ones to make a comparison. The market is full of defects; so is the government. For some things the government works better and for some things the market works better.

Representative government may be the best even if, sub specie aeternitatis, it is not very good. Further, representation is not necessarily by way of a legislature. In a very real sense the president of the United States is a representative of the average voter, just as much as is Congress. The Roman consul in command of an army could reasonably be called a representative of the voters who had elected him and who were now functioning as soldiers in his army.[19]

Indeed there is another way of getting representation, a method that was used by many classical democracies, which is the use of lots. Today, we use this only in the form of a jury, but we could select a House of Representatives by simply having a computer print out 435 randomly selected names. It would have to be rotated frequently as indeed similar groups were in Athens.

As far as I know, except for juries, this technique is not used or even proposed in the modern world. The reason may be simply tradition, with the tradition having shifted over 2000 years. Aristotle thought it was the perfect democratic system. It certainly assured that the representative assembly was a good mirror of the electorate.

We have discovered that there are many things about representatives that we do not know. This is not surprising granted the fact that what I would regard as a reasonably scientific approach to politics is a very new field, but still it is disappointing.

Another area where we use representation very widely is the corporation.

19. It is a little known fact, but the Confederate Army in the American Civil War, which on a man for man basis was clearly better than the Northern one, had elected officers up to and including Captains.

In this case the individual voters, i.e., the stockholders, are usually even less well-informed than the average voter for governmental officials. It works reasonably well for two reasons. First, the objective of most corporations is simply to make money, and second, it is fairly easy to tell whether the corporation is doing so. That being so the people at the top who represent the stockholders know that they can be removed and almost certainly will be removed if the company loses money.[20] It would be nice if we could do the same with our representatives politically.

The basic problem here is that it is very difficult to tell whether the representatives are achieving the rather badly specified objectives of the voters they represent. The voters themselves do not have clear ideas unlike the voters of corporations who do know what they want the corporation to do. Thus, the possibility, and indeed probability, that the politician will be removed from office if he is thought to be unsuccessful is of much less value in disciplining him than is the rather simple procedure of the corporation.

Bush, during the period when he was president and not actively campaigning, certainly did not expect that he would be criticized during the campaign for the particular things he was criticized for. He was surprised when the Democrats attacked him in many cases from the right, rather than from the left. Nevertheless, he lost, though his principal opponent did not do very well either; 43% of the vote is far from an overwhelming vote of confidence.

Representation in recent times has begun to have a rather different meaning than it did before. Specifically, the representative is beginning to be somebody who represents his citizens in their contacts with the administrative side of the government. In other words, in a way the representatives have taken over part of the duties of the executive branch.

Congressmen now maintain large staffs[21] which assist the congressmen directly in campaigning. To a large extent, however, they are engaged in what is called constituency work. If you do not receive your social security check you complain to the congressman and one of his assistants takes care of the matter.[22] This is obviously a representative activity since they do represent

20. This was dictated on the day that IBM announced that it was going to have a new Chairman of the Board.

21. Interestingly, in hiring this staff the congressman is exempted from all of the civil service regulations, including the ones prohibiting racial discrimination.

22. It should be said that this large staff also engages in a number of other activities. The constituency work together with these other items are the basic reason that congressmen tend to stay in office as long as they do. It costs about two million dollars per year to provide what

their constituents. On the other hand, it is not what is traditionally meant by representation.

It should be said that this seems to be more highly developed in the United States than elsewhere, but other countries are rapidly following us. Furthermore, France, in any event, frequently has a large overlap between the representative from the district and the high officials within the district government itself. The fact mentioned earlier, that for a considerable period of time the Mayor of Paris was also Prime Minister of France, illustrates this.

It is possible that in the United States an individual congressman's potential for being re-elected is far more influenced by this kind of work than it is by anything else. He in essence substitutes for the higher members of the executive branch in administering the government.

As William Niskanen pointed out, if the congressman devotes his time and energy to becoming well informed about legislation, in essence he is generating a public good for the other congressmen. On the other hand, if he devotes his energy to constituency work, he is generating a private good for himself. It is well known that private goods tend to drive out public goods, and that people tend to free-ride on others' activity. Thus it is not surprising that congressmen are apt to put more time into representing their constituencies directly by this kind of method than indirectly by considering the public interest with respect to legislation.

It can be said here that in the United States representation has taken another twist. In this case I think most other countries are farther advanced. The issuance of regulations by career civil servants, or to some extent by presidential appointees, produces a larger body of law than that passed by the legislature.

The legislature designates some part of the government to draw up legislation and provides that they will be binding on the citizen without any further congressional action. This is clearly moving representation from the congressman to other officials, most of whom are not elected, and many of whom are career civil servants.

When I was in law school it was still thought a little dubious that all of this was constitutional. At that time, the 1930s, it was thought that probably the battle was all over and Congress could do it. It is interesting that recently there have been a few signs that possibly this issue will be reconsidered. Of

---

amounts to a special campaign fund for each congressman and opposition candidates never have anywhere near that much.

course, it is impossible for Congress, or indeed for anyone else, to know and work on this vast body of regulations, but perhaps we would be better off if we did not have them.

In any event, the only possible justification for having what amounts to binding rules drawn up by civil servants is that somehow or other they also represent the citizens. It is thought to be a highly technical matter and wise and virtuous civil servants will take care of it, rather than wise and virtuous congressmen. It should be said there are other similarities between their activity and the regular representatives. They also tend to push strongly for various special interests, in particular their own, and are the subject of very vigorous lobbying activity.

This article has not solved very many problems. It is a survey of a very difficult issue and an issue which in general has not yet been solved by research. I am not criticizing the existing research, but it has tended to deal with minor problems around the edge of the main problems. This is necessary for a start and my hope is that having cleared up a lot of the minor problems we will now go on to the major problems. This article is a small first step in that direction.

VOTING, DIFFERENT METHODS AND GENERAL CONSIDERATIONS

In earlier chapters I have argued that the American Constitution is not particularly majoritarian. Let me now discuss the general issue of majoritarian votes. The first thing to be said is that if there are more than two possible alternatives, and there almost always are, then we have to discuss the method that actually guarantees a majority vote for one of them. For example, all alternatives will be submitted to the voters who each select one. The top two then go into a runoff election. There are various other methods. These will be temporarily deferred. I will for the time being discuss the situation in which there are only two alternatives.

I have mentioned several cases in which I believe a minority would have lost in a simple majority vote, but it would be costly for them, and the gain for the winners would not be great. The Germans in 1933 would probably have voted for various discriminations against the Jews. In this particular area and almost throughout the entire reign of Stalin, there was mild discrimination against the Jews in Russia without any signs of public protest. At the very end Stalin had started his campaign to literally wipe them out. If he had lived another year the Jewish population would have been markedly smaller.[1]

Once again, there does not seem to be any sign of a popular opposition. Still, the ordinary Russian's willingness to discriminate against the Jews is not as plain as in the case of Germans, because after all there was no freedom of expression, while in Germany there had been before 1933.[2]

In order to avoid invidious comparisons, I should say that I was alive in the United States before World War II, and mild but genuine discrimination against Jews occurred quite regularly. Harvard and the other leading schools had quotas for the number of Jews that they would admit, rather like today they have for Chinese and other orientals. There was nothing equivalent to

Reprinted, with permission, from *On Voting: A Public Choice Approach* (Cheltenham, U.K., and Brookfield, Vt.: Edward Elgar Publishing, 1998), 157–69.

1. His campaign highlighted Jewish doctors. It is conceivable that the campaign accelerated his death by removing Jews from his personal medical staff.

2. Hitler did not actually win the election before he came into power, but he did well, and his original rise to power was completely constitutional. Needless to say, he did not find the constitution a serious hindrance once he got power.

affirmative action so within their quota they always selected the best candidates which may be one reason for the academic dominance of Jews today.[3]

All of this is vastly different from what we saw in Germany or Russia, but once again there was no sign of the population as a whole objecting to it, and it might well, if it had come up, have been voted into law by a majority. There are other cases. I mention again slavery in the early history of the United States, and indeed slavery throughout history. Up to about 1750 few thought slavery raised moral problems,[4] and opposition for moral reasons was generally regarded as eccentric.

For a modern example consider the position of prohibition in the United States. This went through in a constitutional manner, which means effectively much more than a simple majority, and it was eventually given up because it was realized there was a large number of people whose feeling against prohibition was strong enough so that they were willing to break the law. The people who favored prohibition apparently did not feel so strongly.

In all of these cases I believe there was a minority that felt strongly, and a majority which felt not so strongly. Thus a simple majority vote would inflict more injury through imposing difficulties for the minority than the gain to the majority. If we had used the demand revealing process which permits people to express the intensity of their feelings as well as the direction, we can feel confident the outcome would have been the reverse.

Considering slavery, we can digress to wonder why the slaves were not simply bought by the abolitionists. It would have required some kind of credit operation to make this work out. In Greek and Roman times the law on slavery fluctuated a good deal, but during periods in which they were not at war, and hence there was not a free source of new slaves, it tended to be simple for a slave to purchase his own freedom. In essence, his master permitted him to buy it on credit, and the law was designed to make this easy. An old friend of mine, John Moes, put it that his body was more valuable to him than it was to anyone else because he had a sentimental attachment to it. He would be willing to work harder to pay off the mortgage on himself than as a slave.

Apparently something like this developed in the United States, because most of the Southern states passed laws prohibiting freeing of slaves. In spite

3. The orientals probably will have the same dominance in the next generation.

4. Both Alexander Hamilton and Benjamin Franklin were members of abolition societies. They dropped their scruples at the constitutional convention. Jefferson and Madison were both slaveowners, in Jefferson's case, on a large scale.

of these laws a number of profit-maximizing entrepreneurs like the owners of the Tredagar Iron Works in Richmond found it paid to violate the law, and give some of their employees their freedom in return for harder work. Needless to say the arrangement would not be legally enforceable, but the slave if he had raised the issue would have been held by the court simply to be a slave, because it was illegal in Virginia to free slaves.

It seems likely that one of the important reasons for the American South prohibiting freeing of slaves was the difference in skin color. In a society where almost all blacks were slaves it was difficult for a slave to simply move someplace else, and act as a free citizen. Thus, prohibiting the development of a large free black community improved the protection of the property in the "peculiar institution." Here again we have a case which seems likely that simple majority voting would have given a result which inflicted more pain than the reverse result.

Of course you have the question of who should be permitted to vote which I have discussed before. As a quick review, until recently there were adults, sane, and with no criminal record, living in most democracies but unable to vote.[5] People may talk about requiring all adults to be able to vote as a necessary condition for democracy. Mostly they are perfectly willing to concede that Lincoln, who did not even have a majority, was a democratic President, and would be surprised if you told them that the United States, by their definition of democracy, was not a democracy until the 1960s.

I will interject here that a rather sophisticated admirer of democracy said that it was a democracy if something approaching a majority of the adult population could vote. Women, in general, were not permitted to vote until World War I.[6] There were normally other small categories of people who could not vote, farm laborers in England, for example. Thus under his definition there would have been practically no genuine democracies until this century. Still, this definition clearly brings in Japan in 1941, and Germany in 1914. The view which is being pushed by many political scientists that democracies do not get into wars with other democracies, with this definition, is clearly untrue.

Let us think about these matters a little and assume that the demand revealing process or some other procedure is imposed so that people can weigh their preferences. It is possible that an arrangement to purchase the Southern

5. You may not like using the term "democracy" for the United States in let us say 1789, but once again this book is about voting, not about the meaning of democracy.

6. They did not receive full franchise in England until the 1931 election.

slaves and free them subject to a fairly large special tax to reimburse the federal government for payment to their masters would have achieved general approval in the United States any time after 1820. Of course the Northern abolitionists were violently opposed to paying anything for the slaves, although obviously purchasing them all and freeing them without any compensation whatsoever would have been much cheaper than the Civil War.

This has been a digression. Let us go to the problem of obtaining a simple majority when there are more than two possible alternatives. If we are to guarantee a majority there must be some procedure to reduce the number of alternatives to two, and this procedure may have a number of fairly severe difficulties.

Let me begin with something suggested by Lewis Carroll which was simply that if there was no majority, the voting be suspended for a short period of time while the people thought the matter over and discussed it. Then another vote be held. It was apparently intended that his process would be continued until a majority was obtained or everybody gave up.

It could be said that where there is no majority we just will not enact anything, but this sneaks another alternative in. Doing nothing is always a possibility, and logically should be put into the voting series as it is in terms of the final vote in all parliamentary procedures. Doing nothing if there is no single majority vote is equivalent to agreeing with one of the alternatives and giving that alternative, doing nothing, a superior position. We will see shortly that something like this is quite common.

I pause here and summarize what I take is the current conventional wisdom among students in the area. Since I myself agree with it, the term "conventional wisdom" in this case is not intended to be an insult.

There is no known voting method which can be said to guarantee a majority which is not the result of random factors, like order of voting if there are many alternatives, and the preferences are reasonably diverse. We can arrange things in such a way that the alternatives are winnowed down, and there is eventually only a pair. Then there can be a choice by majority vote. The winnowing down process, and we will turn to that in a moment, is subject to so many difficulties that referring to the winner as having a majority over all of the other alternatives, is simply foolish.

One of the standard methods of cutting down the alternatives to two, which is familiar to most Americans, is to have two major parties and have each of them put up their candidates or policies. The founding fathers were strongly opposed to parties, but we have during most of our history two fairly strong parties. They change from time to time. The Republicans did not exist before 1854. There normally have been a number of minor parties, like prohibitionist, socialist, etc.

Up until the 1968 election it was legally extremely difficult for anyone except for the two main parties to get on the ballot. Wallace, as part of his presidential campaign, conducted an intensive and intelligent set of legal actions with the result that this blockade which in essence had been enacted by the two parties as a sort of cartel restriction has been lifted. Since then third parties have been not very successful, but at least possible. Wallace himself, John Anderson, and Perot have succeeded in getting on the ballot throughout the country and getting a significant number of votes. Further, a number of minor parties like the Libertarians have taken advantage of this to get on the ballot throughout most of the country even though they do not get a great number of votes.

The presidential candidates are largely elected by a very confused primary process running from state to state with people in the later-voting states tending to be really left out of the process. Primaries have only recently become dominant in presidential choice, but have been for a long time common at a lower level. In this case the members of two separate parties vote among themselves for who will represent them in the upcoming election. If we confine ourselves to these parties alone, this does not guarantee us a sensible contest. Goldwater and McGovern both obtained nominations in their own parties although in both cases they were obviously doomed before the campaign even began.[7]

I have not here gone through every single method that is used to whittle the choice down to two so that we are guaranteed a majority; however I do not think that anyone will question my view that all of them have fairly severe defects from a strict majoritarian perspective.[8] Of course, as mentioned in the first chapter, Americans tend to take anything we are accustomed to as being equivalent to majority voting.

7. In the case of McGovern this may not be true. He campaigned as a far left Democrat having made remarks to reporters and so forth that it was harder to get nominated in the Democratic Party than it was to win the election. As soon as he was nominated he made an effort to shift sharply to the right, but discovered that because of the things he had said in his nominating campaign he could not pull it off. Thus he probably thought that the position of the far left he assumed in order to get the Democratic nomination would not handicap him later in the presidential election itself, although of course it did.

8. This is true no matter how many votes are needed for election.

There is by the way another procedure that is used in a few countries to obtain a majority in the legislature even if not elsewhere. In these countries whichever party gets the largest number of members of the legislature (say the Democrats had 40 percent, the Republicans 35, and Perot's followers 25 percent of the members of the House) would be given a bonus set of seats in order to guarantee it a majority. This, of course, is totally different from our procedures and it is hard to argue that it is the result truthfully of an election process, but it does guarantee a majority in the legislature as long as party discipline holds up.

I now turn to a very common method which for some obscure reason I do not think that most people realize is a solution to the above problem, even if it is not a wonderfully good solution. I turn again to the referendum process. This is actually a choice between two alternatives: the proposed referendum and doing nothing. Normally, either the act proposed gets a majority or in many cases something more than a simple majority, say two-thirds, or the status quo remains in effect. Thus, we have a choice between two alternatives and if the proposal or the status quo wins, this solves the problem.[9]

There are two technical problems. The first is that the order in which the voting is undertaken can be very important. The second is that there is no obvious reason why the one that is accepted could not, when it became a part of the status quo, be beaten by one of the ones that had not been presented to the voters. This is in a way a restatement of the first objection.

A variant on this is the basic method that democracy uses in dealing with policy questions, and as we shall see below it was used to some extent by Venice in dealing with elections. It is also the basic method that is used by the parties in selecting the presidential candidate, although in that case it is concealed.

It used to be that the actual decision was made in the presidential nominating conventions, and this sometimes required a large number of votes, 124 in one Democratic convention when they required a two-thirds majority to nominate.[10] Today it is simply a bit of history.

If we look at legislation we find that something like what I have just described occurs. A complex proposal usually has many, many different clauses,

9. In Arizona, judges are periodically subjected to an election process in which the voters vote for their continuance in office or their removal. This is rather like the referendum voting process.

10. This was to protect the democratic solid South from an unfriendly president.

pork scattered around among the constituencies, etc., and when it is brought to Congress, it is either voted up or voted down. If we consider only that one vote, there is no Arrow problem. But the actual bill presented must be chosen by some other process.[11]

Once again it would be possible to go through a vast collection of amendments, sub-amendments, etc., but that is not what happens. It is true that in the Senate there are sometimes a number of amendments offered, but basically the bill is produced by somebody, not necessarily the relevant committee; it may be the leadership or even the leadership in the minority party. As produced, it is already a complex matter, and there are not very many changes actually voted on. Basically, it is voted up or voted down.

There is a great deal of careful anecdotal historical research about particular bills by political scientists. They do not seem to have any theory except one offered by Shepsley which is that the committee makes up its mind and then if it makes the proper trades, it will go through. There are several problems with this, one of which is the committee itself is a voting body, and we simply move from one voting body to another. Shepsley, in private conversation, answered this by saying that the chairman actually controlled it. I do not believe that but it is true the chairman has more influence than the average member.

In fact, only a few of the possible alternatives will actually be put before the legislature, normally only one, and that one will either pass or fail, because that is the way voting is run. The process reduces the alternatives to two, refusing to consider many possibilities in the voting process.

I am not alleging that the committees systematically eliminate alternatives which are better than the ones that they finally end up with. What I am alleging is that no one (including committee members) knows how they reach their conclusion, and we do not know whether some of the alternatives that are eliminated in the discussion inside committee might not beat the one they finally adopt. There is possibly a different distribution of post offices which

11. I have been reading *The New York Times*, as I write this book, and the front page carried a box about the bizarre things that had gotten into the main spending bill of the session. On page 12 there was another collection on the same topic as a continuation of the box. One of the items contained in this appropriation bill was intended to settle a quarrel between Rhode Island and the Narragansett Indian tribe. People responsible for all of this boasted that they had only accepted half of the proposals made by individual members of Congress. There does not seem to have been any formal voting process anywhere in this selection. October 3, 1996.

would get it through at a lower cost. There are collections of potential loopholes in the federal income tax law which might purchase more votes than the present ones. We simply do not know.

What we do know is the people who do this in the committees, and for that matter in the leadership and on the floor, are reasonably skilled, but they do not have complete information about the preferences of the other people who will be voting. Nor do we actually know how they make their decisions.

Is there weighted voting with weights varying from time to time? If one person feels strongly, can he impose something on other people who object to it, but not very strongly? We do not know with respect to any given bill, although the careful empirical study by the political scientists might give us a pretty good idea with respect to those particular bills which have been studied. They are a very small minority of all bills.

Going further I would like to talk briefly about a suggestion of Dennis Mueller called "voting by veto." In this system all of the people are qualified to vote. Let us assume that the 435 members of the House of Representatives each propose a motion on some particular subject. There are now 435 motions, plus the status quo or 436 total alternatives. Each individual[12] then selects one of this mass of alternatives and vetoes it. After 435 vetoes there will be one left which could be the status quo, or one of the others.

Mueller's argument for this is not that it gets the ideal outcome. Granted this system, all of the 435 are motivated to propose propositions which will not be vetoed by any single member of the remaining 434. He feels this would mean that all of the decisions would be "moderate."

Note, this is not necessarily a wonderful voting method, but it at least tells us where the various propositions come from. The individual congressmen would need very good ideas as to the prejudice of other people. In other words, their preference functions would not actually be independent of each other and the mathematics which assumes independence is invalid here. Further, it is not particularly likely that any of the proposed alternatives would actually be the first choice of anybody.

The reason that I have brought this up, is that I believe what actually goes on in the legislature before it gets to the floor does have some resemblance to this. I believe that general ideas are suggested, and then individual mem-

12. The order in which they are called might be important, but we will ignore the matter here.

bers of the house leadership, etc. switch their votes on receipt of various special favors. They could either vote for or against in return for payment.

It is not necessary to get everybody in, the majority will do, or in the Senate 60 percent, and it will be sensible to consider both Houses and the President. The whole process, including the conference committees, should be taken into account by the people attempting to get some general program through.

This is a realistic account of what happens, and it will be seen that it is not very closely duplicated by the existing mathematical theory. Further, it is extremely difficult to test empirically because the individual congressman will be voting for the whole package of items, and each congressman may in fact be motivated by the fact that he likes one particular sub-part of the packet, and dislikes another. Another congressman who also likes one sub-packet and dislikes another may have different packets.

So far the readers may think that I have led them into an impasse, and I do not quarrel with that judgment. The existing theory of voting is more straightforward than this. My point has been that this simple straightforward theory we now have is only part of the entire theory which we should hope to have. The major aspiration of this book is to stimulate research in areas where at the moment we do not know very much. I regret that I have to admit I am merely suggesting research. I cannot offer an idea of my own on how to engage in this research. Nevertheless, I think such research is highly desirable.

It will not surprise any student in this area, but I think that I should emphasize that matters of agenda control, the order of which things are voted on, are as important as the actual voting. I would like to give one striking example. When the United Nations was first organized, the interests of the Union of South Africa in the United Nations were taken care of by Great Britain. At substantially every meeting of the United Nations a proposal was made condemning South Africa. The British arranged that it was far enough down the agenda so that it was never voted on.

After a while a South African foreign minister who was more interested in his domestic political position than in the well-being of South Africa wanted to go to the UN and make a speech. He insisted that the South African matter be moved up to the top of the agenda, made his speech, and harvested an almost unanimous resolution of condemnation. From that meeting on, South Africa was condemned at each meeting of the UN General Assembly.

This was a particularly striking example of intelligent agenda control by the British representatives, and hopelessly stupid agenda control by the foreign minister of South Africa. Of course it may have improved his political standing in South Africa, and that may have been his major objective.

There are now journals specializing in public choice. Mainly they run articles in what has been called normal science as opposed to revolutionary science. This is not a criticism as most sciences are in the normal step-by-step process, and we owe the great advances we now have over Egypt 3000 B.C. to this step-by-step process. Still, we would like radical improvements.

I am not in a position to recommend any particular radical improvement, although I would like them. For the time being all that I can predict is continuing our step-by-step progress. We undeniably have made considerable progress by this method. I would like to close by pointing out that we have already made a good start. Everyone should hope for radical improvements. Everyone should keep their eyes open in the hope that they will find them.

A BOUQUET OF VOTING METHODS

I will here discuss a list of different voting methods that have been used in various places. It will not be a complete listing. To be complete would take much more space than this book, but it will give you an idea of the variety of the voting methods which are possible.

Let me begin with the voting method which Aristotle thought was the most stupid he had heard of. In this procedure the judges of the election were moved into a room which was next to an open square where the voting took place, but the window overlooking the square was high enough so that the judges could not see the voters. The voters then assembled in the square, and various candidates were brought in and the voters cheered. The judges would decide which candidate had the loudest cheers, and that would be the one elected.

To repeat, Aristotle thought this was the most stupid method, but we Americans would tend to think that the method which was very common all over the Mediterranean at the time was equally bad: voting by tribes. The citizens of Rome, let us say, in their assembly would line up by their tribes, and each tribe would cast a vote according to the desires of a majority of the people then present from the tribe. The actual outcome would then depend on the majority of the tribes. This would permit three people who were the only representatives of one tribe to cast as powerful a vote as say 200 representing another. It resembled the American Senate in this respect.

Let us turn from this election system to the one which substantially any historical investigation would show up as the best. Venice had only a very slowly changing constitution from about 800 to Napoleon's conquest of it around 1800 A.D., roughly 1,000 years. It was stable, had no coups, and gave what was generally thought to be the best government in Europe at the time. Of course the competition was not exactly stiff.

Further, a city which consisted essentially of a sandbar not only became a great and wealthy trading nation but built up a sizeable empire, and was able to take on great powers in war. Altogether, it was a very successful government, and to this day the city in the lagoons is one of the most beauti-

Reprinted, with permission, from *On Voting: A Public Choice Approach* (Cheltenham, U.K., and Brookfield, Vt.: Edward Elgar Publishing, 1998), 170–84.

ful places in the world in spite of its very unfavorable situation. Its art and architecture more than make up.

The highest official in the Venetian government was the Doge, and his election after about 1200 A.D. followed a procedure which we are likely today to find rather odd.

> The ducal election lasted five days, with two stages of the process allotted to each day. Thirty members of the Great Council, exclusive of patricians under thirty years of age, were selected by lot. Retiring to a separate chamber, this group of thirty reduced themselves by lot to nine, who then elected forty men by a majority of at least seven votes each. After electing the forty, the nine returned to the hall of the Great Council with their list of nominees, "without looking at, speaking or making a sign to anyone." (Sanuto, *Cronachetta*, p. 71.)
>
> These nominees were announced to the chamber and checked to insure that no clan had more than one representative, a precaution followed at every stage of the election. The group of forty assembled in a separate room and reduced their number by sortition to the twelve men who were to elect the next group of twenty-five by at least seven votes apiece; although forbidden to nominate themselves, the twelve could elect a member of the previous group of forty. The twenty-five were reduced by lot to nine, who elected forty-five patricians by the usual majority of seven votes. The forty-five drew lots to select eleven of their number, and the Eleven (the *Undici*) elected the Forty-one (the *Quarantuno*) that then elected the doge by at least twenty-five votes.[1]

The actual election was not carried on as we would expect. The 41 each wrote down a name and put it in a jar. One was drawn. The person that was drawn, if he was a member of the group, and any of his relatives if they were members of the 41 left, and the remainder discussed his qualifications. After a suitable period of time he was brought back in, and would answer questions, and perhaps make a short speech. If he then received 25 votes he was the Doge; if he did not, another name was drawn. You will note that the majority is roughly 60 percent. In general, somebody within the original 41 names would be elected Doge, but if no one was then the process would be repeated.

1. Finlay, Robert. *Politics in Renaissance Venice.* New Brunswick, N.J.: Rutgers University Press (1980), p. 140.

It is not only there that above-majority voting was used in Venice. Complicated "motions to alter electoral procedures or grant petitions often required a favorable vote of two-thirds, three-fourths, or even five-sixths of the patricians present in the assembly."[2] The reader will no doubt have noticed that none of these methods involved placing one proposal against another. They involved taking up proposals one at a time, and putting them against the status quo. The status quo in the case of the election is that there was no Doge.

The use of random allocation in the election of the Doge had the basic purpose of preventing the type of factualism which tore most Italian cities apart. It was successful for many centuries.

These were unusual forms of voting, although certainly the success of the organizations which used them is a strong argument in their favor. Even today we do not feel as confident in the strength of our armed forces as did the citizens of the Roman Republic.

Now, let us turn to other kinds of voting. The first one I would like to discuss is one in which the different voters have different numbers of votes. The obvious case of this is the British House of Commons before 1830. This came from essentially a minor accident in the way the thing was designed.

The seats in Parliament were held by various districts and constituencies, each of which had two. In general, these constituencies had been designed a long time before, and their populations were not equal. The House of Pitt actually owned six seats in the House of Commons by owning the real estate upon which the alleged cities or districts existed. They owned, among other things, the famous Old Sarum which was a plowed field that sent two members to Parliament. Other members of the aristocracy also held many votes, but there were actually a few places where a sizeable number of people voted for their representative.

Burke in the earlier part of his career represented Bristol, which had over 4,000 voters and was the most populous constituency. He voted against certain changes in the tax law which would greatly benefit Bristol. His citizens threw him out, and he spent the rest of his career representing a rotten borough.

Anyone seeking amusement as well as information is advised to read Namier's *Structure of British Politics at the Accession of George III.*[3] It is essen-

2. Ibid., p. 141.

3. Namier, Sir Lewis Bernstein, *The Structure of Politics at the Accession of George III*. New York: St. Martin's, and London: Macmillan (1957).

tially a listing of the various constituencies in England with all that Namier could find about how they sent their representatives to Parliament. The one that impressed me most was one in which public spirited citizens in a northern constituency put their two seats of Parliament up to auction. The money derived was used to repair roads in the constituency. Other tales in Namier's book are perhaps not quite so amusing, but they do indicate that popular voting was not exactly the norm.

I have already mentioned that the power of the voters varies a good deal in the American Senate. Probably the place in which inequality of voters is most common is in the election of the board of directors of a corporation. It is of some interest that this system actually comes from about the same time that Burke was having difficulty with the voters of Bristol.

Lord Clive, being a wealthy man, bought a lot of stock in the Honorable East India Company and talked some of his friends into doing so too. They divided their stock up among a number of their friends who could be depended upon to vote as they wished and return the stock after a while. At this time all stockholders simply had one vote. Clive and his friends were called "splitters." Opponents also split, but as a result corporations began providing that there was one vote per share instead of one vote per head. In any event, today almost all corporations are arranged in such a way that you get as many votes as you have shares.

The existence of "corporate democracy" is frequently doubted because it is certainly true that the stockholders[4] pay little attention to their corporation's business. If they become unhappy with it, normally they just sell their stock rather than waiting until the next election and voting against the current board. Still, stockholder approval, which is mainly in terms of profits, is absolutely vital to the management.

The reason that it is vital to the management is not that usually there will be stockholder efforts to throw the management out, but that the existence of stockholder dissatisfaction whether it is indicated by selling the stock, which means that the stock declines in value, or by just complaining, means that there is an opportunity for a corporate raider.

The raiders will, if they decide that some corporation is not producing adequate profit, try and buy it out, fire the present management, put a new management in. Then when the stock goes up, they sell it and go on to another corporation. This mechanism first explicated by Henry Manne is the basic way that corporations work.

4. Including me.

In the United States for a long time this was very easy; in other countries, Germany and Japan for example, this was hard to do with the result that their corporations were not as continuously pressed to behave in a profit maximizing manner as ours were.

The managements of corporations, needless to say, do not like this system, and they have over the years developed various methods of trying to make it hard to buy the corporation's stock and fire them. Ignoring temporarily those things that are done by the corporation itself, one of the things that they have done is attempt to get various governments to pass rules making it difficult.

Interestingly enough, in recent years they have succeeded in sneaking some provisions providing for super tax into the federal government corporation and individual income tax. These special provisions raise substantially no money, but they do mean that it is harder to throw an inefficient corporate management out, and hence reduce the total efficiency of our economy to some extent.

Mainly countries use voting systems in which the people who can vote have only one vote apiece. Not everybody can vote, for example the House of Lords in England. The equivalents that have been appointed in Australia and Canada are not elected officials, nor, for that matter, are the members of the Supreme Court of the United States, who are probably more important in our government than the House of Representatives.

We now turn to more normal methods of voting, at least more normal in the present day. The first of these is what I call the English system, in which the legislature is selected by voting in each constituency. Normally one person will be selected to represent that constituency, whether that constituency is the state of California, the state of Alaska in the Senate, or a more or less equal-sized constituency in the House. We already discussed at some length the way that this kind of thing can go wrong because of the fact that there may be more than two candidates. On the other hand, the whittling down to two can go badly wrong. This has been adequately discussed before, but the reader should keep it in mind.

Another method which has gained some approval is approval voting. The voter is confronted with a list of possible nominees, and marks those that are above his minimum requirement, i.e., those that he approves. This has been discussed together with the strategic methods of cheating on it earlier on in the book, and there is not much to add here, except that it is very convenient for the learned societies that face some kind of rebellion.

The rebels might conceivably get more first choice votes than the members of the establishment who are nominated by the society, but most people will approve of the members of the society who are nominated, and not all of them will approve of the rebels. In consequence, the establishment will normally win. I believe this is the reason that it has been adopted by a number of the learned societies.

The second method that I would like to discuss is proportional representation, but before I begin discussing it as it exists in general in the world, I would like to talk about two systems which no longer exist, and one purely theoretical proposal that I have made and another made by Tollison, etc.

First is one that was used in Illinois when I was a boy. The lower house of the legislature was elected three to a constituency. The voters had three votes which could be cast either one vote for each of three people, one and a half for each of two people, or three votes for one person. Illinois was mainly on the two-party system, and the two parties did have pretty much control over who ran for their seats in the legislature.

The system provided a strategic problem. Rockford, where I was brought up, was primarily, but not entirely, a Republican city, and for a long time the Republican Party nominated two, both of whom were elected, and the Democrats also two, only one of whom would be elected. At one point the Republicans became ambitious and nominated three, and the Democrats stuck to two, with the result that the two Democrats were elected, and only one of the three Republicans, although to repeat, the Republicans outnumbered Democrats at that time and place. As far as I know this system has never been used anywhere else, although something like it has recently been adopted by some cities in the south.[5] The second system that I would like to talk about was developed in Japan, and I have no idea exactly how it got started. It was a function of the post-war Japanese constitution, not the prewar. In this case they had constituencies, most of which would send more than one representative to the legislature, three to five on average. Voters all had one vote, and the consequence of this was that the representatives of the various parties in essence competed with each other because the party discipline was not by any means perfect.

It resulted in the development of the cliques, which so dominated Japanese politics. The Liberal Democrats, for example, were actually a sort of federation of cliques. The clique leader raised money for campaigning, and his followers campaigned in some, usually not all, of the constituencies, against

5. See "All for One" by Samuel Issacharoff and Richard H. Pildes, *The New Republic*, Nov. 18, 1996, p. 10.

the followers of other leaders. It seems to me that in silliness it competes with the Greek system mentioned above. It has now been replaced by a different system that we will discuss below, and until at least one or two elections have been run under the new system the outcome is quite unpredictable.

We now return to the types of proportional representation I mentioned above. The first one which I invented and put in *Toward a Mathematics of Politics*[6] is simply that the members of the legislature have different numbers of votes, depending on how many people have voted for them. I went further and assumed that we have computers, and people could quickly change their representative at any time. The present system developed in the late Middle Ages in which many high political figures actually could not do simple arithmetic.[7] It does not seem to have much argument for it except that it is easy if you do not have computers. With computers there is no reason why each member of the legislature should have the same number of votes or why people cannot change their representative from time to time.

To go farther as I did earlier, it is quite possible to have many more representatives than can sit in one room. In the article I actually suggested that since my mother was retired and living in Florida, my sister and I and her husband could all designate my mother as our representative, and she could sit and watch the proceedings on television and from time to time cast four votes.

Whether or not you think that this is a good idea, it is certainly feasible today. I would argue that the proportional representation systems that I will discuss below are in essence rather crude efforts to reach something like that system.

The next system that I would like to turn to was invented by Robert Tollison.[8] In this case, by an ingenious and radical technique, each person was guaranteed an equal weight in government in the sense that they would actually be able to put at least some bills through. For example a clique of 10 percent of the voters, if they lost on one issue, would have the weight of their votes automatically increased for the next vote and so on, until eventually this 10 percent got their will even if their position was different from

6. Tullock, Gordon. *Toward a Mathematics of Politics*. Chapter 10. Ann Arbor: University of Michigan Press (1967).

7. Hence the court of the exchequer.

8. Mueller, Dennis, Tom Willit, and Robert Tollison. "On Equalizing the Distribution of Political Influence." *Journal of Political Economy* (March/April 1974): 414–22.

everyone else. In other words the number of bills passed by each individual clique would be roughly its own strength, although they could get together either formally or informally.

Neither of the two above systems has been used, but proportional representation is in fact in use in general throughout the world, and I would like to begin with the version that was discussed by Lewis Carroll. Originally that was what was meant by proportional representation, but now it is only used in a few odd places like Cambridge, Massachusetts, Australia, and Ireland. It was also adopted in New York for the regional school boards and has caused a great deal of trouble.

In this system you have, let us say, five openings on a board to be elected. Various people run, and the voter is required to rank all the people that run from first preference, second preference, etc., on down. The method in which the votes are counted is rather complicated and in early days meant that the votes took almost an infinite amount of time to be computed. Now with computers it is fairly fast, but New York, when it adopted the system for the school boards, apparently did not know that computers existed, and hence the long delays in finding out who won is one of the complaints about it.

Basically, if there are five people to be elected and ten candidates, the first choices of all the voters are looked at, and if any one of the candidates has one-sixth plus one of the votes, that person is declared elected. The one-sixth plus one is called the droop quota. Normally this candidate would have more than just one-sixth plus one, and hence some of his votes would be switched to his second choice.

The exact way in which this is done varies. Let us assume that it is done randomly. The counting is then done again, and if there is somebody else with the "droop quota" mentioned above he is declared elected and the same process gone through.

Normally eventually we will reach a situation in which there are no excess votes to be distributed. At that point the candidate with the least votes is eliminated, and his votes are distributed to his second preference. All of this is continued until five people have been elected. For some reason this system seems to be quite popular, but I have never understood why. It means not that everybody has a choice particularly, but that everybody's vote somewhere or other will be counted. It may however be given to somebody that he detests, but is not from his standpoint the worst person on the ballot. On the other hand it is quite possible that somebody's vote would be involved in electing his first, second, and third choices. To call this equal seems to me bizarre.

To repeat, this is in fact used in a few places and in general, in places where they come fairly close to having a two-party system, with the result that the system does not have all that bad an effect. The New York school board situation is in this respect exceptional.

Another form of proportional representation is very widely used, and it has already been described briefly in the earlier part of the book. One or another variant of it, and we will discuss three here, is used in a clear majority of democracies. In all three a number of different legislative seats are grouped together in one large bundle. In some cases the number is the entire membership of the lower house of the legislature, and in other cases it is perhaps 15 to 20 legislators. The parties then nominate candidates for these positions, and the nomination procedure is usually informal and need not be discussed here. The voter then checks one party.

The parties then receive the same share of the total number of seats in the legislature to their share of the vote. Thus the legislature will have the same percentage of people from each party as in the population.[9] This system provides what is sometimes referred to as a "mirror of the people." More often than not it produces more than two parties in the legislature, although not always.

If no party gets a majority, which is a common event, some kind of compromise coalition has to be hammered together. It is rather like the situation of the United States when the president is of one party and the two houses of legislature the other. In that event there is no true party control.

In most cases the members of the legislature are appointed by simply going to the top of the list of names that the party has submitted, and going down the appropriate number. If there are 20 seats in this particular district, and the given party has received one-quarter of the votes, it will get 5 seats, and these will be the 5 at the top of the list. This gives the party machine a great deal of power, and in most cases it is exercised rather arbitrarily. There does not seem to be any case in which the government has insisted that this be dealt with by a primary, or something of that sort.

There are two places in which the voters have more say than what I have

9. There are problems of rounding error here, and there are various ways of dealing with them. None of them are very successful, but none of them are disastrous.

described above. In Switzerland, you can go down the list of your favorite party, and strike out 1 or maybe 2 of the names. You then write, above the names you struck out, the name of another candidate on the list whom you particularly favor. The candidates who are actually selected will be determined by those voters who have taken the trouble to do this rather than by the party machine.

If the party had 25 percent of the votes, and was going to get 5 out of 20 representatives, those 5 would be the ones that had the most of these "cumulation" votes by individuals.

This system is interesting, as it turns out not very many of the voters bother to cumulate. This means that those voters who are particularly interested in politics are much more powerful than those who are not. It is a self-selection in terms of political interest, and probably the voters who cumulate are better informed than the others. In a way we have a voluntary division of the voters into two categories, an upper and a lower, with anybody who wishes to spend a little extra time voting, being in the upper.

Italy had, until the recent reforms, a system in which you were permitted in addition to marking the party on the ballot to simply check five of its nominees, and the number of such checks was used to select who would actually occupy that party's seats. This system had a peculiar by-product. The Communist Party was highly disciplined during most of its history, although not now, and designated whom individual voters would vote for. By telling the voters a separate combination of which ones they were to check, they were able to tell whether each had in fact carried out instructions. You could simply inspect the ballot and see whether the combination assigned to a given party member had occurred.

Germany after World War II, when they drew up their new constitution, produced a compromise between the single-member constituency and the proportional representation, which I think has nothing to say for it, but it has been copied by Italy, New Zealand, Japan, and Russia.

Under this system something like half of the members of the legislature are elected in the constituencies according to the English system described above. The other half are elected by proportional representation. Each citizen casts two votes, one for the candidate from his constituency and the other a proportional vote for the party. The result of these are two quite disparate bodies of candidates who have been elected, but they meet in the same hall and vote in the ordinary way. To repeat what I have said above, I cannot think of anything much to be said for this except that it is a compromise. This in my opinion bizarre procedure has been copied by New Zealand, Japan, and Russia. Apparently they all like compromise and do not know very much about voting theory.

Personally, I would like a two-chamber legislature with one chamber elected according to the English system and the other according to the proportional representation system. The reader can immediately say that I too am a compromiser, and in a way I am. The compromise is not between these two forms of voting, however. I would like a more than majority, two-thirds to three-quarters, to pass bills. It seems very difficult to talk people into even considering this, but I think that my two-house legislature raised in this way might be more readily saleable politically. It would have the same net effect because the two-house members being elected differently would require effectively more than 50 percent of the population to elect a majority in both houses. Thus I am compromising, but a different compromise than the one that I criticized above.

I obviously should not leave this topic without mentioning my favorite form of voting, which is demand revealing. This is a system which permits the individual to indicate the intensity of his desires. Since a Nobel Prize has just been awarded to a man who did some preliminary work in this area, I suppose it is more popular than it used to be, but basically no one has actually adopted it except for a few American bureaucracies where the actual inventor, Ed Clarke, was employed. I am not going to go through it here because I have written so much on it before.[10] Basically, his system means that you indicate how strongly you feel, as well as what alternative you favor. It is a very clever system which makes it unwise for you to misinform people as to the intensity of your preferences. To repeat, I am not going to discuss this here. There is plenty of material in print on it, and it does not seem likely that it will be widely adopted in the near future.

There are a number of other voting methods which have been suggested, Mueller's voting by veto for example; an exhaustive list would take another book, so I will stop here. If the reader is still curious, I should warn him that research in the field is both tedious and likely to be erroneous. Basic sources frequently misdescribe voting methods for reasons that are mysterious to me. In any event, I leave it here.

10. Tideman, T. Nicolaus, and Gordon Tullock. "A New and Superior Process for Making Social Choices." *Journal of Political Economy* 84(6) (October 1976): 1145–59. The reader can easily find out how it works there.

INDEX

References to bibliographic information appear in italics.

The typeface used for the text of this book is Galliard, an old-style face designed by Matthew Carter in 1978, in the spirit of a sixteenth-century French typeface of Robert Granjon. The display type is Meta Book, a variant of Meta, designed by Erik Spiekermann in the 1990s.

This book is printed on paper that is acid-free and meets the requirements of the American National Standard for Permanence of Paper for Printed Library Materials, z39.48-1992. ♾

Book design by Richard Hendel, Chapel Hill, North Carolina
Typography by G&S Typesetters, Inc., Austin, Texas
Printed and bound by Edwards Brothers, Inc., Ann Arbor, Michigan